D1599185

The Rise of
Middle-Class Culture in
Nineteenth-Century
Spain

THE RISE OF MIDDLE-CLASS CULTURE IN NINETEENTH-CENTURY SPAIN

JESUS CRUZ

LOUISIANA STATE UNIVERSITY PRESS
BATON ROUGE

 # 7206 34809

Published with assistance from the Spanish Ministry of Culture

Published by Louisiana State University Press
Copyright © 2011 by Louisiana State University Press
All rights reserved
Manufactured in the United States of America
First printing

DESIGNER: Amanda McDonald Scallan
TYPEFACE: Minion Pro
PRINTER: McNaughton & Gunn, Inc.
BINDER: Acme Bookbinding, Inc.

Library of Congress Cataloging-in-Publication Data
Cruz, Jesus.
  The rise of middle-class culture in nineteenth-century Spain / Jesus Cruz.
     p. cm.
  Includes bibliographical references and index.
  ISBN 978-0-8071-3919-6 (cloth : alk. paper) — ISBN 978-0-8071-3921-9 (epub) — ISBN 978-0-8071-3920-2 (pdf) — ISBN 978-0-8071-3922-6 (mobi) 1. Middle class—Spain—History—19th century. 2. Spain—Social conditions—19th century. 3. Spain—Civilization—19th century. I. Title.
  HT690.S7C784 2011
  305.5′5094609034—dc23   2011016091

To Cindy and Cristina (mis chicas)
for your support and patience

CONTENTS

The Rise of
Middle-Class Culture in
Nineteenth-Century
Spain

Bourgeois Culture and Modernity

THE author of a conduct book entitled *Elegance in Social Treatment,* published in Spain at the end of the nineteenth century, wrote the following in reference to the celebration of January 6, the Epiphany of the Three Kings: "In recent years, it has become fashionable in Spain to celebrate the holiday of the Three Kings with the following ritual: at dessert time a child dressed as a medieval page enters the dining room with slices of cake covered by a white cloth. One of the pieces contains a tiny porcelain doll. Each person at the table receives a slice, and the one whose slice contains the miniature will have the honor of selecting a 'queen of the festival' among the ladies."[1]

The writer was referring to a form of celebration adopted by the upper classes, a very small segment of the late nineteenth-century Spanish social body. He was describing the introduction of this ritual in some Spanish homes and was encouraging its adoption as a sign of elegance and distinction. The tradition of baking of a cake to celebrate Epiphany with a hidden object inside to play what was known as the "game of surprise" was not Spanish. Although in its most remote origins it seems to have been connected to the Roman commemoration of the winter solstice, the tradition in the form described by our author originated in medieval France, and its transformation into a family ritual occurred in more recent times. In France it was and still is customary to bake a cake—called *gateau des rois* during the Old Regime and *galette des rois* at present—to celebrate the Epiphany of the Three Kings. It seems that beginning in the seventeenth century this form of celebration enjoyed popularity in France, spreading from palaces and monasteries to the homes of humbler classes. The rich hid a small jewel in the cake, the poor a lima bean; everyone played the "game of surprise" and designated a queen or a king for that special day. In Spain the tradition of the *gateau des rois* was introduced by the Bourbons but never spread beyond court circles. It was not until the end of the nineteenth century that bourgeois families, imitating the French, adopted this way to celebrate, which became quite popular despite the fact that it was imported. A similar process has occurred with many other adopted Christmas traditions.

The cake with the surprise remains a popular way to celebrate the holiday of the Three Kings in the Hispanic world. In Spain, where the day is a national holiday, it is customary to eat the *roscón de reyes* at breakfast or as dessert with the traditional family dinner. The custom is also observed in many parts of Latin America where the Epiphany of the Three Kings is celebrated as a national holiday. The *roscón de reyes,* the Hispanic version of the French *gateau des rois,* has become an important source of income after the New Year's celebration for bakers in countries such as Spain and Mexico, much like the *galette des rois* is for French bakers. If we ask Spaniards or Mexicans about the *roscón* or *rosca de reyes,* most people will answer that it is authentic to their traditions. Surely most people are not aware that this ritual was imported from a foreign country about one hundred years ago by a minority who believed that it lent them elegance and distinction. The *roscón de reyes* is a clear example of a custom brought to Spain by the well-to-do who were desirous of imitating the French bourgeois lifestyle and that has evolved into an act of mass consumption and a popular tradition considered genuinely Spanish.[2] This is but one example among many habits introduced in the nineteenth century that have shaped the present-day lifestyle of Spaniards.

Who were the introducers of imported styles, and what were they pursuing? The life story of the author of the above-cited conduct manual provides some clues to help us answer those questions. The manual was signed by Viscountess Bestard de la Torre, one of the highfalutin pseudonyms used by Alfredo Pallardó (1851–1928), a well-known Catalonian journalist and playwright who specialized in social chronicles and etiquette manuals. The majority of his articles and essays were devoted to divulging behavioral norms, manners, values, and tastes that he considered necessary for the creation of a modern polite society in Spain. Pallardó himself was a self-made man. Of working-class origins, he started his professional life as a typesetter, attained a college degree when he was middle-aged, and ended up a well-known writer and prosperous bourgeois. Pallardó represents a clear case of embourgeoisement. He was one of the many voices of that social group dedicated to promoting the benefits of the bourgeois lifestyle, which they considered essential for Spain's incorporation into modernity.

The bourgeois customs adopted over the course of the nineteenth century have shaped present-day Spanish lifestyles. The example of the *roscón de reyes* is one among many practices and traditions that characterize the way of living of the majority of today's Spaniards. Consequently, it is not an exaggeration to say that Spanish society has gone through a process of embourgeoisement. In present-day colloquial Spanish it is not uncommon to use the term "bourgeois" or "embourgeoisement" to refer to somebody who has partially or totally adopted a specific lifestyle. Usually that adoption results from a rise in that person's income accompanied by increased consumption of luxury items. On occasion these statements in regard to a friend's or acquaintance's embourgeoisement may have a connotation of social critique, but frequently they contain a hint of admiration or even jealousy. In any case, when Spaniards use these qualifiers they are placing somebody within a particular social category on the basis of his or her taste, habits, or appearance. In sum, bourgeois, bourgeoisie, and embourgeoisement are concepts that define a lifestyle, or, in other words, a culture. That culture, the bourgeois culture based on consumption, prevails among contemporary Spaniards.

This book examines the spread of bourgeois culture in Spain, a process that started in the nineteenth century, as it did in the rest of the Western world. It is true that the roots of this historical development can be traced back to the Renaissance, but it was during the nineteenth century that bourgeois culture became hegemonic. The making of bourgeois society, or middle-class society, resulted from a long and complex historical process with diverse rhythms and circumstances in each country depending on historical conditions. However, despite these differences in time and framework, and despite the variety of scenarios and results, there exists a common ground of shared experiences that gives coherence to this historical process that resulted in the formation of middle-class consumer societies. At some point in this historical development, all countries underwent a profound alteration of their political and legal structures that brought about the creation of new nation-states. These countries also experienced a process of economic transformation that ushered in market economies, in some cases in anticipation of the political and legal changes, in others as its consequence. One of the central aspects of the creation of the new society was the modeling of new identities that embodied the value system and lifestyles of the bourgeois dominant groups.[3]

In Spain, as in the rest of Europe, only traces remain of nineteenth-century bourgeois families—their last names may be influential in certain circles or may appear in the social columns. Nevertheless, the fact that they were the creators of Spain's contemporary lifestyle can be evidenced in many aspects of daily experience. They introduced values such as respect for intimacy, a taste for comfort, and a commitment to sports as a means to improve health and beauty or to make a profit. They popularized summer vacations as something entertaining, invigorating, and even profitable, and promoted travel as an educational and recreational experience. They valued entertainment as a means of personal enjoyment and enrichment, as well as an avenue for social relations. In sum, the nineteenth-century bourgeois promoted a hedonistic culture that ultimately freed luxury of moral censure as long as it benefited wide sectors of the social body. According to their value system, to furnish a home with elegance, to dress following the dictates of fashion magazines, or to adopt certain habits imported from societies considered more advanced was not only pleasurable, but necessary for social progress. While they did not dispute the existence of class distinctions, they adhered to the utilitarian principle according to which social progress meant bringing the benefits of their way of life to the most individuals possible. For the bourgeois this was the road to happiness. All these practices and values have survived the passage of time and provide contemporary societies their distinctive traits. It is true that present-day societies have lost the conventional formalism that characterized social treatment during the nineteenth century, and that many of these rigid rules of etiquette today seem affected and even discriminatory. Returning to the example of the *roscón de reyes,* certainly no one still dresses a child in a medieval costume to distribute the slices of cake, nor do they designate a queen among the ladies. However, most Spaniards celebrate the Three Kings holiday by eating the cake for breakfast, dessert, or *merienda.* What in the nineteenth century was a practice conferring distinction imported by a style-conscious minority has become in the twenty-first century a tradition characteristic of the modern middle-class consumer society.

In the pages that follow we will study the making of this lifestyle—what is generally known as bourgeois culture. We will explore its main components, and consider how a good portion of them have shaped present-day Spanish society. The book's thesis is that the middle-class culture that contributed to the democratic stability and economic prosperity since 1975 in Spain originated in the nineteenth century. All scholars concur in considering the nineteenth century in Spain as the century of the bourgeoisie. However, Spanish nineteenth-century middle classes have been mainly studied for their politics and their structural weaknesses rather than their cultural habits. The predominant paradigm up to the 1980s presented a nineteenth century characterized by political instability, economic failure, and social frustration. Spain lagged behind the most modern countries of the West in part due to the weakness, incompetence, and selfishness of its bourgeoisie.[4] During the last two decades, that point of view has been the object of a thorough revision. The studies of David Ringrose, Juan Pablo Fusi Aizpurúa, and Jordi Palafox Gámir, among others, present new historical evidence that questions the assumption that Spain was an exceptional case of failed modernization.[5] Recent research from the perspective of cultural studies, literary analysis, and visual culture provides new understandings of the nature of Spanish modernity by considering the Spanish case in its specific historical context and in its diversity of manifestations.[6] This book adds new perspectives on that revisionist task and demonstrates that during the nineteenth century a solid middle-class culture established its roots in Spain, like in other parts of Europe. As Noël Valis has pointed out, there is at times a disparity "between the perception of middleclassness and the economic, material conditions required to produce it. Here, however, it is necessary to stress that awareness of being middle class and the adoption of certain life styles and attitudes can and do exist even when the economic structure lags behind, that is, when there is a perception of being modern despite insufficient modernization. This, I think, is the case for Spain in the nineteenth century."[7]

Three main arguments constitute the foundation of the book's central thesis. First, over the course of the nineteenth century, the dominant groups in Spain, as in other parts of Europe, strove to introduce a variety of social practices that were in the process of being established in the most developed societies of the West. In principle, this effort pursued the consolidation of a new middle class that would provide balance to a society deeply split between rich and poor, a source of equilibrium that would curtail social unrest. Bourgeois cultural practices were promoted by the use of three basic means: the elaboration and dissemination of new rules of conduct aimed at establishing a dominant code of behavior, the promotion of consumer culture as a means of facilitating economic growth and bringing about collective happiness, and the establishment of a material culture with distinctive symbolic components that provided class identity.

Second, the spread of bourgeois culture deeply transformed the life of Spaniards in the long run. However, due to its cultural nature, it was a smooth and gradual transformation, with continuous episodes of negotiation, rarely the consequence of revolutionary occurrences. Bourgeois culture substituted, transformed, or adapted many practices of estate society, but as opposed to political and legal change, the results never appeared as sudden or radical. We will see, for instance, how some practices from aristocratic lifestyles were admired, embraced, and tailored by the bourgeoisie. The abolition of aristocratic privileges or the suppression of the guilds were dramatic decisions that generated the sensation of living a revolutionary moment. However, that feeling of radical change dissipates when considering transformations in lifestyles, because these may occur over a longer period of time.

Third, if in the long run bourgeois culture has become hegemonic in today's Spain, in the midterm the results of its implantation were insufficient and much slower than in other parts of the West. The diverse components that make up the bourgeois cultural system constituted a substantial part of the discourse of modernity. Social agents involved in its promotion measured their success based on the logic of utilitarian liberalism. In a society that sanctioned equality before the law and the liberty of the individual, but at the same time protected private property and social divisions, the only way to ensure social stability was by promoting economic well-being for the greatest possible number of individuals. According to this scheme, the contentment of a large middle class would serve as the best antidote for social conflict and political instability. In British Victorian society, in the United States, and in parts of northern Europe that scheme proved to be effective, but in the case of southern, central, and eastern Europe, insufficient economic growth delayed the expansion of the middle classes and was one of the causes of social and political instability well into the twentieth century.[8] The case of Spain is a clear example of this historical development.[9]

The use of the words "bourgeois" and "bourgeoisie," and their derivative, "embourgeoisement," in the context of the making of modern Spanish society requires clarification. In contemporary Spanish the terms "bourgeoisie" and "bourgeois" have various meanings. Most commonly they refer to a middle-class citizen with enough income to enjoy a comfortable lifestyle. There is, however, another connotation that identifies "bourgeois" with that which is mediocre, conventional, and unsophisticated. According to this usage, "embourgeoisement" is synonymous with conformity and lack of spiritual elevation. There is a final connotation that uses the term "bourgeoisie" to refer to the class of capitalists in opposition to the proletariat. In the political language of Marxism, a bourgeois is anyone considered to be an exploiter of the working classes. According to this conception, the bourgeoisie arose as a class during the Middle Ages, and since then strove to take over the means of production. After achieving that goal, the bourgeoisie clashed with the nobility in a revolutionary process that started in the second half of the eighteenth century. For Karl Marx the bourgeoisie was the main social force behind the fall of the Old Regime, the establishment of the new liberal state, and the economic and social order known as capitalism.

Spanish historiography of the 1970s promoted the use of "bourgeoisie" and "bourgeois" according to their meanings in the Marxist tradition. The bourgeoisie was presented as a well-structured social class whose main feature was its antagonism toward the feudal nobility. As a consequence of that clash the bourgeoisie carried out a revolution—the bourgeois revolution—that according to some Spanish historians happened between 1833 and 1868, the years of the conflictive building of the liberal state and the disentailment of church and seignneurial property.[10] The bourgeois revolution paradigm, extensively applied during the 1960s by European historiography, was useful for understanding the dimensions of the transcendental historical change that took place in Spain during the mid-nineteenth century. It helped to place Spain on the map of the cycle of the "Atlantic revolutions" initiated by the American and the French revolutions. Nonetheless, it was a theoretical model, and its application to the specific case of each country was frequently forced. For that reason, during the 1980s and 1990s the bourgeois revolution paradigm was the object of constant revision. On the one hand, revisionism resulted from a better knowledge of the particular historical circumstances of each country. In Spain, for instance, a number of innovative studies about the making of regional and national bourgeoisies have swept away traditional approaches.[11] On the other hand, the revisionist effort has come about due to new ways of understanding the concepts of social class and social identity, a consequence of the change in methodological approaches within the social sciences and the humanities.

Part of the revisionist effort deals with the history of the very concept of bourgeoisie. The terms "bourgeois" and "bourgeoisie" began to appear in European political terminology after the occurrence of the episodes characterized as "bourgeois revolutions." In France, according to Sarah Maza, during the French Revolution and in the successive revolutionary events up to 1848, no political party, group, or individual claimed to be bourgeois or to represent that social class. The term "bourgeois" in post-revolutionary historiography refers to an imagined reality that distorts historical evidence. "Bourgeois" and "bourgeoisie," according to Maza, constituted an imaginary "other" opposed to the values and expectations of the nation, a negative stereotype manipulated to ignite patriotic passion.[12] The argument is suggestive but excessive, despite being supported with admirable erudition. After all, the French intellectuals and politicians were the first to use the term "bourgeoisie" to refer to the new social class linked to the changes of modernity. Although Maza's argument is controversial, her contribution adds new substance to revisionist scholarship concerning the history of the bourgeoisie in modern Europe.[13]

In the case of Spain, Pedro Álvarez de Miranda writes, the history of the terms "bourgeois" and "bourgeoisie" is complex "because they have had different meanings across time, and their usage has been erratic."[14] They were originally used during the Middle Ages to refer to a person who lived in a city, but the terms disappeared from Spanish texts written during the early modern period. Their use has been recorded in some texts written in Spanish and published in the Low Countries at the end of the sixteenth and during the seventeenth century, always referring to social situations of that region. Justo Serna and Anaclet Pons point out the inclusion of the term *burgo* in the *Tesoro de la lengua castellana o española* by Sebastián de Cobarruvias published in 1611, though they find contradictions in its meaning: "On one hand Cobarruvias seems to connect *burgo* with its urban origin, on the other, he underlines its rural, remote, mountainous, or agrarian connotations. It gets even more confusing when he deals with the etymology of the term that he considers alternatively to be Visigoth or Arabic."[15] Despite its disappearance from written Spanish, the word remained in the *Diccionario de Autoridades* with its medieval meaning and as a term borrowed from French. "It is a word," the dictionary points out, "taken from the French 'bourgeois' and recently introduced here," but it is not found in any written text until well into the nineteenth century. The concept will come back into written Spanish during the last third of the nineteenth century, this time used heavily in the political literature of the 1868 revolution, clearly marked by foreign connotations.[16] That concept of bourgeoisie as it appears in political pamphlets, party declarations, and the partisan press is the one that will prevail in the political thought and discourse of contemporary Spain. It is the usage that, in a general sense, serves to identify the middle classes, but it can also have negative connotations when referring to the social class that exploits and oppresses the proletariat. "Bourgeois" and "bourgeoisie" were reintroduced in literary language by realist novelists. Benito Pérez Galdós, Armando Palacio Valdés, and Leopoldo Alas (who wrote under the pseudonym Clarín), among others, used these terms extensively and contributed to their transmission to popular language with the connotations they have at present. It seems that in Spain, as in France, the bourgeoisie was more the consequence of nineteenth-century revolutions than their cause.

The concept of the middle class, however, was used before the terms "bourgeois" and "bourgeoisie" in a more straightforward and consistent manner.[17] During the early modern period, the terms *mediano* and *mediania* were used to identify the social segment situated between the nobility and the commoners. The word *mediano* was not uncommon in the abundant advisory literature sent to the king with proposals to resolve the economic troubles of the monarchy, as some writers argued for the promotion of *medianos* as a feasible remedy.[18] It was in the early nineteenth century when the concept of the middle class started to be broadly used with the meaning it has at present. There were references to the middle classes in the history books dealing with the resistance against Napoleon, and above all in the debates surrounding the first constitutional parliament in 1812.[19] The term was frequently used in political debates during the 1820 revolutionary cycle. The middle classes became the central subject of most of the social references by journalists, writers, and academics of romanticism and liberalism. Ramón Mesonero Romanos, in his popular memoirs, identifies himself as a member of the middle classes based on the social position and background of his family.[20] In his writings, as well as in the texts of Mariano José Larra and other writers of the time, the middle class is portrayed as the sponsor of the new liberal state and the support of its economic and social foundations. "The middle classes," wrote Manuel Bretón de los Herreros, "visibly neutralize the social extremes; this phenomenon results in part from the progress of civilization, in part from the influence of political institutions."[21]

The extensive literature on conduct published during the nineteenth century—the books on courtesy, etiquette, and taste—clearly state in their introductory chapters that they are written for, and in most cases by, the middle classes. Until the end of the century, when the term "bourgeoisie" was recovered by political, journalistic, and literary language, "middle class" was the concept broadly used in Spain to refer to the urban, educated, and well-established social groups. Later, during the 1930s and especially in the 1960s, the influence of Marxist thought within broad segments of the scholarly community spread the use of "bourgeois" and "bourgeoisie," differentiating these terms from "middle class," which they considered to be a scientifically imprecise and politically incorrect notion.[22] Following the tradition of nineteenth-century liberalism, recently recovered by revisionist historiography, this book uses "bourgeois," "bourgeoisie," and "middle class" to refer to the same groups. In the social context of nineteenth-century Spain, the "bourgeoisie" or "middle classes" was the diverse social conglomerate situated between the old nobility and the working classes. These individuals and families range from the wealthy capitalists to the modest middle class with limited income but pretentious lifestyles, and also include members of the bourgeoisie that attained aristocratic titles. In sum, in this book the terms "bourgeois," "bourgeoisie," and "middle class" refer to the same social reality, abandoning the linguistic restrictions imposed in the past by Marxist scholarship.

As Peter Gay has pointed out, the nineteenth-century European bourgeoisie—he uses the term "Victorian bourgeoisie"—was sizable, diverse, and deeply fissured. "The historian," writes Gay, "attempting to understand that bourgeoisie must come to terms with pervasive conflicts among those who defined themselves as 'middle class' as much as the qualities that made them kin."[23] Using a similar interpretative approach, Raffaele Romanelli considers "bourgeoisie" to be a "relational" term. It is useful for pedagogical purposes as it serves to describe a social group with certain similarities—it does not, however, define a totally homogenous class in regard to its members' behavior and social integration.[24] It may well be that the divisions among the group known as bourgeoisie in regard to political positions and ideological allegiances are irreconcilable. The Spanish case is a clear example of this, given the continued disagreements and confrontations among nineteenth-century liberals (i.e., radicals, moderates, progressives, republicans, Catalan and Basque nationalists, etc.), not counting those bourgeois who endorsed and promoted working-class revolutionary projects. The Marxist principle according to which class identity matches ideological adscription is broadly questioned. Given these considerations, does it make sense to talk of bourgeoisie or a middle class or a working class? Clearly, the answer is "yes." These generalizations have pedagogical application, and the researcher cannot ignore them. But beyond their pedagogical functionality, there is sufficient space in recent social theory, and in its application to the study of history, to be able to function with a concept of the bourgeoisie that combines the diversity of ideological commitments of each bourgeois individual with the reality of a shared lifestyle.

It is more suitable to consider this social group—or social conglomerate— from the perspective of their attitudes, their social rituals, their tastes, their ways of socializing, and their symbols—in a word, their culture—instead of their political positions or their income levels. We have already seen this in reference to terminology. The word "bourgeoisie" became popularized in practically all the European languages and there soon appeared autochthonous forms and a multiplicity of subcategories and derivatives, such as *petit bourgeoisie, Grossbürgertum, aburguesamiento,* and the like. In the English-speaking world, nevertheless, the term "bourgeoisie" never caught on. Great Britain and Anglo-Saxon America used the term "middle class," and it became a key concept of contemporary social thought. There arose another element of bourgeois culture: the idea of the self-made man, the belief in a society open to the opportunity to advance oneself. Of course, equality of opportunity was quite uneven in the diverse geography of the Western world. There is no doubt that where there was lesser presence of the Old Regime there was greater margin for social ascent, but there were societies more or less open, and in general they all tended to exaggerate their degree of openness.

The culture of the self-made man became revered myth in Anglo-Saxon societies. Samuel Smiles and Horatio Alger created a hagiography of perfect joyous bourgeois.[25] The Carnegies and Rockefellers were the real cases that helped to create the myth of the American Dream, and were probably the most authentic and appealing examples. But European countries can also boast of illustrious self-made men who left their mark in the collective imagination. Many of them—especially in former times—decided to disguise their humble backgrounds with impressive aristocratic titles, a testimony to the fact that the revolutions had not dissipated the atavistic prestige of the nobility. The Marquise of Manzanedo, one of the prominent *hombres de pro,* as they are known in Spain, came from a family of rustic mountain people from the province of Santander. The first Count of Güell was even less distinguished: he came from a family of tradesmen who made their fortune in colonial trade. The Marquise of Salamanca, who became one of the richest men in Europe, hailed from a provincial middle-class family.[26] In sum, we can track the bourgeois influence in the legacy of a value system and lifestyle reflected in dozens of manuals of courtesy, etiquette, and good taste; in the fashion magazines, novels, and paintings that are exhibited in museums; in photos that still hang in many homes; and in many other sources.

The most distinctive trait of the history of the nineteenth-century Spanish bourgeoisie or middle class was its small size. The available data about social structure are partial, but all historians agree that the urban middle classes, even counting the rural middle classes, comprised a reduced portion of the social body. Up until the first third of the twentieth century, Spain was still mainly a rural country, with an urban network that was growing, but at a much slower pace than its counterparts in northern and central Europe. Spanish cities grew at a faster rate than rural zones, but by 1900 the percent of dwellers in urban nuclei with more than twenty thousand inhabitants was 21 percent compared to 39 percent in France and 75 percent in Great Britain. But it is also true that demographic growth in general—from 10.5 million in 1800 to 18.6 in 1900—occurred in urban centers and was due in part to expansion of the middle classes.[27]

It is difficult to locate those middle classes on the social map of the period. The source traditionally used by historians to estimate who belonged to the middle classes is the electoral census. Under liberal electoral law the right to vote was restricted to those with a specific level of yearly income. Adrian Shubert estimates that by the mid-nineteenth century more than 3 percent of the total population was in the middle class based on the electoral censuses, while all indicators point to a sizable increase in this figure in the second half of the century. According to Shubert, the data from electoral censuses are insufficient because they do not include large sectors of the urban and rural petit bourgeoisie and the professional classes. At the same time, he stresses the qualitative impact of the growth in the second half of the nineteenth century since this took place in areas where there was greater economic and social dynamism.[28] It was in that period, as Francisco Villacorta Baños has demonstrated, that professional groups and the diverse bureaucracies of

Spanish society were consolidated, representing a key segment of the new middle classes.[29]

The studies of David Ringrose and Ángel Bahamonde Magro have shown that in Madrid beginning in the second half of the eighteenth century there took place a consolidation of the group connected to the bureaucracy, to provisioning the city, and to state contracts and finances; this group constituted the social nucleus that would drive the liberal revolution and shape the bourgeoisie in the second half of the nineteenth century.[30] Integrated by members of the provincial gentry (hidalguía), this group originated as a class of notables who controlled the mechanisms of ascent through networks based on relations of kinship, regional solidarities, and patronage.[31] The new framework of social relations ushered in by liberalism beginning in 1833 and the growth of the state created social opportunities for the definitive consolidation of a powerful bourgeoisie. Barcelona, in contrast to Madrid, always had a marked bourgeois character. It had an old bourgeoisie in the traditional sense of the term: an urban class dedicated to commerce and industry. The bourgeoisie of Barcelona consolidated in the nineteenth century and, as we will see in the following chapters, had a defining impact on the city's character.[32]

Although these statistics are important, the numerical insufficiency of the nineteenth century bourgeoisie was not a defining factor in regard to its historical impact.[33] As important as the numbers was the influence of bourgeois attitudes: the feeling of being middle class, the desire to perceive oneself as modern despite insufficient modernization. Regardless of their small numbers and structural weakness, the bourgeoisie began to assemble a *modus vivendi* that appealed to the masses. This way of life, this culture that at the beginning of the nineteenth century was in a process of gestation, became the hegemonic culture by the end of the century. People were particularly attracted to consumption as a vehicle to improve their living conditions. Up until the 1960s, the level of consumption of Spanish society was well below that of other developed societies. Nevertheless, the culture of consumption continued to be hegemonic and, for better or for worse, contemporary Spain has become a typical modern consumer society. The leitmotiv of this study will be the examination of the process of transformation of bourgeois culture into the hegemonic culture over the course of the nineteenth century, based on the consideration of its continuity into the twenty-first century.[34]

Although sections of this book are based on a quantitative method, overall it is a study of cultural history. Its conception derives from an interest in classic themes of the social history agenda, and in the course of its evolution its focus became the provision of replies from the perspective of "new" cultural history.[35] "Now is the time for the history of culture. Social history, economic history, and political history have all had their day," wrote Jesús Martínez Martín in a recent book about the cultural origins of liberal Spanish society. He adds that he is talking about "history of culture not in the sense of the history of ideas and high culture, but rather of cultural practices . . . a new way of looking at history inspired by methods from anthropology and linguistics," which in Spain is still in its early stages.[36] The present study continues in this vein; its main objective is the study of cultural practices of the nineteenth-century Spanish bourgeoisie. We will examine how these practices aggregated until they constituted a cultural system, and how that system appealed to large segments of society, eventually becoming hegemonic. Overall this book presents an analysis of the struggles that characterized Spain's uneven process of transitioning into modernity. Episodes like the Civil War can be explained in part due to the insufficient implantation of middle-class culture in Spanish society. Nevertheless, this book follows the approach of Fusi Aizpurúa, Palafox Gámir, and Ringrose, who believe that in the long run the response of Spanish society to the challenges of modernity was produced in the context of comparative normality and not exceptionality.[37]

The adoption by historians in the 1970s of methods from anthropology and historical sociology has produced fascinating results in what has been called the "cultural turn."[38] One of the consequences of the new methodology was that the concept of social class was freed from the straitjacket imposed by orthodox Marxist theory. E. P. Thompson's classic study of the English working class offered new perspectives for the definition of class identity, taking into account the role of norms, habits, customs, and symbols. In a similar line, French historiography carried out by Jacques Le Goff, Emmanuel Le Roy Ladurie, and others, began to produce rigorous and creative results combining the time-honored social history tradition of the *Annales* with a type of cultural history called history of mentalities. If the *Annales* promoted the practice of a total history, the incorporation of theoretical and methodological tools on the part of the inspiring social theorists Norbert Elias, Clifford Geertz, Pierre Bourdieu, and Anthony Giddens has made possible a multidisciplinary and multi-thematic approach to historical analysis. What is the common thread in historical studies that encompass themes as diverse as religion, sports, reading practices, and diplomacy? Undoubtedly it is an interest in the symbolic, the attempt to explain historical phenomena by means of reading and interpreting symbols. While cultural history has benefited greatly from the methodological instruments of anthropology and sociology, it is by no means a new discovery—in fact, this approach to interpreting the past first arose in the context of the Enlightenment.

"Culture" is the key word. "Culture" and "cultural history" are concepts that encompass multiple meanings and diverse applications. In its most traditional definition, "culture" derives from "cultivate" and refers to the qualities that perfect human talents. Thus, the classic study of cultural history addressed the evolution and status of human knowledge. The notion of culture from an anthropological and sociological perspective was first developed during the late Enlightenment and was portrayed by the romantics. This notion—the one that interests us here—understands as culture the lifestyle of a group of human beings. Lifestyle is a cluster of conventional models of thought and behavior that includes value systems, beliefs, norms of conduct, and even forms of political organization and economic activity. These models of thought and behavior are transmitted from one generation to the next by means of a learning process, never through genetic inheritance. Thus culture is something that is malleable and should not be considered outside its economic and social context.[39] Above all, culture is a process, not a fixed condition, and thus the emphasis that some anthropologists—in particular, Geertz and Anthony Cohen—place on considering culture as a cluster of symbols that take on meaning within the specific context in which they are produced.[40] The individuals who constitute a culture make use of these symbols to give meaning to their thoughts and actions. This conception of culture is very useful for the cultural historian, but it should be used with caution due to the complexities involved in its application to specific aspects of historical analysis. In our case, for example, it helps to explain the meaning of certain modes of behavior, the symbolism of which can only be understood within the context of Spanish society. Valis's analysis of the different meanings of *cursilería*—a typical Spanish concept saturated with symbolism in its cultural context—is convincingly based on Cohen's understanding of culture.[41] This symbolic approach is most useful in a microanalysis—what Geertz defines as "thick description." It is very well suited to the object and focus of investigation in certain disciplines such as linguistics, communications, and literary criticism, but its use is more problematic in other disciplines that must take into account factors whose symbolism is difficult to interpret, as is the case with historical analysis. A case in point is the impact on fashion of factors with minimal symbolic content such as price increases or the imposition of laws that affect the textile industry.

The theoretical framework, or the intellectual legacy, that inspires this investigation comes fundamentally from the work of Elias and Bourdieu. Elias is known for his emphases on the progressive view of historical development, the role of self-control, and the importance of behavior norms in the making of culture, what he calls "the civilizing process." His master work about the evolution of courtesy in the Western world, published in 1939 and rediscovered in the 1970s, continues to be a source of inspiration, especially for scholars who study Spain for which the history of courtesy is in its infancy.[42] According to Elias's model, courtesy norms—based on the exercise of self-control—began to be established in western Europe starting in the Middle Ages, and were the most salient aspect of a civilizing process that culminated in our modern society. Elias envisioned a connection between the civilizing process and certain social and political developments, such as the centralization of the state and the domestication of the military nobility. Although his research does not go beyond the eighteenth century, it projects a vision of the history of the occidental world that has continuity into modern times. Chapter 2 of this book is dedicated to the study of the evolution of models of conduct in Spain from the eighteenth century to around 1900. Following, in large part, Elias's model, this chapter looks at the rise and consolidation of the bourgeois ideal in social behavior.

Bourdieu's theory provides three fundamental concepts for the development of the analysis presented in this book: social field, cultural capital, and *habitus*. Bourdieu discusses the traditional concept of social class understood as a specific group of individuals who adopt an ideological position based on economic status.[43] Social reality is actually much more complex. Instead of specific social classes, we have to speak of social groups or "social fields," which can be composed of individuals with diverse economic situations.[44] These social fields function within a stratified system of social positions. The mobility of individuals or groups within a social field is not based solely on the accumulation of economic capital, but requires other types of accumulation, basically what Bourdieu calls cultural capital and symbolic capital.[45] The main source of cultural capital, according to Bourdieu, is education, something that in recent history has constituted the bourgeoisie's decisive instrument for exercising their domination. Education complements money in the accumulation of the necessary symbolic capital to obtain social distinction and exercise social preeminence. Within Bourdieu's model, in order to understand the genesis of modern societies, culture is as important as money. This explains the importance of Bourdieu for those who are attempting to explain the history of contemporary society taking into account the role of "culture."

The final component of Bourdieu's theory that I want to discuss is the notion of *habitus,* a concept adopted from Elias, Johann Carl Friedrich Gauss, and Max Weber. By *habitus* Bourdieu understands those internal structures of perception, thought, and action that are relatively autonomous and change at a slower pace than political and economic structures. *Habitus* is deeply rooted in human consciousness through customs and norms. Even in circumstances in which historians perceive revolutionary changes, this *habitus* is barely altered.[46] The notion of *habitus* is at the heart of this study. It helps, for instance, to understand the fascination shown by the nineteenth-century European bourgeois toward some manners and values of the old aristocracy, and their preservation in bourgeois norms of behavior.

Bourdieu has had a profound influence on the historiography resulting from the cultural turn in specific fields such as the history of material culture and consumption. A substantial portion of this book explores stories of bourgeois material culture and the beginnings of modern consumerism in Spain. What is known in the Anglo-Saxon world as "material culture"—equivalent in the Hispanic world to a combination of museum studies, archaeology, and anthropology—has remained an area more or less independent of historiography until recent years. Economic historians were the first to turn their attention toward the study of objects, but as commodities of consumption and not for their symbolic value. Beginning in the 1980s, cultural historians have been discovering the possibilities offered by material culture for their field of study. This has resulted in an increase in multidisciplinary studies—in the last decades dozens have been produced, some of them very influential.[47]

Much the same has occurred with the history of the origins of modern consumption. The purely economic aspects of consumption—those involved with supply and demand and the origins of industrialization—have been amply studied by economic historians. For their part, anthropologists and sociologists have addressed the symbolic and psychological implications of consumption. Additionally, in the early 1980s a group of historians suggested in a polemic essay that the origins of modern consumption could be situated in a specific time and place, the initiation of a "consumption revolution" motivated by cultural impulses. The time was ripe for this debate, and two decades later it is still raging.[48] Chapter 3 of this book addresses the rise of the bourgeois home in Spain from the perspective of the history of household material culture and the origins of modern consumer culture. Chapter 4 studies patterns of bourgeois consumption over the course of the nineteenth century. It places the Spanish case in the context of the debates of the consumer revolution and looks at the spread of modern fashion, advertising, and the evolution of the Spanish shop from the traditional store to the department store.

In recent years, urban history has also been influenced by the cultural turn and the history of material culture. Several new studies have focused on the transformation of the European urban landscape in the mid-nineteenth century from the perspective of its symbolic content.[49] Spain presents an interesting case in regard to urban history and urban modernity as reflected in the recent studies by Deborah Parsons, Daniel Frost, and Joan Ramón Resina.[50] Although its urban population grew at a slow rate in comparison to those of central and northern Europe, urban planning in Spain was extremely dynamic. Many cities developed innovative and imaginative projects of expansion (*ensanches*); some were implemented while others remained at the planning stages or were only partially executed. Chapter 5 presents this planning frenzy as a basic expression of the rise of the bourgeois city in Spain.

Finally, chapter 6 will cover the origins of modern leisure in Spain and its contribution to the creation of the bourgeois public sphere, the consumer society, and the imagined nation. Music, theater, museums, sports, amusement parks, tourism, and the like constitute essential components of today's middle-class way of life, the origins of which are in the nineteenth century.

The development of cultural history has generated a heightened interest in the history of the lifestyles of the bourgeoisie or the middle classes, especially from the perspective of their material culture and behavior. From the late 1980s, French, British, and North American historiography has been the most prolific in this vein of research.[51] Despite this recent activity, Linda Young notes that overall less attention has been paid to middle classes than to the working classes and the peasantry. For this reason, she states, much work remains to be done.[52]

Spanish historiography bears out Young's observation, as the lion's share of contemporary Spanish social history studies has been dedicated to the working classes. Nevertheless, since the 1980s there have appeared several studies about the formation of the bourgeoisie as a social class from the eighteenth century to the mid-twentieth century. For the most part, these are studies of social history focusing on the role of the middle classes in the bourgeois revolution and the consolidation of the capitalist system in Spain. Thus, they address phenomena related to social ascent, such as mechanisms of accumulation of wealth, the nature of businesses, and strategies of reproduction and ideological positioning in the context of the liberal-bourgeois revolution.[53] Some of these studies have considered aspects of bourgeois culture, albeit in a tangential manner. Since the beginning of the 1990s, studies of the bourgeoisie have become more cultural. A case in point is the book by Anaclet Pons and Justo Serna about the nineteenth-century bourgeoisie of Valencia. This pioneering and suggestive work, which includes a rigorous treatment of sources, as well as the most recent by these two authors, *Diario de un Burgués*, have served as an inspiration for parts of this study.[54] Equally inspiring has been the above mentioned books by Valis and Frost. From the perspective of the culture of *cursilería,* Valis's study addresses themes such as the anxiety of the Spanish middle classes in regard to the challenges of modernity and the debates concerning the intellectual origins of Spanish national identity.[55] Based on his analysis of the writings of nineteenth-century urban reformers, Frost provides a persuasive study of the role of bourgeois culture in the complex modernization of Madrid.

In sum, returning to the above mentioned comments made by Jesús Martínez Martín, cultural history is "a new way to do history" that is only beginning to develop among Spanish historians of the modern period. May this work help foment this development.

CHAPTER 2

Bourgeois Conduct and the Making of Polite Society

S PAIN produced 44 courtesy and etiquette books in the eighteenth century—much fewer than the number of similar publications printed in England and France over the same period of time: 287 and 216, respectively. Yet, between 1820 and 1900, Spanish presses produced close to 300 volumes on self-improvement, rivaling the 335 and 403 in England and France, respectively.[1] This marked acceleration in publications of this genre reflects an important social shift in nineteenth-century Spain, as dominant groups began adopting the social conventions of modernizing Western societies. Most of the conduct texts that were published in Spain before 1850 were translations from French, English, and Italian, despite the fact that in previous centuries Spanish authors such as Antonio de Guevara and Baltasar Gracián contributed to European courtesy literature with originality and success. Articulating standards shared by a broader European society, this literature—referred to as *urbanidad* (urbanity)—offered a picture of modern gentility. By enunciating and prescribing rules of refined behavior in accessible publications, these new conduct manuals were central to the making of bourgeois society. This chapter studies the content of that literature and its contribution to the spread of the bourgeois conduct ideals in nineteenth-century Spain. It focuses on what it meant to be a bourgeois in Spanish society, and how that meaning changed over the course of the nineteenth century.

One of the developments of the cultural turn in historical scholarship has been the recovery of Norbert Elias's thesis of the "civilizing process," and the acknowledgment that courtesy literature offers rich evidence for studying the evolution of social conduct.[2] Elias intrigued literary scholars with his analysis of self-restraint in early modern and modern European societies. His idea that manners were utilized by dominant groups to establish cultural systems and implement social control provided a useful model for analyzing literary texts, particularly the modern novel.[3] Similarly, the creation and transformation of conduct imaginaries has been an essential thread in interdisciplinary approaches such as gender studies, feminist theory, and cultural studies.[4] Historians of society, culture, and *mentalité* have also studied the evolution of courtesy for what it reveals about social behavior, symbolic meaning, and material culture. Since courtesy is a system of social conventions, changes of form and audience are meaningfully connected to social, economic, and political transformations.[5]

Recent scholarship on courtesy has largely omitted Spain from its transnational, comparative, and interdisciplinary view. Among those who study the nineteenth century, perhaps the most prominent work on courtesy focuses on Victorian Britain and America. These studies, largely interested in ideology, have juxtaposed the Victorian value system with present-day moral decay.[6] Contributions from the Continent tend to focus more broadly. For instance, the working initiatives sponsored by Alain Montandon at the Université Blaise-Pascal in Clermont-Ferrand have enriched the field by uncovering new cases within the European territory and contrasting them with the better known histories of courtesy in England and France. Spain is among the lesser-studied areas, and studies of Spanish conduct literature have been fragmented and limited in scope and only cover isolated periods of time.[7] This chapter addresses this gap in the historiography of Spanish manners with a brief history of courtesy in the nineteenth century.[8]

FROM THE IDEAL OF COURTIER TO THE IDEAL OF URBANE

Throughout the eighteenth century, Spain and its colonies practiced conduct patterns based on Italian traditions codified in Baldesar Castiglione's *Book of the Courtier* (1528). Mercedes Blanco suggests that during the sixteenth and seventeenth centuries Baltasar Gracián and Antonio de Guevara customized Castiglione's model to create a distinctly Spanish form of courtier entirely focused on the nobility.[9] In the eighteenth century, conduct manuals were still produced mainly to satisfy the demand of a select segment of society— the educational institutions (*seminarios de nobles*) and private tutors of noble families. Unlike England and France, there is no evidence in Spain of the existence of a growing audience that demanded literature of manners;

urbanity texts were not yet a required component in the curriculum of primary and secondary schools. The most published authors of that period wrote to teach nobles how to behave in court circles, and the manners and values they articulated reinforced the inherent divisions of estate society. Authors did not create exportable, distinctive Spanish models as they had in the past. The most reedited manuals were by French authors: François de Callières's *La urbanidad y la cortesía universal que se practica entre las personas de distinción* and the Marquis of Caraccioli's *El verdadero mentor o educación de la nobleza,* first published in Spanish translation in 1762 and 1787, respectively.[10] François de Callières, Lord of Rochelay and de Gigny (1645–1717), was a well known diplomat in the court of Louis XIV whose conceptions on social interaction stemmed from the world of the seventeenth-century French court. Louis-Antoine Caraccioli, Marquis of Caraccioli, is described by Elizabeth Amann as one of the great bibliographical curiosities of the eighteenth century. The author of numerous books that sold well in France, he was among those authors most translated into Spanish during the period, thanks to the work of Francisco Mariano Nipho. His popularity in the Hispanic world, writes Amann, "undoubtedly relates to his moderate, Catholic spin of Enlightenment ideas."[11] Caraccioli was a moderate conservative, well-received by the Catholic clergy, whose renown came to an end with the French Revolution.

Courtesy manuals published within this context share three recurring themes. First, they show an obsession with social hierarchy: the main rule of this traditional urbanity was to be aware of social rank, to behave with deference toward superiors and condescension toward inferiors. Second, the rules of both individual and collective conduct were determined by the moral principles of Catholicism. Third, norms of behavior were designed to guide the performance of those navigating the complex sites of absolute monarchy, whether interacting with the king or members of the aristocracy in the court or the salons of the royal administration.

By the mid-eighteenth century, some Spanish *ilustrado* (enlightened) writers questioned the basis of predominant (Renaissance) models of conduct with a new alternative discourse. Such contestations appeared in essays or press articles, but not as manuals in book form. This was a discourse of bourgeois civility inspired by the English culture of gentility and the French model of *l'honnête home* formulated during the seventeenth century by Nicolas Faret and Chevalier de Méré.[12] Proponents of this revision of prevalent conduct patterns retained the traditional Spanish term *urbanidad* (urbanity), but with additional new meanings. First, they discussed what it meant to be "urbane." Their main claim was that notions of being urbane in ancient Rome, which valued the practice of genuine, unaffected civility, were corrupted by the fabricated formality required in the behavior norms of the court. Second, they argued that urbanity should not be exclusive to noble courtier interaction but rather should extend to the functioning of the whole social body. Thus, the condition of being urbane or attaining urbanity should be available to all members of society. As a result of this discussion, the prevalent courtier urbanity came to be considered artificial and false, and revisionists advocated that it be replaced by a different style of urbanity exempt from duplicity and flattery. Defined in opposition to old practices, the *ilustrado* discourse on manners introduced an alternative vocabulary with terms acquired from gentility and *savoir vivre*, such as polite society, civility, etiquette, and *buen tono* (the Spanish translation from the French concept of *bon ton*, meaning "refinement").

SIGNS OF THE NEW BOURGEOIS CIVILITY IN EIGHTEENTH-CENTURY SPAIN: AUTHENTIC VERSUS THEATRICAL URBANITY

In Spain the discourse of bourgeois civility started to reveal itself in a veiled form in some texts of the eighteenth-century Enlightenment. Father Benito Jerónimo de Feijóo in the essay "Verdadera y falsa urbanidad" (Sincere and artificial urbanity) published in his *Teatro Crítico* around 1740, was the first to establish the central concept of *ilustrado* urbanity: that the condition of being urbane was not exclusive to the courtier nobility.[13] Courtesy, explained Feijóo, comes from "court," and "the court" is the place where "all practices of urbanity are performed with greater rigor than anywhere else." He even considered urbanity to be a virtue or a "virtuous habit, that directs a man in actions and words to make gentle and pleasant his trade and interaction with other men." Consequently, its practice, stated Feijóo, had to be above all sincere.[14] Was this precept always upheld? Did individuals always practice a virtuous urbanity and thus an authentic one? Here is where Feijóo found the principal challenge to his ideal of urbanity and where he proposed his alternative model of social conduct. Unfortunately, wrote Feijóo, many individuals practice a superficial and intentional form of courtesy. Hypocrisy abounds in manners; countless use courtesy for the purpose of flattery and double meaning is the norm. Feijóo defined this insincere way of practicing courtesy as "false or theatrical urbanity" because it was superficial and hypocritical, and contrasted it with "authentic or sincere urbanity," a condition that arises naturally among members of civilized society. "Authentic urbanity," according to Feijóo, was natural unlike acquired urbanity and thus ceased to be the exclusive patrimony of the courtier who had been educated in its practice. This form of urbanity could be obtained by anyone who put in practice the virtuous habit of polite behavior. Clearly, Feijóo's concepts challenged traditional thinking that restricted urbanity to the sphere of the courtier. For Feijóo, as for other enlightened European thinkers of the time, urbanity was a necessary instrument for civilized coexistence, which all members of a given society without distinction of rank should practice.

Feijóo insisted that authentic urbanity predominated over false urbanity in the Spanish royal court. He disagreed with those who held a negative view of the Spanish court, considering it to be dominated by a culture of adulation and fostering fraud, favoritism, and the negation of merit. To the contrary, he believed that for the most part members of the Spanish court were honest servants and trustworthy people, nobler and more decent the closer they were to the king. In defense of this position he wrote:

> Neither my talent, nor my fate, have permitted me to interact with the highest (government) ministers; but I have heard from sincere and knowledgeable individuals, who have interacted with them, speak of them in positive terms, whether about their performance, or about their intentions . . . With inferior ministers (which I understand the magistrates of the provinces to be) I have had plenty of contact; and contrary to some views, I find them the best people with whom I have interacted. I do not deny that may be a few of little honesty, or of much greed but they are not the norm. Judging from those who are magistrates of the provinces, I deduce what those of the court are like. It seems natural that the greater the theater and the more sublime the position, so much more inspiring is it to them the honor of not having committed some despicable act.[15]

Where could that false urbanity that led to deception and to corruption be found? According to Feijóo, it existed also in the court; it was the common practice of *pretendientes* (pretenders), the clique that frequented all absolutist administrations consisting of young individuals and lobbyists who circulated around the waiting rooms of the ministries in search of employment, political favors, or personal privileges. Feijóo referred to them as a "militia of Satan that for the most part serves the devil without pay."[16]

Thus, Feijóo's concept of urbanity combined innovative and traditional elements. He was traditional insofar as he considered the court as the main public space for the practice of courtesy. However, the type of courtesy he proposed was innovative because it was no longer exclusive to the noble courtier. As opposed to the belief that courtesy could only be attained by persons of education and breeding, Feijóo conceived courtesy as an exercise of common sense that everyone could and should access. He described these desirable attributes in the following manner: "A solid discrete spirit, even-tempered without abjectness, inclined by temper and by ruling to please as long as it does not oppose reason, accompanied by a clear judgment or the common wisdom that dictates what to say or how to act according to the circumstances, all these simple attributes without the need of arduous learning will generally seem good for habitual interactions."[17] Feijóo considered himself to be the best example of a commoner who had acquired gentility because he was capable of performing without difficulty in courtier circles, despite the fact that he had been born in a remote Galician village, that he followed a career that in the formative years of his life kept him away from the mundane world, and that his timid character was incompatible with the hustle and bustle of courtier circles.

The ideal personality of an "urbane" individual consisted of three orders of attributes: a moral character, appropriate social behavior, and knowledge of manners. The attributes of morality and behavior were strongly interconnected and constituted the essence of polite conduct. For Feijóo, a refined individual was one who held strict moral values, behaved according to the rules established by society and politics, and applied both morality and behavior to the art of social interaction. Besides these general attributes, a refined person needed to possess certain qualities necessary to succeed in polite circles. The first was caution, understood as the capacity of any individual to carefully weigh his words. In Feijóo's world, the art of conversation was imperative; knowing how to converse was a guaranty of social success. The second was authenticity. The urbane fled from hypocrisy and always sought refuge in truth. "Is there a more inurbane thing than a lie?" speculated Feijóo. The lying individual was to be despised as the archetype of false or theatrical urbanity. The last moral quality essential to attain urbanity was the practice of discretion, which meant fleeing from shameless behavior, defined as the attitude of those who take the liberty to say whatever they feel.[18] The urbane individual should avoid being obstinate in his judgments and opinions. Stubbornness, wrote Feijóo, is opposed to the spirit of civility insofar as it promotes intransigence and obstructs communication.[19]

Feijóo's advice concerning social conduct was limited to two specific practices: visits and the writing of letters. In the new society developing in the eighteenth century visiting was becoming one of the most common forms of sociability among the well-to-do classes. Visiting was an essential obligation of what was considered polite behavior. To be visited was perceived as an unmistakable sign of social integration and preeminence. The genuinely refined man or woman had to be fully familiar with the etiquette of visits: when it was appropriate and when it was untimely to visit and how to behave during the visit.

Finally, Feijóo addressed the art of writing letters, an act as valued in social interaction as the command of conversation. Letters were used to establish ties of affection and to show respect. Feijóo delivered two basic pieces of advice regarding how and when to correspond by letter. First, he counseled that utmost attention be given to style, whether the letter be written in Castilian or Latin. Second, he warned against the abuse of correspondence by letter. Writing a letter is like visiting, explained Feijóo. Excessive writing, just as excessive visiting, becomes tedious.

In sum, Feijóo's essay can be interpreted as a sort of manual of civility with a moralizing aim and an ethical content. His intention was not to write a new treatise on behavior that revised classic ideas, but rather to provide a critique of the use of established practices of courtesy by certain social groups. This tendency was shared by other *ilustrado* authors who formulated similar ideas in a variety of genres other than the expected conduct manual.

One of the *ilustrado* authors was José Clavijo y Fajardo, a follower of Jean-Jacques Rousseau's ideas who addressed these issues in *El pensador,* a journal published weekly between 1762 and 1767. In his journal, Clavijo penned dissenting observations on society and politics, as he analyzed, reflected on, and adapted the thoughts of French and British authors such as John Locke, Rousseau, Montesquieu, and Isaac Newton. In "Pensamiento XV" he expressed his opposition to the prevalent practices of courteous treatment that he considered ridiculously deferential and out of touch with reality. Yet, Clavijo did not call for the suppression of existent forms of social treatment, nor did he propose abolition of the nobility. "The noblemen and the gentlemen," he wrote, "should receive the treatment that custom or privilege has allotted them. Their hierarchy is in possession of these distinctions and does well to conserve them."[20] But he considered that nobility had the obligation to do what was necessary to deserve such forms of address. What Clavijo proposed in his article was to abandon flattery and artifice, and instead adopt an etiquette that recognized individual merits. He argued that deference should be based on civic behavior and respect individual talent, and social status should not be inherited with family names or coats of arms. Clavijo, like Feijóo, called for a renewed urbanity, open to all social classes, stripped of artificiality, and free of subjugation to the rule of irrational hierarchy. Both men promoted a code of behavior based on the recognition of natural human potential, individual merit, and civility. Feijóo's and Clavijo's conceptions of urbanity were expressions of *ilustrado* programs of social change, and, more specifically, of the extended claim for the suppression of the privileges of the nobility of blood, a social practice that many *ilustrados* considered an obstacle to national progress.

During the first half of the nineteenth century, *ilustrado* principles fostered a refurbished code of urbanity that revised traditional conceptions. This reformulated urbanity was the instrument used by ascendant bourgeois groups to implement domination. Proponents of bourgeois urbanity aimed to establish the behavior norms required to become a person of distinction within the social space shaped by the liberal revolution. Bourgeois urbanity did not fully suppress Old Regime conduct norms; rather, it adapted them to the conditions of a society that valued individual merit over inheritance. In its early formulations, bourgeois urbanity was decidedly exclusive; it established the *sociedad de buen tono*, a redefined version of polite society. *Sociedad de buen tono* was composed of select members of the new liberal community—still a social minority of privileged groups with access to education and other social and economic resources. The main difference from the past was that under the new conditions good manners became a form of cultural capital available to wider segments of society. Modern codes of conduct would promote civic virtue in the newly established republics of citizens. Deference toward pre-established social hierarchy was replaced by a new notion of social "distinction." In the past, distinction as well as urbanity were qualities inherent to the condition of nobility. Under nineteenth-century conduct codes, potentially everyone could and should be urbane; however, only those who achieved what was stipulated in the literature of urbanity could attain distinction. Religion would no longer provide the exclusive moral guidance for conduct. Spanish manuals generally recommended that citizens be good Catholics, but religious practice was no longer a central component of urbanity. Similarly, polite conduct was relocated to new arenas of bourgeois sociability such as the home, the theater, the café, the street, the race track, the vacation resort, the athenaeum, the casino, and the political meeting place, thereby displacing the court and its adjacent spaces of power.[21]

EL HOMBRE FINO AL GUSTO DEL DÍA AND THE MAKING OF NINETEENTH-CENTURY POLITE SOCIETY

The new urbanity began to appear in conduct manuals after 1820. Unlike the sundry writings of the previous century, the new discourse was transmitted to the public in a clear, focused, and structured form. These manuals reflected a concerted effort by a rising bourgeois populace to convey normative messages regarding rules of social behavior. The first of these publications was a manual written by Mariano Rementería y Fica and published in 1829, *El hombre fino al gusto del día: Manual completo de urbanidad cortesía y buen tono*.[22] Rementería's *El hombre fino* (The refined man) provided a model that would be reproduced throughout the nineteenth century.[23] It went through several editions, and was printed in revised versions up to the 1880s. *El hombre fino* introduced the ideals of conduct that men and women should presumably follow to succeed socially, thus providing the prototypical portrait of the nineteenth-century bourgeois.

Some years ago Russell Sebold noted the importance of this book for two reasons. First, it is the first Spanish text that uses the term "dandy," much before its inclusion in the dictionary of Juan Corominas (1855). Rementería elevated the concept of the dandy (*dandi* once it was incorporated into Castilian) to an archetype of conduct that was adopted by the members of the dominant Spanish society. Second, the content of Rementería's manual had a significant impact on the culture of the dominant society of the period. Sebold demonstrates the influence of *El hombre fino* in literature of the *costumbrista* genre, specifically in some of the articles of Mariano José Larra, such as "El Castellano Viejo" (The Old Castilian) and "La Sociedad" (The Society).[24] Additionally Rementería used the term *etiqueta* (etiquette) for the first time to refer to the protocol for social interaction outside the environment of the royal court.[25] In the courtier tradition, etiquette was the collection of rules, uses, and customs to be observed in the royal court. The new etiquette, introduced in the English and French manuals of courtesy in the second half of the eighteenth century, referred to the protocol for public and private social interaction that the male and female members of polite society were expected to follow. The new etiquette, which can be described as bourgeois-civic, differed from traditional etiquette in several ways. First, its practice did not represent an obligation based on a rule or the law, but rather was an expectation. Next, it was used throughout the bourgeois public sphere, from royal palaces to private parlors. And finally, it established a symbolic language of social distinction that was implemented by new dominant groups (the bourgeoisie, dignitaries, old aristocrats, etc.) to establish barriers of social differentiation.[26]

El hombre fino introduced the ideals of conduct that men and women were advised to follow in order to succeed socially. What were the basic elements of the conduct model that Rementería's manual described? First of all, the book unabashedly favored the practice of emulation. From its first pages it advocated emulation of everything European, especially everything French. The introduction states that the book is a translation of two French manuals published in Paris because this city is the "center of civilization and sociability, of frivolity and lavish spending . . . supreme tribunal of taste. Today one comes to this capital to learn the delicate art of urbanity, of grace, and of politics, that just like our cuisine and our language are becoming more European."[27] The two French courtesy manuals published during the 1820s were the *Code civil, manual complet de la politesse* by Horace Raisson and *L'art de briller en societé* by P. Cuisin. Nonetheless, neither Rementería nor the writers who came after him simply transferred French behavioral patterns to the Spanish context. Each writer revised the imported volume's content to meet the needs of their own audiences. For example, when Rementería discussed etiquette for theaters, he referred to Spanish plays and actors of his time. When commenting on the appropriate conduct for social gatherings with artists, his examples and references were classic and modern Spanish painters.

In the Spanish version of the manuals, the refined gentleman's acts of courtesy, etiquette, and politeness were placed in the spaces of sociability corresponding to the new bourgeois private and public spheres. The *hombre fino* was pictured variously in his home among his equals, in the house of his superiors, in the house of artists, at the theater, at dances, at a wedding, traveling, at the table, in his dressing room, and riding a horse. Interestingly, he was not placed in church except to attend ceremonies that were more social in nature than religious. The space for which ideal rules of conduct were dictated was no longer the court, the university, or the seminary, but rather what would be known as *sociedad de buen tono* (polite society). Rementería describes that society as "the gathering of men that due to their incomes, social position, and the nature of their occupations mutually professed to each other the duties of urbanity."[28] Although it was a selective space, no one was denied a priori the right to form part of it. "We live in a period," wrote Rementería, "in which talent and ingenuity compete with fortune and birth; for that reason this treatise is directed at all who are interested in acquiring refinement." Nineteenth-century polite society was placed within the reach of everyone except the uncivilized. "Polite gathering," stated Rementería, "is nothing but an ideal similar to an open republic whose members are found in all classes . . . in the highest classes as in the poorest. Appropriate manners, generous feelings, conduct, and knowledge; these are the qualities that can make anyone into a member of any polite society."[29] Refinement was seen as a capital that, in theory, was attainable by everyone regardless of birth and wealth. *El hombre fino al gusto del día* imparted the knowledge needed to attain that cultural capital. Rementería depicts the attributes of the refined man, focusing on three fundamental areas of social performance: behavior, distinction, and sociability. Let us look at how Rementería conceives the essence of *el hombre fino* in regard to each one of these three areas.

Behavior

The first attribute of Rementería's *hombre fino* was to behave according to the tradition of the honorable Spanish gentleman, always genteel with women and generous with his family."[30] The self-respecting polite man had to be subject to the demands of ladies, endeavoring to comply with their desires. When ladies were not present, while the atmosphere could be more natural and less attenuated, nonetheless the refined man had to distinguish himself by his civility. He was advised not to be solemn, but rather pleasant and light-hearted, depending of course on the occasion, and above all distinguished and honorable.

In tune with the most central aspect of urbanity, Rementería dedicated considerable space to the subject of conversation. The refined man had to have command of the art of conversation, an essential attribute in a verbal society like the nineteenth century. "There is nothing more difficult in the world," wrote Rementería, "than artfully sustaining a conversation. The *hombre fino* always tries to avoid disputes or pointed opinions that could be unpleasant for his interlocutors, and he has to know how to listen. When conversing with someone, he does not allow himself to be distracted and turn his eyes to the tapestry or to the paintings on the wall, nor does he demonstrate impatience by touching his nose or the tip of his tie or the buttons of his vest. He never interrupts a conversation, swears, insults, gossips, harbors secrets, behaves impetuously, cuts off his interlocutor, shouts, or lies."[31]

Besides being a good conversationalist, the fashionable gentleman had to behave according to standards of virtuousness. Traditional rules of urbanity demanded the practice of virtue, but in modern gentility the goal was not to earn the forgiveness of God but rather to triumph in polite society. Two virtues were required: prudence and generosity. We have already looked at the first in regard to the subject of conversation. The second did not signify traditional Catholic generosity, understood as the practice of charity, but rather the generosity that shows a certain nobility of the soul. For example, an act of generosity was not to refuse to play a team game with a companion who is known for being bad at it. To be generous meant also to be magnanimous. The fashionable man pays his respects by giving gifts on the appropriate occasions, while avoiding exaggeration and the suspicion of having hidden intentions. Finally, in *sociedad de buen tono* there was nothing worse than being stingy or indiscrete.[32]

Distinction

The drive to attain elegance was the newest part of modern bourgeois civility and fed into the culture of modern consumption. "In our time," Rementería wrote, "classes are not differentiated by their clothes, but by the manner in which they wear these clothes."[33] As distinction replaced Old Regime pre-established social hierarchies, urbane men and women needed to acquire the appropriate markers of refinement. There is no doubt that traditional forms of elevated status, such as lineage, aristocratic title, or wealth, provided some measure of distinction, but being distinguished in the nineteenth century meant more than that. The *hombre fino* and the *mujer fina* followed fashion with discretion, avoiding exaggeration and reading fashion magazines, conduct books, and other sources of information. They adopted the most recent fashions and were the first to know when something was no longer current.[34] The urbane individual was a modern consumer who visited shops, read European magazines, and cared about the cleanliness of his or her clothes and body.

Personal grooming was particularly important for the *dandi*. Using loose and comfortable clothes was considered elegant, while tight clothes were for artisans. A beard or a moustache was recommended for a more masculine look. The most distinctive part of man's dress was his necktie; indeed, his quality was judged by his choice of tie. Rementería cited a total of twenty-two different ways of knotting a necktie, declaring France and England had compete manuals dedicated to this skill. The knot had to be fastened in accordance with the people and places that the *dandi* would come across during the day. There was a knot for dances (fixed with a pin), the Byron-style knot for the theater (the two ends form a knot under the beard), the hunting knot (tight for the rigors of the cold or looser in summer), the gourmet style (a very simple knot for meals), the sentimental knot in the shape of a flower (for a date with a lady), and the most shocking, the Gordian knot (a very complicated knot ideal for visits). There was an oriental-style knot, small and shaped like a half moon, and an American knot, the simplest of all. Vests and pants were also recommended for each occasion. Black pants were ideal for the evening, but they were not to reach past the ankle so that the black silk socks could be seen. For formal occasions a white vest was recommended. Jackets differed according to the season—one was not allowed to dispense with them in the summer. The same was true for gloves—their use was required outside the house and was recommended inside to protect one's hands. The preferred color for gloves was black except for weddings, when they always had to be white.

Of special importance in the care of one's appearance was hygiene, enhanced by the use of cosmetics. Hygiene was not only related to health, but also to appearance, and cosmetics were considered an indispensable aid. For the first time a manual of urbanity recommended procedures such as the cleaning of one's teeth with a special formula: "rinse the mouth with warm water bleached with some drops of liquor or of eau de cologne . . . brushing [the teeth] inside and outside with a soft brush, two times per week, using crushed charcoal passed through a silk sift." Also, one could use a toothpaste "made from charcoal and quinine powder mixed with a bit of cream of tartar, all combined with carbonized honey so that it forms a paste to be applied with a toothbrush or with the tip of the finger."[35]

The *dandi* is also identified by the use of what Rementería calls "certain whimsical objects," necessary accessories for the completion of the outfit, such as canes, umbrellas, watches, and hats. The watch had to be placed in the pocket of the vest, or worn with a gold chain around the neck and underneath the vest, passing it through the third or fourth buttonhole. Watches of silver or studded with diamonds were considered to be in bad taste, even ridiculous. Glasses were not to be used unless they were strictly necessary, although the monocle was considered to be a very elegant object.

Lastly, Rementería advises the *dandi* to consume tobacco because "it is recognized that the smoke that is exhaled from the leaves from Havana is beneficial to one's health and keeps the teeth and mouth healthy, nowadays the majority of men smoke, although, the refined man does not do it in the street, he smokes in his house and in the morning, never in the presence of ladies unless it is with their permission . . . he never does it from a pipe unless he is the captain of a regiment of hussars."[36]

Sociability

Finally, Rementería dictates a collection of rules for social interaction. The worldly man moved in a broad constellation of new spaces of sociability that emerged in both the private and public bourgeois spheres. Foremost was his house, where public or semi-public functions took place, such as receiving guests in the visits demanded by polite sociability, organizing celebrations, and sponsoring social functions. All the manuals of the new bourgeois civility emphasized the home as a transitional space between the public sphere and the private sphere. Although the home was considered a sacred and inviolable domain, it was not described as a hidden area, foreign to social life. For that reason, its decoration, aesthetic appeal, and comfort were fundamental to the new bourgeois lifestyle and the construction of bourgeois identity. The manuals of *urbanidad,* etiquette, and social elegance published since the beginning of the nineteenth century included chapters dedicated to the family home, describing the codes of conduct to be followed, how to decorate it, and the appropriate home for the refined man and woman, a significant difference compared to the texts of courtier urbanity of the past.

Beyond the home, the refined man was present in an unprecedented variety of spaces of sociability. Rementería takes these new spaces into account with rules about the behavior and protocol necessary for visits; dates; dances; the theater; literary, philanthropic, and political meetings; the houses of artists; a day in the countryside; celebrations; public strolls; horseback rides; and places of vacation.

THE REFINED WOMAN

New urbanity publications were gender specific. In addition to books dictating male conduct, there were a significant number of manuals for women. Spanish writers looked to Victorian society for models of ideal femininity. The refined woman was situated first and foremost in the home, taking care of all things related to domestic activity, but she also had a relevant space in polite society, or in the *beau monde*.

If the principal goal of the refined man was to make himself pleasant to his fellow men in order to be respected and triumph socially, the refined woman was measured by her virtue, whether it be in polite society or within the home. First of all, a woman was expected to be honest, a virtue shared with the men who prided themselves on being urbane. In particular, women had to display virtues that were considered specific to the "fair sex," namely, sweetness, affability, propriety, and modesty. These virtues complemented those that formed the ideal of conduct for the refined man: vigor, energy, and activity.

What in the nineteenth century was known as polite society was that broad area of social life in which the bourgeoisie and the nobility interacted. Within this environment at least three stratified social circles could be distinguished: the petit bourgeoisie, the bourgeois society of politeness, and the aristocratic-bourgeois *beau monde*. In accordance with the dominant social conceptions of the period this diverse conglomerate had a common denominator—the gathering of notable or distinguished individuals who interacted according to the rules of urbanity.[37] While both men and women had access to polite society, the gender lines were rigidly demarcated. The majority of conduct writers conceived polite society as a space dominated by men, as was the case for society in general. Women, wrote Rementería, "are the adornment of society, a polite society without women rather quickly ends up as a political gathering or Masonic club" and therefore loses some of its urbanity.[38]

The presence of women was desirable insofar as they encouraged a greater degree of urbanity. Without them polite society would be different but would not cease to exist. The attitude that women were dispensable in polite society would change throughout the century, affording women greater prominence and relevance. In 1829, for instance, Rementería recommended that the refined man take care when conversing with a lady so as not to introduce topics related to politics, science, and the like, which could be boring for his female interlocutor. This type of advice would disappear from texts written at the end of the century, which took note of women's broader spheres of interest: "the recommendations that women should speak only of knickknacks are being refuted every day . . . no longer is any branch of literature, art . . . unknown to them."[39]

The refined lady, just like the refined man, kept up with the trends of the time, but the woman had to do so with simplicity, combining fashion with modesty.[40] She was expected to pay special attention to her beauty, although she should avoid succumbing to excesses that consumed time and money. Her main responsibility was to tend to the domestic economy; order and industriousness were not considered incompatible with an urbane social life. While the refined woman had considerable domestic help at her disposal, she was in charge of the administration of the home. The well-educated woman "ought to know how to do everything incumbent on her sex without need of help . . . all types of domestic labors, from overseeing the pantry to even preparing the food by herself from time to time."[41] Such is how María del Pilar Sinués expressed the woman's role in her periodical *El ángel del hogar* (The angel in the house) and in some of her works of fiction, which presented the ideal of feminine conduct among the Spanish middle classes in the second half of the nineteenth century. Regardless of her social status, a mother, according to Sinués, had the same duty: to educate her children in the habits of modesty and good judgment.[42]

An important aspect of the ideal of conduct that the manuals of urbanity presented was women's appearance, considered fundamental to judging character, and more so for women than men. A woman was advised to pay careful attention to her posture at all times, keeping her head and body upright when standing and sitting in a modest posture, not on her side, or crossing her legs, or putting her feet on the crosspieces of chairs. She needed to avoid postures that betrayed superiority, melancholy, or sarcasm, maintaining a fixed smile or a solemn or sad expression.[43] An ill-directed gaze, a show of distraction, a fidgeting of the head, the excessive use of a fan, and the like were signs that could be negatively interpreted by those present at a social function as they could denote audacity or excessive concern for one's appearance.[44] An honest posture, wrote Fernando Bertrán de Lis, "allows the decency of one's habits to be seen, and contributes to one's health and grace through an ease with one's body."[45]

A woman's virtue was measured by her ability to be modest and submissive in all acts of sociability. She was not to initiate conversations, or raise her voice in excess or gesture. Silence, reserve, and modesty were seen as valued qualities that made a woman more attractive. On strolls, she was to be accompanied by other women or her husband. A young woman could stroll with her father or mother, a relative, or a trustworthy person, and she was to offer her escort her right arm and the cleaner side of the path. In the event that her parents stopped to talk with some acquaintances, the young woman should distance herself so as to not to overhear the conversation. When passing by a man, she must never turn her head toward him or insinuate curiosity or interest. In an unexpected encounter she would never be the first to stop to talk with a gentleman unless he was elderly.[46] The refined woman had to be familiar with all the rules of etiquette in order to function in polite society. It was essential that she be an expert in all the dances and the complicated protocol of society balls as well as the etiquette of dinner parties and the rules of urbanity governing the table. Likewise, she had to be familiar with the set of rules for visits, the most important social activity of bourgeois society, which would become almost the complete responsibility of the wife.

Over the course of the century, polite society in Spain, as in the rest of the Western world, became more feminized, although within the limits of traditional gender divisions, as the woman came to represent the family in *sociedad de buen tono*.[47] Jose Manjarrés, an art professor at the School of High Arts of Barcelona and author of a successful conduct manual for young ladies published in 1854, maintained that in polite society the woman "is the representative of family since the man, in most occasions, remains separated from it."[48] As Catherine Jagoe has pointed out, the centrality of domestic life in bourgeois society gave women an unprecedented social presence.[49] The wife, considered the *ángel del hogar* (angel in the house), although in a role of legal subordination with respect to the men of the household, would gradually become the foundation that sustained vital aspects of the new bourgeois society. While women were still secondary within the private realm of the nuclear family, conduct manuals depicted the new roles assigned to women in polite society that enhanced their presence in the nineteenth-century Spanish public sphere. By the end of the century, polite society was inconceivable without women, as women took on new roles, acquiring well-deserved respectability, pointing toward the changes in gender relationship that would occur in the twentieth century.

ETIQUETTE, RITUALS, AND SOCIABILITY

As in other parts of western Europe, in Spain after 1850 the emphasis of conduct literature shifted to the promotion of etiquette.[50] Etiquette served to reinforce the barriers of social differentiation in bourgeois society.[51] Rules of behavior became more conservative in accord with the definitive consolidation of the bourgeoisie as the dominant social group during the period of the Restoration (after 1874). At the beginning of the century, the discourse of bourgeois conduct aimed to facilitate the construction of a new social space in which social domination was not exclusive to the nobility, but rather shared with the ascendant middle classes. As we saw in Rementería's *El hombre fino*, the adoption of a meritocratic form of urbanity was encouraged in order to make polite society accessible to ascendant groups. However, by midcentury these notions of *ilustrado* and liberal urbanity were replaced by stricter codes of behavior that resembled those of the Old Regime society. Via the introduction of restrictive etiquette norms, fin-de-siècle codes restored aristocratic rituals and symbolism and gave a more central role to religion. This reformulation of urbanity aimed to facilitate the enclosure of the Restoration's new dominant groups and to reinforce established social hierarchies.[52] The conduct literature genre became more specialized as it began to differentiate between two distinctive kinds of books: the etiquette, taste, and manners manuals for mundane readers avid to learn about what was required to be part of the *beau monde*; and urbanity texts (*manuales de urbanidad*) written to teach civic and moral values to youth in schools. Etiquette codes also became more universalized, adaptable to the international audiences of western Europe and North and South America. Manuals such as the French Ermance Dufaux's *El buen gusto en el trato social* were translated and sold to Spanish-speaking audiences without need of substantial adaptation. Nonetheless, in comparison to the first half of the nineteenth century, after 1850 the number of conduct manuals translated from foreign languages was greatly reduced as by this time Spanish authors produced most of the conduct literature for their countrymen and women.

The polite social world of the high bourgeoisie and the old and new aristocracies prevailed in the dominant Spanish society of the Restoration, as well as in most European countries. In this society, behaviors judged to be "impertinent, inappropriate, and vulgar" were purposefully excluded by the adoption of new rules of etiquette.[53] Charles Day, a successful Anglo-American writer on manners, stated in the mid nineteenth century that "etiquette is the wall rose by polite society for self-protection."[54] The only way ascendant groups could break through that barrier was by learning increasingly complicated etiquette codes required by the *sociedad de buen tono*. This reality explains the growth in publication of etiquette and manners manuals, as they were desperately demanded by newcomers desiring to gain access to polite society. In her book on good taste, Dufaux wrote that a manual was the best way for a newly rich man or his wife to learn that "when receiving visits at home it was considered vulgar to wear street clothes, or that using a knife and fork to eat asparagus was a clear sign of social ineptness."[55] Bourgeois society would gradually organize itself via a complex framework of social rituals and practices of sociability, all of which were regulated by the rules of the new etiquette and extended to new circles of social activity, such as the worlds of business, art, and leisure.

Although in Spain the strict commitment to the rules that marked the new etiquette would not reach the levels of formality like those in Victorian England, the dominant Spanish groups did not fail to adopt elaborate forms of social protocol. The most characteristic ceremony of bourgeois life was the visit.[56] The social life of nineteenth-century well-to-do Spanish families consisted of a continuous coming and going from one's home to the homes of members of the same social circle. In this regular form of sociability, families, friends, and socialites created occasions for sharing pleasures, conflicts, sufferings, and negotiations. Each country established codes pertaining to the visit in accordance with its particular customs and traditions. In England, for example, visits always had to be announced in advance by means of a visiting card which, in turn, required a reply; the failure to reply meant an invitation had not been extended.[57] In Spain, however, the use of visiting cards was considered excessively formal and was reserved for specific occasions. For example, in the case of offering condolences, the visitor was not obliged to converse with the family of the deceased—one could simply leave a card.[58] Leaving a card was also required if one made a visit and no one was at home. When sufficient friendship existed, Spaniards accepted informal visits without a prior announcement, but for acquaintances or more formal encounters, it was customary to set a specific day of the week or month for entertaining, with the aim of avoiding inopportune visits.[59] For this reason, Spanish manuals of *urbanidad* and etiquette distinguished between formal visits, which followed a specific protocol, and friendly or private ones, for which the rules were less rigid.

Good taste recommended visiting between four and six in the afternoon, with the earlier hours being more formal. Nevertheless, the possibility of visiting in the morning was not ruled out for friendly visits. What was not accepted under any condition was visiting during meal times or *la siesta*. In bourgeois society to receive many visits as well as to be a welcomed visitor in many houses was an unquestionable sign of social success; the lack of an intense social life denoted failure, whether it was due to a lack of status or elegance. Any individual or family with social aspirations had to be familiar with visiting etiquette. The young man in the process of entering society had to know, for example, that upon entering a home for a visit, he must remove his hat, but he should not hand it over to the domestic help without first having greeted the lady of the house. She should always be the first person to be greeted with a bowing of the head and the formulaic expression of courtesy, "Señora a los pies de usted" (At your feet, my Lady). During a visit he should not offer his hand to someone who was his superior; he could only do so with peers, friends, and inferiors, as the shake of hands was considered a sign of friendship and protection.[60] In fact, the act of shaking hands, so normal in contemporary interaction, was an innovation in nineteenth-century social manners and had many restrictions. The visitor would only take the seat that the host and hostess had offered him and after they had been seated. He should not take the initiative with conversation but instead follow the conversation established by the hosts or by other visitors of higher social rank, age, or intimacy.[61]

Visits would become parts of the social routines controlled by the woman. The decision about the arrangement, days, and reciprocity was the responsibility of wives. To obtain social success they had to govern a house with an intense social life; be visited by acquaintances, friends, and relatives; and belong to a family that was well received in wide range of social circles. It was customary to set aside one afternoon each week, or at least every fifteen days, for receiving visitors. The day designated for visits could only be canceled for reasons of great importance. Depending on the social level of the house, visitors would be announced by a footman or servant. The lady of the house was in charge of receiving visitors unless she was indisposed. Good taste prescribed that guests be received in the parlor, but in less spacious bourgeois homes it was acceptable to receive visitors in the study or the dining room. The well-informed wife would know that serving refreshments in this type of social function was not advised, unless the visit was for a saint's day or birthday. "Serving food at any time and for any occasion," wrote one author, "was a habit of the nouveau riche, because they saw it as a sign of prosperity although for those who practiced good taste it was a clear sign of vulgarity."[62]

The dress code for visits stipulated modest elegance. A gentleman would never wear a tail coat if the visit was before seven in the evening or a frock coat if the visit was after seven. Ladies were expected to avoid excessive jewelry, as it was reserved for dances, the opera, or receptions. If a lady was single, good taste dictated that she not wear any jewelry. Authors of etiquette manuals even addressed the issue of pets. "In recent times," wrote one author, "some people take their little dog when they visit; although we have nothing against this habit, it is not advisable to bring pets on our visits."[63]

Among the more pleasant and de rigueur visits were those for saints' days and New Year.[64] Visits on saints' days were characteristic of Catholic countries and, judging by literary testimonies as these of Mesonero Romanos, during the nineteenth century they became required social practice among the well-to-do classes of Spain. The visits paid at the beginning of January to wish a Happy New Year represented a social ritual of the Western space that some societies, such as the French, strictly followed, although that practice has been lost in today's world.[65] Skipping a visit to a sick friend or to offer condolences was considered a grave breach of courtesy. Wedding visits, which were paid by the new couple six weeks after their marriage to all who had attended the ceremony, were also considered obligatory—not doing so justified breaking off relations. However, the recently married couple was exempt from all social obligations during those six weeks after the wedding, "even to the extreme that if a friend sees them in the theater or in the street he can pretend that he doesn't know them."[66]

Visits of friendship were social acts in which individuals showed their affection for their closest friends at the same time that they cemented their own social circle. A good bourgeois had to pay as much or more attention to this modality of visits as to the formal ones. These visits were always short, lasting between fifteen minutes and half an hour.

Even though the act of visiting constituted the most common occasion of sociability among the well-to-do classes in the entire Western world, it was also a part of new bourgeois civility that revealed the cultural differences of distinct nations. The English and the Danish would never visit in order to wish one a good day as would the Spanish and the Italians. Most authors stated that the Spanish favored a less formal, more straightforward style of interaction than the northern Europeans. Bestard de la Torre (Alfredo Pallardó), for example, found the English custom of constantly introducing each other when in groups to be excessively rigid. In Spain, one introduction was sufficient, although a certain protocol was always observed. He also attacked the "cold and even ridiculous greeting" customary in England and recommended maintaining the pleasant and adequate traditions of Spanish gallantry.[67] As the century advanced, urbanity gradually became more Spanish and less emulative of foreign manners, a transformation that can be understood as part of the ongoing process of Spanish society to construct a national identity.[68]

While visits represented the principal component of the busy and fruitful nineteenth-century parlor life, there were other forms of gathering that were carried out in compliance with the rules of bourgeois civility. Dinner practices were a case in point. The table has always been an essential component of urbanity, and everything related to behavior and etiquette for dinners, banquets, soirees, and the like was enormously complicated and was an essential part of the cultural capital to be assimilated by the members of polite society.[69] Rules of behavior changed over time. For example, in the past the napkin was pinned in a buttonhole of the clothing, while in the nineteenth century putting it over the knees was sufficient. At the beginning of the century cutting the bread at the table with a knife was the rule, while at the end of the century tearing it into pieces and distributing it among the diners was the elegant thing to do. In the eighteenth century, hot coffee could be poured from the cup to the saucer, while in the nineteenth this was considered vulgar, as was the custom of holding a spoonful of soup in one hand and the fork in the other. Good manners dictated that hosts issue verbal or written dinner invitations with plenty of notice and that the guests respond within twenty-four hours. The most consummate act of urbanity was the "visit of digestion"—the recurrent visit of the dinner guest within the subsequent eight days to praise the meal.[70]

Weddings, baptisms, and saints' days were the most common family social rituals in the nineteenth century. While first communions had not yet come into fashion, baptism was the quintessential family party, including relatives and intimate friends and establishing the bond of godfatherhood. Any family with the slightest economic means at their disposal held a dinner party to celebrate this ritual. To have godchildren was a sign of social recognition, and thus etiquette advised always accepting a request to be a godfather or godmother.

Weddings were family celebrations with important symbolic value. How elaborate the wedding and prior rituals were depended on the social rank of the couple. For upper-class families, the first step was courtship. Norms of politesse recommended that an older relative or close friend act as mediator between families; his role was to publicize the existence of a formal relationship. The next step was the ceremony of *petición de mano* (engagement) for which etiquette was quite strict. The wedding ring was presented at the *esponsales* (betrothal), which was celebrated with a formal dinner or banquet with the close families of the engaged. Some courtesy books recommended following the French custom of the *trousseau,* a public display of presents made to the bride by the groom and her intimate friends. The last ceremony before the wedding was the *capitulaciones,* a legal act to formalize the engagement with a written document signed by a public notary. At that stage, etiquette recommended another banquet in which the groom offered a *canastilla* (small basket) with presents for the bride, after which invitations were sent. The following Sunday after *capitulaciones,* the priest publicly announced the wedding.

Up to the last third of the nineteenth century, the tradition among upper classes was not to set a specific day for the ceremony of marriage, holding an intimate wedding at night or in the early morning.[71] Tumultuous and bustling weddings were seen as appropriate for peasants and craftsmen. The upper classes gave more attention to the ceremony of preparation than the wedding itself.[72] After the 1870s, it became more fashionable to celebrate the wedding in the morning with a lunch served in a restaurant. By then, the etiquette of the wedding was more elaborate; according to conduct manuals, a distinguished wedding required bridesmaids, ushers, and one or more flower girls. Within a month of the wedding ceremony, invitees were obliged to visit the newly married couple to extend their congratulations and thanks for the invitation. Couples honeymooned for at least a week, if possible, at fashionable destinations such as Paris or London.[73]

Dancing was an important part of polite social interaction. Balls were special occasions where individuals displayed distinction, sociability, power, and luxury. A ball provided entertainment, opportunity to make acquaintances, occasions for sentimental encounters, and moments for conversation about politics and business. In the past grand balls were restricted to the royal courts and their high aristocracies. Beginning in the Renaissance, nobility and bourgeois, imitating the courtier tradition, held ballroom dances in the family dwelling or other extra-courtier public spaces. This expansion of the rituals of the European courts to the circles of polite society formed by the nobility and the incipient bourgeoisie led to the appearance of a body of literature relating to dance, first in Italy at the beginning of the seventeenth century with the publication of Cesare Negri's manual, *Nuove invenzioni di balli,* and then in the rest of Europe. Negri's work, which arrived in Spain in 1630 as a handwritten translation, marks the beginning of the cycle in which courtier dance would become the instrument of social distinction in the circles of dominant society.[74] In Spain this development grew throughout the eighteenth century, and in the nineteenth century the social ball expanded from the wealthy circles of aristocratic palaces to the more modest circles of the provincial clubs and petit-bourgeois dwellings.[75] "In a parlor with a piano," wrote the author of a courtesy manual, "dance is the best accompaniment to a soirée that has started through conversation, card games, a poetry reading, musical performance, and even sometimes the show of needlework of the young ladies."[76] However, in all formal or occasional balls a universal etiquette prevailed based on the respect that the gentlemen had to display toward the ladies. For example, always dancing with the same partner was highly impolite. The master of the house, or the person in charge, had the responsibility of assuring that no lady was excluded and that all had the opportunity to be invited to dance.[77] If the dance in question was a private one, and even if it was well attended, the gentlemen could never evade heading first of all to the lady of the house in order to place themselves at her feet. The gentlemen would make their requests to dance following a very strict formula and would never dare to make an offer if they did not know how to dance the piece. For that reason, a condition of refinement was to know how to dance. The minuet, the pavane, the contradance, and the allemande were dances from the past that in the nineteenth century were replaced by the waltz, the polka, the mazurka, and the irreplaceable cotillion to close the party.[78]

In addition to acquiring knowledge about polite conduct for parlors, dining rooms, ballrooms, and other family ceremonies, the *hombre fino* and the *mujer fina* also learned how to behave in the new bourgeois public sphere.

In the nineteenth century, social life most commonly occurred at home or in the public or semi-public areas of the family dwelling. However, in time it became more common for polite citizens to find themselves in social situations outside the household. Diversification of public spaces for sociability was an unequivocal sign of the incorporation into modernity.[79] The most popular bourgeois public spaces in nineteenth-century Spain were the theater, the café, and the traditional *paseo*.[80] Etiquette in the theater had some curious aspects; for example, applauding in excess was considered inelegant. Rementería even recommended not applauding in order to avoid being confused with "paid applauders." Shouting "bravo" was sufficient for recognizing the merit of the playwrights.[81] Within the premises of the theater, men would never wear a hat and would bear in mind the classic rules of gallantry to be used with ladies: yield better seats in the box, stand whenever a lady entered or left, and so on. In the café, the refined man had to remove his hat upon entering. If an empty table could not be found, he was permitted to share one, after first extending a polite request to the person or persons occupying it. To gain the waiter's attention by tapping on the table or with one's cane was recommended, shouting was not allowed.[82] Among the new spaces of sociability that were gaining prominence throughout the nineteenth century were vacation resorts and places of retreat for short stays. Vacations, as we practice them in today's society, are an invention of the nineteenth-century bourgeoisie. Manuals of etiquette also started to provide rules of behavior for picnics. Additionally, as the century advanced one could find recommendations about the conduct to be followed in spas and sea sides, as well as etiquette rules for literary and artistic circles, political meetings, concerts, museums, parks, libraries, casinos, and temples.

Urbanity of the Body: Hygiene, Fashion, and Beautification

The new urbanity focused on the body. Fitness and stature were central to the bourgeois ideal, and each manual included prescriptions for *la toilette*, the process of attaining a fit body and an elegant appearance.[83] In the discourse of the new urbanity the concept of stylishness is differentiated from that of previous periods in several aspects. First, stylishness is presented as the most consummate expression of the new culture of consumption, which was exempt from the moral concerns and social prejudices of the past. As the next two chapters demonstrate, in Spain, like in the rest of the Western world, the presence of a new culture of consumption is perceivable beginning with the second half of the eighteenth century. The culture of modern consumption—the idea that the prosperity and happiness of a community is directly linked to its capacity to produce and possess material objects—took hold in Spain during the nineteenth century. Conduct and taste literature reflects this tendency in the advice it provided for the decoration of the home, a theme we will address in the next chapter. Much attention was paid to attaining elegance through the appropriate care of the body. To be stylish or elegant meant not only to be in tune with current fashion, but also to be clean and in good physical shape. Hygiene became a bourgeois obsession, and was clearly linked to the progress made in medical science during the nineteenth century.[84] The word "hygiene," understood as "the medical science dedicated to the conservation of health," appeared in 1837 for the first time in the dictionary of the Spanish *Real Academia*. The first treatise on public hygiene published in Spain was that of Jean Baptiste Pressavin around 1800. The concept was incorporated early in the urbanity texts published in Spain and subsequently in the discourse on diverse aspects of education: domestic economy, morality, and the like.[85]

Hygiene, declared the treatises on urbanity, besides enhancing one's image, "is known to provide health, well-being, and longevity."[86] What was the nineteenth century's ideal archetype of bodily beautification and hygiene? Care of the complexion was foremost, and individuals who did not have a fair and glowing facial complexion—considered not only a sign of beauty, but also of good health and character—were advised to recur to artificial treatment. At the same time, authors discouraged the excessive use of artificial cosmetics, advising natural methods such as the avoidance of exposure to sunlight and cleaning the face with a mixture of water with herbal tea or wine. Care for the hair was also highlighted. Individuals were instructed to comb their hair daily using a fine-toothed comb to avoid parasites; however, washing the hair with soap was not considered beneficial. Brushing one's teeth using crushed charcoal, cream of tartar, and, later in the century, commercial mouthwashes was recommended. After the face, stylish people, especially women, paid attention to their figures. The nineteenth century was the era of the corset, and recommendations and commentaries on qualities and uses of this garment were always present. Some *dandis* even went so far as to use chest padding and hip girdles to cut a more stylish figure, although some authors regarded this practice with suspicion. However, having a good figure did not mean being thin, as extreme thinness was considered a sign of poor physical constitution and these individuals were advised to conceal it through the use of thick clothing. "How many women," wrote Horace Raisson, "toil and fret to put on weight! Some live on nothing but vegetable stew, others eat nothing but bread crumbs at the risk of having indigestion, and lastly, some spend the better part of the day in bed. And what results do these remedies produce? None. So then it is better that they content themselves with their slenderness than become victims of pointless desires and continuous privations."[87]

The hands and fingernails required special attention since, like the face, they are "parts of the body that are constantly on display."[88] Most of the time hands were to be protected by gloves, an essential element of stylishness and distinction characteristic of the upper classes. Toward the end of the century, gloves were considered a hygienic garment, since they protected the hands from dirt and prevented contagion. There was a pair of gloves for every occasion, and some authors recommended using them inside the house, even while sleeping. At the beginning of the century black gloves were stylish, but by the end of the century they were reserved for mourning. For black tie events white was the ideal color for men and amber for women. For the promenade, colors varied depending on the season and the fashion. According to the literature on etiquette, the stylish individual would only remove his or her gloves at the table, while gambling or writing, and on a few other occasions.[89]

Finally, concern for the care of the body led to the popularization of sports and the development of cosmetics, two very characteristic elements of modern society. As the century advanced, the literature on urbanity and taste gradually put greater emphasis on sports as a vehicle for beautification and good health. At the beginning of the century, manuals referred to the more classic sports that were linked to the upper classes, such as horseback riding and fencing, but by end of the century, there was a marked cultural change in this area. In *Arte de saber vivir* (The art of knowing how to live), a text intended for men and women but with an undeniable feminist touch, Carmen Burgos dedicated an entire chapter to sports. While Burgos recognized that sports were a novelty with defenders and detractors, she insisted that in modern society they were fully in tune with cultural changes and that they were supplementary to femininity. She greatly expanded the list of cited sports, adding biking, swimming, tennis, skating, target practice, car racing, and even hot air ballooning. Burgos discussed the merits and disadvantages of each sport, as well as the proper attire and etiquette. She highlighted the benefits of swimming, horseback riding, and rowing—the fact that they had to be practiced without a corset was an added benefit, lending a sensation of freedom. Finally, Burgos noted that cycling was becoming very fashionable and undoubtedly had a beneficial impact; nevertheless, she recommended that young ladies consult with their doctor before beginning to practice it.[90]

FIN-DE-SIÈCLE URBANITY AND ETIQUETTE

At the dawn of the twentieth century, Spain had an extended polite society composed of the social conglomerate that constituted the dominant Spanish society of the Restoration. At the top was the old aristocracy of noble blood, followed by the new aristocracy of money and merit, and the grand bourgeoisie linked to business, politics, and high administration; the middle ranks included the bourgeoisie of professions, commerce, agriculture, and the new industry; the bottom ranks consisted of the petite bourgeoisie of the office, the small businesses, and even from some types of workshop. In this conglomerate the individuals and groups interacted among themselves according to the guidelines for behavior and style as prescribed in the literature on urbanity, etiquette, and taste. It was not because they were all avid readers of conduct literature, but rather because their standard of behavior was the reflection, and at the same time the expression, of the style of life practiced by those at the top. As one writer of the period pointed out, the aristocracy and the grand bourgeoisie set the guidelines for style and manners, and the middle classes emulated them. "The modest and pretentious bourgeoisie," wrote Melchor Almagro San Martín, "those with employment, and students, know at least by sight, the ladies of high society as much as they do the famous sopranos, comic actors, bullfighters, and politicians."[91]

The civic-bourgeois ideal of conduct was hegemonic in Spanish society at the beginning of the twentieth century. *Urbanidad* had become an obligatory subject in schools, and literature on urbanity, etiquette, good taste, and civility continued to be produced. In a general sense the goal of *urbanidad*, such as it had been defined since the eighteenth century, was the creation of civilized, responsible, disciplined, and elegant citizens. While this cultural system emanated from the dominant groups and its principal followers were the middle classes, its proponents tried to impose it upon the whole society.

In a social space increasingly more open to opportunities, urbanity supplied the cultural resources for social ascent to those who sought to improve their position, and to the whole social body it was an instrument for civic integration. Nevertheless, in Spain as in the rest of Europe, at the beginning of the twentieth century the discourse of urbanity was gradually becoming more diversified, reflecting the fact that society was becoming more complex.

While alternative discourses of urbanity were developing in Spain, the dominant discourse became more conservative, in a word, more "Victorian." It pursued, above all, the promotion of an elitism aimed at putting each individual in his or her place in order to preserve the social dominance of the highest members of society.[92] To achieve this goal, the upper classes of late nineteenth-century Spain urbanity emphasized the moralistic content of urbanity, recovering the role of religion, and Catholic morality. Earlier manuals like Rementería's lacked meaningful references to Catholic moral doctrine and did not consider religious duties to be an obligation of the refined individual. However, religious references were not missing from any of the fin-de-siècle texts on etiquette. New editions of *El hombre fino* published after 1850 adopted a discourse that took greater inspiration from the thought and moral doctrine of Catholicism. These versions proposed a code of decorum that was aimed at promoting not only "decency, and respect for others and oneself," but also "deference toward divine matters."[93] Manuals presented respect to propriety as an antidote for "the poison of revolution" because, they declared, when revolution occurs, respect, decency, and modesty disappear. The return of religious moral doctrine to the discourse on etiquette was an expression of political reconciliation between liberalism and Catholicism, befitting the maturation of bourgeois society. Fin-de-siècle conduct books reintroduced among their rules the obligation of complying with the church's mandates not as a social obligation, but rather out of sincere devotion. They also dictated rules on governing behavior in churches, in religious ceremonies, and when addressing ecclesiastic dignitaries.[94]

Besides the recuperation of religion, fin-de-siècle urbanity emphasized the practice of elegance, by means of etiquette and stylishness, with the aim of fostering elitism. As has already been pointed out, the titled aristocracy became once again the mirror of society.

Finally, dominant urbanity became more nationalistic, emphasizing the adoption of traits that reflected national identity or national character, and establishing etiquette for patriotic acts involving the national flag, the national anthem, military parades, and so on. In sum, in Spain, as in the rest of the Western world, urbanity inspired by the spirit of the Enlightenment and the influence of Jeremy Bentham and John Stuart Mill's liberalism was replaced by the moralistic and aristocratic concepts of the Victorian ideal.[95]

At the same time that the Victorian ideal encompassed many nuances, new manuals were written to serve the needs of the more diverse and complex late nineteenth-century Spanish society. An example of this nuanced discourse is found in rules of urbanity for women in which feminist thought can be discerned. Such was the case with some of the writings of Alfredo Pallardó and, above all, Carmen Burgos. The modern woman, according to Pallardó, besides being a mother and wife had to have an intense social life and "be familiar with and do all types of women's sports, as a means of acquiring physical beauty."[96] Burgos recommended women acquire a variety of skills needed in modern life such as knowing how to drive small carriages for outings to the countryside or around the city, operating a firearm in case she needed to defend herself, or riding a bicycle. Her conduct and taste manuals captured this proto-feminist line of thought, which would continue developing in the future in works by Emilia Pardo Bazán and Concepción Arenal.[97]

At the beginning of the twentieth century, the spectrum of Spanish literature on urbanity broadened to serve the demands of a more diverse and complex society. In Spain, as in the rest of the Western world, courtesy literature written since the Renaissance consisted of basic manuals aiming to educate men and women. With the passage of time, authors wrote conduct texts for specific groups—the most common group being the clergy—which incorporated information about specific etiquette norms as well as advice pertaining to morals and behavior. As the nineteenth century advanced, this panorama gradually broadened to encompass many of the newly established spaces of bourgeois activity. First, authors began to incorporate advice for the practitioners of certain occupations, such as public officials, lawyers, doctors, and artists. By the last third of the century, authors started writing etiquette manuals for business and sports. The best example of the diversification of the discourse on *urbanidad* is the enormous variety of texts dedicated to children's education. This is an aspect of the history of Spanish urbanity that deserves specific treatment, the extension and complexity of which exceeds the limits of this book. One must bear in mind that the texts of urbanity for children constituted the largest share of this genre after 1800. Teaching urbanity in schools was the best way to educate responsible individuals in accordance with the bourgeois ideal of conduct. Children were instructed to become virtuous citizens, good Catholics, lovers of order, individuals respectful of private property, and model fathers and mothers. They were also guided to be fashionable, clean, and in good physical shape. As the century advanced, the ideal of conduct for children was subject to variants deriving from the diversity of views stemming from the new political ideologies of the time. Catholic schools and conservative circles promoted a conduct literature that projected traditional conceptions that were sometimes rooted in the old noble-courtier tradition. Manuals within this context reflected conservative and sometimes anti-liberal points of view. Other less widely distributed texts took positions more inclined toward secularism or Christian humanism and progressive thought. In the last third of the century, the first school texts inspired by republicanism and Catalan nationalism appeared.[98] This diversification of ideological contents in children's urbanity texts, a subject that became mandatory in the Spanish school, reflected the conflicts of the bourgeoisie in the process of building the public sphere, as well as their anxieties before the new social and economic challenges of pre–World War I society.

CONCLUSION

As in other countries in western Europe, changes in the ideal of conduct that shaped polite society in nineteenth-century Spain emerged from a mix of aristocratic traditions and new bourgeois norms. By 1900, Spain had a well-established *sociedad de buen tono* that in many ways mirrored others in Europe. This *sociedad de buen tono* became the dominant society, dictating behavioral norms through fashion and refinement, or *buen tono*. It was a social body still characterized by a somewhat atavistic attachment to the values, manners, and symbols of traditional aristocratic culture. But at the same time, politeness had moved to social spaces no longer dominated by birth, and norms of conduct spread to ever-widening segments of society.

The expansion of new bourgeois civility in nineteenth-century Spain stemmed from adaptation of ideas imported from France and Britain. This importation of manners and styles from Europe's wealthier countries reflected the elites' interest in making Spain current with standards of courtesy and etiquette shared by the most modernized Western societies. This adoption of foreign manners affirmed Spain's Europeanism (*Europeísmo*) by demonstrating the dominant bourgeois society's wish to import modernity to Spain. Europeanism was a leitmotif in the discourses of Spanish bourgeois modernizers. Even in today's Spain, a fragmented community with diverse nationalities and a problematic national identity, Europeanism constitutes a common identity, a legacy inherited in part from the proponents of new bourgeois urbanity.

Homes from the Inside

IN June 1866, a new weekly publication called *El Hogar* appeared in Madrid. It was presented to the public as a periodical "on the advances in domestic living, hygiene, culinary arts, magazines, poetry, stories, anecdotes, novelties, fashion, advertisements, and public spectacles." More than a fashionable magazine, *El Hogar* was also a newsletter. Its editor, Don José Ferrer y González, was both founder and owner of an agency that helped people hire domestic servants. This agency sought to guarantee the quality of maids and butlers and contribute to the "improvement of life in the middle class home." Don José wrote for a clearly defined audience. *El Hogar* was for that social segment "that enjoys an honest well-being, those who Horace defined as the golden middle ground; who manage to live in a shelter protected from life's hardships, who enjoy the flow of a tranquil existence adorned by simple and honest pleasures . . . and acquire their social prestige on the basis of talent and merit."[1]

Don José's agency not only connected servants and families; it also helped households maintain the quality of their staff by providing the "means to improve the education of maids and butlers." Domestic servants were required to study "specific readings that contribute to work habits and moral formation, as well as other qualities essential for good servants such as fidelity, prudence, and circumspection."[2] Don José maintained a personnel archive to make the selection process easier and more efficient, and the agency also offered periodic visits to supervise households using their services. While it was not the first Spanish publication dedicated to the interests of the bourgeois family, *El Hogar* incorporated the most innovative aspects of what would come to be known in Spain as *economía doméstica* (domestic economy).[3]

Since the 1830s, authors writing about the family in Spanish periodicals had focused their attention on issues of morality and religiosity. *El Hogar* broke with that tradition by transplanting family life into the context of modern consumerism. Many of its articles depicted the home as a place where scientific and technological innovations converged. In a sense, it reconfigured the home as a central component of capitalism, although *El Hogar* presented domestic space as a sacred domain. In this vision, the home was a haven, fostering practices of privacy, individuality, and intimacy. Attention to domestic life became a manifestation of respect to the main principles of the bourgeois spirit, with ordered domestic life being the very foundation of social order. This connection that *El Hogar* presented—between the home and technology, science, consumerism, privacy, and social peace—was innovative, and it exemplifies the manner in which the culture of nineteenth-century bourgeois domesticity took root in Spain. This chapter analyzes the different elements that merged to form the ideal of the bourgeois home in Spain, how that ideal was created, and its historical evolution in theory and reality. To examine the making of the ideal home we will look at a variety of literary and periodical sources—mainly conduct literature. For the study of the bourgeois home as a material reality we will examine a sample of probate inventories from Madrid's notarial archives.

In her recent study of the Victorian home in England, Judith Flanders writes that "political and social history, both encompass the one thing we all share: that at the end of the day, after ruling empires or finishing the last shift at the factory, we all go back to our homes."[4] While this statement might apply to any age, the Victorians brought the ideology of "home" to the fore in a way that was new. That idea of *el hogar* was a fundamental component of nineteenth-century Western bourgeois identity. It embodied the main symbolic elements of bourgeois lifestyle: family life and material refinement. The family provided individual fulfillment and a basis for collective order, while the bourgeois house, its abundant material culture indicating social position, served as an expression of the right of privacy and a foundation for a new capitalist economy based on consumption. In western Europe, the home-centered culture of domesticity became a perfect instrument for the construction of bourgeois group identity.

A developing culture of domesticity has often been interpreted as a sign of a country's modernization. Since the 1980s, there has been increasing interest in the study of domesticity from a variety of disciplinary perspectives and geographic contexts. Scholars of society, art, architecture, and design theory link the historical origins of domesticity to the development of capitalism and individualism. Witold Rybczynsky, in his classic study tracing the history of "home" as an idea, finds domesticity originating in the seventeenth-century Dutch city and maturing in nineteenth-century Anglo-American Victorian society.[5] The most extensive historiography on domesticity comes out of literary criticism. Early manifestations of domesticity were written, whether in the format of moral literature or modern journalism. The first approaches to scholarship on domesticity emerged from studies of eighteenth- and nineteenth-century novels and journalism. Gender, feminist, and women's studies have provided substance to its definition, mainly by articulating the debate on women's roles within the private and public spheres.[6] The culture of domesticity is often aligned with the eighteenth-century rise of the bourgeois public sphere. Eve Bannet, for instance, perceives a "domestic revolution" in the discourse of eighteenth-century women writers who produced early manifestations of feminist thought.[7] Diana Archibald defines domesticity as a pan-Western phenomenon rooted in shared religious, social, and economic practices.[8] Beyond the literary text, manifestations of domesticity have been studied by art historians in various forms of visual culture such as paintings, engravings, and drawings that have been in circulation since the seventeenth century.[9] The history of domesticity has been explored from diverse and interdisciplinary angles, including relatively new fields such as material culture, consumer studies, and, in a broader sense, cultural history.

In Spain, the culture of domesticity originated and evolved in much the same way as it did in the rest of Europe, although it took hold more slowly given the particularities of Spanish social and economic development. While its roots extend back to the Renaissance, its transformation into a hegemonic practice did not happen until the second half of the nineteenth century, much later than in England and France. Not unlike in other countries, domesticity in Spain was driven by three major impulses: changes in religious thought; advances in technology, industrialization, and consumer culture; and evolving values and attitudes carried out initially by the Enlightenment and later by romanticism with its deep impact on affective relations between the sexes.

Catholicism has always prioritized the home. In the Catholic tradition, virtue is in marriage and in the effort of the couple, especially the wife, to maintain a harmonious domestic life. In Spain, this responsibility has been promulgated actively since the sixteenth century with a variety of popular texts such as Fray Luis de León's book, *La perfecta casada* (The perfect wife). The principles and teachings of *La perfecta casada* were reinforced during the nineteenth century by theorists such as Antonio Claret and Severo Catalina.[10] Religious literature interpreted the home as a refuge intended to house the practices of all Christian virtues, a protected space for peace and harmony that stood in contrast to an outside world full of dangers and temptations—especially for women.

The second major development in the culture of domesticity was the advance of technology, industrialization, and consumption. Neil Mckendrick's compelling thesis about the origins of consumer revolution in late eighteenth-century England sparked a flurry of debate among historians, who have only recently begun to investigate patterns studied for decades by economists, anthropologists, and sociologists.[11] Explanations remain complicated. Did modern patterns of consumption arise as a consequence of increased supplies of manufactured goods owing to the Industrial Revolution? Or did consumers—spurred by psychological impulses to emulate, remain fashionable, and distinguish themselves socially—provide the main stimulus for industrialization? These are fundamental questions in an ongoing debate. The only thing that seems certain is that mass modern consumerism in Western societies originated in the eighteenth century.

In Spain mass consumerism was not fully evidenced until the mid-twentieth century. Yet, while Spain did not fully become a middle-class consumer society until the 1950s, in some regions and especially in urban areas there has been a significant middle-class presence since the mid-nineteenth century. In these geographic spaces bourgeois social groups embraced and promoted a culture of consumption, comfort, and domestic hygiene before the country's industrialization. That gradual embrace of consumer culture and the ideology of domesticity set the foundations of a process with a long-term impact.

The writings of Mariano José Larra and, to an even greater degree, those of Ramón Mesonero Romanos, reflect a growing interest in improving domestic interiors and urban infrastructure during the romantic period. Mesonero Romano's article "Las casas por dentro" included in his book *Escenas Matritenses* (1832) depicted a pessimistic panorama-like view of the comfort and sanitation of Madrid's middle-class apartments. His intent was to call attention to the disparity between homes in Madrid and those of the most advanced cities in northern Europe. Recognizing some improvement in the decoration, furnishing, and interior layout of newer houses compared to those built forty years earlier, he maintained that there was much work to be done to improve common areas, plumbing, and other services. Many of his suggestions and complaints were taken into account in the construction of new buildings in Madrid's expanded areas (*ensanches*) developed after the 1860s. Similarly, new apartments in the *eixample* (enlargement) in Barcelona came equipped with modern coal stoves, water closets, and other up-to-date features in addition to running water and gas. New technologies, mainly of industrial production, began to be introduced in homes in order to improve living conditions. The best indication of this progress was the proliferation, after 1840, of new home and family periodicals, and manuals dedicated to domestic economy such as *El Hogar*.[12]

The third impulse contributing to the rise of domesticity in Spain was the change in the conceptualization of love and sexuality between the sexes after the Enlightenment and romanticism changed the meaning of family relations. Marriages based on love began to supplant prearranged marriages as affirmations of freedom and individualism against the tyranny of patriarchy. Spanish financier and politician Francisco de Cabarrús wrote in 1795, "Perform weddings under the most absolute freedom," because the best marriage is founded on "spontaneous choices, in the compatibility of temperaments and characters; in a word, on these indefinable elements that compose love preference."[13] Stephanie Coontz, in a recent book, referred to this change as a "love revolution" that appeared in the eighteenth century and blossomed in Victorian society with the model of the "angel of the house," which maintained that a virtuous wife should be rewarded by her husband's sincere affection.[14] Affectivity became an indispensable component of the happiness, welfare, and continuity of the family, not only between husband and wife but also in the relation between parents, children, and other family members.

Historians point to several causes for this historical shift in emotional values. Demographic growth after the eighteenth century played an important role. Reduced infant mortality provoked a change in the relations between parents and children, largely because children became less dangerous and potentially devastating to bear.[15] Urban growth also had a noticeable impact on family relations. In cities, separation between the workplace and the home was greater than in the countryside, and this distance enriched the intimacy of family time. Cities also provided better access to education, health care, and employment, factors that contributed to familial welfare. These developments were slow to reach Spain, and their spread was uneven, so their impact on demographic structure was not marked until the twentieth century. The lion's share of Spanish population growth, from 10.5 million in 1800 to 18.6 million in 1900, happened in the country's big cities. In that hundred-year time span the population of Madrid increased by 318 percent, and Barcelona's by 218 percent. By the end of the nineteenth century, although urbanization levels in Spain were below that of most industrialized societies of northern and central Europe, in relative terms this represented substantial growth.[16] These demographic changes brought cultural transformations. By 1900, the culture of domesticity was hegemonic in major Spanish cities. Notwithstanding the persistence of structural backwardness, new ideas and attitudes circulated freely in a society willing to embrace change.

The culture of domesticity, like gentility, was transmitted as a social ideal in a diverse range of written texts and visual materials. Domesticity was also a material reality present in the everyday life of an increasing number of new bourgeois homes. This chapter explores both developments: the evolution of the bourgeois domestic ideal in Spain and its materialization in the transformation of the Spanish bourgeois home.

Although founded in the religious literature of the Counter-Reformation, modern ideals of domesticity in Spain matured in the journalism, conduct literature, domestic fiction, and realist novels that appeared in the nineteenth century. Writing about domesticity depicted a variety of themes, arguments, situations, and episodic characterizations of daily life that created idealized images of Spanish bourgeois domesticity. Such writing had been excluded from the Spanish literary canon until recently, when scholarship from women's history, gender studies, and feminism began revealing this literary culture.[17] For instance, Alda Blanco describes domestic literature as commercially successful at midcentury, owing to a demanding audience of female readers. Blanco presents numerous texts reflecting the sensitivities, concerns, attitudes, and reactions of nineteenth-century Spanish women. These texts celebrate female identities at a time when tradition and law still relegated women to a position of social subordination.[18]

The domestic novel, along with newspaper articles and conduct manuals, emerged as a cultural platform for a new ideal of femininity that would come to characterize the developing Spanish bourgeoisie. These books represented middle-class women as repositories of morality and virtue prevalent in society.[19] Following the Victorian model, "virtuous writers" introduced in Spain the archetype of the "angel in the house." In this view, the wife exemplified maternal submission—pure, devout, generous, dedicated to domestic duties, loyal to her husband, and displaying strength and forbearance toward his moral weaknesses. This idealized image of femininity incorporated all the components of the traditional Christian wife resituated in a modern bourgeois family.[20]

In the discourse of the "virtuous writers," women were morally superior to men. Husbands could overcome their moral failings by treating wives with loyalty and affection, thus maintaining a solid marriage and contributing to familial harmony. As such, men preserved their preeminence over the family's material life, as they provided income, owned the property, and represented the family within the public sphere, especially in the arenas of politics and the economy. Given how very concrete male power was, it is difficult to gauge the everyday value of women's virtue. Did women benefit from the position of moral superiority attributed to them by the creators and defenders of the "angel in the house" concept? Did women gain in stature by becoming the pillars of home life in a society deeply oriented toward the promotion of domesticity, or on the contrary, did this tendency favoring segregation in the private sphere make women's access to politics and business even more difficult? These questions continue to be debated among scholars who specialize in nineteenth-century women's studies.

Realist and naturalist novels of the late nineteenth century developed further the moral and social implications of the domestic ideal. Authors put new emphasis on the material aspects of domesticity: the home served not only as a space for the practice of morality and virtue, but also as a symbol of distinction. Many of Benito Pérez Galdós's novels are prime examples of this new tendency. *Tormento* (1884), for instance, narrates a tortuous love relationship between the modest and poor female protagonist Amparo (Tormento) and the successful businessman Agustín Caballero. Amparo embodies the ideal of the virtuous woman: humble, decent, unaffected, submissive, attractive, and sexually pure. For Agustín Caballero, an epitome of the Spanish self-made man and Madrid's financial bourgeoisie, she was an archetypal "angel in the home," perfectly attuned with his social position and beliefs about what a wife should be. Pérez Galdós depicts Amparo and Agustín's relationship as a domestic ideal: "he loved her with a tranquil love, the eyes of his soul dwelling more on the charms of a homely life . . . his greatest desire was to have a family and live a completely law-abiding life, surrounded by honourableness, comfort, peace, savouring the fulfillment of his duties in the company of people who loved and honoured him . . . It was an English kind of love, deep, secure and unshakable, firmly established on the basis of domestic ideas."[21] This notion of an "English kind of love" references the emulative content of nineteenth-century Spanish ideals of domesticity.

Beyond its moral manifestations, *Tormento* also presents domesticity as a symbol of social position. Agustín Caballero's apartment, located in an elegant new building on Arenal Street in Madrid, was situated on the first floor, evidence of the couple's social position. In Spain, the first floor (denominated the *principal*), is one level above the street, and the street level is referred to as *la planta baja*. Distinguished families inhabited the first floors of apartment buildings, and that level was an even greater factor of distinction than the location of the apartment within the city. In buildings without an elevator the *principal* was close enough to the street for comfortable access, but at the same time offered protection from the filth, noise, and social promiscuity of bustling streets. In Madrid apartment complexes, as in those of all European cities, class hierarchy was represented inversely to the floors of a building, with the poor inhabiting the upper floors. To underscore the point about their social position, Caballero's apartment was located on Arenal Street: a prime site, close to Plaza Mayor, the business district of nineteenth-century Madrid, and on the symbolic axis connecting the Royal Palace to the Carrera de San Jerónimo, the street of the parliament, as well as to the Retiro Gardens and the area of the new *ensanche* of Barrio de Salamanca.

Another novel, Narcis Oller's *La febre d'or,* describes mid-nineteenth-century Barcelona as a universe of domesticity similar to what Pérez Galdós portrayed in Madrid. Oller's novel reflects the structural differences between Barcelona and Madrid resulting from Catalonia's more industrialized economy. While Agustín Caballero was a typical *indiano* whose wealth originated in Spain's oversees colonial possessions, Gil Foix (Gilet) was a craftsman who prospered from the bustling trade between Barcelona and its hinterland. Oller's main characters are manufacturers, financiers, well-to-do craftsmen, commercial farmers, and new aristocrats, as opposed to the government employees, politicians, bankers, aristocrats, merchants, and successful retailers that compose the social spectrum of Pérez Galdós's novels. Nonetheless, the values of domesticity are essentially the same for both authors. Gil Foix achieved his quick social ascent by moving his home from Carrer Gíriti, a dark and enclosed corner of the old city, to a new building in distinguished Carrer Ample. The new house where he established his family home and business also had a magnificent entrance—open to the street, luminous, and covered with marble. With the name of the firm on a large wooden panel with golden lettering, the impressive entrance opened to wide marble steps covered with a lavish red carpet, extending from the street to the doors of the Foix offices and home. A doorman sporting a sumptuous uniform with stripes and golden buttons welcomed clients and visitors. The narrator marveled: "That was richness! That was pleasure! Everything in the new place attracted clients as honey attracts flies."[22]

The most noteworthy aspect of Caballero's and Foix's new dwellings were their tasteful interior decorations and their modernity, what Pérez Galdós terms their "comfortable disposition, following the English manner," once again referencing the prestige of the English example. The Foixes delighted in impressing their guests with a stylishly appointed apartment chock full of new rugs, curtains, chairs, bibelots, side tables, and stools, placed there by a professional decorator, referencing the norm in aristocratic circles. Although Agustín Caballero, the utilitarian bourgeois hero of Pérez Galdos's novel, prioritized comfort and hygiene, the rooms in his home were decorated with stylish pieces of furniture that emphasized function over frivolity. Caballero was especially proud of his new technical devices still scarce in mid-nineteenth-century Madrid apartments, an indication that "over the miserable village was starting to shine the modern capital." The most remarkable of these devices was a "gigantic kitchen stove," which Pérez Galdós calls "a huge iron contraption, product of pure English industry, with various hotplates, small doors, compartments, and metallic pieces, able to provide hot water for the whole apartment that only needed wheels and it would look like a locomotive."[23] There was running water in the bathroom and a modern circular shower with a large showerhead that provoked the embarrassment of some prudish female guests as the image came to their mind that "an unclothed person would stand under that grater and that water would come out forthwith . . . It is a shocking thing, a shocking thing!"[24]

These modern houses depicted the trilogy of elements in the domesticity ideal of the bourgeois home: they afforded social distinction, they bestowed comfort, and, above all, they provided shelter for privacy, affection, loyalty, honesty, and elegant simplicity. Realist fiction was not the only literary venue touting Spain's domestic impulse. It can also be seen in a diverse number of texts related to conduct, taste, and consumption, such as etiquette manuals, guides to domestic economy, and periodical publications on fashion and decoration.

THE CHOICE OF RESIDENCE: BOURGEOIS HOME IDEALS

One of the functions of manuals espousing norms of etiquette and manners was to provide advice on the ideal home. It is noteworthy that this kind of advice pairing the home with established standards of social conduct first appeared in Spanish manuals in the second half of the nineteenth century. Eighteenth-century and early nineteenth-century *urbanidad* books did not include chapters or sections describing the ideal house, and references to domestic space were always secondary. For instance, in the manual by Mariano Rementería y Fica there are extensive references to domesticity but there is no advice in regard to the characteristics of the appropriate house. There are only indirect references. For instance, a chapter about the *hombre fino* at home with his family suggests that he follow the English idea of being "at home": to enjoy the pleasures and benefits of intimacy and consider the domestic a sacred space. The most important place in the home for men was the office, described as an ideal room for daily reading and reflection. Attention to all the family members is central to the conduct norm for the *hombre fino*: he "has to know how to spend an afternoon at home, in the company of wife and children or with his sister; it is his duty to entertain the grandfather playing chess, and if necessary also play with the children."[25]

The first *urbanidad* manual to include a section providing advice on adequate house choices was published in 1850 in one of the revised and expanded editions of *El hombre fino*.[26] The anonymous author wrote that "in the rooms of our ancestors," symmetry, order, comfort, and hygiene were not matters of concern, which was "just the opposite of our present day priorities." Natural light was filtered through windows consisting of small pieces of glass held in place by lead strips, making it difficult to see interiors. Rough wood or tile floors were too uneven to be polished with wax. Rooms were not connected rationally with corridors, and they had bumpy floors, crooked ceilings, and patched walls. In contrast, modern interiors should be comfortable, elegant, and, above all, orderly. "Order in the house is a reflection of orderly life of the owner."[27]

While elegant families chose first floors of buildings, a single man could choose based on personal interest; it did not matter whether it was on a *principal* floor or in an attic as long as it was decorated with taste. A bachelor home consisting of two rooms was adequate—a bedroom with a dressing table for daily grooming and a second room that functioned as parlor, living room, and study. In this case, the manual recommended practical decoration with bookshelves, a writing desk with filing cabinets, a dining table, a sofa, and several chairs.

Unlike bachelors, married men "with children and ambitions" must have homes on the first floor or near to it—never higher than the third level.[28] Conduct manuals recommended that houses have at least one bedroom for the couple and another for the children, a dining room, a study for the husband, and a parlor for social gatherings. This was the minimum number of spaces required to assume a bourgeois lifestyle. Domestic service was another uncontested necessity. Interior rooms, rooms by the kitchen, and attics were appropriate rooms for servants. It was also ideal to have room for a horse barn and a coach at the street level. Importantly, the author of *Nuevo manual de urbanidad* specified that his advice was for the average middle-class family. He intentionally omitted the description of home interiors of "opulent people, opera singers, famous actresses, bankers, powerful businessmen, and members of high ranks of state bureaucracy."[29]

In the second half of the nineteenth century, the home became both an essential expression of bourgeois identity and a fundamental component of a growing consumer society. Volumes about etiquette, manners, and good taste reflected this transformation with substantial portions of their contents. Authors pointed out that the choice of the right house reflected social status, a distinguished education, and good taste. Of course, choice was determined by the acquisitive power of each family, but the advice in all manuals was to make the maximum financial sacrifice to afford the best possible house.[30] This advice clearly endorsed new houses that met standards of rationality, sanitation, and comfort. Continental European conduct literature favored the urban apartment lifestyle in multilevel buildings with a preference for new construction in the recently developed *ensanches* away from the historical downtown. In Great Britain and the United States the ideal home was a single-family dwelling of two or three stories with back and front yards. Unlike the continental model, this kind of architectural preference produced a distinctive pattern, with middle and upper classes in the suburbs and the lower classes in the inner city. In any event, authors of advice manuals championed new buildings based on the criterion of the rational distribution of interior spaces: "In absolute opposition to good taste," wrote Ermance Dufaux, "are those houses where to get to the parlor one has to pass through private rooms."[31]

The ideal home required the creation of intimate interior spaces. In such havens family members could exercise their right to privacy. Advice manuals recommended that each family member have her or his own room and that it be furnished and decorated according to individual taste, personality, and gender. Thus the walls of a young lady's room would be painted in her favorite colors, the bookshelves would contain her preferred readings, and the décor of the room would reflect her gender and social rank. The study, decorated according to male taste, would be a repository for documents, books, and objects related to the father's profession as well as to his status as the family patriarch. Although all rooms were supposed to have an antechamber, this was not possible in most homes due to space restrictions so homeowners were advised to install doors to ensure intimacy. Doors were unquestionably a necessity for bedrooms, but the manuals went on to suggest installing them in most familial rooms, such as the dining room, the study, and the family room. "Could any distinguished family," wrote Dufaux, "allow that a servant or visitor intentionally or by accident invade the intimacy of a family dinner or a family conversation due to the lack of doors to separate rooms in the house?"[32]

In addition to promoting privacy, conduct books emphasized the importance of decoration and prescribed what was and was not acceptable in the ideal home. Many of these manuals espousing etiquette and manners also served as guides for home decoration and fashionable clothing. French-style furniture was preferred over English in Spain. If possible, Dufaux advised, pieces of furniture should be antiques, authentic and preferably inherited because that pointed to the family's history.[33] Homeowners were advised to maintain uniformity of style and period in their decoration, despite the cost of doing so. It was supposed to look effortless. All authors cautioned against excessive decoration and pretentious ornaments. Gold was not to be used for decorations—the color was appropriate for cafés or theaters but not private spaces. Hanging paper or tapestries on the walls, and using rugs in all rooms, lent seriousness to the house. Some objects were appropriate only in specific rooms. For instance, a piano or a harp belonged in a parlor, family photos or portraits in the family room or the study. More versatile pieces of furniture such as console tables and stools were deemed appropriate decoration for parlors, bedrooms, and halls.

By the turn of the twentieth century, there were numerous Spanish publications centered on lifestyle and the home, as well as other aspects of the domestic economy. In addition to manuals related to etiquette, manners, and good taste, there were a number of periodical publications targeted to female readers. These contained many illustrations and featured articles on decoration, architecture, urbanism, and other themes connected to domestic consumption and the home. In Barcelona, for instance, the *Almanaques de la casa,* a supplement of the magazine *El Eco de la Moda,* dedicated each issue to specific aspects of domestic life such as cooking, sewing, etiquette, decoration, and technological innovations for the home. Some of these issues, compiled in a volume by E. Richardin and P. Lamb y Cia, offered ideal houses specifically designed for certain populations of women like newlyweds, housewives, and single women in the process of forming a family.[34] *La Última Moda,* a magazine printed by the publisher and bookseller Rubiños, first appeared in Madrid in 1888. It included a supplement entitled *La casa donde habitamos* (the house where we live), which would be frequently quoted by the authors of conduct and manners texts.[35]

These magazines published a fair number of advertisements on their pages, which was a departure from earlier publications of this type. Articles describing dream houses, offering advice on decorating, and appraising symbolic social value appeared alongside ads for new products that directed readers to particular stores. With such visual materials, publishers could pair textual description with matching images. Illustrations and pictures were readily adopted for magazines and advertisements as well as supplements, catalogues, and almanacs. Like etiquette and manners, domestic economy was also a popular topic in the developing culture of domesticity. Schooling for girls had traditionally included *urbanidad* as a subject matter, but by the late nineteenth century domestic economy became part of the curriculum at the same time that it continued to be of interest to the female middle-class public in general.[36]

This burgeoning advice literature describes what was considered to be the ideal bourgeois fin de siècle home. Three fundamental changes distinguished this ideal home from its pre-1850 counterpart: greater emphasis on the functionality of domestic space, an increased concern with hygiene, and new technical and industrial innovations intended to make domestic life more comfortable. Some writers and decorators, for instance, downplayed the importance of a big room exclusively for receiving visitors, the *sala del estrado* found in traditional Spanish houses. The modern house offered a study for the husband and a *gabinete* (living or family room) for the wife where they could entertain in either a formal or a more intimate manner depending on their relationship with the visitors.[37] The *gabinete* was described as a room for the enjoyment of the company of friends and kin, and especially for family intimacy. The idea of having a room for the reception of visitors still existed, but now it was designed to be cozier, more habitable, more functional.[38]

There is no doubt that this shift became possible owing to the development of new middle-class houses in the new urban *ensanches*. In most cases, these houses had less square footage than the old *caserones* (big houses) in historical downtowns, but they possessed a more rational floor plan.[39] "What is the point of having a richly decorated parlor where no member of the family ever enters and is never used for any purpose?" wrote a journalist providing advice for young couples. "Wouldn't it be better to have an unpretentiously decorated room, cozy, welcoming, where the family gets together and is also used to receive visits?"[40] Similar advice was given for interior furnishing. The same journalist wrote: "It is no longer conceivable to use a piece of furniture in a room only because it is beautiful, expensive, or unique. Each object has to have a function and also be decorative. Does a flower vase make any sense without flowers?"[41] New middle-class homes should be furnished according to the lifestyle and needs of their families.

Matters of hygiene were critical in discussions of the way middle-class homes were designed. Advice writers cautioned people to avoid buildings that did not possess an adequate sewage system. Many buildings still had main entrances passing over open drains connected to the city sewage system. Obviously, these foul-smelling drains were totally unacceptable. Interior ventilation and illumination were additional concerns. Experts recommended that houses possess enough windows to ensure adequate air circulation and allow the entry of natural light—especially in bedrooms, the parlor, and the *gabinete*. Buildings with small interior patios or those in which a small patio was the only source of ventilation were to be avoided. Interior patios "build up moisture and filter bad odors and unhealthy airs from drains, horse barns, and coal storage rooms."[42]

Hygienic design and furnishing of bedrooms was particularly important. High ceilings would increase air circulation, and ideally bedrooms were to be situated "facing east to take in morning sunlight and have two windows on opposite sides to permit air flow. These windows should remain open at least two hours every day." Even in winter it was advised to keep bedroom windows open until two hours before bedtime.[43] Sanitation was also critical in choices of bedding. Authors recommended the use of iron beds instead of wood, as wood could become infested with bedbugs. Bed canopies were totally out of fashion, not because of aesthetics, but rather because they were obstacles to proper aeration. Straw, corn leaves, and even feathers were not recommended materials for mattresses, as they were considered dusty and prone to parasites and moisture. Instead, writers recommended the use of a single wool or horsehair mattress on a spring bed.[44] Revising recent practices, rugs and tapestries were not advised; a small side rug by the bed was sufficient. Of particular importance was the cleanliness of sheets, blankets, pillows, and bedcovers. Sheets should be marked to indicate the end for the feet, and beds would ideally remain unmade for at least two hours every morning with the bedroom window open for ventilation.

Last but not least, kitchens and bathrooms in ideal houses boasted new devices implementing the latest industrial and technological developments. By the end of the nineteenth century, an elegant house was unthinkable without adequate nighttime illumination, preferably gas. In newspapers and magazines there were advertisements sponsored by sellers of Spanish-made products for domestic gas lighting. The best-known was *La Parisien,* which also supplied gas furnaces and modern coal heaters to replace the traditional charcoal braziers, coffee pots and stoves that ran on alcohol, and many other products for "the modern kitchen."[45] Bathrooms showcased technological innovation in the new house. "Today," wrote Carmen Burgos around 1897, "to have a bathroom is considered the grand innovation *du temps.* This room is still rare in most houses in provincial cities and nonexistent in rural areas, but they are more frequent in the major cities where twenty years ago they were a luxury and today are seen as something natural."[46] In the bathroom, or water closet, the two essential components of domesticity—comfort and hygiene—united.

Bathrooms proudly incorporated numerous new industrial products and technical devices, such as flushing tanks, toilets, sinks, bathtubs, showers, and water and air heaters. Writers, journalists, and doctors began promoting the benefits of the English custom of a daily bath, especially for women. It is difficult to know how many people heeded that advice, but even if it was only a small minority in the wealthy and well-educated circles, this suggestion, as most of those described above, circulated extensively in late nineteenth-century manuals, magazines, and newspapers. This kind of ubiquitous advice signaled the dissemination and growing acceptance of the culture of domesticity within Spanish society. While it is impossible to quantify the number of Spanish households that actually incorporated a substantial portion of the elements of the ideal bourgeois home by the beginning of the twentieth century, it is possible to attain a sample extracted from historical research. The pages that follow consider evolving material culture in the middle- and upper-class Spanish *casa* through analysis of Madrid's archival records.

THE MATERIAL REALITY OF BOURGEOIS HOMES

Since homes constitute both ideal and material realities, efforts to understand what they mean benefit greatly from analysis that combines both ways of looking at them.[47] As an idea, the nineteenth-century home was represented as a space embodying all beneficial outcomes from the culture of domesticity and consumer culture, as well as an essential instrument for the acquisition of social distinction. As a reality, the home is always the result of compromise between social aspirations, daily requirements, and economic possibility.[48] In its material dimension the home becomes humanized, resembling a prop through which scholars can learn about lifestyles, identities, values, and incomes. To study the evolution of the Spanish home as a material reality, this section analyzes evidence from 814 probate inventories of middle-class families who lived in Madrid between the first half of the eighteenth century and the mid-nineteenth century (Table 1).[49] The selection of this particular group reflects the fact that in the literature of the time, as well as in recent historical works, this social segment tends to be associated with the main changes in consumer behavior.

The sample by occupation extracted from Madrid represents changes taking place in Spanish society at large. During the nineteenth century, Madrid was the largest urban center in Spain. It had grown steadily since 1561, the date of its de facto transformation into the imperial capital of the Spanish monarchy. During the seventeenth century and after the court moved to Madrid, the city attracted a society consisting of nobles, bureaucrats, and professionals, a social

TABLE 1

The Sample: Social Distribution by Occupation in Bourgeois Probate Inventories

	1700–1758	1793–1820	1874–90
Upper ranks			
Rentiers	24	22	23
High levels, administration	34	29	29
Commerce/Finance	28	47	43
Middle ranks			
Middle ranks, administration	39	48	23
Professions	28	35	47
Commerce	27	21	41
Low ranks			
Low levels, administration	20	28	14
Shopkeepers	37	19	16
Master artisans	25	31	36
Total	262	280	272

Source: Author's compilation with information from the Archivo Histórico de Protocolos de Madrid (AHPM).

conglomerate whose living depended on the provision of services to the state.[50] Besides being the capital of the Spanish Empire, nineteenth-century Madrid became vibrant commercially when it became Spain's main financial center. Whereas prosperity and economic dynamism in Barcelona were founded on its powerful industrial sector, Madrid had two main economic sectors that for the most part functioned independently. As state capital, it was connected to the big operations of state administration: state contracts for public projects, military supply, and state finances. The other source of economic activity stemmed from the demand for services generated by the city itself, such as construction, trade, and maintenance.[51] Despite fundamental differences between Madrid's and Barcelona's economic structures, the cities had something in common: both sheltered Spain's largest portion of dominant social groups.

Probate inventories from Madrid's Notarial Archives offer a very detailed source for the study of household material culture as well as for the reconstruction of long-term changes in household consumption habits.[52] In Spain, these legal documents were drafted to avoid disputes among heirs after the death of an individual, or when the family assets were extensive and complex.[53] One advantage to using probate inventories is the amount of detailed information they contain and, in most cases, the precision of their contents. After about 1775, inventories filed in Madrid were required by law to itemize a deceased person's belongings along with their appraised value. This was not required in other parts of Spain. In addition, in the eighteenth century some notaries elaborated household inventories by summarizing the contents of each room, offering detailed descriptions of the home's interior. Previously, officials undertaking the inventory had classified objects according to their function or materials, for instance, wood, kitchen, silver, or bed wear. In contrast, inventories that provide a room-by-room description offer snapshots of household interiors.

Madrid's probate inventories provide evidence that when compiled makes it possible to decode meanings, tastes, the function of objects and spaces, and other details that help us understand how people lived. Nevertheless, it is important to recognize what inventories cannot explain. For example, since they are usually made after the death of an elderly individual, inventories tend to document a family at the end of its lifecycle. As a consequence, most inventories describe the material culture of old people, those who have already acquired a solid patrimony but whose decorative objects, clothing, and furniture were likely to have fallen out of fashion. Furthermore, inventories are a static source, made at the time of an individual's death, and do not provide information on the process of making the family assets. Finally, there always exists a possible margin of error due to tampering; for instance, it is impossible to know whether widows or another heirs removed objects such as jewelry and cash. For this reason, Kathryn Burns advises scholars to approach Spanish notarized documents as historical artifacts—spaces where negotiations once took place around a notarial template, leaving traces of understandings that often belie the wording of the text and reflect the ethos of a historical moment.[54]

Madrid inventories demonstrate Burns's cautionary warning. In 1800, they were organized differently than they had been in 1700. In the infrequent cases when older inventories are organized according to rooms, they refer only to main rooms or use generic titles such as "parlor," *estrado,* and "kitchen." In the room-by-room itemization featured in later inventories, notaries labeled rooms according to their function, distinguishing between "main parlor," "kitchen," and "room for maids." This was a new way of perceiving objects and interior spaces. These inventories transmit the sense of a more rationalized interior plan. It is impossible to know why this change in inventory composition occurred. It may have demonstrated improvements in professional standards of notaries, or the adoption of new laws requiring detailed appraisals. It is unlikely that inventories responded to the physical alteration of floor plans in apartments in Madrid. After all, the amount of new construction within the city was very limited until the development of the *ensanche* in the second half of the nineteenth century, and many of the homes inventoried had not changed in the last fifty years. What seems most feasible is that changes in probate inventories reflected new ways of perceiving the family household among notaries and their customers. That shift in perceptions, a new way of conceiving the home, becomes clear in these room-by-room inventories.

Studies of Madrid's urban history show minor variations in the distribution of urban space from the time the city became the capital of the Spanish monarchy in 1561 up to the 1860s.[55] As noted earlier, some nineteenth-century authors remained critical of the comfort and decorative taste of many middle-class Madrid homes, especially in comparison to their counterparts in northern Europe.[56] However, household interiors were changing significantly during this time. Archival evidence demonstrates change toward a more rational distribution of interior space and functionality, and the impact of new ideas about furnishing and comfort. By considering the inventories in the sample, it is possible to interpret modifications in the distribution of interior household spaces. The room-by-room listings provide a rich source for analyzing changes in the furnishing and decoration of these spaces. Since these changes responded to either cultural, political, or economic impulses, a brief comparative analysis of the historical reasons behind those changes and their impact on Spanish history will help provide context.

Many upper- and middle-class homes in early eighteenth-century Madrid retained distinctive features of medieval and Renaissance interiors. Furniture was sparsely distributed, lacking in variety and limited in number. Both high- and lower-income families possessed similar pieces of furniture such as chests, chairs, and stools. The difference was in quality, not in form and function. The different types of chests—*arcas arcones* and *cofres*—were versions of a piece of furniture that always had the same function: to store clothes, objects, and even food. The chest was the forerunner of the armoire, already in existence in the seventeenth century though infrequent in Spanish homes. Choices of furnishings were based more on availability and functionality than on an interest in fashion.[57]

In traditional houses, the bedroom was not a private space: it was the main room and the bed was the highest appraised and most appreciated piece of furniture.[58] Historically, distinguished people received visitors in their bedroom, sometimes while they were in bed.[59] Bedroom furnishings were valued highly in late seventeenth-century Madrid inventories.[60] In 1682, an inventory taken after the death of Pascual García Recada, a high-ranking staff member of the Royal Treasury, included as the most highly appraised objects a bed with a canopy and curtains, bed wear, bed heaters, bedroom braziers, and rugs.[61] In the inventory of Angeles Rueda, widow of a servant in the king's entourage, the bedroom objects—bed, armoire, cotton bed covers, and canopy—were worth more than half of the total value of all the appraised possessions.[62]

One feature that set seventeenth-century Spanish homes apart from their European counterparts was the existence of a gender-divided space in the living room known as the *estrado* or *sala del estrado*. Commonly referred to in Hispanic plays, novels, travel accounts, and memoirs, the *estrado* was a space reserved for women, where wives, daughters, maids, and occasionally female kin and friends spent many hours doing needlework and talking about women's affairs. It was raised from the floor by means of a wooden or cork platform, and separated from the rest of the room by a slender railing. Its space was furnished with cushions, stools, pillows, low chairs, oriental rugs, curtains, and small pieces of furniture used to store needles, pins, scissors, thread, and other objects related to female domestic activities.[63]

Although museums and collectors possess pieces of furniture characteristic of the *estrado*, historically accurate reproductions are difficult as accounts are sketchy and there is no visual evidence. When inventories refer to *estrado* or *sala del estrado*, they describe an area within a larger room, not the contents of a particular section. An example is the inventory of Francisco de Burgos filed in 1677. De Burgos was a wholesaler in Madrid with a title that identified him as a member of the local Inquisition tribunal. Based on his occupation and the possessions listed in the inventory, he belonged to the middle ranks of Madrid's society. While the inventory is organized according to categories of objects, surprisingly there is a specific section entitled "sala del estrado." Some of the objects described and appraised—curtains, several pillows of green damask, and a Turkish rug in good condition—are typical of the *estrado*. However, the same section includes sheets, bed covers, and clothes: items that would not belong in the *estrado*.[64] It is frequent to find inventories including appraised objects classified as belonging to the *estrado*: "estrado side table," "estrado chair," "estrado rug," "estrado pillow," and so on.[65]

The tradition of the *estrado* was exported to the colonies and, like many colonial influences, it survived in some areas as a peculiarity of *criollo* lifestyles even after it had disappeared in Spain. In his *Recuerdos de Provincia*, written around 1850, Domingo Faustino Sarmiento describes the importance of *estrado* in the Argentine *criollo* home where he was born. The house had two main areas: "one was the bedroom of my parents, and the other, larger area was a parlor in which there was an *estrado* furnished with pillows in the tradition of the Arabic divan preserved among Spanish people." In the *estrado* his mother spent long hours sewing and embroidering. Sarmiento describes his mother's disappointment when his sisters, in the name of modernity, decided to dismantle the *estrado*: the old woman "was not accustomed to work seated on a high chair."[66] This long-standing tradition in interior design is difficult to trace back to its roots in Spain, and there are no studies on medieval household material culture that clarify its origins. That Sarmiento links the *estrado* with Arabic culture suggests that its tradition extended beyond the Hispanic world.[67]

One of the characteristics of the beginning of the culture of domesticity in northern Europe was the existence of new spaces with specific functions in the interior of the house. Among the earliest were rooms and antechambers exclusively for women, where female members of the household gathered to embroider, receive visitors, play music, and serve food. The presence of these areas has been well documented in the case of Italian Renaissance palaces and country homes of the English gentry.[68] Like the Spanish *estrado,* these spaces were decorated according to female taste and reflected their various functions. In wealthy Venetian households, for instance, there was a type of chair called *pro muliere* of smaller dimensions than a regular armchair, placed in bedrooms and designed for women's use in performing traditional female tasks.[69] Italian *pro muliere* chairs resemble Spanish *estrado* chairs that have been preserved in Spanish museums and collections. Based on the presence of these customized chairs, the *estrado,* more than a medieval atavism, could be considered a stage in the transition to the modern home insofar as it possessed two of its most distinctive features: specialization of interior spaces and recognition of intimacy.[70]

Literary accounts indicate that the original function of the *estrado* was beginning to fall out of use by the end of the seventeenth century.[71] The boundaries between male and female spaces within the living room were becoming blurred, and admission of men to the *estrado* to socialize with their female counterparts became an accepted practice, reflecting changing attitudes about domestic sociability. Although the *estrado* did not disappear from Spanish homes until the early nineteenth century, fewer and fewer homes had them and their original function had diminished.

After 1750, there was a tendency toward rationalization in the distribution of interior spaces, as rooms began to assume specific functions. Most inventoried descriptions of household interiors from the early eighteenth century suggest limited privacy, a lack of defined areas for domestic and public socialization, and poorly delineated divisions between family spaces, the spaces occupied by servants, and working spaces.[72] However, after 1750, inventories began to distribute domestic spaces according to the functionality of each room.[73] In many cases this change reflects only the use of new terminology to define preexisting spaces in old homes. In other words, what changed was not the physical distribution of interiors, but rather the way in which these were perceived, described, or organized. This transition marks an important cultural shift in the way essential aspects of everyday life were conceived.

The transformation of Spanish attitudes toward domestic life was marked by the widespread use of three kinds of rooms: the *gabinete* (living room), the *sala* or *sala principal* (parlor), and the *pieza de comer* (dining room). The *gabinete* was a well defined space for the privacy of everyday family activities, while other rooms were designated for public social gathering. Initially, the meaning of *gabinete* was connected to *estrado*. The dictionary *Real Academia Española* registers an interesting evolution for the word *gabinete*, which comes from the French word for *cabinet*. At the beginning of the eighteenth century, it refers to a room in the house, while the 1734 edition defines it as "the room, in palaces or houses of principal people, in the most private areas, for their retreat or for dealing with personal business." *Gabinete* also referred to "the room that ladies use for hair dressing and make-up, the walls of which are decorated with mirrors, small paintings, miniatures, and other bric-a-bracs that give the room an air of joy and brightness." The 1803 edition was even more precise in its definition of *gabinete*: "a room for ostentation [sic], smaller than the *sala de estrado,* considered its continuation, though with improved taste and quality of its decoration." Moving forward in time, the 1914 edition includes two meanings: "room by the *sala de estrado,* of smaller dimensions but in its proximity," and "drawing room where the ladies of the house entertain their visitors." It was not until 1950 that *gabinete* is defined as a "smaller room in the house to receive informal visits" although this was the main purpose of that room in middle-class houses from the beginning of the nineteenth century.

Notarial evidence illustrates this transition in interior design. For instance, the inventory of Castile Council member Cristobal de la Mata, filed in 1801, contains a description of a room called *gabinete* that was adjacent to other room called *sala del estrado.* The *gabinete* was furnished with ten chairs of good quality wood with damask upholstery, one sofa seating four with upholstery matching the chairs, two braziers, two tables of imitation mahogany, and curtains. The notary wrote that that was "the room of the house used by the widow and daughters of the deceased." The *sala del estrado* was similarly decorated although with fewer functional pieces of furniture. It held a total of thirty-six chairs in three twelve-piece sets, each set of a different quality: one dozen with damask upholstery, another dozen of the common *sillas de Vitoria,* and another dozen small chairs. The room had a sofa with damask cushions, a large central table, some corner tables, paintings on the wall, and damask curtains on the windows. On the large table there was a magnificent clock imported from England with bronze ornaments and quality woods, the most valuable item in the room. As the inventory reveals, Cristobal de la Mata's house illustrates a transition between the traditional *estrado* house and the modern bourgeois home. The *sala del estrado* was not the typical space found in seventeenth-century and earlier houses; rather, it was a conventional eighteenth-century parlor for the purpose of social gathering. [74]

The *gabinete,* a private space reserved for the women of the household, thus performed the functions of the traditional *estrado,* but it was decorated with the furnishings of a modern living or family room. Two things are clear in the evolution of the *gabinete.* First, it remained a private room, for either women or the entire family. Second, this room always had a marked female character. The fact that it was considered a transformation of the *estrado* underscores the idea that the history of the *estrado* cannot be interpreted as a medieval atavism peculiar to Spain and linked to its medieval Islamic past. Its development into a space dedicated to the privacy of the family followed a path similar to the transition of household interiors in France. In the homes of well-off families it played an active role in the transformation from the old noble household to the modern bourgeois home. The *gabinete* in Spanish homes was the equivalent of the *petit salon* in French houses and the drawing room in Victorian homes. It was a central location in the bourgeois home where the family gathered, the wife governed over domestic issues, and close friends and kin visited. In sum, it was a room that embodied the values and practices of domesticity.[75] The *gabinete* is the forerunner of the modern family room, a space for the privacy of the family in contrast to the parlor or living room, which was reserved for public social gatherings. This distinction between private and public areas within the house is evidence of the assimilation of new concepts of individualism and civility by the Spanish middle ranks.

Functional specialization of household interiors reflected a new concern for order and spatial control that was achieved largely through household objects and their distribution. Inventories depict a significant process of transformation in furnishings during the first half of the eighteenth century. Early eighteenth-century records reflect continuity from medieval and Renaissance notions of furnishing: few pieces of furniture, a lack of functionalism, and minimal specialization. Later inventories show sustained growth in the amount of domestic goods—such as furniture, decorative objects, and clothing—in proportion to the total assets itemized per family (Table 2). The main increases took place in items such as linens, furniture, and the decorations of interior spaces, especially walls and alcoves. The average middle-class home presents the traditional *vargueño* or *bargueño*—essentially a writing desk, but with multiple uses, from writing to storage—as the most common piece of furniture. *Vargueños* were expensive because they were highly decorative.[76] As an alternative, those who could not afford *vargueños* used *papeleras* or *escribanías*, also types of desks, but smaller, more austere, and, of course, less expensive. There were few chairs in proportion to the dimensions of the interiors. Decorative elements were also limited with the exception of the *estrados* and *oratorios*. In general, walls were covered with inexpensive reproductions of paintings and engravings of religious themes. Wealthier houses had mirrors, tapestries, and more expensive original paintings. Small tables—*bufetes*—and large numbers of chests completed the typical furnishing elements.

TABLE 2

Domestic Assets as a Proportion of the Total Assets in the Probate Inventories of
Madrid Middle Classes (in percentages)

	1700–1758	1793–1820	1874–90	
	Domestic*	Domestic	Domestic	Total Cases
Upper ranks	19.33	22.70	20.83	270
Middle ranks	48.02	51.10	56.97	323
Low ranks	58.36	56.23	61.30	221
Total cases				814

* This category includes personal goods such as clothes, furniture, linens, china, books, and the
like.
Source: Author's compilation with information from the Archivo Histórico de Protocolos de
Madrid (AHPM).

Inventories of average homes around 1758 show important elements of
transition. First, there were changes in terminology: *bufetes* were now called
mesas (tables); *vargueños, papeleras,* and *escribanías* were now called *escritorios*
(writing desks). But alterations were not just changes in name; the homes also
had new types of furniture. Wardrobes, chests of drawers, and sofas appear in
inventories for the first time. Decorative elements such as mirrors are reflected
in 77 percent of the inventories, walls begin to be decorated with paper and
cloth, and there are also more wooden friezes, statues with religious motifs,
folding screens to separate spaces, glass windows and doors, and, in a few cases,
cornucopias (wall candle mirrors). Cornucopias were the most idiosyncratic
decorative element of the late eighteenth and early nineteenth centuries. Named
after the horn of plenty due to their design, they best characterized the change
in middle-class household material culture. Rarely were they found in poor
houses, which were still illuminated by the traditional oil *candil* and candles
made of animal fat.

This tendency toward functional specialization in furniture began after 1765
and continued up to the 1880s. Inventories from the later period depict greater

diversification in furnishings, and, in particular, a remarkable number of new objects, decorative as well as functional, accumulated in the households. More than 76 percent of them list sofas, love seats, armchairs, more numerous and varied chairs, wardrobes, folding tables, cornucopias, side tables, candlesticks, clocks, braziers, and more elaborate beds replacing the simple wooden ones. Slightly more than 40 percent of inventories include items such as night tables, desks, chest of drawers, sideboards, dressing tables, game tables, consoles, and a large variety of new tableware items such as soup bowls, *chocolateras* (hot chocolate pots), gravy bowls, salad bowls, china, and glassware. Also more frequent, undoubtedly as a form of investment, is the possession of pieces of furniture made of rich imported woods such as mahogany, ebony, and rosewood. Inventories also point to significant changes in textiles that will be analyzed in the next chapter.

By the mid-nineteenth century, the lifestyles and consumer habits of Madrid's middle classes were substantially different than they had been one hundred years before. A change of this magnitude in consumer behavior is unprecedented in Spanish history. Historians studying the evolution of consumer practices in the West since the sixteenth century describe periods of limited improvement in living standards and a consequent increase in consumerism.[77] These cycles were connected to the expansion of Atlantic markets and the circulation of a limited number of products, mainly textiles and stimulants such as coffee, cocoa, and tea. Recent studies have questioned the view that consumer society was an exclusively Western phenomenon linked to the advent and expansion of modernity, as many oriental societies experienced similar developments since the Middle Ages.[78] Nonetheless, starting in the eighteenth century, the expansion of new forms of consumption in the West is unquestionable.

Consumer revolution seems less applicable in Spain, where consumption practices remained weak and restricted to a small segment of society up to the twentieth century. Changes in consumer behavior appear to have affected society and culture more than the economy.[79] The consumer revolution thesis referred to the spread of consumer habits of the rich to the lower ranks of society, especially the working classes. Change resulted from three essential developments: increased industrial output, sustained improvement of living standards, and emulation of the well-off. In England and its colonies that process began after 1750. By the end of that century, writes Neil Mckendrick,

English men and women consumed like never before, and that rampant consumption resulted from the desire of the lower ranks to emulate lifestyles of the upper ranks.[80] However, in Spain emulative consumption was limited to a small portion of society due to the failure of the economy to improve living standards for the lower ranks. Nonetheless, the benefits attained by the upper and middle classes from slow but sustained economic growth that characterized the central years of the nineteenth century were strong enough to bring about a substantial sense of change.

HOUSEHOLD MATERIAL CULTURE AND THE MAKING OF MIDDLE-CLASS IDENTITIES

So far we have explored general changes in the distribution of interior spaces and house furnishings during the eighteenth century. Turning to the nineteenth-century bourgeois home, this discussion begins with a typology of Madrilenian bourgeois homes. Observing the evolution of that model across the century makes it possible to interpret significance in these alterations, especially changes related to the function and the decoration of rooms. Objects that the family chose to place in different areas of the home are critical because they reflected a family's acquisitive power, decorative taste, and use of interior spaces. Functions assigned to rooms projected the assimilation of values, symbols, and meanings of domesticity. Focusing on selected objects and associated uses helps reveal information about a given owner's lifestyle and group identity.[81] This analysis is based on nineteenth-century probate inventories, but concentrated on a smaller but significant number—forty-six cases—including high-ranking politicians who held positions as ministers and/or deputies along with members of the high ranks of the financial bourgeoisie, professionals, and merchants (Table 3).

The old bourgeois house in Madrid's historic downtown provides an appropriate starting point. In early nineteenth-century society, before the growth of the *ensanches,* this was the typical residence of affluent groups. Mainly on the first and second floors of old buildings, this kind of home was described extensively in *costumbrista* literature and later, the realist novel. Because they appear so frequently in Pérez Galdós's novels, they have been referred to as *viviendas galdosianas* (Galdosian houses). These houses were located on the main arteries of old Madrid, near the axis connecting Retiro

TABLE 3

Value of Inventories, 1800–1866 (*reales de vellón*)

Net Assets	Ministers	%	Deputies	%
1–500,000	4	18.2	0	0
500,000–1,000,000	2	9.1	2	20
1,000,000–1,500,000	4	18.2	0	0
1,500,000–2,000,000	2	9.1	2	20
2,000,000–5,000,000	3	13.7	5	50
5,000,000-10,000,000	4	18.2	0	0
10,000,000+	3	13.5	1	10
Total cases	22		10	
Median	1,755,235		2,700,000	

Value of Inventories of Bankers, Merchants, and Professionals, 1866–84 (*reales de vellón*)

Net Assets	Professionals	%	Bankers and Merchants	%
1–500,000	8	100	2	33.3
500,000–1,000,000	0		3	50
1,000,000–1,500,000	0		0	0
1,500,000–2,000,000	0		1	16.7
Total cases	8		6	
Median	86,642		675,312	

Source: Archivo Histórico de Protocolos de Madrid (AHPM).

Gardens and Paseo del Prado with the Royal Palace, with more located in the business district of San Bernardo Street and the Plaza Mayor. These areas of the city reflected Madrid's status as a political, administrative, commercial, and financial center. It was a natural location for politicians, bureaucrats, merchants, bankers, and, of course, the old nobility. This part of Madrid contained three types of bourgeois dwellings: mansions, midsize homes of the middle classes, and more modest homes of the petit-bourgeoisie.

The Dutari Fagoaga family house on Mayor Street, close to the Plaza Mayor and Puerta del Sol, exhibited all the characteristics of an old bourgeois style.

The Dutaris, of Basque origin, were a typical ascendant family. They arrived in Madrid in the second half of the eighteenth century and made a substantial fortune with businesses trading in wool, supplying the army, and finance. By the first third of the nineteenth century, there were Dutaris and Fagoagas in the upper ranks of the state administration and the selective posts of private banking; some were prestigious professionals and even members of the church hierarchy.[82] The Dutari home occupied a *principal* floor of an old building at the beginning of Mayor Street. It was an old-style commercial family dwelling, with twenty rooms, plus offices, a shop, and warehouses. Characteristic of the practice of traditional merchant families, the Dutari home was attached to the business's main banking offices; a shop that sold spices, wool fabrics, and haberdashery; and the warehouses that stored commercial products. Most of these dependencies were at the street level, but some offices were in the first floor and attached to the family dwelling.

The big Dutari household had a spatial distribution typical of homes in old Madrid. While the floor plan followed the pattern established in the eighteenth century—hall, parlor, and *gabinete*—there were several rooms that did not fit into a scheme of the rational distribution of spaces; for instance, a room called *pieza colgada,* an irregular space between the kitchen and a bedroom with no clear function. The inventory of the house also describes hallways and a long corridor wide enough to include various pieces of furniture. A room with a small private chapel was another feature of the Dutari house that represented the past, although this was more characteristic of seigniorial palaces or the countryside large houses of the provincial nobility.

Along with these traditional elements the Dutari house incorporated many aspects of modern living. It was decorated stylishly according to the taste of the times, with luxury and comfort in mind. The floor plan, described in the inventory, included differentiated public and private areas in the home's interior. The public area consisted of a hall, a main parlor, and an antechamber; these combined spaces provided seating for forty-eight people. The walls were decorated with expensive paintings, and as expected, there were cornucopias, damask curtains, tapestries, and side tables topped with porcelain figures, vases, and clocks. The private area of the house featured a *gabinete,* decorated with a sofa upholstered in silk, an oriental rug, *cabriole* chairs, and numerous Chinese porcelain figures—probably the personal collection of one of the family members. Each of the principal rooms had braziers for heating in winter, a sign of comfort and a luxury that only the wealthy could afford. Details indicate that the Dutari Fagoaga family was very religious: the elder son entered a monastery and renounced his inheritance, and the house was filled with religious objects, including religious paintings, relics, figures of saints, the Virgin, and Jesus, and stoups for holy water.[83]

Another house, owned by Pedro Otondo, a prosecutor in the Contaduría, a high tribunal court in the state Treasury, provides a good example of a typical midsize middle-class home. Otondo lived with his three daughters and wife María Gorbea on Arenal Street not far from the residence of the Dutaris. The inventory dates from 1818, after both husband and wife died within a short period of time. Otondo's assets were assessed at 632,000 *reales,* a midsize fortune mainly in cash, a good portion of which came from María's dowry. María Gorbea belonged to a family of Basque origin who owned a prosperous hardware store in Madrid. There is no doubt that the marriage of Otondo to Gorbea constituted a perfect match: Otondo provided the social prestige of his professional position and his rank within the nobility, and the Gorbeas contributed María's sizable dowry to ensure the family a respectable financial status.

The Otondos offer a good example of a middle-class family life in Madrid in the early nineteenth century. Their household consisted of nine rooms plus three small storerooms. The entrance hall and the parlor were decorated similarly to those public rooms in the Dutari family home, although the objects in the Otondo residence were of lesser quality and lower value. In the hall there were two side tables and a table for playing cards with a reliquary on top—a curious mix of religiosity and leisure activity. The Otondos were as religious as the Dutaris, and every room in the house, except the kitchen and storage areas, boasted religious decorative motifs: images, paintings, and prints. In the parlor there were chairs, stools, a sofa upholstered in silk, and a piano that was the most highly appraised object in the house. For a bourgeois family with three daughters the piano must have been a prized object, perfect for evening social gatherings where the girls could show off their musical skills to guests in their social circle.

Fitting for a family with so many women, the Otondos' home featured a *gabinete* that the notary listed in the inventory as "the room of the lady." This room was decorated with small side tables, two consoles, several chairs, a sofa, some small decorative boxes, and a dressing table. This *gabinete* resembles the *estrado* in its feminine decoration and character; however, it had elements—

side tables and console—of a more complex functionality within the house. In contrast to the *gabinete* there was a *sala de despacho* (office) with unequivocally masculine decoration. In this room the notary listed an *escribanía* (writing desk), an armchair, a clock, a large map on the wall, and several armoires that stored books and documents. In the private area of the house the notary registered bedrooms for the young ladies, for the couple, and for the maids. The family used the attic of the building for storage; here the inventory, filed in late spring, listed braziers and brazier tables stored until winter months. Although there is no description of a bathroom in the house, the notary appraised a bath tub at 120 *reales* and several copper pots for carrying hot water along with other objects for personal grooming.[84]

By the mid-nineteenth century, middle-class homes in old buildings in downtown Madrid were considered inadequate for modern standards of living. Mesonero Romanos described them as barely acceptable—full of awkward features, uncomfortable, and unhygienic. Like similar buildings in other old cities in continental Europe, these old buildings housed a diverse group of people of varied social status. The social mix was obviously not ideal, but there were many more shortcomings. Most buildings did not have doormen—an indispensable symbol of distinction in the new middle-class buildings—and their dark entrances tended to get occupied by local artisans. Access to the apartments was by means of old and generally dingy stairs.[85] In other words, the space between the street and the apartments was not clean, ordered, comfortable, or elegant. Inadequate entryways to old buildings were a glaring example of how these residences failed to meet the standards of what was considered appropriate.

Due to inadequacies with old buildings, demographic growth, and new notions of social organization, the affluent classes began to abandon the old centers of European cities to settle in socially homogenous suburbs.[86] In Madrid and Barcelona this trend started in the 1840s and was fully established by the last third of the century.[87] New residential areas arose in suburban areas such as the *eixample* in Barcelona, and the Salamanca and Argüelles barrios in Madrid, perfect for bourgeois aspirations and lifestyles with all the elements required for the modern lifestyle.[88] In these neighborhoods there were two new forms of bourgeois house: the *hotel*, similar to the typical Victorian house, and the residence known as *piso*, the equivalent of the French *apartement*. These new residences were characterized by the rational arrangement of space aimed at promoting social distinction, privacy, and comfort. The *hotel* was the preferred residence of the new and old aristocracy and the upper bourgeoisie. Some builders and urban planners tried to promote an intermediate version of hotel called *hotelito*. The *hotelito* was supposed to be a Spanish version of the typical middle-class Victorian house and was intended for the well-off segments of the urban middle classes. However, since *hotelitos* were expensive to build and maintain and did not totally fit in Spanish lifestyles, this kind of home was not as successful in Spain as it was in northern Europe.

The prototypical bourgeois home in mid nineteenth-century Spanish cities was the apartment, or *piso,* in the new buildings of the *ensanches.* Apartments offered all the elements described in the conduct manuals and publications on lifestyle. All middle-class *pisos* after the 1860s followed a basic structure, with three main living spaces: the parlor, the *gabinete,* and the bedroom. When it departed from this basic configuration, the *piso* was as diverse as the bourgeoisie itself. As we will see in the next chapter, the *piso* could be smaller, larger, more up to date in technology and comfort, or more austere; in any case, new houses were designed as symbols of social position and as transmitters of modernity that projected the identities of their inhabitants.[89]

As we have seen, one of the developments driving the rationalization of interior spaces was the distinction between private and public or semi-public areas in the home.[90] This division reflected two main elements of the liberal ideal as it pertained to lifestyle: the private, as an expression of respect for ordered individualism, and the semi-public, as necessary space for civic interaction. Each home in our sample presents a differentiation between a "front stage," oriented toward public or semi-public activities, and a "back stage," dedicated to the privacy of family life.[91] The "front stage" consisted of a series of spaces of varying sizes that served as a transition between the bustling public sphere outside and the quiet harmony of family life inside.

In large single-family dwellings, *palacetes* and *hoteles,* the availability of space allowed for an extended transitional area. A visitor to the palace of Prime Minister and liberal politician Ramón María de Narváez in the heart of Madrid would go through a large hall, a billiard room, a long corridor, and a gallery before arriving at a large parlor followed by a living room. The prime minister's study marked the boundary between the public and private wings of the house. Narváez established his residence in one of Madrid's more emblematic buildings: the Casa de Cisneros, a palace near the city hall built in

1537 by Benito Jiménez de Cisneros, a nephew of the famous cardinal.[92] When Prime Minister Narváez decided to establish his residence there, the palace was an inhospitable space that needed updating to become a family residence. Improvements to the structure, recorded in the inventory filed in 1869, provide an intimate look at the modern domestic interior Narváez created.

Despite the Casa de Cisneros's palatial dimensions, the notarial description of the private areas reveals a comfortable bourgeois home, with pleasant spaces for the family's private life. There is a room described as a *salón diario* (day parlor) near the main office of the minister with all the trappings of a classic *gabinete*. That *salón* established the boundaries between the public section, consisting of the administrative palace, and the private part where the family lived. It functioned as a typical middle-class family room but with decoration suitable for the palace of a first minister. The room had two sofas, seven chairs, and ten armchairs all in damask with matching pillows. There were two corner tables, two consoles, two special tables for playing cards and other games, and a writing desk with bookshelves, all made of the best-quality woods. The most highly apprised object was a bronze clock that adorned one of the consoles. Two oval mirrors and a Pleyel upright piano provided the finishing, romantic touches to this *salón diario* of a powerful emblematic family of Madrid Isabelino.[93]

In the typical Madrid *piso,* this "front stage" was less spectacular but always an essential component of the middle-class home. Most included a small entrance hall (*recibimiento*), followed by a parlor (*sala*) and a dining room (*comedor*). Behind those were the private rooms of the family and the domestic staff. The dining room and the study or library room were semi-private areas that marked the division between the "front stage" and the "back stage." Of course, this ideal floor plan had many exceptions. The Madrid residence of Joaquín María Ferrer y Cafranga, a member of the *progresista* liberal party and minister of the Spanish Treasury, illustrates the difficulty of adapting a seventeenth-century apartment to nineteenth-century criteria.[94] Although the interior spaces functioned according to modern norms, the distribution of private and public areas was irregular: its two parlors were not directly accessible from the entrance hall, and private rooms were mixed with semi-private rooms, making it necessary to pass through private rooms to access semi-private rooms. It was not always possible, or desirable, to conform to the ideals of domestic life and architecture.

The "front stage" was intended for society. Its function was to provide an arena for the public and semi-public rituals that characterized bourgeois life. In the homes of the upper ranks it constituted a clear continuation of the public salons, waiting areas, and corridors of the Royal Palace, the Ministry buildings, the parliament, and the stock exchange. They were designed and decorated for the purpose of hosting large parties and gatherings with many guests—balls, dinners, and even musical and literary performances. There, political decisions were made, profitable business transactions were arranged, and treacherous ruins and political downfalls were hatched. The *salón grande de recepciones* (grand parlor for receptions) in Narvaéz's *palacete* was of this sort. It was a large room preceded by a long gallery decorated with mahogany benches, mirrors, and rugs. The grand salon seated about forty people in numerous sofas, chairs, and stools placed in different parts of the room. Illuminated by six lamps, of nine lights each, and a big chandelier in the middle, it was heated by two chimneys and decorated with a variety of mahogany tables, consoles, chests of drawers, clocks, porcelain vases, mirrors, curtains of taffeta, and English rugs with a prevalence of crimson colors.[95]

In smaller homes these "front stages" functioned as venues for public as well as more intimate events. Members of the political elite, for instance, used parlors for formal afternoon visits of friends and family, evening *tertulias,* and periodic celebrations such as birthdays, anniversaries, name days, and promotions. These spaces were furnished in a fairly standard way: one or two sofas, several armchairs or straight chairs to provide seating for about twenty people, side tables adjacent to the sofas and armchairs, corner tables, rugs, mirrors, consoles, Chinese jars, chandeliers, clocks, small marble and ivory sculptures, and often a piano. Lively colors such as crimsons, burgundies, and blues graced the damasks, velvets, and muslins of the upholstery, curtains, tassels, and wall coverings. While these "front stages" were arranged with functionality in mind, they were also luxurious.

In all the inventories studied, parlors were the rooms with the highest overall appraisals. They featured furniture made of expensive woods, predominantly mahogany and rosewood, but also ebony, cedar, and walnut. Expensive rugs and ornate window treatments and decorative objects graced surfaces. Fine Chinese, English, and French porcelain jars were displayed alongside porcelain, clay, wood, and metal figures representing warriors and animals. Common were chandeliers, miniature boxes, games, vases for flowers, clocks, and functional items such as glasses, cups, and coffee and tea sets. This lavish decoration presented a dramatic contrast to the austerity of traditional Spanish interior decoration.[96] These objects constitute a semiotic universe of meaning understood by contemporaries. For instance, there was a general lack of religious themes present amid a world of cherished trinkets. Religious motifs remained in some wall paintings, but eventually they would be found only in isolated pieces of decoration.

In contrast to the "front stage," the "back stage" was reserved for the privacy of family life. Rooms in this part of the home were meant to provide intimacy, comfort, and informality for the consanguineal members of the family group. Those who did not form part of this group, yet were admitted into the private areas, were treated with familiarity and informality; they were the closest friends, some of whom were considered members of the family. At the same time, this atmosphere of informality was limited by the restrictions imposed by the authoritarian and gender-divided nature of the nineteenth-century bourgeois family. "Back stage" space was segregated according to a hierarchy imposed by the dominance of male over female and master over servant.[97]

The prototypical room of the familial "back stage" in Madrid homes was the *gabinete* (family or living room). As mentioned above, this room began to appear in inventories after 1750 as a substitute for the traditional Spanish *estrado*. In some Madrid homes *gabinetes* were still located near bedrooms or in areas separated from the bedroom by a door with glass panels, curtain, or folding screen. Typically, the *gabinete* was a common space used for daily meals, family conversation, playing, reading, and praying. While both the dining room and the *gabinete* were for family living, the latter was more oriented toward female activities. Women would spend most of their time there doing needlework, caring for the children, reading and writing, or receiving visits from the most intimate kin and friends. Middle-class female characters in the novels of Pérez Galdós and Palacio Valdés are portrayed in *gabinetes* with decoration that reflects some of their main psychological features.[98]

Probate records underscore the domestic nature of the *gabinete*. In the home of Manuel Cortina, who served in several liberal cabinets, its decoration reveals the interests and pastimes of the women in his family—with the sofa, armchairs, and occasional chairs we find a sewing box, a small sewing table, and small shelves holding books of religion and fashion. José Garcia de la Torre's *gabinete* was decorated with framed embroideries made by his wife and daughters.[99] The *gabinete* in the house of attorney Clemente Escudero, inventoried in 1874, had two functions: it was the family room and the widow's dressing room. The room was furnished with chairs, armchairs, tables, a dressing table, and an armoire listed as *una librería de señora* (woman's bookshelves). This combination of functions in single rooms becomes more frequent in the houses of lower social station. The 1872 inventory of Julián Fernández, owner of a grocery store on La Madera street, describes a traditional bourgeois home in Madrid's historic downtown with the business attached to the family dwelling. The Fernández home was decorated tastefully with fine pieces of furniture: armchairs, mahogany tables, decorative objects, religious figures, and paintings. At the same time, the house was small and single rooms served diverse functions. The elegant parlor also had a chest of drawers to store bed linens. The only sofa inventoried was in the master bedroom. There was no *gabinete,* since the parlor functioned as both family room and living room.[100]

Objects in the *gabinete* present distinctive features that enable us to examine the construction of new middle-class identities. What the decoding of these signs reveals is the ambivalence that characterizes this process in Spain, as in the rest of the Western world. This room, more than any other, symbolized the triumph of the family as an essential pillar of social order in liberal Europe and America.[101] *Gabinetes* were decorated by and for the family. In the majority of cases studied, this room incorporated a space reserved for the display of family memorabilia, frequently portraits and photographs, but also medals, diplomas, and genealogical objects such as family trees, coats of arms, and pictures of ancestors. The visual association with family members reveals new perceptions of the role of the individual within the structure of the nuclear family. Most painted portraits and photos were of immediate members of the family—parents, daughters, sons, and grandparents—but at the same time the taste for genealogy suggests the persistence of a culture strongly committed to the practices of familism.

On occasion, decorative objects also suggest political and religious ambivalence. In general, the presence of religious motifs in nineteenth-century Spanish interiors is less frequent than it was in previous centuries. The Spanish had customarily decorated their walls with paintings, engravings, or inexpensive prints of religious images and themes, along with reliquaries, ex votos, and a universe of religious trinkets. Yet, by this time the industry producing religious items was in decline. Religious motifs were sometimes displayed alongside an iconography of revolutionary political symbols. For instance, in the *gabinete* of the Gil de Santibáñez family, who were bankers in the circle of *progresista* liberalism, a large statue of Juan Alvarez Mendizábal (sponsor of Spanish disentailment of church property), shared room space with an image of the Virgin of El Pilar (symbol of the most traditional Spanish Catholicism).[102] The liberal minister Manuel Cortina combined imagery of regional virgins with images of family members and mythological motifs.[103]

Many families displayed objects symbolizing regional identities. Madrid was a city of immigrants and a substantial portion of its middle class came from different parts of Spain and its colonies. For instance, several rooms of the Otondo home displayed figures of Mexican virgins such as the Virgin of Guadalupe and Our Lady of México. It is possible that the Otondos had a connection with that territory, since it was still part of the Spanish Empire when the inventory was filed. It was common to find symbols related to provincial cults, traditions, and landscapes. The Basque engineer Carlos Aguirre y Labroche, a Madrid-based agent of the Bilbao Iron Roche Company, decorated the walls of his *gabinete* with a big picture of Bilbao along with oil on canvas portraits of family members and lithographs of horses copied from an English artist.[104]

Beyond the familial *gabinete* and dining room, there was typically a series of rooms characterized by signs of privacy, intimacy, and individualism. For instance, the function and decoration of rooms identified with proper names— such as *la pieza de María* (María's bedroom)—seem to have been determined in part by the personal taste and values of the occupant. We find rooms that demonstrate the progress made by Madrid's middle classes toward achieving desirable aspects of the bourgeois lifestyle, such as new technology and individualized objects and living spaces. Rooms in the "back stage" became more overtly comfortable throughout the course of the century. Iron stoves replaced traditional braziers in family areas and bedrooms, making interiors much warmer in winter. The number of braziers and especially of fireplaces was also higher. The use of rugs, bed heaters, quilts, chamber pots, and iron beds with wool mattresses over bed springs increased notably. But the most significant improvement in the material culture of bedrooms related to the increased number of objects for personal hygiene such as pitchers, wash basins, bath tubs, and bidets.

Individualization of rooms in the nineteenth century was an ongoing trend, but it occurred in the context of a gendered division of interiors. Rooms that best represent this differentiation are the female dressing room and the male study, spaces that appear in about 77 percent of the homes studied. The dressing room was clearly a woman's space, and always located in the "back stage" far from the main areas of the home. In contrast to the remote location of the dressing room, the study (*despacho*) was strategically located and judging from inventory evidence it was the second most important room of the home (after the parlor). The study was clearly a male space, reserved for the head of the family, who used the location to manage the private and public affairs of the family. It was decorated with objects symbolizing his role as head of the household: artworks, books, heirlooms, and important family documents.

Occupying a more private area of the family residence, the lady's bedroom was filled with objects that indicated the gendered division of roles within the household. In contrast to the variety and importance of the objects studied, the lady of the house tended to furnish her room with relative simplicity: a dresser with drawers, a gold-framed mirror, family portraits, inexpensive paintings, and engravings of religious motifs. There were no books, no writing desks, no armchairs, no clocks—only objects that conveyed her subordinate role within the family hierarchy.[105] For example, the banker Felipe Rávara had two studies containing locked armoires that stored money, legal documents, and important family correspondence. His inventory listed a room called "the room of the ladies," obviously for the use of Don Felipe's wife and daughters, which was decorated with engravings featuring religious scenes, chairs, mirrors, closets, two small tables, a dresser, and a musical instrument.[106] These examples demonstrate that the nineteenth-century middle-class private sphere was indeed relegated and divided by gender.

Ultimately, evidence from notarial sources proves that real homes inhabited by historical families approached the ideal of the bourgeois home as it was described in conduct literature, in journalism, and in literary fiction. The process that transformed the domestic spaces of dominant groups and brought about the modern home began in Spain during the mid-eighteenth century. In that transition we find the development of the essential components of present-day middle-class life: domesticity, intimacy, privacy, hygiene, and comfort. Spain developed similarly to other Western countries in this process of transformation, albeit at a slower rate compared to northern Europe and the United States. Indeed, as late as 1950, the number of Spaniards living in comfortable and well-equipped homes was still modest in comparison to people in France and Britain. In the long term, however, slow transformations inside the home have been underway in both ideas and material culture long enough to constitute a tradition in itself.

CHAPTER 4

El buen tono and the World of Goods

O N January 10, 1882, the first issue of *La Moda Ilustrada,* a fashion magazine published in Madrid, included an advertisement for a gift shop called El Buen Tono. "Mr. Alvarez Vivigo, owner of this prestigious store," read the commercial, "wants to report the display of a large and varied inventory of men's ties appropriate for the season, all sorts of wedding presents, greeting cards, bronze decorations for ladies' boudoirs, deluxe cigarette holders, wallets, toiletry bags for ladies, card cases, opera glasses, purses, shell cigarette cases with gold and silver incrustations, canes, umbrellas, fans . . . and a multitude of rich and capricious objects that can compete with the best available in other gift shops of this capital."[1] El Buen Tono gift shop was located at 20 Arenal Street, in the heart of Madrid's commercial district, and it is not a coincidence that both the shop and the editorial offices of the above-mentioned fashion magazine shared the same address. El Buen Tono, a distinctive name emblematic of the sort of store it aspired to be, carried a selection of fashionable clothes, elegant objects, and decorative bric-a-bracs that epitomized the material universe of the *hombre fino* and *mujer fina.* The advertised items held symbolic meaning, as they signified social status and a certain lifestyle. They were part of the variety of objects considered necessary acquisitions by those who strove to be identified as members of bourgeois polite society, a society characterized—unlike any other before it—by its attachment to the consumption of goods. As has been pointed out by Douglas Goodman and Mirelle Cohen, "middle class culture is consumer culture, since the spread of modern consumerism was the consequence of those social groups struggling to rig themselves out with the paraphernalia of gentility during the nineteenth century."[2]

This chapter expands on the preceding chapter's study of the origins and expansion of modern consumer culture in Spain during the nineteenth century. So far we have considered the making of the bourgeois home in the context of the dissemination of the ideals of domesticity. Now we will delve deeper into this story by looking at the role of garment consumption, fashion, and the history of retailing as central aspects of the nineteenth-century bourgeois world and Spanish incorporation into modernity.

CONSUMER CULTURE AND THE "CONSUMER REVOLUTION" IN SPAIN

Scholars studying the origins of modern consumer culture, or modern consumerism, agree for the most part that modern consumer society emerged in western Europe before the Industrial Revolution and contributed to its advent. Current debates center on the determination of the when, the why, the how, and the where, and seek the appropriate terminology to define the complexities of this historical process. Regarding the "when," there seems to be a general consensus in identifying the early modern period with the inception of modern consumerism. While the consumption of objects is fundamental to human nature and has existed from the very beginnings of the history of humanity, studies show that after the sixteenth century Europeans began to produce, exchange, and possess objects like never before. This modern form of consumption differed from the past in that it was more widely shared by social groups and was not exclusive to the upper classes. The early stages of this process were linked to the expansion of the international markets with the commercialization of colonial products such as sugar, tea, coffee, cocoa, and calicoes. In the second half of the eighteenth century, the first consumer societies rose in determined regions of Europe, and over the course of the nineteenth century modern consumer culture expanded to most of the Western world.

The explanation of the "why" and the "how" of this rise in consumer demand has generated more controversy. In a very general sense most scholars accept the linking of consumer culture with the growth of Western capitalism beginning with the age of European expansion. The development of commercial economies in early modern Europe brought about a consumer apparatus evident in the explosion of shops, the increasing use of new marketing techniques, and the availability of credit and new affordable commodities. The shopkeeper and his methods established the first interactions of the new consumer society.[3] But the growth of commercial activities has also been interpreted as a *symptom* or *consequence* rather than a *cause* of the rise of consumer practices. For a significant group of historians the main force that ignited modern consumerism was cultural. Beyond economic growth and a slow but sustained improvement in living standards, consumption rose due to the human tendency of emulation. Neil Mckendrick argued that the English "consumer revolution" resulted from the willingness of the lower ranks to emulate upper ranks' lifestyles.[4] Those who subscribe to the emulation thesis follow the intellectual tradition begun by American sociologist Thorstein Veblen, who emphasized the role of human psychology and cultural behavior in economic change. "Culturalists" place the moment of the intensification of consumer behavior in the mid-eighteenth and early nineteenth centuries, and for the most part accept the use of the term "consumer revolution" to define that historical process. The consumer revolution involved a profound change in perceptions and attitudes that altered traditional patterns of demand and had a direct impact on industrialization. For some it was a sort of trickle-down effect as the middle and lower classes began to replicate aristocratic fashion and lifestyles. Other historians emphasize the role of the Enlightenment, arguing that its praise of material progress promoted a set of values consistent with the belief that having comfortable houses and buying elegant clothing and furniture constituted an acceptable goal in life. This validation of consumerism was continued by liberalism and romanticism's defense of individual rights, freedoms, emotions, and appreciation of moral and physical beauty. According to Colin Campbell, it was contact with romantic values acquired in particular through the reading of the new emotion-laden novels that most explicitly spurred consumerism.[5]

The notion of a "consumer revolution" provoked mainly by cultural, intellectual, and institutional reasons that preceded and set the ground for the Industrial Revolution has been broadly contested by economic historians, who rarely consider demand to be a factor in long-term economic change. Jan De Vries in the most recent contribution to the consumer debate offers an alternative model that combines the role played by cultural change with other economic factors generally neglected by cultural historians such as salaries, prices, budgetary constraints, and the balance between supply and demand. De Vries, in line with the cultural approach, detects the rise of new consumer aspirations during the eighteenth century, despite stagnant salaries and high prices. The increase in demand took place fundamentally at the level of the household economy. Household members fostered a new attachment to the world of goods; they made consumer decisions that stimulated both the growth of demand and the supply of marketed commodities, developments that impacted labor, prices, and transaction costs. The connection between alterations in household behavior and macro-economic change constituted an "industrious revolution," a concept that De Vries considers more adequate than "consumer revolution," to encompass the richness and complexity of the historical shift toward the modern consumer society.

De Vries' provocative and intriguing thesis brings us to the final consideration in the consumer debate and the one that is most central to this chapter: the question of the "where." According to De Vries, the "industrious revolution," like the consumer revolution, was an exclusively European occurrence. A few scholars have questioned this proposition of European dominance, offering a multiplicity of examples of consumption patterns in other parts of the world—mainly early modern China and Japan—that show compelling similarities with what was happening in the West.[6] Notwithstanding the similarities, their arguments have been received with skepticism by the dominant Western clique. The fundamental difference between Western and oriental forms of consumption, Europeanists reply, is that in Europe the Industrial Revolution and the rise of consumption went hand in hand and gave birth to today's hegemonic consumer culture. The historical origins of modern consumer societies are unequivocally in the West; they matured first in northern and western Europe during the eighteenth century. De Vries is categorical about this point: "the industrious revolution and the household organization linked to it had their chief impact in a restricted zone of indefinite boundaries. It is best observed in north Western Europe: England, the Low Countries, and parts of France and Germany . . . neither Eastern Europe nor the Mediterranean zones participate fully in its main developments."[7] Thus, although Spain played a central role in the age of European expansion and in the articulation of the Atlantic market, it has been largely overlooked by most scholars of the consumer debate, at least until recent times.

Research into the origins of modern consumer culture in Spain still remains in its early stages. The goal of this chapter is to present new evidence of Spain's role in the making of modern consumer society. First, we will look at how the case of Spain provides new substance to the discussion of the role played by middle-class emulation in the spread of new consumer attitudes. Second, this chapter will present the case of a country on the European periphery that possessed a longstanding consumer culture rooted in the early modern period despite the fact that it did not become a mass consumer society until the twentieth century.

Carmen Martín Gaite's study of the love customs in late eighteenth-century Spain, published more than three decades ago, detected the existence of a new sensitivity toward the use of material goods that implied noticeable changes in the attitudes of men and women of the middle and upper ranks toward fashion and taste.[8] Her claim was based on evidence extracted from literary sources of the period. As we saw in previous chapters, the discussion of the social, political, and economic impact of this new culture constituted one of the favorite topics of discussion among eighteenth-century Spanish writers. For some, this new materialism was a dangerous sign of moral decline and social subversion. Followers of the new fashions and manners were accused of emptiness, amorality, and dissolution. They were portrayed as snobs without personal criteria who were supplanting healthy Spanish traditions and Christian values with foreign vices and dissolute habits and taste.[9] For others, an open attitude toward the consumption of material objects was a sign of progress and modernization, a trend to be endorsed as beneficial for the general utility. Whether the tone is supportive or disparaging, we find in the second half of the eighteenth century a significant number of plays, novels, treatises, and journals that have characters displaying new sensitivities toward consumption.[10] Based on this evidence, Martín Gaite placed the origins of Spanish consumer society in the second half of the eighteenth century.

Several major studies published in recent years show compelling evidence that corroborates Martín Gaite's perceptions, with examples of Spain's involvement in the early modern surge in Western consumerism. Marcy Norton's work on the origins of chocolate and tobacco consumption not only details the role played by the Spanish and Portuguese in the adoption of new consumer habits and the commodification of new products, it also offers provocative new arguments to explain how and why Europeans engaged in the consumption of these two stimulants. Contrary to traditional assumptions that the habits of drinking chocolate and smoking tobacco were initiated by Europeans during the late seventeenth and eighteenth centuries, Norton asserts that Spanish colonizers first consumed these products in the sixteenth century. And the reasons why Iberians engaged in the pleasures provided by the consumption of tobacco and chocolate were more along the lines of emulation and adaptation than the desire to create exclusive European habits. Initially, colonizers imitated ancient recipes and consumption rituals of indigenous Mesoamerican groups. With the passage of time, Europeans adapted these practices to their religious beliefs, scientific assumptions, and cultural and economic systems and transferred them to their places of origin.[11] Before coffee and tea became popular in Europe, chocolate was the most common stimulant drink, and the Iberians its major consumers.

Beyond this inexplicably forgotten Spanish contribution to Western consumer culture, a number of studies show a moderate but sustained rise of consumer practices among Spaniards between 1750 and 1860. What we know so far comes from research conducted in two significant Spanish regions: Catalonia and Old Castile. Catalonia is central to this discussion because it was the first case of early industrialization in an overwhelmingly agrarian Spain. The Valladolid-Palencia-Santander axis in Old Castile, the other region of focus, is also meaningful because during the nineteenth century it enjoyed a profitable agrarian economic system based on the production of cereals and the industrial processing and commercialization of flour.[12]

Early studies of the Catalonian case are based on the analysis of bridal trousseaus, which constitute a type of legal document that was customary among a broad spectrum of social groups and reflects consumer patterns of textile products. Jaume Torras, Montserrat Durán, and Lídia Torra's detailed study of trousseaus from the city of Igualada between 1600 and 1800 shows a sustained growth in the number of pieces of clothing and bedding items brought by brides to their new households.[13] Lídia Torra expands the sample to include the cities of Figueres and Mataró and adds to the trousseaus evidence from 1,845 probate inventories as the main source. Her study reveals that between 1750 and 1800 family wardrobes were not only better supplied but they were also more varied in regard to the type and quality of fabrics.[14] Belén Moreno Claverías's analysis of eighteenth-century middle-class inventories in the region of Penedés also reveals a general increase in household consumption throughout the course of the century. She points out the difference in consumer patterns between farmers and members of the professional and commercial groups. While the former were more austere, the latter were more inclined to conspicuous consumption of items that projected social status.[15] These authors link the rise in consumerism in Catalonia to the region's early industrialization by presenting evidence of the connections between the consumer subject, the market, and the supplier. Bride trousseaus and family inventories grew in size and variety, and a substantial portion of the new stocks were made of Catalan fabrics. At the same time Catalan merchants were developing new forms of commercialization by the establishment of innovative shops and the creation of merchant networks that transcended regional boundaries.[16]

Marta Vicente, in a recent study of the eighteenth-century Catalan textile industry, demonstrates the extent of the connection between Catalan industrial development, commercial networks, and consumption patterns. Vicente reveals the appearance of a new demand for calico fabrics among Spanish women beginning in the first third of the eighteenth century, and links this process to a combination of diverse economic and cultural changes. Since the end of the seventeenth century, Catalan and Castilian merchants were importing, mainly from England, a variety of new cotton fabrics. This availability of more affordable textiles brought about a process of democratization of fashion; more women and men than ever before wanted to follow fashion by wearing calico fabrics, causing a spectacular growth of demand.[17] At the same time *ilustrado* writers such as Sempere Guarinos, Gaspar Melchor Jovellanos, Luis Cañuelo, and Francisco Romà y Rosell, among others, following their counterparts in other parts of the West, embraced modern doctrines that espoused the utility of beneficial luxury. In their late eighteenth-century writings they encouraged new attitudes toward luxury, fashion, and consumption as factors for economic growth.[18] Marta Vicente states that in Spain and the Spanish colonies, like in other parts of the Western world, these economic and cultural developments brought about a "calico craze." The demand generated by this new collective mindset was a central factor in the expansion of Catalan cotton manufacture. She also emphasizes the role of the household economy in this process and its projection to the Spanish American colonial markets in the 1780s. Family was at the very foundation of the Catalan factory and a key factor in the development of this early process of industrialization. Barcelona calico factories were for the most part small or midsize workshops operated by a family workforce within family dwellings. Even large factories were organized following family schemes, with an internal structure of separate rooms where groups of workers belonging to a family unit worked together, and in many cases these familial groups lived under the same roof in the factory house.[19] Vicente's Catalan families could fit into De Vries' pattern of northern European industrious households and their industriousness had similar effects: it animated the rise of demand and the spread of consumer culture, at least on a local scale.

Studies of the Castilian case focus mainly on the consumption of textile products between 1750 and 1860 and describe patterns of consumer expansion and diversification not unlike those seen in Catalonia. While Castile experienced sustained expansion from the last third of the eighteenth century, consumer activity intensified mainly during the 1830s. The sources used are also similar to those examined by scholars of Catalonia—bridal trousseaus and probate inventories—but cover a broader geographic region and combine rural and urban areas. While they include a broad array of social rank—from lower to upper—the bulk of cases are from the middle classes. Máximo García Fernández and Rosa María Dávila compare trousseaus from the city of Valladolid with agrarian towns in the countryside, specifically Peñafiel and Olmedo. Over time both urban and rural brides were bringing to their marriages a greater amount of items. The increase was proportionally higher in the city than in the countryside, and occurred especially in the number of women's clothes and undergarments, as opposed to other household items such as bedding and table linen. Women's dresses and undergarments formed more than 83 percent of countryside trousseaus, while in the city the portion was about 67 percent. Apparently, in the villages keeping up with external appearances was of greater concern than having a comfortable home.[20] Fernando Ramos Palencia studies the consumption of textile products in the region of Palencia by looking at probate inventories of members of the middle ranks. His analysis focuses on the family unit and takes into consideration a series of variables such as the total value of fortunes, annual incomes, the level of urbanization, and the occupation of the head of the household. In Palencia the consumption of textiles rose moderately in both the countryside and the city. The average number of textile pieces per family grew from forty-eight items in 1750 to sixty-seven in 1830, clothes and undergarments being the largest component of this growth. Some of these new textile products in the wardrobes of Palentine families were cotton fabrics of Catalan origin, but a substantial portion were manufactured locally in household workshops. Ramos argues that accumulation of textile products did not result from a significant growth of family income, but rather from a reallocation of household resources. What led people to purchase more clothes instead of other items was a change in the management of the family budget based on new assumptions in regards to family priorities. Taking these factors into account, Ramos concludes that some elements in Palencia's consumer rise resemble Jan De Vries' model of the "industrious revolution."[21] The final example comes from the study by Andrés Hoyo Aparicio and Ramón Maruri Villanueva of the Santander region (Cantabria). It also covers rural and urban spaces, concentrates on the middle classes, and uses probate inventories as main source of information. The authors discovered in both the city and the countryside patterns of consumer expansion in textile products similar to the case of Valladolid. Starting around 1820, the wardrobes of well-established farmers and bourgeois urbanites included elements of new nineteenth-century male clothing styles: jackets, pants, and vests. Hoyo and Maruri look beyond clothes and fabrics to emphasize changes in a diversity of household items such as furniture, kitchenware, and decorative fixtures. The interiors of middle-class homes in the city of Santander evolved in a fashion similar to that of the Madrid homes studied in the previous chapter. Homes inventoried between 1820 and 1840 were better decorated and more comfortable than those inventoried around 1750. These changes were evident in the inventories of both countryside and city homes, although in the rural areas the progress made was more modest. While the evolution of prices, salaries, and market conditions are taken into account to explain the rise in consumerism, Hoyo and Maruri highlight the role of cultural change to explain Santander's progress toward becoming a modern consumer society.[22]

The consumer trends seen in Catalonia and Old Castile between 1750 and 1860 are comparable to those found in our study sample of 814 inventories from upper and middle-class Madrid families in the eighteenth and nineteenth centuries. In the previous chapter we saw evidence of change in the way home interiors were distributed, furnished, and decorated. The findings presented there are similar to what Ramón Maruri Villanueva describes for the case of Santander.[23] The transformation of the home into a modern bourgeois one can be understood in the context of the spread of the culture of domesticity. Now let us return to the contents of family probate inventories to examine the evolution in the consumption of textiles.

Madrid inventories differentiate between two categories of textile items: domestic use and individual clothing. The first, labeled *ropa blanca/ropa de casa*, included items such as table linens, bedding, and curtains. The second, called *vestidos*, incorporated clothes, shoes, and hats. Although eighteenth-century inventories are consistent in keeping this distinction, it becomes less frequent over the course of the nineteenth century. The value of personal clothing in comparison to domestic goods varied according to the family income. Inventories of wealthy households display higher appraisals of curtains, linen, and cloth covering the walls, while in lower-income inventories the value of personal clothing frequently surpasses the value of domestic textile items. In addition to this difference, all inventories present a significant increase in the consumption of domestic textile products (Table 4). Tableware and bedding are the categories in which the increase in consumption is most evident. Pillow covers and pillows are absent in a significant portion of mid-eighteenth-century inventories, but they appear in almost all inventories of the second half of the nineteenth century. Mattresses and blankets increased in quality over time. Straw and animal hair mattresses were not uncommon up to 1820, but they almost disappeared from middle-class bedrooms in the second half of the nineteenth century, when wool prevailed. Popular low-quality wool blankets, known as *mantas de Salamanca,* were gradually replaced by blankets made of imported wools and cotton as well as quilts. The attention given to tableware reflects the importance of table rituals and manners in bourgeois society. Not only do inventories show larger stocks of tablecloths and napkins, but also a greater interest in itemizing these according to their quality and function. After 1850, notaries created a second category for kitchen tablecloths of lower value and daily use to distinguish them from tablecloths reserved for special occasions. There were also separate categories for napkins—dessert and dinner or lunch napkins—and diverse types of glassware, silverware, saucepans, and plates. Curtains—considered a luxury in the eighteenth century—became an indispensable decorative item in the nineteenth-century bourgeois home. Of course, inventories list a large range of qualities and designs, but even the most modest homes had curtains to provide privacy, comfort, and decoration.

Personal wardrobes grew over time. By 1880, households contained a greater number of jackets, skirts, winter coats, underwear, and hats than one hundred years earlier. Patterns of dress became more uniform over the course of time, especially for men. Eighteenth-century male wardrobes in our sample included coats, waistcoats, and breeches—the three classic components of eighteenth-century male dress. However, it was not unusual for coats and waistcoats to be absent in inventories of the lower social segments. In contrast, in the second half of the nineteenth century, all inventories in the sample, without distinction of owner's social rank, itemized jackets, vests, and pants—which took the place

TABLE 4

Frequencies of Possession of Domestic Goods in Middle-Class Madrid Probate Inventories (in percentages)

	1700–1758	*1793–1820*	*1874–90*
Curtains	56	77	92
Pillows	43	85	98
Mattresses	93	100	100
Bedspreads	78	87	97
Blankets	92	90	95
Tableware	48	78	100
Total inventories: 814	(262)	(280)	(272)

Source: Author's compilation with information from the Archivo Histórico de Protocolos de Madrid (AHPM).

of the coat, the waistcoat, and the breeches of the eighteenth century (Table 5). At the same time, the color, quality, and design of male attire became more uniform. Jackets, pants, hats, and ties were black, white, or neutral, sometimes striped. Women's clothing admitted more variations, but in general dress styles became more standardized. Scholars of fashion note that the nineteenth century marks a trend toward democratization of patterns of dress in the Western world, and that trend is evident in our study sample.

Inventories reveal substantial changes over time in the type and quality of fabrics used in clothing and for other domestic purposes (Table 6). Linen, traditionally used for expensive products such as sheets and pillow covers, became a fairly common fabric for undergarments. Despite this new use, inventories show no overall increase in the consumption of linen products—its demand remained stable throughout the nineteenth century. While wool was traditionally the preferred fabric for clothes and domestic items, inventories show a steady decline in wool products over the period of study. Silk, the most expensive, refined, and desired fabric in early modern Europe, continued to be exclusive and in demand. Despite the elevated cost and restricted supply

TABLE 5

Frequency of Dress Components in Male Inventories (in percentages)

	1700–1758	1793–1820	1874–90
Coat/jacket (*casaca/levita*)	61	73	100
Waistcoat/vest (*chupa/chaleco*)	57	71	100
Breeches/pants (*calzón/pantalones*)	72	78	100
Stockings (*medias/calcetines*)	100	100	100

Source: Author's compilation of information from the Archivo Histórico de Protocolos de Madrid (AHPM).

of silk, greater numbers of middle-class individuals were able to have access to it. Cotton was the textile in greatest demand among nineteenth-century Spaniards and was used for a wide variety of purposes. After the second half of the eighteenth century, all inventories display a greater use of cotton products in household items such as bedspreads, tableware, curtains, and wall coverings. Cotton was very popular for the manufacture of clothes, and almost all female wardrobes contained numerous items made with muslin or percale. Muslin was used extensively for shirts, petticoats, traditional Spanish *mantillas,* bonnets, aprons, girdles, shawls, scarves, corsets, and other women's items, as well as men's shirts, pillow cases, sheets, and handkerchiefs. *Indianas,* the variety of calicoes most in demand, were used to cover interior walls, and to make colorful and fashionable vests (*chalecos*), shirts, sashes, and shawls. *Cotones, cotonías, mahones, bombasíes,* and corduroys completed the collection of cotton fabrics that formed part of this new consumer universe characteristic of the Madrid middle ranks in the transition from the eighteenth to the nineteenth centuries.

The cases of Catalonia, Madrid, and Old Castile demonstrate that significant segments of Spanish society were participating in the late eighteenth-century consumer takeoff in the West. It is important to take these regions into account because, up to the present, historical studies on early modern and modern consumer expansion have been based on evidence from north Atlantic

TABLE 6

Textile Fabrics of Items in the Probate Inventories of Madrid Middle Classes (in percentages)

	1700–1758	1793–1820	1874–90
Wool	57	42	39
Cotton	6	25	41
Silk	12	10	14
Linen	43	41	42
Total inventories: 814	(262)	(280)	(272)

Source: Author's compilation with information from the Archivo Histórico de Protocolos de Madrid (AHPM).

countries. Since the late 1980s, inventory studies based in England, Scotland, colonial America, Belgium, Germany, the Netherlands, and France have been revealing the rise, with each generation, of the number, range, and quality of material possessions.[24] Inventories from Spanish households display similar patterns. Our data show that new consumer aspirations and the spread of new material cultures also occurred in the Mediterranean region. It is obvious that in Spain this development was not linked to a process of industrialization on a national scale as it was in England and other parts of northern Europe. It also had a restricted social impact in Spain: studies on the evolution of living standards in Spain describe a highly polarized society for most of the nineteenth century. In Old Castile, where we have seen increased consumerism in the cities and the countryside, between 1780 and 1860 the salaries of agrarian and industrial workers remained stagnant and far below those in northern Europe. "The agrarian capitalism characteristic of that region," states Javier Moreno Lázaro, "brought about growth and benefits to a limited segment of society while deepening the gap between poor and rich. It helped to elevate middle class living standards to the levels of most advanced European societies, but at the expense of impoverishing the working class."[25] Thus, consumer expansion in nineteenth-century Spain occurred mainly among the middle and upper classes, and there is no evidence to sustain the claim of a consumer revolution.[26] While historians talk about the consolidation of mass consumer societies in the north of Europe during the second half of the nineteenth century, in Spain the first signs of mass consumerism were not evident until the 1920s, and they were restricted to specific regions and large cities. But is also a well known fact that stagnation of salaries affected all Western countries, even the most advanced economies and those at the epicenter of the Industrial Revolution. Known wage data, states De Vries, suggest that ordinary workers could do more than survive, and as the eighteenth century gave way to the nineteenth they show mostly distress and decline.[27] It is true that the Spanish bourgeoisie was smaller in number and less leading-edge in regard to consumer habits than their counterparts in northern Europe. But despite these limitations and differences, Spain experienced sufficient transformation to claim a berth within the group of Western societies that gave birth to modern consumer society.

Catalonia, which showed signs of economic and social dynamism by the first third of the eighteenth century, constituted the earliest case of an industrial and consumer society in modern Spain.[28] That dynamism was evident in the leading role played by Barcelona in the modernization of the Spanish city. Between 1860 and 1930, Barcelona's streets, buildings, and public spaces became vibrant examples of avant-garde bourgeois urban modernity. Catalan industrialization also benefited Spanish intraregional markets and consumer cultures, as it expanded the availability of textile products and resulted in the increased use of cotton fabrics in Madrid and Old Castile. In Madrid, for instance, during the second half of the eighteenth century a significant number of shops specializing in the sale of Catalan textile products were established. Known as *tiendas de géneros catalanes* (stores of Catalan textiles), they were owned by a growing community of Catalan merchants, many of them members of manufacturing families.[29] Like other merchant groups in Madrid, the Catalonians formed a tight colony with strong signs of regional identity. According to some contemporary sources, their businesses were very profitable, and the Catalans were a group in expansion within Madrid business circles.[30] In 1797, there were fourteen major shops in Madrid commercializing Catalonian-made textiles. Firms such as Nadal y Guarda, Tutau, Masvidal, Lanchas, and Llovera occupied a distinctive place within Madrid's retailing business.[31] In 1830, most of the luxury textile commerce of Madrid was still in the hands of merchant families from the northern regions of Spain—Basques, Cantabrians, and Riojans; Catalonian merchants accounted for only 7 percent of the textile business. However, by 1856, the Catalonians represented about 17 percent of Madrid textile shop owners, constituting the largest regional minority. This shift coincided with a second stage of mechanization of the Catalan textile industry.[32]

Catalan industrial and commercial buildup brought about lower prices for cotton products, making them affordable for wider social groups. Affordability was a factor in the expansion of consumption. Spain, along with the rest of Europe, benefited from a long-term process of the reduction of the price of linen, wool, and cotton fabrics that began in the seventeenth century.[33] Increased supply coupled with growing demand explains the rise in Catalan and Castilian consumerism. On the supply side, Catalan industry was boosted by improved technology at that same time that Madrid merchants enhanced distribution networks and marketing techniques and practiced price restraint. Demand also played a significant role despite the fact that Spain's economy was still predominantly agrarian with limited local industry and markets in the process of development. As mentioned above, the first extensive references to changes in taste and consumer habits can be found in literary and political texts written mainly during the second half of the eighteenth century. Satirical journalists, playwrights, and enlightened economists were the first to publicize the Spanish consumer subject. Comedies, novels, and newspaper articles featured characters who adopted new consumer attitudes that went against established traditions or resulted in excessive spending. These public debates reflected cultural, social, and political changes that brought about the spread of modern consumer culture in modern Spain.

In the 1820s, after the brief disruption caused by the Peninsular War, the spread of consumer culture entered a new stage as it became an integral part of the making of nineteenth-century bourgeois identity. Boosting consumerism were new forms of supply linked to technological advances and the development of innovative and efficient methods of distribution. At the same time, the new middle classes energized the demand side as they embraced consumer habits connected to the formation of new bourgeois public and private spheres. The making of the bourgeois home with its display of new material culture was the principal factor in the rise of consumer culture in the private sphere. In the public domain, new tastes in fashion were the main reason for increased consumerism. The *hombre fino* and the *mujer fina* were the new consumer subjects in need of acquiring an array of new symbolic objects in order to perform in the diverse spaces for social interaction of the bourgeois public sphere. In addition to innovative clothing styles and new textile fabrics, Madrid inventories reveal that bourgeois individuals and families acquired a variety of objects that constituted the paraphernalia of gentility (Table 7). As we saw in the study of the function of different rooms in the bourgeois home, pianos were one of these artifacts of refinement. However, pianos were expensive and they only appear in a restricted number of inventories. For instance, the grand piano manufactured by Pleyel that the banker Manuel Gil de Santibañez had in the parlor of his apartment was appraised at 5,000 reales—the estimated yearly income of a low-middle-class family.[34] More common were the less expensive upright pianos like the one owned by the family of the civil engineer Constantino Germán Cavero appraised at 400 reales.[35] Although upright pianos were more affordable, this musical instrument was still a costly item out of reach of many middle-class families. While pianos were only for the most classy, pocket watches became very popular and were owned by almost everyone in the middle ranks. For many families a pocket watch was a symbol of distinction and a profitable investment. In the inventory of Nicasio Guijarro, an accountant in the public administration, three pocket watches of the variety called *savonette* were the highest appraised objects.[36] This pattern was common in cases of the lower ranks in our sample. The usual protocol was to itemize pocket watches with reference to quality, design, and brand. The money lender Domingo Aldama Zulueta, for example, owned a Cartier watch and a *savonette,* again the most valuable objects in his inventory.[37] Card cases became a necessary item in the ceremony of the visit, the most required practice of *buen tono*. The possession of this sort of small container for diverse purposes such as the storage of jewelry, cards, cosmetics, and other personal objects became a characteristic of the nineteenth-century bourgeois material universe. Finally, our inventories display an increasing amount of objects of gentility used for the embellishment and care of the body. Gloves, regarded as both a sign of refinement and as necessary to the practice of hygiene, were a prime example of an item deemed essential. Conduct and taste manuals recommended the use of gloves to keep one's hands clean and delicate; the condition of hands was perhaps the most immediate distinguishing sign of social class. Most male inventories itemized canes, top hats, and swallow-tailed coats, objects that were imperative for certain late nineteenth-century bourgeois social gatherings.

TABLE 7

Objects of Refinement/Gentility in the Probate Inventories of Madrid Middle Classes (in percentages)

	1800–1820	*1874–90*
Pianos	13	37
Watches	26	72
Cufflinks/earrings	46	93
Gloves	31	97
Umbrellas and parasols	12	68
Family portraits/photographs	16	43
Cosmetics utensils	41	88
Card cases and toiletry bags	3	65
Total inventories in the sample: 542	(270)	(272)

Source: Author's compilation with information from the Archivo Histórico de Protocolos de Madrid (AHPM).

All inventories, male and female, display an assortment of new utensils and products, such as brushes for hair and clothing, razors, toothbrushes, soaps, toiletry bags, and grooming scissors, reflecting the increasing obsession of the middle classes with the care of the body. In sum, our sample of nineteenth-century bourgeois Madrid families presents solid evidence of the spread of consumer culture in nineteenth-century Spain. This development is also evidenced in the birth and consolidation of a Spanish fashion industry after 1850, which we will analyze in the following section.

FASHIONING THE SPANISH MIDDLE CLASSES

Scholars agree that fashion has been a major force behind the spread of modern consumer culture.[38] There is less agreement, however, in regard to the historical moment when fashion became a factor for the spread of consumerism. Some track the beginning of Western culture's concern with fashion to the sixteenth-century court of Elizabeth I. It was here where these historians first see a conception of fashion that would spread to the middle class.[39] Others identify the origins of modern fashion in the Italian courts of the fourteenth century.[40] Revising these opinions, recent scholarship presents convincing evidence that the early manifestations of fashion as we experience it today appeared in late seventeenth-century France. It was first seen in the confection of dolls wearing aristocratic French fashions, and then in the printing of engravings (fashion plates) displaying court clothing styles that were sold as collections or inserted in magazines.[41] The plates of high society characters designed and printed by engravers such as Jean Dieu de Saint-Jean and the Bonnart family, and the fashion comments and images included in the gazette *Mercure Galant* around 1670, were the first manifestations of modern fashion culture. However, these early initiatives did not have continuity. The true launch of the fashion system as we know it today did not occur until the second half of the eighteenth century with the diffusion in France and England of the illustrated newspapers and, above all, the fashion magazine. Jennifer M. Jones cites *Le Corrier de la Nouveté* (France, 1758) and Joseph Boudier de Villemert's *Le Courier de la Mode* (France, 1768–70) as the first publications established with the exclusive objective of presenting the latest fashions.[42] *The Lady's Magazine, or Entertaining Companion for the Fair Sex* (England, 1770–1832) pioneered fashion publication in English, and Jean Antoine Brun's *Cabinet des Modes* (France, 1785–86) completed the European constellation of early fashion publishing. The *Journal des Luxus und der Moden* (Weimar, 1786–1827) for Germanic audiences and *La Donna Galante ed Erudita: Giornale Dedicato al Bel Sesso* (1786–88) for the Italians were adapted copies of the *Cabinet des Modes*.[43]

In Spain the first fashion plates—the collections of engravings by Juan de la Cruz, Marcos Téllez, A. Rodriguez, and others—were not produced until the last third of the eighteenth century, one hundred years later than in France. According to Valeriano Bozal, two factors explain this delay: the underdevelopment of the Spanish engraving industry and the lack of consumer demand for such products. The publication and commercialization of fashion engravings after 1770 can be interpreted as a sign of the onset of Spanish consumer expansion. These plates were sold in bookstores to a wide clientele of educated Spaniards who were interested in collecting, decorating, and keeping abreast of matters of taste.[44] As in the rest of Europe, since the mid-eighteenth century the daily presses of Madrid, Barcelona, and Cadiz included sporadic comments on fashion and early samples of advertising in Spain. The *Diario Mercantil de Cádiz* (1802–37), for instance, occasionally included a supplement entitled *Correo de las Damas* (Courier of Ladies) with information on the fashions of Paris and London.[45] In 1822, the liberal journalist León de Amarita published *El Periódico de las Damas* (Periodical of the Ladies), the first magazine dedicated to female audiences with extensive comments on fashion and fashion plates borrowed from the French *L'Observateur des Modes*. *El Periódico* was an ambitious weekly project of forty plus pages that survived only a few months.[46] The first Spanish publication with financial continuity focusing on fashion, *Correo de las Damas,* did not appear in Madrid until 1833, sixty-five years later than its counterpart in France.[47]

The nineteenth-century illustrated press in general and the fashion magazine in particular brought about the codification and commercialization of taste and made fashion available to wider audiences. Like most specialized publications of the time fashion periodicals served a variety of purposes. Magazines were, above all, profit-making entrepreneurial initiatives aimed at promoting consumer habits. They pursued the creation of a new kind of consumer, one who would embrace the attitudes, values, and dispositions of the dominant bourgeoisie. Fashion magazines and illustrated publications, along with conduct and domestic economy manuals, formed part of the public sphere and were major vehicles for the diffusion of bourgeois culture. Fashion texts guided readers regarding how to dress, where to go, how to act, and what to say, according to the criteria established by the upper classes. Their main audiences were the educated and affluent members of the upper and middle classes, those who could read, understand, and afford the cultural and material pleasures publicized in their pages. From an ideological perspective, major segments of the nineteenth-century fashion press espoused and divulged the conservative values, principles, and worldviews of Victorian culture. In countries such as Spain and Italy, these Victorian values were comingled with moral principles from the Catholic tradition. Images and texts were chosen to appeal to the female public, the main subject of fashion up to the twentieth century. Despite their conservative and gender-based content, these publishing initiatives were unequivocal carriers of modernity because they created the fashion system as it exists today: an industry with wide economic and cultural ramifications. The main innovation of the fashion press was its combination of information, images, and ideology in a single publication that could be purchased by a large audience. With the introduction of the fashion sketch, the magazine invented modern style based on the reading and interpretation of forms instead of the characteristics and quality of the materials. The fashion sketch became a major reference of what was fashionable.[48] Because the engraving transmits incomplete realities, fashion entered what Patrizia Calefato characterizes as the realm of the not important, where "the accessory becomes the essential: the length of the shirt, the form of a shoe heel, the shape of a neck etc."[49] Beyond the introduction of new approaches to the fashioning of the body and the house, these publications served as vehicles for the promotion of refined high culture, sociability, and leisure. In addition to the regular articles on fashion trends and commentary about fashion sketches, magazines included sections on theater, art, music, and literary pieces—short stories, poems, and serialized novels. Finally, it is crucial to note the role of advertising in the contribution of fashion periodicals to the making of consumer society. Commercials were rare in early magazines, but became more and more frequent and creative over time, eventually constituting a substantial portion of the publishing content.

The nineteenth-century Spanish illustrated press in general and fashion publications in particular follow the pattern described above. The Spanish fashion press developed more slowly than its counterparts in northern Europe and Italy, and the volume of publications was lower as one could expect from a country that still had high illiteracy rates and a weak middle class. Nevertheless, the social functions, technological aspects, and overall historical transcendence of this aspect of nineteenth-century modernization in Spain were comparable to that in the rest of Europe. For this reason, in recent years Spanish scholarship has been paying more attention to the study of the social, cultural, and economic impact of nineteenth-century periodicals. The majority of the research on fashion publishing has been carried out by literary critics from the perspective of women's, feminist, and gender studies with a focus on nineteenth-century representations of womanhood, gender relations, and the position of women in the bourgeois public sphere.[50] These studies detect a fundamental change in the 1840s, driven in part by the arrival of female writers on the Spanish literary scene. Their newly achieved literary prominence coincided with the political transformations of the Spanish state in the direction of liberalism, the consolidation of an incipient capitalist economy, and the spread of romanticism with its individualistic attitudes and creative sensitivities. Most of these women writers contributed to the expansion of female journalism, including fashion magazines. Studies demonstrate that most female periodicals, particularly the fashion press, served to enforce the continuation of a gender-divided society. With a few exceptions female contributors did not subvert that status quo; rather, they produced didactic or informative texts praising Victorian and Catholic values of domesticity, motherhood, and purity as they advocated the woman's role as the main pillar of the ideal bourgeois family. Paradoxically, writes Gloria Espigado, this apology of the excellence of the female sex in defending faith and family laid groundwork that would open new avenues for women.[51] Female authors demanded access to higher education for women, raised women's profile in areas of the public sphere, and promoted a female market in which some of them acted as managerial agents. In our study of fashion periodicals we will focus on two of their main functions: the hegemonization of bourgeois values and the spread of consumer and business culture.

The Spanish fashion magazine, as well other types of illustrated periodicals, changed substantially in format, content, organization, and circulation over the course of the century, reflecting broader historical transitions in Spanish politics, technology, culture, and economics. The surge in fashion publishing after 1833 occurred at a moment of political liberalization that was beneficial for the press in general. Mercedes Roig Castellanos mentions the failed launch of two fashion periodicals in 1795 and 1804 due to censorship.[52] Cadiz and Madrid boasted the first magazines, while Barcelona shared with Madrid the bulk of fashion publishing by the end of the century. This shift is consonant with the evolution of nineteenth-century Spanish social and economic reality in which Catalonia became the most industrialized region with a stronger bourgeoisie.

Originally magazines were oriented toward the promotion of taste via literary accounts, social notes, and commentary on theater, music, and artistic events. Starting in the 1850s, most publications adopted a new orientation known as *salón y moda* (parlor and fashion), which emphasized the material aspects of lifestyles. This evolution was coupled with a substantial improvement in the visual quality of the printed text, a result of advances in printing technology, especially the use of photogravure for fashion plates and commercials. By the end of the century, the fashion magazine was more commercial, devoting substantial space to the description of fashion products and dress patterns, and introducing advertisements. A few of these publications proved to be profitable in the long run. This entrepreneurial success, although restricted to geographic areas and social groups, was nonetheless unequivocal proof of the spread of consumer culture and technological progress in Spain. More research must be done on the impact of the sewing machine in the development of the fashion magazine. Paper patterns to be used with sewing machines were first seen in Spanish magazines in the early 1860s, about the same time as in France, shortly after American and English sewing machines were first sold in Spain. In 1872, the Catalonian mechanic Miquel Escuder i Castellà designed the Aurora, the first Spanish sewing machine based on the technology of Wheeler & Weber and Wilson. Escuder's success in manufacturing the Aurora helped make fashion more available to Spanish women.

Throughout the nineteenth century, Spanish fashion periodicals and the general fashion system continued to follow French, and, to a lesser extent, English patterns. Journalists, consumers, and the sartorial world emulated with fascination the dictates of Paris fashion. Spain was not an exception in its dependence on France, which extended beyond style to culture, the economy, and even technology. The Count of Ségur wrote in 1818 that the fashion from Paris was the only sovereign whose orders, caprices, and fantasies were never questioned, even by the most obstinate.[53] French hegemony in matters of fashion was only challenged by Great Britain. Up to the twentieth century, both countries remained as the dominant paradigms of fashion and lifestyles that other societies strove to reproduce. When one considers the fashion press, it is clear that emulation played a major role in the making of the modern Western fashion system. For instance, the first successful Spanish fashion periodical *Correo de las Damas: Periódico de Música, Amena Literatura, Teatros y Modas,* inaugurated on June 3, 1833, was a replica of the French magazines *Petit Courrier des Dames* (1821–68) and the *Journal des Dames et des Modes* (1797–1839).[54] It borrowed from these two periodicals the format, sections of the text, and, above all, the images. Other less successful magazines of the same period were *La Mariposa: Periódico de Buen Tono y Modas,* and *El Buen Tono.* Both appeared in 1839 and lasted only a few months. *El Buen Tono* was a poor imitation of the influential and successful French periodical *Le Bon Ton* (1834–84), which employed the very best artists with fashion plate expertise of the time. Magazines published in the Germanic region, Italy, eastern Europe, and America were inspired by or simply reproduced French originals. Even one of the most successful early English fashion magazines, John Bell's *La Belle Assemblée,* also called *Bell's Court and Fashionable Magazine* (1806–68), was clearly shaped by French influences.[55] In Spain, magazines, like conduct manuals, adapted foreign contents to the idiosyncrasies of Spanish audiences; nonetheless, the reproduction from French and English periodicals of images, literary texts, advertising logos, and even cooking recipes was a constant throughout the century.

The proponents of fashion publishing displayed a modernizing rhetoric and attitude despite the elitist character and conservative disposition of most of their publications. Angel Lavagna, founder and editor of *Correo de las Damas,* clearly expressed this disposition in the first issue of the journal. "Periodicals," wrote Lavagna, "are a measurement of the prosperity and enlightenment of a people. Fortunately our current government is aware of that reality and is endorsing a variety of publishing initiatives the goal of which is to spread knowledge and healthy ideas, fundamental pillars for the welfare of the nation."[56] Lavagna presented *Correo* as a type of journalism that already existed in the most prosperous nations of Europe but that was almost unknown in Spain. Hence his magazine aimed to fill a cultural gap that separated Spain from other parts of Europe. Lavagna was confident that the political and social conditions of Spain were ripe for his initiative, and, indeed the periodical may have survived for two years thanks to the subscription of numerous members of Madrid's new liberal establishment. A list of subscribers in the December 1835 issue counted 260, including many well-known names from Madrid's dominant society of the time. Topping the list were Queen Isabel II, who at that time was only five years old, her mother the queen-regent, and other members of the royal family. Sixty-one percent of the subscribers were men and 38 percent were women. While *Correo* also occasionally covered information about gentlemen's fashion, it was overwhelmingly female oriented. The higher portion of male subscribers probably reflects the fact that this was a family magazine, and that in the family the man figures as the head of the household in charge of soliciting and paying for the subscription. The list reflects a substantial presence of the aristocracy, boasting fifty-seven names with a title, 22 percent of the total list. The bulk of subscribers, 78 percent, were members of the bourgeoisie of Madrid, with a few from the Castilian provinces. Among the names in the list we find some of the main representatives of the two wings of Spanish liberalism. Representing the moderates there are the names of former first minister Francisco Martínez de la Rosa, the Count of Toreno, and Francisco Cea Bermudez, among others. The presence of progressives was even more noticeable, beginning with the name of the current first minister, José Alvarez Mendizábal, in the company of many others in his circle of politicians and businessmen, such as Gaspar de Remisa, Andrés Finat, Jaime Ceriola, Modesto Cortázar, and others.[57]

The 1840s and 1850s saw the expansion of the fashion periodical genre in Spain. The two most successful periodicals of the century appeared during that period: *La Moda*, later called *La Moda Elegante Ilustrada*, originated in Cádiz in 1842, and *El Correo de la Moda*, which started in Madrid in 1851 and was the first long-lasting magazine edited by women. In Madrid, Cadiz, Seville, Cordoba, and Valencia at least twenty new fashion periodicals appeared during the two decades.[58] Although the majority of these periodicals had a short life due to financial difficulties, their existence indicates an increased demand for information about taste, manners, and arts, as well as progress toward the goal of new liberal dominant groups to create a unified culture of concurring values, styles, and manners.[59]

When comparing Spanish fashion periodicals with the European and North American ones of the period, most scholars concur in the finding of a higher aristocratic tone in Spanish publications, at least until the mid-1850s. Pablo Pena states that Spanish magazines of the romantic age promoted the idea of a woman who lived in a world of leisure equipped to seduce in the *sociedad de buen tono* (polite society), in the theater, the parlor, the opera, the promenade, the ball, and, above all, the visit.[60] This understanding of the function and impact of mid-nineteenth-century Spanish fashion periodicals is only partially accurate. It does not take into account the fact that these publications began to include articles aiming to educate middle-class women on how to deal with the uncertainties of the modern capitalist system in which rapid ascent and family bankruptcy went sometimes hand in hand. In contrast with the assessment of Pena, Iñigo Sánchez Llama emphasizes the pedagogical function of the magazines, arguing that along with fashion reviews, literary bites, and mundane comments, fashion periodicals included advice to help women make rational consumer decisions. Also for the first time in that type of literature, in articles written by and for women, Sánchez Llama points to a steady claim in favor of the creation of educational initiatives to prepare middle-class women to compete in the job market.[61]

El Correo de la Moda: Periódico del Bello Sexo (1851–93) and *La Moda Elegante Ilustrada: Periódico de las Familias* (1842–1927) are milestones in the development of a consumer-oriented society in Spain after 1860. Both periodicals were successful business enterprises that reached broad audiences and survived for an extended period of time. After the explosion of publishing initiatives that characterized the 1850s, the number of magazines in circulation during the 1860s and beyond would be reduced; however, these periodicals enjoyed a better financial situation and remained in circulation for longer periods of time.[62] Although it is difficult to measure the specific impact they might have had in fostering a democratization of consumption, we can look at the contents of the most important ones and establish some connections with our findings from probate inventories.

Both *El Correo de la Moda* and *La Moda Elegante Ilustrada* expanded their audiences during the 1860s thanks to a series of common features. First, they combined balanced information on consumer and cultural trends and reached a broad middle-class audience in the Spanish-speaking space. Second, they included on their editorial staffs the best journalists available in the field. It is not a coincidence to find articles in both periodicals written by Angela Grassi and Joaquina García Balmaseda, who were the editors of *El Correo de la Moda* in 1867 and 1883, respectively, and Pilar Sinués de Marco, who founded and managed *El ángel del hogar* (1864–69). Other well-known women writers of the period such as Faustina Sáez de Melgar, Fernán Caballero (Cecilia Böhl de Faber), Gertrudis Gómez de Avellaneda, and Emilia Serrano de Wilson were regular contributors to both magazines. But at the end of the day the key for the continuity of these periodicals was not the value of their literary content but the quality of their consumer information, as pointed out in an article published in 1907 in the *Ilustración Española y Americana* to commemorate the anniversary of *La Moda Elegante Ilustrada*.[63] Where the two periodicals excelled and established a commercial competition was in the inclusion of high-quality fashion plates and paper patterns imported from Paris and London. Paper patterns were of special interest to the editors. They frequently declared that the main goal of their periodicals was to supply Spanish women with practical tools to allow them to reproduce high fashion for themselves and their families.[64]

La Moda Elegante Ilustrada won the commercial battle during the 1880s, becoming one of the most successful publishing enterprises in the history of the Spanish press. The story of this periodical illustrates the evolution of the fashion press in Spain and its role in the spread of consumer culture. It is also an interesting piece of the history of nineteenth-century incipient Spanish industrialization as well as business history. The magazine was founded by

Francisco Flores Arenas in 1842 in Cádiz, when the city was still an Atlantic commercial node with a dynamic middle class.[65] In 1858, the periodical was purchased by Abelardo de Carlos, a young and ambitious journalist who transformed it from a local periodical into an international product. De Carlos was a talented entrepreneur from the middle class who was forced to work when he lost his father at the age of fourteen. Before starting his own business, he worked in publishing houses in Cádiz, Málaga, and La Habana, where he acquired an international background and established connections that were vital for his future entrepreneurial achievements.[66] Under de Carlos *La Moda Elegante* was transformed from a women's literary periodical that published information on fashion and local cultural and social events, to a fashion magazine with a cosmopolitan tone that provided consumer education. The transformation was initiated in 1861 with the declaration of a "new editorial epoch," the goal of which was to supply the best fashion plates from Paris and to include information on household consumption.[67] De Carlos followed the model of the French magazine *La Mode Illustrée,* the leading publication in the field between 1860 and 1872. He purchased engravings from that French periodical because they were larger, more detailed, and much more artistically hand-colored than those of its competitors in England, France, and America. De Carlos established partnerships with a variety of French writers, tailors, fashion designers, and engravers, who sent their contributions to *La Moda Elegante Ilustrada*. He also imported marketing techniques from France and England. For instance, the magazine was sold in two supplementary editions, one called "economic," at a lower price, and the other called "luxurious"—a more expensive version that included additional plates and paper patterns. In 1868, coinciding with the opening of a new democratic era in Spain, de Carlos moved his printing enterprise from Cádiz to Madrid. Over time Cádiz had become isolated from the expanding peninsular markets, and the move to the capital was a step forward to address new patterns of demand and have access to more up-to-date technology. In 1869, de Carlos started the new editorial adventure of *La Ilustración Española y Americana.* By the time of his death in 1884, Abelardo de Carlos was one of the most influential press entrepreneurs in Spain. According to the testimony of José Castro y Serrano around 1888, *La Moda Elegante* sold about one million issues per year to subscribers in Spain, Cuba, Mexico, Argentina, and other parts of Spanish-speaking America. Adding to this figure the sales of *La Ilustración Española,* Abelardo de Carlos distributed about two million magazines per year, providing employment to a staff of more than three hundred people, most of whom worked at the editorial headquarters in Madrid.[68]

Beginning in 1861, about two-thirds of the content of *La Moda Elegante Ilustrada* dealt with fashion trends, focusing on clothing styles for men, women, and children. The magazine regularly included instructions for needlework techniques, including crochet, cross-stitch, brocade, needlepoint, and tatting. Attention was paid to decorative details and the characteristics of the different textiles in each piece. While the magazine's aim was to guide its readers in the reproduction of exclusive and exquisite fashion, at the same time it always provided tips on how to control expenses; for instance, it regularly suggested affordable materials that could substitute for costly ones. Indeed, one of the recurrent themes in fashion literature was the tragic consequences of prodigality for individuals and their families. The remainder of the magazine was dedicated to tales of manners and morality, installments of serial novels, poems, articles with advice on diverse matters of domestic economy, a section with crossword and other types of puzzles, and reviews of theater, music, and art. In the mid-1870s, the editors introduced information on objects and accessories other than clothes and hats. The magazine of the 1880s included extensive text and images related to gentility objects such as parasols, purses, fans, baskets, walking canes, tableware, jewelry boxes, stools, rugs, pillows, tables, chairs, and armoires.[69] Thus, by the 1880s, *La Moda Elegante Ilustrada* featured the same paraphernalia of gentility we saw in the study of the probate inventories of Madrid bourgeois families.

The pattern of *La Moda Elegante Ilustrada* would be reproduced by ambitious and not always successful publishing initiatives during the last decades of the nineteenth century. By this time, fashion periodicals were competing among themselves to supply more and better consumer information. An example of a magazine that aimed to cater to consumers was *La Moda Ilustrada,* launched in Madrid in 1882 by Ramón Ferry, a journalist connected to the world of fashion retailing. The intention of Ferry was to compete with *La Moda Elegante Ilustrada* by offering a unique product with more paper patterns to cover the demand of a larger number of subscribers. Although beautifully designed with a wide display of appealing advertisements, the magazine lasted for less than a year because the final product was not that innovative and could not generate enough appeal as to lure subscribers from other periodicals. More successful was the revamped *La Guirnalda,* which originated in Madrid in 1867 as a very traditional ladies magazine of moral and religious content. In the 1870s, the editor added two new sections dealing with fashion trends and dressmaking. After 1880, the magazine engaged the services of a French engraver and included fashion plates and paper patterns along with the advertisement of sewing machines, Madrid shops, and even services at the Printemps department store in Paris for Spanish-speaking customers. Along with these timely updates, *La Guirnalda* developed aggressive marketing methods and offered very competitive prices, charging about 30 percent less than *La Moda Elegante Ilustrada.* It included many extras such as lottery tickets in the December issue for the traditional Spanish Christmas draw.[70] The magazine's format was flexible; its three sections—fashion plates, dressmaking patterns, and literary pieces—could be purchased separately or in combination. Its literary content boasted the highest quality of the genre, including installments of Benito Pérez Galdos's novels and *Episodios Nacionales* beginning in 1880. *La Guirnalda* survived until the mid-1880s with a customer base of middle-class women and individuals connected to the sartorial industry. Also catering to the sartorial industry were *El Figurín Artístico* (1882–84), published in Barcelona by the *Colegio Central de Corte para Señoritas* (Central School of Dressmaking for Young Ladies), and *La Moda de Madrid* (1884–87), edited and marketed by the professional association of tailors known as *La Confianza* (the Confidence).

By the end of the century, there were four well established fashion periodicals that lasted into the twentieth century. All had a broad base of clientele that extended beyond Spain and Portugal to Spanish America. Two of these publishing enterprises were established in Madrid: the aforementioned *La Moda Elegante Ilustrada* and *La Última Moda: Revista Ilustrada Hispano Americana* (1888–1927), a new magazine edited by the prolific conservative journalist Julio Nombela. The remaining two sprang up in Barcelona; they were *El Salón de la Moda* (1884–1911) and *El Eco de la Moda* (1897–1928). In the late 1860s, Barcelona emerged as a new Spanish center of fashion culture, competing with Madrid and displacing Cadiz from the role it had played as an Andalusian fashion hub up to mid-nineteenth century.[71] The fact that Spain had enough readers to sustain four major fashion publishing enterprises is proof of the increased interest in fashion, style, and consumption. Thus, although the Spanish fashion industry was still far behind those of the most developed nations in the West—a group that now included Germany and the United States—the success of these magazines is an indication of significant progress, especially in Barcelona and Madrid.

The four magazines had several common features. First of all, they continued to emphasize the commercialization of imported fashion, mainly from France. Indeed, the most innovative of the four, *El Eco de la Moda,* administered by the Librería Francesa (French Bookstore) in Barcelona, was a Spanish version of the French periodical *Le Petit Echo de la Mode.* Images were an essential component of all of the periodicals, as they boasted an increased use of color engravings and photography. *La Última Moda* and *Salón de la Moda* incorporated detailed accounts of the social life of Madrid's and Barcelona's high society circles. Along with *La Moda Elegante Ilustrada,* they reflected the conventional culture of the Restoration's dominant society with its mix of aristocratic and bourgeois manners and styles. The tenor of *El Eco de la Moda* was less aristocratic; its contents were principally oriented toward modern bourgeois lifestyles. The reader of this magazine could find illustrated informative pieces on matters such as how to play tennis, how to organize a menu, where to go for summer vacation, how to clean tough stains from clothes and upholstery, how to decorate the home for the Christmas season, and what to wear for a night at the opera. It was not totally devoid of aristocratic pretensions—the latest news about the doings of the *beau monde* of Paris, Barcelona, or Madrid could be found alongside articles on how to eliminate unpleasant odors from alcoves, or what drinks to serve in a special social occasion.[72] *El Eco de la Moda* also sponsored more progressive representations of women, showing images of women engaged in outdoor sports such as biking and tennis as well as providing fashion plates and paper patterns for trousers to be used for these activities.[73] In addition, it published articles addressing feminist debates of the time, such as the pros and cons of the use of the corset and whether women should be involved in politics.[74] All in all, the magazine endorsed the image of a socially active and well-informed woman, without relinquishing her role as the "angel in the house."

The expansion of pages dedicated to advertisement highlights the increasingly commercial and consumer character of late nineteenth-century fashion periodicals. Commercial advertisement that reflected the values, aspirations, and anxieties of the bourgeoisie appeared in Spain at the same time as in other parts of Europe. The first Spanish eighteenth-century daily papers in

Madrid, Barcelona, and Cadiz included written commercials—*avisos*—in their classifieds section. As early as 1762, Barcelona journalist Pedro Angel Tarazona served as what could be considered the first advertising agent in Spain: he opened an agency offering a free service for the inclusion of commercials in the papers he owned.[75] Nonetheless, advertisement was not established as a profitable business in Spain until the mid-nineteenth century—more or less at the same time as in the rest of Europe—when the owners of periodicals started to charge an established fee to publish commercials.[76] Lori Anne Loebb has studied the case of Victorian England. Between 1850 and 1880, Loebb reports, a combination of factors produced an unparalleled advertising craze. Some of the factors she mentions, such as new techniques of illustration, the expansion of a middle-class market, and the rise of the illustrated press, also apply to the case of Spain.[77] Beginning in 1860, the number of commercial ads rose significantly in Spanish newspapers and middle-class illustrated magazines. Some of these commercials were better designed and more effective with appealing images. Fashion magazines joined this trend somewhat late—not until the early 1880s— perhaps because advertising lacked respectability in the eyes of the editors or more likely because the first initiative to improve the genre was via the inclusion of costly high-quality fashion plates instead of commercials. Whatever the reason, the fashion magazine joined the fin-de-siècle advertising craze with an impressive array of texts and images informing readers what things to buy and where to acquire them. Above all, these ads encouraged consumers to obtain the objects that refined men and women supposedly needed to possess to be successful in polite society, such as exotic perfumes, miraculous cosmetic products, elegant clothes, and even the fashionable drinks and food. Displaying the endorsement of international medal awards or suggestive illustrations, magazine commercials also publicized remedies to cure common ailments such as headaches, digestive problems, neuralgia, and fainting. Modern technology linked to the fashion economy, the care of the body, and the comfort of the house was also advertised in fashion periodicals, including items such as sewing machines, bicycles, and bathroom accessories. And most important, the ads invited readers to visit the shops where these products could be purchased. Shop and shopping were central to the making of middle-class consumer society. Let us now consider the evolution of the Spanish high-class shop and shopping to complete our analysis of the spread of bourgeois consumer culture in nineteenth-century Spain.

SHOPS AND SHOPPING IN THE SPANISH CITY:
FROM MADRID TO BARCELONA

The evolution of the shop is central to the making of modern middle-class consumer society. Historians see the physical transformations of shop interiors and exteriors, the adoption of new marketing methods by the shopkeeper, and the spread of the social activity of shopping as major factors in the history of the social and economic modernization of the West.[78] Again, some have characterized this succession of changes as a "retail revolution" that started in the late eighteenth century.[79] According to this view, the "retail revolution" coupled with the "consumer revolution" to bring about the fixed shop and later the large shop and the modern multiple shop complete with the display window, fixed prices, and availability of new imaginative credit formulas. The culmination of the "retail revolution" was the department store, with its atmosphere of cleanliness, comfort, and elegance as well as the use of new marketing techniques such as cash sale, unrestricted accessibility, browsing and window shopping, multiple merchandise lines, and the culture of customer satisfaction. Recent scholarship questions the concept of a retailing "revolutionary" breakthrough. The modern retail system, claim the revisionists, evolved over a long period of time, beginning with the decline of itinerant retailing in the early modern era and culminating with the advent of the department store.[80] Regardless of dissention over the sudden change theory, there is a consensus among scholars that this transition was part of the nineteenth-century modernizing process of Western societies. From the early specialized and restrictive high-class urban shop to the large diversified and open department store, scholars perceive the modern shop as a symbol of bourgeois modernity.[81]

The modernity of the fixed retail shop and shopping as a social activity have been noted by Spanish journalists and writers since the late eighteenth century. The playwright Ramón de la Cruz in *Las escofieteras* (The bonnet makers, 1773) brought the interior of a fashion shop to the scenario of the Spanish theater for the first time. Depicting the daily routine of shoppers, clerks, and the shopkeeper of a bonnet shop in Madrid, the piece parodies the lack of consumer education of Spanish customers and the dishonest habits of the Spanish shopkeeper.[82] The issues and concerns represented in *Las escofieteras* about attitudes toward fashion and consumer practices were treated from a different perspective by other enlightened writers who reflect the preoccupation of prominent segments of Spanish society with the impact of economic change and the challenges for the implementation of modernization. In the nineteenth century, the *tienda* (fixed shop), especially the high-class shop of textiles and home furnishing, appeared in many literary and journalistic texts. While some depict elegant shops that reflect modernity, others show antiquated shops and retailing practices to denounce Spanish economic and social backwardness and to call for remedial action. We find some of the best examples of writings about shops and shopping in the *costumbrista* articles by Ramón Mesonero Romanos and Mariano José Larra published after 1830. For instance, Mesonero's article in the May 8, 1836, issue of *Semanario Pintoresco* praises the charm of a new glove shop on Montera Street in the heart of nineteenth-century Madrid shopping district. The shop is described as an example of the positive change that had been taking place in Madrid's retailing sector since 1800 as well as a contribution to the modernization of the city. The shop with its show window displays and neo-gothic decoration represents, in Mesonero's words, "industry, progress, cooperation, good taste, and the concord of positive intelligence to the service of the community."[83] A few months later, the same author in the same journal writes critically about the lack of shopping arcades in Madrid. Mesonero describes the shopping *passages* built in Paris and London beginning in the eighteenth century as a sign of progress and an example that Madrid should follow.[84] Similar comments, descriptions, and suggestions about the shopping scene are found in literary and journalistic texts over the course of the century, reflecting the centrality of the shop and the social activity of shopping in the modernizing project of the Spanish bourgeoisie. Let us consider the evolution of the Spanish shop and the shopkeeper techniques in Spain in comparison to other parts of the West.

The history of retailing and the transformations of the shop and shopping in nineteenth-century Spain is a much neglected field of study.[85] We can look at the general trends of this story while thinking about a framework for further scholarship. This aspect of the history of Spanish consumer culture presents the same pattern of development as described in the two previous sections. The Spanish shop and the shopkeeper's techniques evolved at a much slower pace than their counterparts in France and Great Britain. Spanish retailers, urban planners, and shoppers looked at retailing innovations from Paris and London with an eye to transferring them to Spain. While Madrid and Cadiz were the first major cities to incorporate innovations in shopping, Barcelona ended up being the only Spanish city that had a shopping life at the level of the major urban centers in the West at the end of the century.

At the beginning of the nineteenth century, the bulk of Spanish retailing still took place at regional fairs, in itinerant markets, or by direct purchase from the artisan producer. The secondhand market remained popular, especially in the countryside, for the purchase of clothing. At the same time, large and medium urban areas of the country saw significant innovations in retailing since the second half of the eighteenth century. In the major cities there were well established commercial areas where the fixed retailed shop was the norm. Most of these shops, however, were still quite traditional in their interior decoration, retailing methods, and managerial organization. The majority of them had no exterior signs or any other public advertising. The only exterior indication of the existence of a store was a sliding door that in the summer allowed for an expansion of the display area. A few stands, a display case, and shelving occupied the interior space, which was generally poorly illuminated and austerely decorated. A religious image invariably adorned the interior, most commonly the Virgin Mary, if not the patron saint of the merchant guild to which the proprietor belonged. Often the lack of light made it difficult to adequately examine the merchandise, leading to frequent accusations of fraud. The poor ventilation produced a strong-smelling atmosphere. Specialization was restricted and many shops had odd combinations of goods, for instance, dry fish alongside writing paper and ribbons. The shop was still a family enterprise run as a patriarchal structure in which the shopkeeper (and patriarch) exercised an uncontested authority.

Despite the antiquated features that persisted in many shops, others modernized their exteriors with display windows and decorated their interiors with mirrors, glass display cases, elegant chairs and side tables, wall ornaments, and appropriate artificial illumination.[86] One such store is described in the 1785 probate inventory of Madrid's retailer and banker Juan Bautista Dutari. The document describes Dutari's haberdashery in Calle Mayor, the area of Madrid where most of the luxury stores were located. The store was attached to the offices of the Dutari banking firm and the spacious and luxurious family dwelling. The shop, occupying the largest space and fronting the street, was richly decorated with chairs and sofas upholstered in damask, wall paintings, curtains, ornamental moldings, gold and silver sconces, mahogany counters, and other decorative items to create an atmosphere of elegance, order, and cleanliness.[87] Dutari's shop was among the select high-class stores in downtown Madrid that were owned by members of the powerful corporation of the Five Major Guilds. A survey conducted by Napoleon Bonaparte's administration in 1810 demonstrated the strength and continuity of that group in the Spanish capital. Some of the shops surveyed were the wealthiest in the Spanish territory, such as the wool textile firms of Francisco Antonio Bringas, the Caballero brothers, and the García de la Prada family.[88] These shops resembled the Parisian *magasin de noveautés* that sprang up in the French capital after 1750.[89] Up to the 1840s, the *magasin de noveautés* was the dominant high-class shop in Madrid, Barcelona, and Cadiz. In this shop customers could sit comfortably in front of a mirror to peruse a French or Spanish fashion magazine to catch up on the latest Parisian styles and make their selections. Some of those stores had been transformed into places where the city's well-to-do socialized. These establishments, Mesonero comments, offered entertainment for the idle, prestige for the aristocracy, and an opportunity for the *nouveau riche* to strut.[90] However, neither Madrid nor Barcelona had yet introduced the shop arcade— the French *galerie*—considered the most advanced shopping venue of the times and the direct antecedent of the multiple shop.

Despite the late arrival of the French arcade to the Spanish city, during the 1820s Madrid and Barcelona benefited from significant innovations in the shopkeeper's retailing methods. First of all, the fixed shop with a window display and lighted interior was becoming the norm, at least in the elegant downtown shopping areas: Puerta del Sol and its surroundings in Madrid, and in Barcelona the old Ramblas and the new Plaça Reial. Ads from the renewed *Diario de Avisos de Madrid* after 1836 provide testimony of this reality. Retailers advertised their products by providing the shop's location and a description of their front window displays, such as "the window display with blue glass" or "the window display with red curtains."[91] Another innovation that can be seen in the *Diario de Avisos* was the extensive supply of ready-made clothing in the Madrid market, and presumably other Spanish cities. Sarmiento Master Tailor, for instance, advertised in March 1836 his store's supply of an extensive array of elegant ready-made clothes for men in different sizes and prices—jackets, swallow-tailed coats, wool pants, and linen underwear.[92] The ready-made clothing business was initiated in 1824 with astonishing success by the mercer Pierre Parissot in his Paris shop; it spread quickly to the rest of Europe and the Spanish tailors and retailers were among the early imitators.[93] Two final innovations complete this picture: the spread of the use of fixed prices and the use of sales (reduced prices) to allure customers. A substantial number of retailers headlined their commercials in the *Diario de Avisos* with *precios fijos* (fixed prices), a technique that was introduced by Paris and London merchants during the eighteenth century but was not broadly used in either city until the 1820s.[94] Some shops, such as the Almacén de San Justo in Madrid, advertised late spring sales with substantial discounts to sell off ready-made winter clothes, thus combining two fairly new marketing techniques.[95]

The first commercial arcades were finally built in Madrid and Barcelona during the 1840s, thus bringing this novelty to Spanish shopping.[96] However, Parisian and Londoner style arcades were never very successful in Spanish cities, perhaps due to the more benign climate of the European south. In any event, once again a transformational new form of shopping arrived in Spain with characteristic delay. By the time that arcades were finally being introduced in Madrid and Barcelona, the French and the British had moved on to a new trend in retailing: the multiple shop, considered the immediate antecedent of the department store.[97]

Before the first multiple shops appeared in Spain during the 1860s, large-scale retailing existed in the form of shops that resembled the French *galerie* or *bazar* and the British "large shop" or "monster shop." There is evidence that the large-shop modality was the main mode of high-class retailing in France and Britain from 1820 to 1840.[98] In Barcelona, Madrid, and other major Spanish cities that type of *tienda* was called *almacén, bazar,* or *galería,* and was not prevalent until the 1850s. The large shop grew in popularity in Spain through the 1870s and continued to prevail in large-scale retailing in many Spanish cities until the twentieth century. An early example of the Spanish large shop was the La Villa de París in Madrid. A 1852 article in the fashion magazine *El Mensajero de las Modas* asserts that these shops, where one could find imported products from France, England, and Belgium, were among the best in Madrid. The owner, Mr. Astrong, was a native of Belgium, where he traveled frequently to keep abreast of the latest European fashions. The stores sold clothes for visiting and for special celebrations, children's clothes, trousseaus, linen, cosmetics, decorative objects, and fabrics.[99] La Ciudad de Barcelona, a store owned by Tomás Isern and located on the Carrera de San Jerónimo, was another popular large shop. A report by the Society of Friends of Madrid in 1867 described it as very spacious, elegant, and well supplied with fashionable ready-made clothes as well as other products of good taste. The report stated that Mr. Isern's store provided employment for 319 people—60 attending the store and 259 making clothes.[100] *Bazares* and *galerías* were also present in Barcelona's commercial center. The Gran Bazar El Cid on Avinyo Street, for instance, sold ready-made clothes for men and women. The store opened to the public in the late 1850s, and by 1882 was a multiple shop with branches in different parts of Spain.[101] El Principal, known for its very competitive prices, was a *bazar de ropas hechas* (bazaar of ready-made clothes) on the Ramblas; its owner was a merchant popularly known as *el feo malagueño* (the ugly man from Málaga).[102] Some drugstores, furniture stores, and hardware stores opened in both cities during the 1860s can be considered large shops. That was the case of Vicente Ferrer y Cia drugstore in Barcelona, which specialized in chemical products, medicines, and paints, as well as the home decoration store ¡Al Bruch! opened in 1881.[103] In Madrid the Gran Bazar La Unión, established during the 1870s at the beginning of Calle Mayor, was a monster three-storey shop with spacious interiors that sold such diverse products as furniture, lamps, cosmetics, watches, toys, gifts, suitcases, and kitchen utensils.[104] By 1880, large drapery, hardware, and furniture shops were common in most Spanish provincial capitals.[105]

The multiple shop, which differed from the large shop in that it consisted of a chain of stores under common ownership in different geographic locations, is considered the forerunner of the department store. Some department stores also evolved from large shops, although there are fewer cases of this transformation. In France and Britain, multiple shops existed as early as 1800 but did not flourish until the 1840s. In Spain, the number of retailers who owned two or more stores in the same city rose significantly between the 1840s and the 1880s. In the 1860s, we see the first record of owners managing stores in two or more cities within Spain. The first known large Spanish chain store was Almacenes El Aguila (The Eagle Stores), founded in 1850 but not established as a national group until later. We do not know where or by whom it was first established, but we have evidence that by 1880 there were four branches of El Aguila stores in Barcelona, Madrid, Cadiz, and Seville that concentrated on the sale of ready-made clothes for men, women, and children. El Aguila was more than a retailing business—it was also an industrial enterprise as it manufactured products to be sold in its stores. All Almacenes were strategically placed in the downtowns of the different cities, and some of the buildings have survived to the present day. In Madrid, for instance, the store was located at the beginning of Preciados Street, the present site of El Corte Inglés, Spain's largest department store. In Seville the building still stands and preserves what was the chain's emblem: two iron eagles gracing the cornice of the main façade. By the early twentieth century, there were Almacenes El Aguila in at least six Spanish cities, with Zaragoza and Palma de Mallorca added to the list. The last El Aguila store, in Barcelona, was destroyed by a suspicious fire on June 6, 1981.[106] This store opened as a department store to the public in 1925 on the corner of Pelai Street and Plaça Universitat. Most likely it was a relocation of the 1870s shop established on Plaça Reial. If this is the case, El Aguila was the longest lasting department store in Spain and it is possible that the chain of Almacenes El Aguila originated in Barcelona. El Aguila is also an example of a multiple store that evolved into a department store. More scholarship needs to be done on the history of this chain as well as on other late nineteenth-century Spanish multiple shops, as these enterprises constitute a poorly known early link in the history of the modern Spanish department store.[107] Nonetheless, based upon information collected so far the history of the Spanish department store has its landmark in Barcelona on October 15, 1881, the day of the grand opening of Almacenes El Siglo (The Century) on number 5 of Rambla dels Estudis Street.[108]

Why are Almacenes el Siglo (soon called Grandes Almacenes el Siglo) of Barcelona considered the first modern department stores in Spain? What was so new and different about them? According to historians who specialize in retailing, a retail business can be categorized as a department store if it has the following characteristics: it offers multiple merchandise lines in more than four different selling departments; is set in a distinctive building of grandiose architecture that has been built exclusively to shelter the store; has spacious, well-lighted, and clean interiors with several floors; invites customers to enter with open doors and friendly service policies; displays the products in display windows, counters, and stands; has centralized cashiers; uses the most up-to-date technology for its maintenance; has a large staff and corporate management; and implements innovative retailing methods such as friendly return policies, long-distance selling, seasonal sales, fashion shows, and sales catalogues.[109] The new Almacenes El Siglo of Barcelona, relocated on the Rambla dels Estudis in October 1881, met all these conditions.

El Siglo Department Store evolved from a large drapery shop and tailoring workshop opened in 1871 on the Rambla of Santa Mónica. The owners, Eduardo Conde and Pablo del Puerto, arrived in Barcelona in 1869 to start a new business with capital they accumulated working for many years in a store in Cuba. On

the island Conde and Puerto not only made small fortunes, but also learned retailing styles and methods imported from the United States. While working for his Cuban patrons, Eduardo Conde visited on several occasions the recently created department stores in Chicago and New York. The manufacturing and retailing business they started in Barcelona, which specialized in the confection of shirts and gloves, grew rapidly to provide employment for seventy store clerks and eight hundred workshop laborers. After ten years they decided to expand, building a new and more diverse store that imitated the Parisian Au Bon Marché and the American department stores that Conde had observed. The new Siglo took up a large portion of the city block between Xuclá Street and the Rambla dels Estudis that formerly had been occupied by a Catholic seminary (Seminario Conciliar). The main façade of the Rambla store had five gates: a principal gate in the center and secondary gates on each side. Between the gates the architect placed large gas lamps—soon replaced by electricity—over marble plates bearing the name of the store and its selling divisions. In the back were four gates, one of which was specially designed to facilitate the access of carts. That entrance for carts was a landscaped yard that had a powerful Siemens gas lamp for night illumination. Tailoring workshops and administrative offices with independent entrances were attached to the building. Originally the store was divided into nineteen sections distributed in spacious rooms on two floors connected by a wide elegant central staircase. Customers could purchase diverse objects such as clothes, suitcases, toys, perfumes, rugs, furs, curtains, umbrellas, linen, bibelots, cards, gloves, and many other commodities for home decoration and travel. The enterprise enjoyed the latest technology, including a central gas unit of Catalonian manufacture, elevators, and sewing machines in the factory. The technical unit and the workshop were managed by the third partner in the consortium, Ricardo Gómez, a mechanical engineer trained in the United States.[110]

Conde and Puerto's store boasted innovations that had never been seen before in Spain. Between 1883 and 1889, they sponsored the publication of a periodical that appeared three times a month. *El Siglo: Periódico Quincenal* had prestigious journalists and graphic designers of the time in its editorial board—Vital Aza, Isidro Sinesio Delgado, and Apeles Mestres, among others. It combined literature, fashion, local information, graphic humor, advertising, and the promotion of the store's products. In 1890, they replaced the magazine with seasonal catalogues featuring the products they offered. The catalogue for the February 1898 seasonal sales, preserved at the Biblioteca Nacional in Madrid, describes a store with twenty-nine sections, ten more than in 1881. There was a new hardware section with diverse products ranging from kitchen and bathroom accessories to heaters for the home, lamps, and silverware. There was even a section that offered the sale of Catholic paraphernalia, such as paintings and imagery of the Virgin, the saints, and baby Jesus; different designs of crucifixes; rosaries; and books of devotion. Another new section focused on photography, offering a variety of cameras and accessories. A new division with furniture had an extensive inventory with pieces for all rooms in the house. In the late nineteenth-century El Siglo, the young sportsman could purchase his bicycle, the elegant lady her fashionable hat, and the science teacher his barometer.[111] The two-storey shop of 1881 had expanded to five levels and had more than doubled its original floor space.[112] It also offered distance selling, reaching remote areas within the Spanish territory. El Siglo continued to expand during the twentieth century. Experiencing ups and downs, it eventually became a chain after 1940 with stores in ten different Spanish cities, some of which remained in business until the 1980s.

In his study of *Au Bon Marché*, Michael Miller points out that the Parisian department store of the late nineteenth century stood as a monument of the bourgeois culture that built it, sustained it, marveled at it, and found its image in it. The department store in general is an expression of bourgeois culture's entrepreneurial drive. Its purpose and organization reaffirmed the culture's commitment to the principle of equal opportunity and bourgeois dedication to productivity. Ultimately, it reflected bourgeois fascination with cleanliness, order, organization, and technology.[113] Many episodes in the history of the Grandes Almacenes El Siglo parallel Miller's findings about the Parisian store. Like most of their French and British counterparts, Eduardo Conde, Pablo del Puerto, and Ricardo Gómez were self-made men who rose to the top through hard work and perseverance. Although Conde was originally from Madrid, he became an icon of late nineteenth-century Catalan bourgeoisie for his entrepreneurial and civic commitments, leaving multiple legacies to the vibrant fin-de-siècle Barcelona. Conde, for instance, sponsored the studies of musician Enrique Granados at the Paris Conservatoire,[114] and his summer residence in northwestern Barcelona now houses the Villa Cecilia Gardens and the Casal de Sarrià Civic Center.

Spain is never mentioned in the historiography of the nineteenth-century origins of the European and American department store. Although it is true that at the beginning of the twentieth century Spain lagged far behind France, Britain, and the United States in regard to retailing and consumer developments, countries such as Italy, Denmark, Austria, and Russia, which opened their first department stores later than Spain, are included. As stated at the beginning of the chapter, until recently Spain has been systematically ignored by scholars of early modern consumer history, despite the fact that Spaniards were the first consumers of chocolate in the West. The history of the making of nineteenth-century bourgeois consumer society includes similar omissions. It is to be hoped that the evidence presented in this chapter will result in a better understanding of the role of Spain in this historical development.

CHAPTER 5

The Bourgeois City

EVEN though, in 1900, Spain was still an agrarian country with a mostly rural population, urban life had experienced an unprecedented transformation throughout the nineteenth century. Quantitatively speaking, the results were modest. At the end of the nineteenth century, only 2 cities, Madrid and Barcelona, had more than half a million inhabitants, whereas the rest of Europe had as many as 25 such cities, of which at least 7 had more than a million inhabitants. Around 1900, 51 percent of Spaniards still lived in population centers of less than 5,000 inhabitants, and 91 percent lived in centers of less than 100,000. In a strictly technical sense, it can be said that only 9 percent of Spaniards lived in wholly urban centers.[1] Even so, the growth at the end of the nineteenth century of some cities like Barcelona, Madrid, Gijón, and Valencia was at a magnitude comparable to that of developments across Europe. But, above all, there was a series of qualitative changes that indicate advances in the urbanizing process. In a context characterized by the persistence of rural life, the inhabitants of the cities exhibited such positive social indicators as sustained mortality rates, greater life expectancy, lower marriage rates, and lower birth rates.[2]

The urbanizing impulse is best seen in the transformation of the urban landscape of a significant number of provincial capitals, as well as that of the most economically, politically, and socially dynamic cities. Since the mid-nineteenth century, many Spanish urban centers followed the standard set by the great European cities and began to break the geographic limits inherited from the Old Regime. The plans for urban extension developed in the second half of the century were in response to the need to improve the living conditions of the cities, and reflect the existence of well-informed urban elites committed to European urbanizing tendencies. The extensions not only illustrate the will of the dominant nineteenth-century groups to modernize, but also constitute the most palpable manifestation of the rise of the bourgeois city. "To modernize," writes Joan Ramon Resina referring to the case of Barcelona, "meant the synchronization of Catalonia with the vanguard of continental societies, but that synchronization had to be expressed spatially."[3] Consequently, Barcelona's *eixample* (extension) project became the comprehensive expression of the efforts of the dominant groups of the city to create images of modernity in the nineteenth century. In the same manner, Deborah Parsons interprets Carlos María Castro's project for the extension (*ensanche*) of Madrid as an initiative meant to create a new city. The new Madrid expressed the ideals of rationality and social order of the new liberal elite, and presented itself as the only possible means to adapt the city to the multiple challenges of modern life.[4]

The extensions (*ensanches*) of the cities were made for various reasons.[5] Since the last years of the eighteenth century, Spanish cities, to a greater or lesser degree, had grown in population, expanded their markets, and experienced administrative changes. As a result, the infrastructure had to be adapted to the new economic and social conditions. From these impulses rose new buildings to house banks, markets, commercial districts, offices, industries, and the like. The extensions were a profitable business for real estate speculators, builders, proprietors, and investors. Scientific and technical development also played a role. It is impossible to imagine the bourgeois city without train stations, organized traffic on its boulevards, or the rails for the trams. But there was also a profound cultural motivation in the new wave of urban planning that began to appear after 1830 in Barcelona and Madrid, and extended to other parts of the country. This chapter argues that the movement that launched the extension of the Spanish cities and their aesthetic, economic, and administrative transformation can be partially understood as an aspect of the development of a bourgeois culture. The concept of nineteenth-century urbanization as a cultural element has gained acceptance in recent years. There is a "spatial turn" that is evident in recently published works that look at the city from the new perspectives and concerns of different areas of investigation.[6] In general, all these works use the material reality that constitutes the city itself as a source of historical interpretation. The interpretation of the material culture constituted by the buildings, streets, gardens, plazas, sewers, and so on serves to depict the historical elements inherent in the processes of nation building. The city is considered a microcosm of the new liberal state, a paradigmatic space in which all the aspects of the relationship between the "new state and the citizen" come together.[7] Some of these investigations interpret the great urban projects of the nineteenth century as the expression of the imperial aspirations of liberal governments.[8]

Of special interest to the present analysis are some works arising from Michel Foucault's concept of the *gouvernementalité* of liberalism.[9] Following the central corollary of Foucault's philosophy, the city is perceived as an extraordinarily efficient instrument of the liberal elites to manipulate the perceptions and behavior of individuals. This perspective interprets the diverse actions linked to urban planning—from the construction of sewers and drains to the opening of great boulevards and public parks—as interventions aimed at conditioning the "liberal subject." They are presented as instruments of sophisticated projects of administrative and social engineering that were much more efficient than the use of political regulation. This historiography places special attention on the role of the senses. For example, as Chris Otter suggests, the bourgeois fascination with clean and open public spaces, with their conformity in space and size, or the introduction of the concept of privacy in interior spaces, reflected a type of sensibility that was very different from that which prevailed in the city of the Old Regime, which was saturated with the senses of proximity and smell—as in today's slums.[10] Even though the Foucauldian approach exaggerates the negative effects of liberal-bourgeois town planning—seen as a deceptive technology of domination—its approach undoubtedly offers intriguing possibilities for interpreting the city of the nineteenth century.[11] This approach is of interest to the argument in this book in that it considers the existence of a direct relationship between administrative action—in this case, town planning—and the universe of individual sensibilities and perceptions.

If we keep in mind the consequences of what has been analyzed in the previous chapters, this approach makes it possible to state that the big city responded mostly to the new basic needs of life—to the new sensibilities established by the bourgeois culture. To be fully put into practice, the ideals of courtesy, community spirit, elegance, comfort, consumption, and domesticity—to mention some of the most recurring—required a new type of city. Refinement, for example, demanded adequate spaces in which to cultivate the new societal norms encouraged by its promoters. The cities should have appropriate outdoor spaces for the members of their polite societies to stroll, meet, greet, observe each other, and practice the rituals appropriate to the occasion. The same was true of interior spaces: cafés, theaters, museums, athenaeums, restaurants, and the like had to be clean, exclusive and, to the extent possible, not lacking in luxuries. They also had to be built so as to preserve the exclusivity of their users and allow them to establish the necessary spatial boundaries with the lower social classes.[12]

All these factors undoubtedly contributed to the rise of the bourgeois city and must be kept in mind in Spain's case. As was stated earlier, the quantitative results of the process of urban growth in nineteenth-century Spain were much more modest than those of neighboring countries. Nevertheless, there was much planning and the appearance of many cities underwent substantial transformations throughout the century. This paradox can only be explained by taking into account that the impulse to urbanize, besides responding to economic, demographic, or political tensions, was also motivated by the will of the new dominant groups to build a city that would suit their evolving notions of life. Urban historians of Spanish cities have not sufficiently taken into account the fact that this impulse was of a cultural nature.[13] These developments can be analyzed through the study of concrete cases, starting with Barcelona and Madrid.

BARCELONA

Barcelona, as an industrial and commercial city, was the most eminently "bourgeois" in nineteenth-century Spain. Its bourgeois identity dates to the late Middle Ages, when the city became the major artisan and mercantile center of Christian Spain and the hub of a trade-based empire.[14] During the twelfth century, the consolidation of a new business class strengthened the role of the city, not only as a center of power, but also as the heart of a maritime empire founded on long-distance commerce, navigation, and military conquest.

In the fourteenth century, Barcelona became the de facto capital of the Kingdom of Aragon and Catalonia, and its empire that extended from the eastern shores of Spain to Greece—including the Balearic Islands, Sardinia, Sicily, and the Kingdom of Naples, in addition to a web of commercial consulates throughout the Mediterranean. In this typical medieval maritime empire Barcelona played a crucial role as the center of consumption and distribution of a region with a surplus of some agrarian products and an ancient and deep-rooted tradition of craftsmanship. The business that brought success to Barcelona's medieval merchants was the exportation of local products and the importation of high-demand products like spices. Barcelona's periods of economic preeminence have always been linked to its agrarian and industrial hinterland. Thanks to a new governing and intellectual class, the city became immersed in a spirit of commercialism and civility that marked its character. Even though Catalonia's commercial imperialism began to show signs of weakening during the mid-fourteenth century and deteriorated in the next century, the commercial and bourgeois character of medieval Barcelona remained its hallmark throughout its history. The identity of the city in later centuries, especially from the nineteenth century on, would-be founded on that past.

The image of Barcelona at the beginning of the nineteenth century as being eminently industrial and commercial—and therefore bourgeois and proletarian—is essentially correct. From mid-1700s on, the city and Catalonia entered a period of economic growth that would become the earliest phase of Spanish industrialization. "The Catalonians," wrote José Cadalso in 1789, "are the most industrious people of Spain. Manufacturing, fishing, navigation, commerce and centers of operation are hardly known in other cities of the peninsula in comparison to those of Catalonia."[15] Once again, Barcelona was the prime mover of this development. A substantial portion of the cotton industries, one of the main products of the new Catalan economy, was located within the city. Its port was the most efficient and profitable means to send manufactured goods and agricultural products to market before the extension of the railroad. The embroidered cotton fabrics—the renowned calicoes (*indianas*)—and brandy were the main products of the beginning of industrialization. In time, industry diversified and a greater variety of goods was exported. The new Catalonian realm was neither regional nor Mediterranean; it was directed toward the interior of the peninsula or toward the American colonies—while they existed—and was evident in the control of the markets. It retained from the past only its mercantile and artisan nature, and the fact that it projected itself through Barcelona, but the social groups that propelled it saw themselves as keepers of its glorious medieval past.

The immediate result of the economic growth of Barcelona, besides enriching the dominant groups, was the increase of the working-class population. In 1717, Barcelona was a city devastated by defeat in the War of Spanish Succession that counted a population of only 34,000 inhabitants. By the beginning of the nineteenth century—in 1802—the city had a population of 115,000 inhabitants. Even though there had been some changes in the interior and the outskirts of the city between those years, the livable limits were still those of the medieval city. The changes in Barcelona's urban landscape throughout the eighteenth century were either aesthetic or administrative, or a combination of both. Among the first was the opening of the Ramblas in 1776, for which one of the medieval walls had to be torn down even though the city remained within its ancient limits. Among the administrative changes was the construction in 1717 of the "ominous" Ciutadella, conceived as a defensive fortification to which was attached a new wall. Many Barcelonians saw this architectural grouping as a symbol of their punishment for having opposed the Bourbons in the War of Spanish Succession, and as an enclave whose function was not to defend the city from outside aggressors but rather to repress any internal uprising against the established order. Before the opening of the boulevards, the remodeling of Barcelona had been initiated by a project partially linked to the fortifications.[16] The opening of the Ramblas and the remodeling plan of the district of Barceloneta by engineer Juan Martín Cermeño was Barcelona's first great modern project in city planning.

The nineteenth century, therefore, was welcomed by an expanding and productive Barcelona in which a new industrial and merchant bourgeoisie was making its appearance as the dominant sector of its social space. Its most outstanding constituents, who had contributed to the establishment of the Enlightenment, would now take the side of liberalism in order to dismantle the Old Regime. As in the rest of Spain, the liberal discourse was fundamentally modernizing and Europeanizing. From the beginning, the leading group in Barcelona felt socially and historically different from its homonyms from Madrid and other parts of the country. Because of their link to commerce and industry, they felt more akin to certain European bourgeoisies that were at their peak. Historically, they saw a link between their medieval glory and their budding industrialization, so they based the industrialized Barcelona and Catalonia of the nineteenth century on the merchant and civil one of the Middle Ages. They also had Catalan, their own distinctive language with a rich literary and cultural tradition. With all these elements, they began to construct a new collective vision that would find its expression in the type of city they would build during the nineteenth century, and in the political, cultural, and social movement that would sponsor the construction.

By 1860, Barcelona looked more like a somber industrial and mining British town than the splendorous Paris of the Second Empire. A city in which lived a bourgeoisie that considered itself the most European of Spanish bourgeoisies had only one avenue, the Ramblas, which was comparable to those of the great European cities. The mood of Barcelona's urban landscape came from its narrow, poorly ventilated, and poorly drained streets of Ribera, San Pere i Santa Caterina, and Raval, which covered three-quarters of the city. On these streets were the textile factories as well as all the other industries of the city.[17] These were neighborhoods made up of densely packed houses, unhealthy dwellings, and sordid streets. Unlike Madrid, Barcelona had not enjoyed the benefits of having courtly spaces, like those adjacent to the Palacio Real or the gardens of the Retiro or the Paseo del Prado. Between 1820 and 1830, the liberal municipal governments, aware of the need to beautify the city, opened Ferran Street and planned the Plaça Reial and the Plaça of San Jaume. These improvements were inspired by the rationalist and aesthetic mentality of liberalism. Ferran Street, paradoxically named after the anti-liberal Ferdinand VII, was laid at a transversal axis to that of the Ramblas in order to add elegance to the most refined area of the city and to create spaces adequate to the needs of its new society. In that section of the Gothic Quarter where the town hall and the Generalitat were located, the opening of the new avenue was meant to give these buildings the splendor that was their due according to the new liberal political vision. To achieve this, they created the Plaça Sant Jaume, an eminently commemorative space, arguably the most symbolic of the modern city. At the other end of the new promenade, a space was opened for the Plaça Reial, which was to be a commercial and residential area. The project took a long time to complete, not being finished until midcentury, when the streets of Jaume I and de la Princesa where added as extensions to Ferran, completing a great transversal axis that joined the old city to the Ciutadella. This stretch combined the new administrative city represented by the Plaça Sant Jaume with the most truly bourgeois one of the Ramblas. Under the supervision of architect Molina i Casamajo, one of the intersections of the Plaça Reial brought together all the elements of the ideal urban bourgeois space: a large open area to guarantee the cleanliness of the air; safe and well-landscaped gardens for the members of refined society to stroll and socialize in; and newly constructed buildings for spacious and comfortable homes as well as stores and commercial offices for the prosperous elite.

Meanwhile the disentailments of Mendizábal were promulgated, and a large number of churches, convents, and cemeteries were auctioned off to the highest bidder. Buildings and spaces of incalculable historic and architectonic value were demolished in the name of economic progress. In their place were built some of the most emblematic buildings of bourgeois Barcelona, among them the Teatro del Liceo. Despite all these improvements, the city was still imprisoned within its oppressive and unpopular walls flanked by the Ciutadella. In 1856, the city had 189,000 inhabitants, 74,000 more than in 1802 and 155,000 more than in 1717, and all lived in an amount of space that had not changed since the low Middle Ages.[18] Factories had become the most characteristic buildings of the lower-class neighborhoods of the old city.[19] Mixed in with the big industrial spaces were diverse small businesses, artisan workshops, taverns, and working-class homes. Some of the large factory buildings had aesthetic value, having been designed by fashionable architects such as Joseph Buizareu, designer of the Porxos d'En Xifré—one of the most emblematic buildings of the early Catalonian bourgeoisie.[20] Essentially, though, their disposition, location, and quality served the criterion of function rather than aesthetics or habitability.

Bordering the north-south axis of the Ramblas and the transversal intersection on the east-west axis of the streets of Ferran, Jaume I, and de la Princesa—in the midst of a host of dirty chimneys, dark corners, and foul-smelling streets—was the refined zone of the city. From the beginning of the nineteenth century to the 1860s, this would be, par excellence, the noble and bourgeois sector of Barcelona, prolonging the peak it had reached in the mid-eighteenth century. All the spaces characteristic of the modern bourgeois sphere—cafés, offices, athenaeums, and bookstores—could be found there. Refined men and women could entertain themselves ambling along the Rambla dels Caputxins enjoying the amenities of the Hotel de Oriente. They could sip drinks in any of its cafés, go to the Plaça Reial to visit their banker to handle financial matters, stop and look at the new store display windows, or enter any of these commercial establishments for news on the latest fashion or to buy something for their homes. In this trajectory, they would enjoy the sober architecture of some eighteenth-century palaces and, in time, the imposing façade of the recently constructed Grand Teatre del Liceu. But once outside the site of the Plaça Reial, the distribution of these spaces became irregular, as if unaware of the criterion of rationality in bourgeois town planning.

In the zone of the port, by the sea, where the Passeig de Colom runs today, was an esplanade known as the Jardí del General. From 1815 to the end of the 1840s, it was the favorite recreation area of Barcelona's refined society. It was the city's first public park and was built by the initiative of General Francisco Castaños, an enlightened military man known for promoting theater and music, especially opera.[21] All these places of expansion, sociability, and business had been built in the irregular medieval city. Just a few blocks away from the Teatre Principal, or the Grand Teatre del Liceu, with no transition, was the realm of workshops, dusty streets, and gloomy neighborhoods. The famous l'Argenteria Street, where a majority of the jewelers' shops could be found, was within the area of artisan shops and factories. The Ciutat Vella (Old Town) was, simply, at the limits of its possibilities; most of it was unhealthy and, above all, it displayed a social promiscuity deemed unacceptable to those whose ideal was refined society. Like most European cities of its time, Barcelona needed to break its old walls to create a new city to meet the tastes and specifications of its new society. Beginning at the end of the 1840s, the city left no stone unturned to make this growth possible. This process was marked by political and administrative controversy, but would bear one of the most original and innovative plans of urban extension of Europe. We will analyze Barcelona's urban extension with a look at its two key moments: the first was the approval of the plan of Ildefons Cerdá's *eixample* (extension) in 1859; the second was the organization of the World's Exposition of 1888.

The first step in the extension process was the demolition of the old walls that liberals, republicans, and Catalan nationalists saw as a symbol of Old Regime oppression. In January 1840, the town council held a contest that raised the question of the benefits of demolishing the walls. Pere Felip Monlau—a republican intellectual who would help introduce, among other things, the social hygiene movement in Spain—won the contest with the slogan "Down with the Walls!"[22] Three years later, during the confusing citizens' uprising of 1843 known as the Jamancia, the revolutionaries tried to turn the Ciutadella into a Spanish Bastille. The protest was orchestrated by elite businessmen displeased with the free trade policies of the progressive government, but the revolt also attracted the working classes, creating an unconventional social and political coalition whose common denominator was the protest against the central government. The revolutionaries marched toward the Ciutadella—where the government troops had dug in—all the while executing symbolic acts of demolition. The response of General Espartero's cannons from the other end of the city was as forceful as it was brutal. For the time being, the walls would remain impassable. In the months following General Baldomero Espartero's repression, the matter of the walls was at the center of most of the political debates and in the minds of the people of Barcelona. But despite all the rebellious commotion, the first effective demolition occurred without any revolutionary stridency. The first opening breached in the 1840s foreshadowed what the city's future expansion would be. The work, which included the demolition of some military barracks and their fortifications—situated in the zone presently occupied by the Plaça de Catalunya—was done in order to complete the Passeig de Gràcia. In the 1820s, this boulevard was envisioned as the natural extension of the Ramblas and was designed with the idea of being the most elegant artery of the city. Such was Barcelona's first great urban remodeling—not to indicate the beginning of the liberation of the oppressed, but rather to build its most luxurious and selective avenue.

The fact that the old city opened itself to the future by way of Gràcia as a continuation of its most exclusive area presents two realities that will mark the development of Barcelona's *eixample*.[23] First, the new city would be built according to the program and interests of the dominant groups—the great bourgeoisie, including the old aristocracy and the emerging middle class— leaving the proletariat on the margins. Second, the agents who made the new Barcelona possible—engineers, architects, proprietors, financiers, and politicians—would adopt French town planning, basically that of Paris, as their model. The opening toward Gràcia meant that Barcelona's expansion began from the location of what was socially, economically, and culturally the most bourgeois sector, that is, it began as an extension of the Ramblas. Despite the fact that in 1854 the radical and proletarian elements of Barcelona took to the streets calling for demolition, the walls were dismantled in an orderly fashion only after formal authorization was obtained from the government in August of the same year.

The Passeig de Gràcia had been opened in 1827, measuring 1,400 meters in length and 40 meters in width. It consisted of five lanes separated by rows of trees. Two of the lanes were for carriages; the other three were for people on foot. Small plazas adorned with fountains and statues were erected in the middle of the boulevard, and kiosks with seats were installed in the walkways to serve drinks.[24] It is not surprising that the area quickly became the favorite place for Barcelona's society to stroll. By the end of the 1840s, the first pleasure gardens bordering the *paseo* had been established—the so-called Jardí de Tívoli and the Criadero. Pleasure gardens became, in the nineteenth century, spaces that were patronized—by the upper and middle classes for the purpose of socializing, promoting culture, and leisurely exercising. These were enclosed spaces located in the city's center or bordering the suburbs; in fact, they were the predecessors of today's amusement parks. In 1853, the middle path of the *passeig* was paved with stones for the carriages, public transportation was improved with the services of omnibuses, gas lamps were installed, a permanent maintenance service was established, and more gardens were opened. The design, the construction, and the functionality given to the Passeig de Gràcia reflected the aesthetic and town planning values of the liberal elites. Beginning in the 1850s, the Passeig de Gràcia became the main artery from which the expansion of the new bourgeois city would be built.

In April 1859, four years after the demolition of the wall was authorized, the town council held another contest, this time to choose a project for the extension of the city. Since the beginning of the century, different groups had been elaborating projects, project drafts, or simply sketches of expansion, but it was not until after 1850 that these projects became worthy of urban development. Miquel Corominas i Ayala, in his studies of the origins of Barcelona's extension (*eixample*), mentions the existence of as many as thirteen, most of them designed by architects. All covered a large area of land and strove to integrate the old city with the land of the Llano de Barcelona, and the most interesting ones had the Passeig de Gràcia as their axis of reference.[25] In the course of the debates, only three of those plans would reach the finals.[26] Two were designed by architects and one by a civil engineer. The bulkiest one, belonging to the architect Miquel Garriga i Roca, included up to six possible versions, the two most interesting of which consisted of an elaborate extension of the Passeig de Gràcia that would join the old city to the municipality of Gràcia.[27] The one that captivated the members of the corporation and won the contest was designed by the municipal architect, Antoni Rovira i Trias. Trias's proposal was the most conservative, and probably the one most influenced by the project being carried out by Baron Haussmann in Paris. The expansion of the new city was conceived as a natural extension of the old by the addition of a grand semicircular boulevard extending from Montjuic to the Ciutadella. Emerging from that boulevard were five big radial avenues in the style of the great Parisian streets, the main one being the Passeig de Gràcia at whose point of origin was located a majestic space made up of three great plazas that would constitute the heart of the new city.[28] The project of the engineer and councilor of the municipal corporation, Ildefons Cerdá i Sunyer, was the least conventional of all those presented. In reference to the ordering of the space allotted, it included the Passeig de Gràcia and the old city, and thus proposed a much more complete extension of the city. The radial system proposed by Rovira i Trias ignored the east-west connections of the area, while Cerdá's accounted for them. Further, it incorporated a totally new urban planning philosophy concerning the distribution and disposition of the surface that could be built upon and the characteristics of the dwellings. This plan won the government's approval, unleashing a storm in a teapot.

In 1994, La Generalitat, the Catalan government, organized an exposition in honor of Cerdá that was seen around the world. Its goal was to present the transcendence of the ideas of the illustrious engineer and his contributions to contemporary urban planning. The exhibition was based on the contents of his plan for Barcelona's *eixample* and its theoretical definition, which is included in a variety of volumes published in recent years. The experts on the history of modern town planning consider Cerdá among its pioneers because of the originality of his proposals and the importance of his legacy. Interestingly, this recognition is relatively recent, since the bulk of his theoretical speculations, so appreciated in present-day town planning, remained untouched in the general archives of the administration until found in 1988 by two young investigators.[29] Cerdá was very controversial among his fellow citizens, and even though he was a member of Barcelona's city council, the approval of his plan by the central government and the rejection of Rovira i Trias's plan caused great trepidation. The members of the municipal corporation preferred Rovira i Trias's plan because it fit better with the vision being adopted by a very influential portion of Barcelona's dominant society. His concept of the new city as an improved expansion of the old, and its emphasis on the aesthetic aspects rather than the technical ones, was better suited to the idea of Catalanism as expressed in the Renaixença. The Catalanists envisioned a Barcelona essentially linked to its brilliant mercantile and artisan medieval past, with a particular culture and a distinct legal status within the Spanish union. Though Cerdá's plan also responded to a bourgeois vision, it was in a different ideological sphere.

Cerdá's opponents portrayed him as a socialist with a technocratic spirit who lacked creativity and was imbued with an intolerable utopianism. "He was a mathematical genius and a man of incredibly bad taste," wrote Josep Pla, compiling testimonies from his contemporaries.[30] Josep Puig i Calafalch, one of the most famous architects of Barcelona of those days who is wholly identified with the spirit of the Renaixença, was of the opinion that Cerdá's plan was disastrous because it left no space for human diversity. He believed that his cellular concept of the city was horrendous, that it would be difficult to find something worse in real life, and that it could only be compared to the most vulgar of South American cities. "Those who defend this plan," stated Puig, "have the most erroneous idea of town planning. They think, for example, that the ideal city is one in which all the citizens feel that they are living under the same conditions." Cerdá's vision, according to Puig, was dehumanizing because it was based on pre-established formulas, on a fictitious concept of the past that lacked concrete historical relations, and on the use of simplistic arguments to resolve enormously complex matters.[31]

These are opinions that have almost completely vanished in Barcelona today. Cerdá was a man of ideas beyond his time, but he was not a socialist in the sense expressed by his detractors. The basic elements of his concept of the city can be connected to the principles and practices of progressivism and the bourgeois republicans of the times. The utopian socialist influence of Henri de Saint-Simon and Robert Owen can be seen in his theory and political activity, but these were not the ideological or intellectual tendencies that most influenced his career. Cerdá was, above all, a positivist, a man who believed in progress through science, a utilitarian who knew perfectly well the value of statistics and believed that happiness was linked to the welfare of the majority. He belonged to a circle of Catalans who were passionate about science and technological advancement, chief among them Narcis Monturiol, inventor of the first mechanically propelled submarine.[32] Cerdá was educated as an engineer at the Escuela de Caminos, an institution immersed in the enlightened tradition of its founders with a majority of the faculty engaged in the promotion of science, technology, and free thinking.[33] Because he was a professional engineer recycled as a town planner, his contribution to this field of knowledge was, above all, practical. The quantity of material—maps, calculations, and notations—associated with the development of the *eixample,* which he elaborated in his day and has been reclaimed from the anonymity of the archives, is impressive. He also left an important theoretical legacy.

Three assumptions determined Cerdá's ideal concept of town planning. The first was that the primary goal of the town planner was to ensure the collective welfare, and that this was only possible through respect for the liberty of the individual and the privacy of the family, the creation of comfortable spaces, the promotion of education and culture, and careful attention to services. The second was that the city should be built with eyes to the future by bearing in mind the latest technological advances, especially mechanization. Cerdá was so fascinated by steam engines and railroads that he had a somewhat fantastic notion, though not totally mistaken, of the flow of traffic in the contemporary city. The third was that the city had to be hygienic. The town planner had to take into account the layout of the buildings to guarantee air circulation, assure the inclusion of medical services, design efficient sewer systems, and make every effort to have green spaces. In his arguments there are no attacks on private property, proposals against the free movement of consumer goods, or remarks about the ideal form of government.[34]

All the studies of recent years agree that the government made the most logical decision because Cerdá's plan was the most sound from a technical, social, and intellectual point of view. First, it offered the most feasible vision for the integration of the land as it was the only one that predicted what the future metropolitan area of Barcelona would be. The best expansion for Barcelona was the one that took into account its character as a port and industrial city with an economy based on exports. For this reason, the land had to be laid out so as to facilitate a viable system of transportation and communications. This was one of the features that Cerdá paid most attention to in the extension project that he submitted for the contest, and he did so even more in later revisions, especially that of 1863. Unlike those of the other projects submitted, the construction layout of Cerdá's plan considered the railroad as the primary mode of transportation. The first railroad line in Spain, from Barcelona to Mataró, was completed in October 1848. The lines to Molins de Rey, Granollers, and Moncada were added in the following years. From the point of view of the contribution of transportation to the economic development of the city and its region, Cerdá's project provided adequate plans to connect the railroads to the ports, the industrial areas, and the lines of communications leading outside the city. It was this vision that subsequently permitted the *eixample* to become in the future the business district for Barcelona's hinterland.[35] The railroad would also be the principal mode of urban transportation. Cerdá proposed integrating homes with an elaborate rail system that would extend the entire length of the city, creating a rapid, environmentally friendly, and safe method of transportation. The main arteries were divided into parallel lines with rails in a center track below street level for train transit and easy access to the riders. But technology evolved much faster than Cerdá imagined; soon, trams would emerge as a more viable alternative to the train for commuting. Nevertheless, Cerdá's foresight left a legacy of properly laid out, wide streets that enabled an easy transition to modern-day methods of transportation.

Second, Cerdá offered the most innovative option for the unfolding of the complex construction operation inherent to the extension project. Cerdá believed that the city's extension should be unlimited and should be seen, not as an expansion of the old city but rather as a solution to it. The *eixample* should facilitate the connection of the old city with its slums packed around the Ciudatella, but it should keep the old city in mind only for the purpose of finding its defects and avoiding them. It should be seen as unlimited because that was the best way to avoid real estate speculation by builders and owners.[36]

The bourgeois character of Cerdá's ideas can be fully seen in his notion of living spaces and their integration into the urban landscape. Just as his devotion to hygiene is evident in his theory of town planning, his concept of living spaces reveals that his ideas and principles can be completely framed in the culture of domesticity. He constantly reiterates in his writings that the family is the basis of society, and that the family home is the foundation of the city. For those reasons, the city should be laid out according to the criterion of fair distribution so that each family has a private space. In the city's general plan, wrote Cerdá, private space constitutes an "inviolable sanctuary that we have called house, which is not of itself an impediment to the existence of certain sites and buildings consecrated to the various public needs of social life." Homes should be constructed so as to guarantee the comfort, health, and relative freedom of the family and each of its members. Its layout should include a series of public rooms, independent rooms, and transition rooms. The purpose of the first and second was to maintain the family's privacy, which Cerdá defined as the freedom of the family. The third ones were spaces of transition between the private and public spheres. And it is here, precisely, that the most innovative part of his plan is found: in his concept of a connection between the public and private spaces, and in the tranquility of this public space constructed for the purpose of guaranteeing a peaceful conviviality in accordance with the principles of bourgeois courtesy.

Cerdá believed that homes in the cities cannot stand alone and be surrounded by nature, as in the countryside, because of lack of space. For that reason, homes need to be grouped together in buildings—a condition that, according to Cerdá, has its advantages and disadvantages. The main advantage is that such proximity favors intellectual activity because it enables close relationships between individuals, the exchange of ideas, and the establishment of norms for coexistence. The principal disadvantage is that it deprives people of the health benefits of living close to nature. For this reason, the best solution would be to create blocks of houses that would combine the advantages of urban sociability with the health benefits of the country. To this end, Cerdá proposed to build blocks that would be open on at least one side, and would be large enough to accommodate community gardens in their interior spaces. The openings of the blocks would allow the circulation of air, thus ventilating the streets and the gardens—a matter that obsessed the hygienists. One distinctive feature of the *eixample*'s blocks is their rectangular shape with chamfered corners. This was meant to facilitate the circulation of air and make transportation faster. Time has proven that at least the second of the two conjectures was correct.

The battle of the extensions was waged between architects and engineers, and their supporters in the state's municipal administration.[37] The first valued more the aesthetic aspects related to the growth of the city; their projects paid heed to monumentality, the balance of the structures, and their style. The architects, being creators of images, felt a greater commitment to giving the new city an identity. The engineers worried about the integration of the territory; their goal was to create spaces that would make livability and development compatible with each other.[38] In the process of the expansion of the modern city, this battle would remain unresolved, as occurred with Barcelona. Even though the engineer's plan for the extension was imposed, the architects played a decisive role in its construction, resulting in Barcelona's well-known art nouveau identity.

Cerdá's urban development assumptions were carried out in their most global content, such as the layout of the streets and blocks, and the distribution of the land, which is more or less the land covered by Barcelona today, but his most concrete developments faced insurmountable obstacles. The most notable was his concept of the open block with ample green spaces in its interior. This was a beautiful idea, but it clashed with the speculative interests of the proprietors and builders. The distance between the plan and reality was also seen in the development of a city with a level of services much inferior to the one proposed. In any case, Cerdá's plan spread to the rest of Spain and became the basis for formulating the "law of extension of towns" passed in 1864.[39] Barcelona, thanks to the motivation of its dominant society and the tenacity of individuals like Ildefons Cerdá, became one of a select group of great European cities that, during the second half of the nineteenth century, acted as veritable laboratories for formulating theories and testing the tenets of modern urban development.

The *eixample* became the expression of bourgeois Barcelona. Cerdá had dreamed of a growth that would not favor only the wealthy; he wished to provide a dignified way of life to the greatest number of families possible. The result did not go beyond the social limits of the petite bourgeoisie on the left side, leaving the right side to the wealthiest, and the *eixample,* as a whole, became the bourgeois district par excellence. It could not be any other way. Barcelona followed in the steps of all the great cities of Europe. Since the approval of the project in 1859 until 1865, the development of the bourgeois city was slow. The first home built after the cornerstone ceremony attended by Queen Isabel II was that of the magnate Gilbert Sans, one of the most representative celebrities of the autochthonous bourgeoisie whose activities were linked to such emblematic developments as the Barcelona-Mataró rail line and the sponsorship of the Gran Teatre del Liceu. These were years of questioning marked by debates and negotiations between the different interest groups: city hall, proprietors, and ministries. This process brought to light the parties that would control the future development of the project, to wit, the construction collectives grouped into the so-called *societats de l'eixample,* the city council, the architects, and the cultural and political Catalanist spirit.

One of the illustrative milestones of the change in trend with regard to the situation in 1859 was the appointment in 1865 of the Catalan poet Victor Balaguer as the one in charge of choosing names for the new streets. Balaguer, one of the greatest representatives of the Renaixença, would redirect the city's identity to the context of the nationalist vision being shaped that intended to recall the medieval city—mercantile and artisan—in its role as an economic, political, and administrative center of a prosperous and extensive regional and imperial space. All of this was perceived as the result of a unique cultural reality that, because of certain historical rights, gave Barcelona a special legal status. Balaguer used the streets of the *eixample* to establish a series of places of memory relating to Catalan identity. Not one name of a person, event, or place that was not related to the historical past of Catalonia or the Crown of Aragon was even considered by the poet.

Between 1865 and 1880, the *eixample* experienced its first stage of expansion and ultimately became the space in which the new city—the expression of the bourgeois ideal of modernity—would be unfurled with all its material and symbolic elements. With the peculiar buildings constructed in the chamfered intersections of Roger de Llúria Street and the construction of the grounds for the World Fair of 1888, the *eixample* started to take shape, having the Passeig de Gràcia as its nerve center. The Barcelona-Sarriá railway line, inaugurated in 1863, divided the new space. *El carril* (the rail), as the people of Barcelona refer to it in jest, becomes the dividing line between a right side where the wealthy bourgeois establish themselves, and a left side reserved for the petite bourgeoisie. It is ironic that it was precisely on the right side that Cerdá's plans favoring a greater social integration were more faithfully followed, specifically the plans concerning the balance between green areas and dwellings, and the plans for creating open blocks with ample space to guarantee the health and operation of urban services.

The Passeig de Gràcia, which, we have already seen, was the place chosen by Barcelona's genteel society as the quarter for cultural and leisure expansion, was developed rapidly. Lluis Permanyer points out that the Passeig de Gràcia was the only existing boulevard in Barcelona that could be compared to those of other European capitals—the Parisian boulevards or that of Castellana in Madrid.[40] This is the reason for the enormous appeal it had for the most powerful families of the city, and for its rapid transformation from a leisure center into the most attractive residential and commercial zone of the city. The distinctive quality of the Passeig de Gràcia, transformed into the heart of the *eixample,* came from the lavish buildings with dwellings in the style of the typical bourgeois *maisons d'appartements* of Paris where Barcelona's fin de siècle upper bourgeois class mingled with the old, aristocratic families.

In the 1870s, the *eixample* became the premier space for real estate investment. These were the years of the *febre d'or,* superbly represented in Narcis Oller's novel. Buying land, erecting buildings, and marketing them was an essential part of that speculative fever in the new Barcelona. The *eixample* attracted much *indiano* capitalism, some of which was of Catalan origin though not the majority. The *indianos* were fleeing from the growing instability of the

Caribbean markets, looking for refuge in the secure investments of the urban extensions of Spanish cities. Of course, the main protagonists of that expansion were the dominant Catalan groups, whether from the city or the province. Oller immortalized the speculators from outside the city in the figure of Gil Foix—the protagonist of *La febre d'or*. Gil, born to a family of craftsmen, decided one day to leave his town in pursuit of the quick and easy wealth available in the big city. The fictitious Gil Foix was a social archetype of the fast-rising bourgeoisie of extravagant taste who inhabited the urban landscape of Barcelona during the second half of the nineteenth century.

The new bourgeois city was materializing day by day in its buildings, its streets, and its interior or exterior spaces used for expansion, culture, or sociability. Everything would be shaped according to the tastes and values imposed by the dominant society. "Charity ennobles; work dignifies," could be read in printed letters attached to the façade of the elegant, neo-classic mansion that the finance and local political magnate, Manuel Girona, built for himself in the heart of the *eixample*. Other icons of the autochthonous bourgeoisie, besides settling down in the *eixample,* contributed to its unfolding as a space for civility and the marketing of leisure. That was Evaristo Arnús's reason for sponsoring the Teatro Lírico Sala-Beethoven, one of the most significant places of Barcelona's social and cultural life during the last third of the nineteenth century, or the promoters of the Maison Dorée, located in present-day Plaça de Catalunya, which, from its inauguration, became the favorite place of Barcelona's high society to socialize.[41]

The expansion of the 1870s was also seen, though more timidly, in the improvement of the infrastructure and the unfolding of the urbanizing process. In June 1872, Barcelona's first tram line was inaugurated. It joined the old city with Gràcia through the *passeig,* thus starting a long period of improvement in urban communications. Also in succeeding years, steps would be taken to solve the problems of bringing in running water, sewers, and other purely urban services. But work on these services was not expedited until after the 1888 World Fair sponsored by the charismatic major Francesc Rius i Taulet. Some historians consider that the achievements of the exhibition were more symbolic than efficient in the implementation of durable initiatives of urban development.[42] The event undoubtedly marked a milestone in the process of construction of the image of modernity that the new bourgeois city pursued. The goal was to place Barcelona on the international map, to take the city out of its role as a secondary urban center. For a segment of the early Catalan nationalist movement it was also a way to strengthen Barcelona's role as the nucleus of a national reality with its own identity. But the exhibition was also successful in carrying out public works that significantly improved Barcelona's urban furnishings. The exhibition required the building of new landscaped zones that remained in the city for the future, the most distinguished of which was that of the Ciutadella. The development of the maritime area was completed in the style it still has today, including the emblematic monument to Columbus. Electric lighting was also brought for the first time to the most important areas, and a series of commemorative monuments were raised, as places of memory dedicated to celebrities, such as the Güells and the Clavés, who were linked to the new city.

In 1889, Barcelona, having successfully presented itself to the international community, proved to itself that its calling to be fully integrated into modernity was having the desired results. From that moment on, and until the 1930s, the bourgeois city, with the *eixample* as its maximum nucleus, would become the heart of a new Barcelona that expanded until it absorbed the neighboring municipalities. If, as we have seen, at the start of this major event the leading part was taken by a controversial engineer, who happened to be one of the founders of modern urban planning, after 1888 was the turn of the architects, among them Josep Puig i Cadafalch, Lluís Doménech i Montaner, and Antoni Gaudi. In the spectacle of construction of the fin de siècle *eixample,* an aesthetic battle was waged in which were synthesized the political debates, the crises of identity, and the cultural conflicts of the dominant Catalan society. It was a game of ostentation, refinement, ambition, and creativity that would finally produce one of the most beloved treasures of European modernism. But that is another long and complex story that belongs to a new historical period.

MADRID

Madrid, first in its role as the capital of an empire and now of the present Spanish state, is a relatively new city. Though the city originated in the Middle Ages, its medieval past was not tied to commerce, industry, or administration, as was the case with the Castilian cities around it as well as Barcelona. In the Middle Ages, Madrid was no more than a small defensive nucleus populated by farmers, soldiers, and craftsmen. Madrid began attaining a certain degree of importance from the late medieval era on precisely because of its appeal to royalty: its geographical location was adequate and its climate was not too extreme. At the dawn of the sixteenth century, Madrid had twelve thousand inhabitants, a considerable amount for that era; nevertheless, it remained a secondary city in the booming urban network established in Castille in the late Middle Ages. Madrid may have remained a subsidiary city had it not been for Phillip II's 1561 decision to convert it into the monarchy's permanent residence. That decision transformed Madrid into an imperial capital without experiencing the intervening process of transition in which the city, evolving naturally, would have served as the economic and administrative center of a region, as had occurred with Barcelona.

Being the seat of the court and the capital of the monarchy, Madrid reaped the benefits of urban initiatives that did not affect Barcelona or other Spanish cities. Nevertheless, until the eighteenth century, it suffered from a lack of urban infrastructure. Even so, there were numerous buildings and spaces associated with the life of the court, the most prominent being the gardens of the Buen Retiro. Aristocrats of all levels and the wealthy gentry went about creating spaces for sociability in the city that, in time, would be developed following the criteria of modern rationalist urban development. The most prominent was the Paseo del Prado, which was situated on the outskirts of the city where the most important roads and royal gardens converged.

The Paseo del Prado and the access routes to the city were redesigned in the time of Charles III during what is considered Madrid's first modern urban development surge.[43] The Prado became the preferred area of the well-to-do classes to go for walks and socialize in the fresh air. The project, known as the Salón del Prado, was carried out through the king's initiative under the supervision of the Conde de Aranda following the design of architect José de Hermosilla. The project created an urban complex that included gardens, fountains, areas for strolling and amusement, lanes for vehicular traffic, and a building conceived as a natural history library with an adjacent botanical garden. It was a remodeling project of enormous symbolism and historical significance in which were condensed many of the ideals of enlightened programs applied to specific concepts of the city and urban development.[44] The Salón del Prado was a step toward creating a monumental Madrid in the style of the great European capitals.

In the redesigning of the Salón del Prado the main components of Madrid's modern identity—a monumental capital, seat of government, financial center, main residence of the aristocracy and refined society, and depository of the national culture—materialized for the first time. Barcelona's identity, as previously seen, was that of a merchant city, industrious and bourgeois, with a brilliant medieval past and a distinct cultural character. The promoters of that identity were aware of the avant-garde role of the economic leadership that the city was acquiring and worked to extend that progress to the fields of politics and culture. From the last quarter of the nineteenth century on, Joan Ramón Resina writes, Catalonia began thinking of itself as a modern society and Barcelona was, at one and the same time, the darkroom and the image of that process.[45] The modernizing efforts had positive results. Barcelona's experience of incorporation into modernity was similar in time, space, and manner to that of other European cities, although it also experienced great frustration at its inability to achieve the preeminent level of national capital. Madrid's case was the opposite; it did not need to fight to acquire the status of national capital since it had been functioning as such since the end of the sixteenth century as a result of a political and administrative decision.

Madrid's challenge in the face of modernity was how to maintain its status as the capital of a European state despite its structural and symbolic insufficiencies. As José Carlos Mainer has pointed out, as a state capital, its role was mainly that of representation. In Madrid, all the citizens were to feel represented as harmonious parts of an organized group.[46] Since the middle of the eighteenth century, all the initiatives of its ruling classes were aimed at overcoming that challenge. As with many European cities, Madrid and Barcelona had to face the challenges posed by their modernization, waging a public struggle for their right to lead the urban hierarchy of the new liberal state. During that long process of creation of the bourgeois city, Barcelona undoubtedly surpassed Madrid in the coherence and novelty of its urban development, but Madrid did not lag behind and managed to retain its political dominance.

Madrid suffered both the positive and negative effects of the French occupation more intensely than Barcelona. The Bonaparte administration took action on some aspects of the city's urban development, but left only a transitory mark. The most relevant act was the prohibition of burials in the churches and the establishment of new cemeteries on the outskirts of the city. Along that same line of intervention aimed at stemming the church's power, they seized and demolished convents with initiatives that anticipated future disentailments. The goal was to open spaces within urban areas saturated by demographic growth and crammed with buildings. The result of those actions was the creation of various public plazas, like Santa Ana and Mostenses, which have survived as some of the most typical squares of old Madrid.[47]

The actions described were, unfortunately, not sufficient. At the dawn of the nineteenth century, Madrid was still, as a whole, a densely populated city with an enormously fragile urban infrastructure and an appearance better suited to a provincial city than to a great European capital. From an economic and social standpoint, the city had experienced extraordinary advances in the second half of the eighteenth century. The reforms introduced during the Enlightenment had produced an administration that was larger, more professional, and more efficient. All these elements favored the city's growth and fostered a certain economic prosperity. Madrid continued to be a city of services whose economy hinged on supplying its population and on state contracts. Except for a few cases, its industrial sector did not surpass the level of craftsmanship because its production was of a self-sufficient nature and was directed mainly at covering the needs of its own population. The principal characteristic of that economy was the persistent deficit of its trade balance: Madrid consumed manufactured goods originating in other Spanish regions and the exterior, agricultural products and capital arising from the income of its well-to-do classes, and the taxes collected by the state.[48]

During the course of the eighteenth century, especially in the second half, enlightened economic theories favored policies tending to suppress market regulation.[49] The supply systems became more efficient, thanks to improvements in transportation, procedures, and financing mechanisms. Although an agricultural revolution did not occur, there was some growth in production and income. This economic relief allowed for greater demand for goods, and although there was no consumer revolution either, the people of Madrid increased their demands for goods, thereby making a small contribution to commercial expansion. All these trends were limited and undoubtedly insufficient, but they did signal a clear change of cycle.[50] Without becoming an industrial city, Madrid transformed into the principal financial emporium for the peninsula and one of its most dynamic commercial centers. These developments had their social repercussions though an industrial bourgeoisie like Barcelona's would not emerge until well into the twentieth century. We have already seen that Madrid's society in the nineteenth century demonstrated certain class survival instincts. The weight of the old landed and powerful aristocracy was felt more in Madrid than in Barcelona. Until well into the century, the dominant groups of the city were comprised of a complex social conglomerate in which social strata, descending from provincial nobility and the old titled nobility, were prominent. But these groups shared that domination with a new bourgeoisie that arose thanks to opportunities that were first provided by enlightened policies and later by liberal ones. This was a complex society with persistent social practices characteristic of traditional societies for the purpose of control and social domination—such as the exploitation of family relationships, patronage, friendship, and common provincial roots—but which showed at the same time an unequivocal inclination toward cultural, political, and economic modernity.[51] It is in that social, political, and economic context—with its conflicts, contradictions, advances, and setbacks—that the new bourgeois city was forged.

The promoters of Madrid's urban transformation, of its metamorphosis into a bourgeois city, were mostly the same ones who promoted the different stages of the construction of the Spanish liberal state. Though there was an administration for the state and another for the city, the interaction between the two had always been more evident in Madrid because of its role as capital, than it had been in Barcelona. A list of mayors of Madrid during the course of the nineteenth century includes a good number of names that transcended national politics: Juan Álvarez Mendizabal, Salustiano Olózaga, and Joaquín María Ferrer y Cafranga are some examples. Construction of the modern bourgeois city was more agitated in Madrid than in Barcelona because of the comings-and-goings of the ever changing national politics. That was the reason Madrid's urban programs lacked the continuity and consistency that was seen in Barcelona; in that respect Madrid came out the loser.

The first systematic formulation of what was to be modern Madrid, in its double role as capital of the state and European city, was developed by Ramón Mesonero Romanos in his *Rápida ojeada sobre el estado de la capital y los medios de mejorarla* (A quick glance at the state of the capital and the means for improving it). The text was included as an appendix in the second edition of his *Manual de Madrid,* published in 1835.[52] Mesonero wrote these pages upon his return from a long trip through Spain and Europe in which he visited various cities, among them Barcelona, with prolonged stays in Paris and London. During that journey he had occasion to observe the urban problems and solutions of the principal urban centers of the time, returning with an idea of what ought to be done in Madrid. While possible actions for improvement of the city's urbanism had been discussed previously, specifically the need for expansion, Mesonero's proposal stands out for various reasons.[53] The first arises from what he represented based upon his social background, his intellectual achievement, and his political position. Mesonero belonged to a typical family integrated into the dominant social conglomerate of the city—the group that has been previously referred to as "the Madrid notables."[54] His ideal city was that of the entire well-to-do society of the mid-nineteenth century. The second reason is his all-inclusive vision, in which, for the first time, is developed an urban plan that formulated a specific model for the city. The third reason is its relevance. Mesonero's proposal affected most of the urban projects carried out during the nineteenth century, partly because of its author's active involvement in the city's government as an elected city councilor.[55] As pointed out by Edward Baker, Mesonero's goal was to offer a proposal to transform Madrid "as yet capital of a stately society . . . into a national and bourgeois capital . . . a center of political, economic and cultural power worthy of a bourgeoisie that values its interests and principles—in a word, its civilization—and that this bourgeoisie be, along with the city which should be its maximum material and symbolic expression, the standard for the entire nation."[56]

The Rápida Ojeada was divided into various sections relating to each area of Madrid's urban developments. Each section reflects the priorities of the developments that Mesonero considered necessary in order to transform Madrid into a city that was to be "of the category of national civilization."[57] The order of those priorities, such as it appears in the original document, expresses the ideal city represented by Mesonero. The first set of actions was directed at attaining a salubrious, comfortable, and aesthetic city. It is not possible to find categories more in keeping with the bourgeoisie's ideal life. By 1830, the city had surpassed the 200,000-inhabitant barrier; notwithstanding, its housing was concentrated within the limits of the old enclosure that surrounded it with its meager infrastructure.[58] Consequently, the first action was to propose an expansion to the north and east, a plan that had first been formulated during the Enlightenment.[59] Mesonero's proposal of expansion was above all plausible, opposed to theoretical magnificence. It was justifiable for reasons of public hygiene: "On the north and east sides the purity of the air is superior and the ground offers less unevenness." The idea of expansion was inserted naturally into the set of concrete projects directed toward achieving a salubrious, comfortable, and monumental city. Within that set of proposals, Mesonero points out two actions as inescapable starting points. One was to resolve, once and for all, Madrid's major infrastructure problem, which was its insufficient provision of water. The other was to improve the mechanisms of supply and the organization, efficiency, and hygiene of its markets. Once these two problems were resolved, the urban projects should be directed at transforming Madrid into a premier capital of "national civilization," that is to say, a habitable city, aesthetic and blessed with the requisite symbolic spaces to fulfill its role as a national monument.

Mesonero imagined this city without ever losing sight of the models of London, Paris, Bordeaux, and even Barcelona and Cádiz. In what constituted the essential part of his proposal, the suggested solutions were of an aesthetic nature, with a marked symbolic content, inspired by the principles of order, organization, and neatness; thus, his projects sought to improve architectural order and street layout. "It should require of all landowners," wrote Mesonero, "the same sacrifices in favor of the general wellbeing, and, in accordance with the laws of the urban police, their consent to the progressive alignment of streets, the cleanliness of façades, the standardization of its architecture and height, and other essential requirements to obtain flattering results."[60] The uniformity and finish of buildings was complemented with ideas for the improvement of illumination and cleanliness of the streets and plazas. As to organization, Mesonero introduced an administrative action plan aimed at implementing order such as he had observed in the large European capitals, which included such measures as creating a system of rational numbering of houses and improving the census of residents. Especially important were the proposals regarding projects directed at development of the symbolic city. Along this line, he presented a plan to establish sites to commemorate historic events and moments of cultural brilliance related to Spain.

Priority projects in the Rápida Ojeada included actions designed to construct a clean, comfortable, and monumental city. That was, essentially, the gist of the information contained in the three remaining sections of the proposal: public safety; work and industry; instruction and recreation. In regards to its security, the clean, comfortable, and aesthetic city required a plan of action to control delinquency and vagrancy. To that end Mesonero proposed combining police action with administrative and charitable interventions.

The measures referring to the improvement of work and industry reflected Mesonero's liberal conservative position. First, he suggested the creation of mechanisms to protect private property and the liberalization of the markets; second, he included a series of considerations and possible solutions to increase the productivity of the working world; and lastly, he expected his ideal city to promote a diversity of cultural institutions that fell entirely within the public bourgeois sphere: athenaeums, academies, museums, assembly halls, libraries, and publishers.

Mesonero's proposals and projects, representing the dominant vision of what modern Madrid would be, marked the beginning of the effective process of construction of the bourgeois city. The following phase began in 1860 with the approval of the Castro Plan de Ensanche (Plan of Extension), and its slow and complicated implementation. In the years that transpired between the end of the Napoleonic invasions and 1860, urban construction advanced intermittently. The construction of the Isabel II Canal, whose first phase was concluded in 1858 after seven years of work, was the most distinguishing feature of the plan for improving the infrastructure. The canal brought water from the Lozoya River to Madrid to solve the urgent problems of water supply to which Mesonero had referred. Also completed were the construction projects for the Plaza de Oriente in a lengthy cycle lasting fifty years. The 1850 inauguration of the first major opera theater, the Teatro Real, along with the creation of zones for commemorative monuments and a promenade, concluded a project that had been proposed numerous times. The works for the Plaza de Oriente exemplify the enormous difficulties entailed in the creation of the symbolic city. To the budgetary problems that accompany any public project, or the technical ones of any significant architectural project, were added those related to the political, intellectual, and cultural debate concerning identities. This complication was fully evident in the desire, brought to light in 1837, to construct a grand pantheon of illustrious men, as proposed by Mesonero. The idea was welcomed unanimously with enthusiasm, and immediately became law. The legislative text established the church of San Francisco el Grande as the chosen space to relocate "with the utmost pomp possible, the remains of the Spaniards who, at least fifty years after their deaths, were considered worthy of this honor by the Parliament." The project, not finished until 1926, suffered so many complications that the end results were very different from those envisioned at its beginning. The debate regarding who deserved the honor of resting in the Pantheon was harsh and drawn out. The technical development was, on occasions, impossible; the search for the ashes of Luis Vives, Miguel de Cervantes, Lópe de Vega, and Diego Velázquez was fruitless. In some cases litigations were initiated, and doubts were cast as to the authenticity of the funereal remains. The budgetary constraint was continuous, the agreement regarding the procedure was distasteful, and the results were never enough. The history of the Panteón de Hombres Ilustres, yet to be written, exemplifies the arduous nature of the creation of the symbolic city. Nevertheless, the supreme memorial to nineteenth-century liberalism, the monument to all those fallen on the second of May at the Paseo del Prado, was completed in 1840. Since 1985, this monument commemorates all those who have died for Spain.[61]

That which Mesonero expounded upon in the Rápida Ojeada was completed with the *Proyecto de mejoras generales* (Project for general *improvements*), written upon his appointment as councilor in 1845. In that second text, Mesonero proposed restorations in the interior of the old city and a moderate expansion on the east side of the Paseo de Recoletos. He also suggested postponement of the great extension of the city. Mesonero did not consider the extension an urgent need as it had been in Barcelona because the amount of space available in the interior of Madrid until the middle of the nineteenth century was much greater. Madrid, because of its tardy industrialization, did not have industrial buildings in its inner urban area, as was the case in Barcelona.[62] Instead, Madrid had an abundance of convents, churches, and noble mansions, many of which had ample spaces for gardens. The successive disentailments since the time of Charles IV, and especially the disentailments between 1820 and 1836, placed on the market some of the properties that would be demolished for the construction of new buildings.[63] A very representative part of the new bourgeois city was constructed in the voids left by the disentailed convents and their gardens during the first two-thirds of the nineteenth century. A stroll around the part of old Madrid near the Plaza Mayor and Puerta del Sol reveals the original bourgeois city that has remained embedded in the old city of the Austrias.[64] The Casas de Cordero, located on the block in Puerta del Sol at the intersection of the streets of Mayor, Correo, and Esparteros, illustrates this development. The building, which presently houses one of the first McDonald's opened in Madrid, was erected on the site of one of the most emblematic convents and popular social gathering places of old city: the convent of San Felipe El Real, founded in 1574. The Casas de

Cordero is a symbol of the bourgeois urbanism that Mesonero defended. They were built in 1842 and 1845 with money from the capitalist Santiago Alonso Cordero, nicknamed "el Maragato." Cordero, a man of humble origin, had made a fortune in the transportation of merchandise to supply the capital.[65] He acquired the convent in one of the auctions of disentailed property with the intention of demolishing it and erecting a building in keeping with the times. The Casas de Cordero was the first great apartment building of the city.[66] In some of the spaces created by the disentailment of churches and convents, the new bourgeoisie built pretentious palaces. Two such palaces that are still standing are the residences of the banker Manuel Gaviria at number 3 Arenal Street and of Francisco de las Rivas, Count of Mudela, at 40 Carrera de San Jerónimo.[67] The parliament (Congreso de los Diputados) building, the Senate building, the old School of Medicine, and the Hospital de San Carlos are, among others, examples of buildings erected during those years on space created by the disentailments.

Madrid, therefore, until the middle of the nineteenth century, had land suitable for building within its ancient walls that was cheaper than the land outside it. This gave the agents of its urban transformation—the proprietors, constructors, and members of the municipal administration, represented by personalities such as Mesonero Romanos—more leeway than the Barcelonians had in the renovation of their old city. Nevertheless, the debate over the necessity of expansion of the city and the characteristics of that expansion had intensified since Mesonero's proposals. The debate would be strongly influenced by the conditions in the real estate market, as well as by the ideological positions of the different agents. Some representatives of progressive liberalism, dating back to the 1840s, leaned toward decisive action by the administrations to expand the city and intervene in its real estate market. In 1846 and 1847, Mendizábal presented a series of ideas regarding urban intervention that did not include elaborate expansion plans; rather, he insisted on the need to expand the city by tearing down the wall constructed in the seventeenth century; and he mentioned concrete actions, such as railroads and construction of hospitals, which needed to be carried out.

In 1845, the engineer Juan Merlo drafted the first plan known as the extension project. It was not an urban plan as such, but rather a drawing in which the limits of the new city and its principal lines of communication were defined. Carlos Sambricio has stressed the long-range influence of this incipient scheme because it established the centrality of Paseo de la Castellana as the hub of the future expansion, and it suggested the reclassification of the rustic farms near the Paseo, implying revaluation and huge profits. The Merlo initiative, published in *La Ilustración,* led to the Royal Order of December 1846, in which Isabel II asked the Madrid council for its opinion regarding this project. The council, with Mesonero as spokesman, while acknowledging the benefits of some of the ideas, considered that the possibilities offered by the old central city were the main priority.[68] Likewise, in 1857, engineer and architect Mariano de Albó argued in favor of the immediate tearing down of the wall, and of a policy aimed at providing for a "reasonable balancing of assets and wealth, so that those assets would yield triple interest, in order to reduce the height of those buildings in the center that are injurious to public health."[69] Albó, like Cerdá in Barcelona, represented the utilitarian, scientific, and positivist bourgeoisie whose concept of the city not only addressed aesthetics, but also the problems of hygiene and social inequality. Mesonero, Merlo, and Albó certainly represented different points of view regarding how construction of the bourgeois city should progress, but not to the point of being irreconcilable since all have in common an unequivocally defense of private property, the market economy, and the real estate business.[70] Perhaps the extension plan drafted by Carlos María de Castro, which was finally accepted in 1860, could be interpreted as a plausible synthesis of all tendencies.

What finally convinced the dominant groups of Madrid that the only possible alternative for modernization was the extension? The details of this part of the city's urban history are, to this day, unclear and require further investigation. Nevertheless, based upon available data, during those years, in the administrative and intellectual spheres of the city and the state, it is probable that a project for investigation and debate was developed that demonstrated the unfeasibility of attaining the desired city—that is, the clean, comfortable, and aesthetic metropolis that would be a mirror of national civilization—without addressing its expansion. Mesonero's proposals were enriched and surpassed by a variety of reports and studies of diverse origin. Some of these, like the *Noticias topográfico-estadísticas sobre la administración de Madrid* (1840), by progressive politician Fermín Caballero, or the *España geográfica, estadística y pintoresca* (1845) by Francisco de Paula Mellado, offered statistical evidence of the congestion of Madrid's interior and its negative impact on hygiene, public order, and image.[71] Others, like the *Diccionario geográfico-estadístico-histórico* by Pascual Madóz (1846), showed the existence of a growing segment of population seeking housing beyond the walls of the city because of the scarcity of space and elevated rents. It was in this context that Mariano de Albó, follower of hygienic trends and a social thinker, upon returning from a temporary exile in the north of Europe, found Madrid unacceptable and decided to write his report defending the urgency of expansion and offering proposals for social improvement. As a result, diverse municipal commissions were formed for the purpose of studying urban action plans. The matter became a state issue, for which the parliament established a Promotional Commission to advance the drafting of an extensions law. As pointed out by Carlos Sambricio, these initiatives meant that the concept of the "modern city" was being created based on the progressive ideals characteristic of that era. The immediate result was the opening of competitions; the approval of the extensions of Barcelona, Madrid, and other Spanish cities; and the approval of the law of extensions in 1864 and codes for development in 1867.[72]

Carlos María de Castro's plan offered the most significant push toward the creation of the bourgeois capital. Its author was a prestigious road engineer, of Andalusian origin, who had intervened in some of the most important public works of the Isabel II era.[73] Castro, unlike Cerdá, was not a theorist. As he pointed out in the descriptive memoir of his project, Cerdá's ideas and proposals were decisive in the formulation of his plan.[74] Castro's proposal made constant references to the expansions and urban projects in Barcelona, London, New York, and Paris, as well as the opinions and proposals of the trends in hygienism and social urbanism. In spite of all the inherent baggage of the rigorous and well-informed professional, Castro developed a project that combined tradition with innovation. His concept of Madrid remained within the framework of a symbolic city fulfilling the role of capital of the state and model of national civilization, yet it also incorporated elements of the most advanced urban concepts of its time. It confirmed the centrality of the Paseo del Prado-Recoletos-Castellana hub to maintain a major connection between the new city and the old. The substantial part of his expansion plan was situated at the north and east of the city, following Mesonero's proposal, although, unlike Barcelona, the new city surrounded the old, maintaining its radial structure in an orthogonal design.

Castro also agreed with Mesonero's concept of the distribution of space in the new Madrid. He envisioned a clearly segregated social distribution as follows: the central area, the Paseo de la Castellana and its vicinity, would be a residential zone for the aristocracy and the upper bourgeoisie; the northeast and west, which were to be the future neighborhoods of Salamanca and Argüelles, would be for the middle classes; Chamberí, the south, and the east, would be for the working classes.[75] Castro also continued the model of the symbolic city, as is evident in the importance given in his *Plan de Ensanche* to the construction of emblematic buildings and monuments. He made comments, for example, on the convenience of constructing a cathedral, of promoting a project for a National Library building, of raising a series of buildings to house museums in strategic locations around the city, and of doing the same with the government ministries.

On the other hand, Castro incorporated into his project elements of the vanguard urbanism of his era. The layout of the city blocks would take wind circulation into account in order to favor ventilation. He believed, as did Cerdá, in the importance of the garden as a transition between the private space of the dwelling and the public street, so there should be gardens in all blocks and throughout the city as plazas. As Deborah Parsons has pointed out, the creation of tree-lined promenades and gardens was not only originated by hygienic preoccupations, but also by the desire of aspiring bourgeois elites to have spaces ideal for refined socializing.[76] Castro was also concerned with social issues, proposing measures for construction of adequate housing and neighborhoods for the working classes. Finally, urban transportation and industry were essential elements of his project. He addressed the distribution of train stations and railways keeping in mind their future development; he considered the width and distribution of the streets based upon the future needs for transportation in the city's interior; and he permanently consecrated the south of Madrid as the city's industrial zone.

As occurred with all extension projects, in Madrid there was a great difference between what was projected and what was accomplished as a result of speculation. Castro, like Cerdá in Barcelona and his emulators in other Spanish cities, left a noticeable legacy of urban transformation. In Madrid, these were the most emblematic neighborhoods of the new middle class: Salamanca, Argüelles, and Castellana. The plan was developed between the Glorious Revolution of 1868 and the decade of the 1920s, but in contrast to the previous phase, this time the number of agents involved in the city's transformation was greater and more complex. The city found itself in the era of large construction firms, of the complex partnerships of financial capitalism, of the real estate market, and of that of the new industry. Still, the predominant concept of the city was substantially the same as the one established in the time of Mesonero Romanos: the great capital, symbol of national civilization, and the salubrious, comfortable, and aesthetic city.

In the last third of the nineteenth century, the new standard bearer of urban Madrid's identity was the journalist and progressive politician Ángel Fernández de los Ríos. By virtue of his publications, *El futuro de Madrid* (1868) and the *Guía urbana de Madrid* (1873), his political activism in the city council, and the influence of his ideas, Fernández de los Ríos played a role similar to that of Mesonero Romanos. The European determination characteristic of Mesonero, Albó, and others was prevalent in Fernández de los Ríos, as has been pointed out by María Pilar González Yanci and Pedro Navascués.[77] He wrote *El futuro de Madrid* during his exile in Paris in the years previous to the Glorious Revolution. Many of the urban solutions he proposed were inspired by those developed by Baron Haussmann in the Paris of the Second Empire. At the same time, his texts differed from Mesonero's in that they had a good dose of utopianism and proposed pompous projects impossible to carry out in the Spain of that time.

To appreciate the progress of the bourgeois city in Madrid it is enough to see the layouts of the city at the beginning of the century and those drawn up by José Pilar Morales and Facundo Cañadas in 1880 and 1900, respectively.[78] The difference can be seen easily in the presence of new buildings and spaces arising in the old city center, and especially in the development of its extension. It is true that the result of so many years of urban development initiatives had fallen short of expectations. The development of the symbolic city was complicated, slow, and often frustrating, as exemplified by the convoluted building of the Panteón de Hombres Ilustres, or the interminable process of construction of the Cathedral of Madrid, concluded at the end of the twentieth century. The results of the extension also fell short of those obtained in Barcelona partly because the real estate speculation of the twentieth century destroyed some of the successes of the end of the nineteenth century. Another factor was the lack of a creative impulse similar to that of modernist Barcelona. Was this a reflection of a dominant society of more conservative tastes, or was it the cost that Madrid had to pay for its dual urban character as capital of the state and a city in search of its own identity?[79] Whichever the case, and despite its failures and shortcomings, the city never shrank from the urban challenges of modernity, with unquestionably positive results in the long run.

EXTENSIONS EVERYWHERE

Barcelona and Madrid set the standard for the construction of the bourgeois or liberal city in Spanish provinces.[80] Urban development of all provincial cases followed similar stages. Processes of extension were implemented once the possibilities for the old city downtowns were exhausted by demographic pressure, the real estate markets, and the desire for modernization of urban dominant groups. In the mid-1850s a Comisión de Fomento (Development Commission) was established in the Spanish parliament for the purpose of discussing the country's need of urban reform. The commission's work, comprehensive yet barely known, reflected the political class's deep preoccupation with this aspect of Spanish reality. Its activities promoted debate on a variety of urban actions in many cities, including Madrid and Barcelona.[81] This commission was also an expression of advances in the fields of hygiene, utilitarian liberalism, and positivism, trends that manifested themselves with the ascent in social prestige—and the increase of the political and intellectual influence—of certain professional groups such as engineers and physicians. The result of the commission's activity was the endorsement of the extensions of Barcelona and Madrid, and the subsequent drafting and approval in June 1864 of the law of Ensanche de Poblaciones (Expansion of Cities) along with the codes for its implementation (April 1867). Those approvals created the necessary legal framework for the formulation of extension plans. In the years between the Restoration (1874) and the Spanish Civil War (1936), the establishment of the bourgeois city throughout Spain would become a reality.

The urban elites of San Sebastian, Bilbao, and Valencia had been demanding action similar to that of Madrid and Barcelona since the 1840s. For that reason, these cities most quickly accepted the possibilities opened by the activities of the Development Commission. San Sebastian's development during the course of the nineteenth century, for example, was shaped by its conversion into the administrative capital of Guipúzcoa and its adoption as the favorite summer vacation spot of the Spanish dominant social groups. From a small village of shop owners and fishermen, it was transformed into a political and administrative center that was also—and most important—the principal bourgeois and cosmopolitan tourist center of nineteenth-century Spain. Tourism and summer vacations ceased to be an aristocratic privilege and became one of the most emblematic elements of middle-class culture. Still, going on vacation to enjoy the northern baths in a stylish locale, preferably San Sebastian, was a privilege reserved to the most affluent. As a result, the city's development was guaranteed by an affluence of money, elegance, and elitism that would not cease until well into the twentieth century. The old village, a wall-enclosed military precinct, went beyond its limits very early—in the first third of the nineteenth century—to begin extending into what is known today as "the romantic city." The city also followed the standards set by Madrid and Barcelona before the approval of the extension laws. In 1862, its city council held a contest in which the elaborate extension plan by architect Antonio Cortázar was selected. With some modifications, the Cortázar project delimited the new city in a plan that, beginning with a lengthening of Mayor Street, established a network of geometric blocks and straight streets in an orthogonal design.[82] With its limits bound by the boulevard and the centenary plaza, it established a distribution of population based upon functions and categories: the native bourgeoisie in the center, the seasonal summer population at the bay, and the artisans and laborers on the periphery.[83]

In contrast to what occurred in Madrid and Barcelona, the San Sebastian extension was a model of speed and relative efficiency. The projects were started as soon as they were approved and were completed by the end of the 1870s. In 1882, a second extension was initiated, known as the eastern extension, which—though not included in Cortázar's project—supposed its continuation on the opposite bank of the Urumea River. Independent of the awkward reality imposed by the social segregation of the city, there still remains in the San Sebastian extension—with all its architectural and symbolic controversies— one of the most significant tokens of the city as a nineteenth-century European center of sea side tourism.[84]

Anaclet Pons and Justo Serna relate how, in Valencia, the matter of extension and the consequent tearing down of the ancient walls was one of the most debated subjects in public opinion since the middle of the century. Those who argued in favor of the extension did so for reasons of public hygiene, denouncing overcrowding and the lack of ventilation in the old city center as direct causes of the periodic outbursts of Asiatic cholera. But they also promoted the extension as a manifestation of progress for a city that had been demonstrating an unmistakable attachment to the innovations and novelties of the century. Thus, "when the telegraphic message authorizing the onset of work on the projects finally arrived on the morning of Saturday, February 18, 1865, the interim civil governor appeared especially diligent in initiating the project that had been delayed for so long." He immediately met with the mayor and council members to inform them of the good news, which had been received with a "Long live the Queen!" and without further delay approved a collective declaration of the commencement of the work necessary to tear down those "ancient and miserable ramparts that tormented the city." Only two days later, on February 20, the destruction of the medieval wall was initiated at the area of the Puerta de San José, with a symbolic ceremony that attracted a large and enthusiastic audience. Those were the beginnings of an urban transformation that garnered great popular support and that finally fulfilled the aspirations of the city's dominant groups. A local journalist wrote in his chronicle the following day that the Valencians could now imagine themselves "transported to the banks of the Sein in Paris, or of the Thames in London, or to the Prado y Retiro in Madrid." It would be impossible to find a more explicit mention of the models upon which the local elite of Valencia based their modernizing aspirations.[85]

In contrast to Barcelona's bourgeoisie, those of Valencia did not aspire to make their city a capital; they were conscious of their subordinate place in the urban network of the liberal state.[86] Yet, as we have seen, its bourgeoisie was unequivocally committed to modernity, so that their vision of the ideal city was simply that of a large, nineteenth-century bourgeois metropolis. The destruction of the wall opened the doors to the realization of that ideal after years of partial results. Cerdá's shadow was also cast over the Valencian extension. While posted there, he had established relations with architects Timoteo Calvo and Sebastián Monleón and, above all, with Antonio Sancho, principal exponent of the first extension project in 1858 who, in spite of his failure, set the foundation for the future projects of 1868 and the more influential one of 1884.[87] In Valencia, the protagonists of the city's urban transformation were the architects, not the engineers. The 1884 plan, carried out by architects José Calvo Tomás, Luis Ferreres Soler, and Joaquín María Arnau Miramón, established the foundations of the truly bourgeois Valencia. Starting at the demolished wall, the city was extended in a checkerboard pattern, having two large avenues as principal axes: the Gran Vía Marqués del Turia and La Gran Vía Fernando el Católico.[88]

Although its completion was arduous and was delayed well into the twentieth century, this area is, to date, the most typically bourgeois part of Valencia, with its latticework of blocks, its old-style boulevards, and its buildings of eclectic architecture of cast iron.[89]

The Bilbao extension plan, drafted by architect Severino de Achúcarro and road engineers Pablo de Alzola and Ernesto Hoffmeyer, was approved in 1876 and, in contrast to what occurred in most other cities, was completed in the years immediately following and was quickly superseded. During the eighteenth century, Bilbao had been molding itself as an eminently commercial city, the center of commercial activity that connected the Atlantic and the peninsular north with Castile and Madrid in the interior. During the nineteenth century, exploitation of the iron mines was added to that activity with the establishment of the first Spanish steelwork industry. The city's urban development responded to the impulse of its rapid growth and reflected the solid establishment of a prosperous bourgeoisie. The built-up part of Bilbao, by virtue of the 1876 plan, with its structure of diagonal axes that converge in an elliptical plaza (Federico Moyúa), presently constitutes the heart of the city. Cerdá's urban influence can be appreciated in its beveled block structure, while its star-shaped configuration points to the Parisian urban influence, or perhaps the survival of certain urban elements of the traditional baroque style.[90]

Other cities were added to the unfolding of bourgeois urbanism as more extension plans were developed starting in the latter years of the nineteenth century and carried out during the twentieth century. The city council of Zaragoza, for example, approved in 1880 an imaginative project formulated by architect Félix Navarro in which Cerdá's influence, and that of German urban theorists Reinhard Baumeister and Josef Stübben, can be seen. Navarro suggested a city in which livability, culture, and work would be integrated, proposing not only salubrious housing and ample streets, but also the establishment of a variety of spaces dedicated to the promotion of science, technology, and art.[91] In León the first extension projects were developed between 1889 and 1897 (Ruiz Salazar), proposing an extension of the city similar to that of Valencia.[92]

That is how the history of the Spanish extensions of the nineteenth century unfolded, with exchanges of proposals and influences, sometimes producing parallel results, and ambitious projects, utopian on occasion, that always frustrated the crude dynamics of the capitalist market. It is a history that has been written in fragments, well known at the local level but lacking, to date, an adequate comprehensive view.[93] The extension of the Spanish cities and the urbanism generated in this process followed standards similar to those of other European countries. Essentially, extensions and urbanism were responses to demographic growth and, above all, the development of the bourgeoisie whose style of life demanded a type of city different from that of the Old Regime. In the Anglo-Saxon countries and in parts of northern Europe, this process was resolved in the suburbanization of the city. In the majority of continental Europe, with France as its principal exponent, the impulse materialized either in remodeling the old city, in extending it, or in adding an appendage that, with some luck, might connect the old section with the new. The Spanish cities belong to the latter category, contributing notably to the shaping of the history of modern European urbanism.

CHAPTER 6

The Pleasures of the Imagination and the Body

IN an article published in 1833, "La fonda nueva," author Mariano José Larra describes a conversation with a French tourist visiting Madrid to learn about Spanish life:

"What country is this?" asked the traveler. "I am sure there will be here great horse racing; we will not miss them."
"Excuse me," answered Fígaro, "we do not have horse racing."
"Don't young people of distinguished families like to race with their own horses?"
"No, they do not race with horses."
"All right, we will go to a country house to take pleasure of the day."
"There are no country houses; we do not take pleasure of the day."
"But, there may be all sorts of different games, like in the rest of Europe . . . I am sure there are pleasure gardens where one can dance; maybe of smaller size . . . I am sure there may be some kind of games for public amusement."
"There is nothing for the public: The public do not play."
"Patience," said the Frenchman, "we will be satisfied by attending the soirees and balls in the houses of respectable families."
"Easy, my friend," interrupted Figaro. "In Madrid there are no social balls, no soirees. *Each* one chats, or prays, or does his will in his own house with a few very close friends, and that's all."[1]

Larra's text offers a definite and disturbing assessment: Madrid is not like Paris, and Spain is not like France or even the rest of Europe. This critique was a recurring theme in his work, argued poignantly in his article "El castellano

Viejo." In Larra's eyes, Spain's weak middle class was the problem. Existing in limited numbers and only in certain areas of Spain, its members did not display refinement, good taste, and gentility. Compared to their French and British counterparts, the Spanish middle classes seemed ignorant about appropriate conduct, and worse, their forms of entertainment and sociability lacked refinement and sophistication.[2] Monday was the only day of the week Madrilenians enjoyed a collective form of public entertainment: the bullfight. "There [to the bullring]," wrote Larra, "everyone comes with pride to manifest their lack of feelings, and to show that their favorite form of entertainment is to fill their eyes with blood, and they laugh, and clap while admiring the slaughter caused by *corrida*."[3]

Larra might have continued his argument against bullfighting, but before he died at twenty-nine his opinions about the availability of civic forms of entertainment and sociability in Madrid had begun to change.[4] In June 1834, one year after "La fonda nueva" appeared, he published "Jardines públicos," an article about the opening in Madrid of a European-style pleasure garden, El Jardin de las Delicias.[5] It opened in May 1834, in the proximity of Madrilenian Paseo de Recoletos, and Larra celebrated the new public space as proof "of a new tendency taken by the city." Had he survived into the 1840s, he might have found further proof of change in the appearance of the first public horse racing track (*hipódromo*) in Madrid's suburbs, as well as new, more sophisticated pleasure gardens promoting refined music and social balls in Barcelona and Madrid.

The enjoyment of entertainments that were decorous, productive, and cultivated—Enlightenment thinkers called them "pleasures of the imagination"—was an attribute that came to be expected in the *hombre fino*.[6] The idea that high culture and entertainment could be spiritually energizing as well as a means to attain social distinction had been debated since antiquity. What had begun to change in the eighteenth century, however, was the social use and meaning of these entertainments.[7] The Renaissance had introduced in Western culture an unprecedented expansion of literature, art, and music. At first it was restricted to royal courts, aristocratic palaces, and their surroundings, but over time high culture became increasingly accessible to the middle ranks of society. John Brewer has explained this shift as the result of two developments in the eighteenth century. The first was economic. Scottish philosophers and political economists began to argue that trade and economic exchange was useful not only because it brought prosperity and welfare, but also because it encouraged refinement and the propagation of good taste.

The second development in the social use and meaning of leisure involved the expansion of urban life. Largely owing to economic growth, cities drew elites to their centers. As a result, royal and princely courts became less significant as exclusive sites of high culture, and refinement became increasingly available to affluent urbanites. As the arts moved to cities, leisure became less courtly and more commercial.[8] Further, the benefit of enjoying high culture was no longer seen as the exclusive patrimony of the nobility. This expansion occurred in the diverse new architectural spaces of bourgeois sociability, such as cafés, theaters, social gatherings, academies, athenaeums, and parks.[9] Liberal revolutions in America and France helped consolidate this cultural shift across western Europe. The enjoyment of life and liberty became an essential part of new definitions of citizenship; rights to education and leisure were codified for the first time in some of new national laws of the early nineteenth century. Ultimately, with the coming of mass society in the early twentieth century, issues related to leisure activities would move to the center of political, social, and economic debates shaping modern consumer society.

This transition from the old society in Spain, which restricted consumption of high culture and enjoyment of leisure to a small social minority, and a new, modern mass society, where consumer products were social rights, occurred during the nineteenth century. "Leisure society" was for the most part a middle-class creation and a fundamental component of the nineteenth-century bourgeois experience.[10] Going to the opera, being present at the opening of an art exhibit, vacationing in a fashionable spa, or gaining membership in a literary club—all were important markers of social distinction and cultural capital.[11] With the progressive ascent of the bourgeoisie through the nineteenth century, leisure activities became essential components of the new bourgeois identity. The proliferation of leisure came to be identified with modernity and national development. In Spain, the availability of cultivated leisure and civilized entertainment became a subject of concern for writers, journalists, and politicians. Mariano José Larra's acrimonious comments in above cited article from the 1830s foreshadowed this outcry.

This chapter describes modern leisure society emerging in nineteenth-century Spain as a result of a growing bourgeois cultural identity. In recent years, social and cultural historians have begun to pay more attention to the role of leisure and consumer culture in Western societies. It is a complicated history that has sparked interdisciplinary research and much debate.[12] Scholars agree that the rise of leisure society constituted one of the clearest manifestations of modernity, and as difficult to fully explain through separate analyses of consumer culture, nationalism, social history, and business history. Commercialization and consumption of leisure in modern Spain have received little attention from scholars. Historians have situated the beginnings of Spanish modern leisure society in the early years of the twentieth century, but this chapter argues that the origins of modern leisure culture emerged out of the bourgeois experience in the nineteenth century.[13]

HIGH CULTURE AND POLITE SOCIABILITY

The first chapters of this book described *sociedad de buen tono* (polite society) in Spain, paying particular attention to the standards of conduct required by those who were considered polite. These men and women from the upper and middle ranks of polite society established benchmarks of fashion, taste, and social distinction. Sharing an integrated system of social rituals, behaviors, and lifestyles, *sociedad de buen tono* emerged in the nineteenth century from new and traditional spaces of sociability—both private and public. These spaces featured cultivated entertainments as a platform for social relations. As such, they became a vital component of nineteenth-century bourgeois culture.

Theater

Nineteenth-century Spanish theater is not renowned for the literary and dramatic quality of its writing and performance. However, as David Gies has pointed out, the nineteenth century was a highly prolific period in Spanish playwriting. It was also a time when theater exerted a market impact on society.[14] Next to bullfighting, theater was the most popular spectacle. Nineteenth-century productions dramatized the ideological conflicts and the culture wars of a society experiencing one of the most complex processes of change in the history of humanity. Even the government noted its important cultural role. Calling it "the thermometer to measure the culture of a nation," the Royal Decree of 1847 ordered the creation of a Spanish National Theater in Madrid and dictated the regulations for all theaters in the Kingdom of Spain.[15]

Theater critic Juan Sureda wrote in 1872, "Theater is the mirror of society, where we can contemplate everyone and everything."[16] These declarations indicate the important cultural role imposed on the stage.

Among more than one thousand plays written over the course of the century, many focus on themes of bourgeois culture: emotional dilemmas, social aspirations, political debates, and economic assumptions of an emerging middle-class identity. Gies identifies three main thematic groups of plays that address the construction of bourgeois identity. Of those three identities— nation, sexuality, and finances—the third relates most closely to our focus on the consolidation of bourgeois culture. Numerous plays deal with financial identities, and comment on changing lifestyles and the maintenance of social status. These plays provide valuable commentary on bourgeois values.[17] For example, *El hombre de mundo* (The man of the world) by Ventura de la Vega appeared in theaters in 1844, a few months after the publication of the famous *Don Juan Tenorio* by José Zorrilla. The title itself references bourgeois culture and middle-class identities: the term *hombre de mundo* was used in conduct literature to refer to the *hombre fino* or *dandi* (the refined man or dandy), the prototype of the perfect bourgeois.

El hombre de mundo was the story of a contrite Don Juan who becomes respectable. Having wasted his youth in debauchery, he admits his wrongdoings and decides to change—he marries, establishes a family, and settles down to work and live according to the moral standards dictated by dominant conduct. As Gies writes, romantic heroes in plays and novels do not work or live average lives. Ventura de la Vega's works mark the transition from romanticism to the post-romantic in drama.[18] The protagonist of *El hombre de mundo* was transformed into a sort of bourgeois Don Juan because adherence to mainstream nineteenth-century morality allowed him to lead an ordered and productive family-oriented life. *El hombre de mundo* ushered in new bourgeois themes that were concerned with personal finances and psychological and material tensions derived from work as well as fashion, elegance, and consumption. These themes dominated the stage during the second half of the nineteenth century, replacing traditional narratives of honor and glory.[19] Returning to Sureda's suggestive metaphor, while nineteenth-century theater may have been a mirror reflecting Spanish society, the middle classes dominated much of that reflection.

The Spanish theater was an important site of social interaction for the theatergoing middle-class public. In his article "El teatro por fuera" (The theater from the outside), published in 1838, Mesonero Romanos described the theater as one of the primary places for the construction of polite society.[20] Instead of viewing the theater from the seats to the stage, he looks at it from the stage. In other words, he understood the theater as a social space rather than a place for passive entertainment.[21] What was the meaning of going to the theater for those who had to pay to get in, sometimes walk a long distance to get there, and endure less than comfortable seats for the duration of the play? We can find the answer in a diversity of literary, journalistic, and personal testimonies left by theatergoers of the times.

Financier, politician, and real estate entrepreneur José de Salamanca penned one such testimony. The Marquis of Salamanca was one of the most prominent members of the ascendant bourgeoisie in nineteenth-century Spain. Elected to the Spanish parliament in 1836, he arrived in Madrid with a new bride, Petronila (Tolita) Livermore.[22] The couple barely knew the city and did not have a social circle. Both came from Málaga, a lively, prosperous, liberal, and cosmopolitan commercial city. They possessed a degree of sophistication and knew the steps needed to gain access to Madrid's polite society. José and Tolita were aware that there were two social activities that could expedite this process: the afternoon and evening promenades at Paseo del Prado and—the more feasible option—attending the theater. Salamanca's biographers describe his fascination with Madrid's theater scene: the society he encountered in the box seats, the business made in the box offices, and the atmosphere of liberty one could find in the backstage.

Salamanca discovered that the theater provided ready access to Madrid's refined society because it provided optimum occasions to encounter Madrid's influential society. One of these circumstances took place in the Theater of La Cruz on June 18, 1837, with the celebration of the queen's allegiance to the new Constitution. Salamanca and his wife took advantage of his status in parliament to attend the performance. The program reflected the importance of the event: fragments of well-known Italian operas were interpreted by the celebrities of the day, and a world premier of an anthem to liberty was composed for the occasion by maestro Ramón Carnicer. But the couple was more interested in what happened off the stage. During the intermissions, Salamanca pointed out to Tolita the most distinguished people in the audience. The royal family—the queen mother, the future queen, and the infants—were all seated in the royal box in the company of the First Minister José de Calatrava. In the front seats they recognized the Ministers Mendizábal and Joaquín María López. The politician and writer Nicomedes Pastor Díaz, seated next to Salamanca, identified other personalities such as María Buschental, the stylish and influential wife of the Brazilian ambassador who sponsored the most elegant and leading salon of the time. At that event Salamanca initiated a long-standing friendship with Pastor Díaz that proved to be decisive for his future business and political career.

The case of the Salamancas typifies the social function played by *teatro por fuera* for ascendant groups. Realist and naturalist novels often point to this reality as they feature bourgeois characters using the theater for social purposes. Benito Pérez Galdos's *Lo Prohibido* describes life amid the upper ranks of Madrid's bourgeoisie. Its protagonist explains how his aunt, "an indolent lady who was not very intelligent, arranged marriages for her daughters with the first pretentious man she encountered in promenades and theaters."[23]

Journalists in major and provincial cities also described theater as a space for social interaction. A writer for *La Luneta,* a well-known theater magazine of the mid-nineteenth century, lamented that a large portion of theater audiences attended merely to gossip and chat. Illustrated with an engraving of an audience gazing at each other and ignoring the stage, the article argued that such indifference was causing a decline in the quality of theatrical productions.[24]

Weekly magazines dedicated to educational or moral improvement generally included theater reviews. For instance, María del Pilar Sinués's *El ángel del hogar* provided weekly reports on the plays performed in Madrid's main theaters. These accounts included information about actors, assessed the quality of performances, critiqued premiers, and, importantly, added gossip about members of the audience. All newspapers featured a section on social events that commonly included theater and music. Often the focus of these articles was not the quality of the performance, the literary value of the play, or the originality of the music. Rather, they highlighted the public attending the spectacle—if they displayed good or bad taste, civility or rudeness, elegance or vulgarity. When the event took place in a provincial city, local reporters highlighted the positive aspects and presented the entertainment as an example of civic progress toward civilization and modernity.[25]

In the 1850s, the first weekly magazines devoted exclusively to celebrity gossip appeared. In these publications, articles about theater highlighted the social dimension of the spectacle over its cultural or literary value. These publications included *El Museo Universal,* and its continuation in *La Ilustración Española y Americana* or *La semana Madrileña, revista de salones, teatros y sport,* which first appeared in 1883. In *La Ilustración Española* Julio Nombela exposed tantalizing news about premiers, the acting profession, and theater-related gossip. Barcelona had its own version, called *La Ilustración Hispano-Americana,* which included Nombela's column, a local chronicle written by José Jaumeandreu, and illustrations by the clever cartoonist Apeles Mestres.

The making of bourgeois culture and the expansion of theater were two aspects of a single historical development. Critics, writers, and managers continually insisted that Spanish theater was in crisis, and their concerns paralleled that of writers, journalists, politicians, and historians who denounced middle-class society. Yet, during the nineteenth century Spain's theatrical repertoire expanded as never before. At the beginning of the century, Madrid had only two main theaters.[26] By 1900, both Madrid and Barcelona had a dozen main theaters, two large opera houses, and a similar number of secondary playhouses covering a variety of spectacles such as plays, circuses, zarzuela, and vaudeville. Other venues included *cafes cantantes* (cafés with musical performances) and private casinos, athenaeums, clubs, aristocratic salons, and family homes. According to data published by the *El Museo Universal* in 1866, there were 318 theaters in Spain with a total of 156,000 seats. In that year the Spanish stage featured 8,410 theater performances, 1,118 operas, and 2,846 zarzuelas.[27] Most provincial capitals built a Teatro Principal to showcase their polite entertainments.

The middle class also influenced the rise of informal theater. At midcentury, professional theater companies competed with clubs (composed of semi-professional performers) sponsored by private or semi-public patrons—from groups of friends to athenaeums, casinos, or even political organizations. In Madrid alone there were more than forty active groups staging home theaters, academies, and circuses.[28] Countrywide data published by *El Museo Universal* recorded 865 private societies (*sociedades de recreo*) presenting theater, music, and dance. Social gatherings in homes of upper- to middle-class families often featured readings from plays or entire presentations—activities that proponents of refinement considered ideal for the creation of polite society. This is why the Villaamils, another Madrilenian low-middle-class family that appears in Pérez Galdós's novel *Miau,* decided to continue sponsoring social evenings at their family dwelling despite their desperate economic situation. Guests at these get-togethers entertained themselves by preparing a play for the Villaamils' home. Women in the family considered these meetings as acts of refinement required to keep up appearances and maintain social status. When Mr. Villaamil lost his job in the state administration and stopped bringing home a monthly income, the family decided to deprive themselves of basic necessities rather than suspending the evening *tertulias* (gatherings).[29]

Another significant development in Spanish theater were the *teatros por horas* (theaters by hours), established after 1850 in Barcelona and Madrid. These playhouses functioned all day long, and sold affordable tickets for differing audiences. These places offered small spectacles, such as vaudevilles, pieces from zarzuelas, comic sketches, and the popular can-can. Jacinto Octavio Picón's novel *Dulce y sabrosa* describes these playhouses as employing mainly young, hopeful women. They needed artistic talent, but only a very small number of these women would ascend to the opera or theater. The world of *teatros por horas* and *cafés cantantes* was more about exploiting female talent than it was about high culture. The proliferation of *teatros por horas* marks the moment in which theater transitioned from a space for the upper and middle classes to a mass spectacle.

The Opera and Classical Music

In November 1859, while attending an opera performance in one of the boxes of the Teatro Real, writer Juan Valera engaged in a discussion with the countess of "X" about whether or not Madrid had a *beau monde*. The writer argued that such a thing did not exist anymore:

> [In the past what was known as *beau monde*] was restricted to those with a title of nobility, whether inherited or acquired, while at present what is called *beau monde* is open to almost everyone who can afford a black tailcoat and a pair of black gloves to wear.
> "How can you say that?" replied the countess with annoyance, "how can you deny what you are seeing around you at this very moment?"
> "Well," said the writer, "the select audience seated in this theater could be considered in such way, but . . . in Spain elegance and distinction

are no longer a privilege exclusive of certain classes. To be elegant and distinguished," added the writer, "as well as to be a member of the nobility, are qualities that at present can be acquired by all Spaniards."[30]

Beyond the differences of criteria the writer and the countess were using concerning the notion of *beau monde,* it was not a coincidence that this conversation took place during an opera performance in Madrid's main theater at the time. In the nineteenth century, the opera was the public space par excellence where polite society gathered. In the orchestra seats and theater boxes one could observe the most complete picture of the new dominant society with all its symbolic and ritualistic apparatus.

Opera began in the seventeenth century under the patronage of royal courts and aristocratic circles, and was restricted to courtiers and nobles up to the nineteenth century. However, by the end of the eighteenth century, this spectacle had become increasingly commercialized, especially in management and regulation, following the changes taking place in Western societies.[31] The nineteenth century was the great century for theater, as we have seen, but this was also true for the opera, due to the quality of productions as well as the social significance of the spectacles. Unlike theater, however, opera had always been an exclusive form of entertainment. There were forms adapted to popular demand—the zarzuela in Spain, the operetta, the music hall, and vaudeville in other parts of the West—but for the most part opera sponsors managed to maintain purity and exclusiveness. Yet, by the end of the nineteenth century, the bourgeoisie controlled its patronage, and opera was one of the public spaces that best represented the nexus between old and new elites.[32]

Dominant groups implemented two strategies to exclude the general public from opera over the course of the century. First, elaborate productions kept ticket prices elevated. Opera supporters demanded luxurious theaters, lavish scenery, ostentatious staging with a large number of singers, highly qualified musicians in the orchestras, and well-paid and extravagant divas. Second, they reduced access at both a symbolic and an administrative level. Opera theater managers implemented restrictive policies for available seats, selling long-term tickets for seats and boxes, sometimes making them available to families or individuals as real estate property. The location of seats always reflected social hierarchy. Strict norms of etiquette regulated attire as well. Habitual audiences contributed to the ethos of exclusiveness by imposing a culture of *connoisseur.*

Attending the opera required that one "understand" its content and execution, implying a level of education only accessible to the socially affluent in the nineteenth century.

Despite elite controls, the Spanish opera was eventually claimed by bourgeois society. A crucial site for social performance, it became a vital space for those in search of social ascent and distinction. At the opera, the upper ranks of the bourgeoisie replaced the old aristocracy; they were now patrons of theaters and theater companies. Although at times the old elites tried to marginalize newcomers, ultimately the power of money prevailed. This displacement of elites was not limited to Europe. The newly ascendant Vanderbilts and Morgans founded The Metropolitan Opera in New York after being denied access to the exclusive Academy of Music.[33] For the middle classes and the petit bourgeoisie, the opera provided a larger return in cultural capital than the theater or other available forms of refined entertainment. The construction and promotion of lavish opera houses became one of the essential commitments of the new liberal governments. The opera was a potent symbol of modernity: powerful, civilized, and prosperous nations possessed a strong opera under the patronage of their ruling groups.

The Spanish opera followed the European pattern, in regard to both its historical origins and its evolution. In the eighteenth century, most operas were performed in Madrid—at the royal palaces, in the royal gardens, and in the disappeared Coliseo de los Caños del Peral.[34] After the Napoleonic wars, fascination with opera grew among urban elites, who sought to imitate the most advanced countries in Europe. The opera spread to other Spanish cities, beginning with Barcelona.[35] Although rising demand for opera was absorbed by the elegant theaters in the cities—the Príncipe and Santa Cruz in Madrid, and the Principal and Santa Cruz in Barcelona—elites wanted a theater exclusively for opera. In Madrid, the idea was backed by courtier, aristocratic, and bourgeois circles who wanted Madrid to become the symbolic capital of the new liberal state. In Barcelona the impetus to build an opera theater matured with the ascent of the bourgeoisie, who wanted to enhance Barcelona's presence within the national and international context and establish its reputation as a great European metropolis. The result of these projects was the construction of the Teatro del Liceo in Barcelona and the Teatro Real in Madrid. These two emblematic initiatives illustrate what was different and what was similar in the struggles by dominant groups of both cities to implement modernity.

Dominant societies of Madrid and Barcelona pursued similar aspirations with this new construction. Opera theaters would provide spaces for the sociability and enjoyment of polite society, and also furnish symbolic stages on which the urban elites could project the values of civility, good taste, and order. Promoters also sought international prestige for their city via this powerful symbol of refinement and development. But beyond this set of parallel objectives, there were significant contrasts, which reflected differences between Madrid's and Barcelona's economy, culture, and society over the course of the nineteenth century. While the Teatro del Liceo has a place in history as one of the main symbols of the determination and dynamism of Catalan bourgeois culture, the Teatro Real represents the complications encountered by Madrid's bourgeoisie in the creation of symbols of national identity.

The Liceo emerged from an initiative by a civic group established in 1837 to promote culture in Barcelona.[36] The group, known as Liceu Filharmònic d'Isabel II, included members of the liberal National Militia, defenders of the constitutional monarchy under Queen Isabel.[37] The affiliates of this original Liceu Filharmònic belonged to Barcelona's middle classes and sought to bring progress to the city through the instruction of music and drama and the organization of concerts and plays. With a dream to build an opera theater, the group designated Joaquin María Gispert, one of the most active members, to act as agent for the purchase of the old convent of Trinitarios in the heart of the historic Barcelona downtown. Gispert belonged to one of the most powerful families of the city's new industrial bourgeoisie, and he had advantageous political connections and solid business skills. The intention was to acquire this premier space in the historic Rambla to build a grand theater and a music conservatory. The group designed an efficient financial system based on private donations and took the first steps toward the construction of the opera theater.

In planning the Liceo, they wanted to build the best theater not only in Barcelona, but also in Spain. It was to compete in its capacity, design, decoration, and program with the most renowned theaters in Europe. The results were spectacular, beyond the most optimistic expectations. The theater was built in only three years, and was completely finished on its opening day, April 4, 1847. The public, wrote the journalist Marc Jesús Bertran, "walked through the lounge, the gallery, the corridors, the backstage rooms; then they came back to the lobby, sat in the comfortable and stylish sofas, stepped on the glistening marble floors, and expressed praise about everything." Besides its tasteful and exquisite decoration, impressive seating, and ample, comfortable lounges and lobby, the building was fully equipped with gas illumination and even an "English kind of restrooms."[38]

This achievement was possible because the society of the Liceo was established as a capitalist enterprise with the solid financial commitment of its members. Founding stockholders were offered the opportunity to purchase seats and boxes as a private estate, occupying half of the theater's capacity. While this form of management provided a stable source of revenue that ensured its continuity, a negative aspect was that the theater was socially segregated from the start and would remain that way.[39]

The Liceo would become a premier cultural institution in Spain. Initially offering a varied program, including opera, zarzuela, ballet, and even the circus, after the 1870s its repertoire consisted exclusively of music—basically opera—with some ballet, classical music, and an occasional operetta. By the second half of the nineteenth century, it was inconceivable to come across an *hombre fino* or a *mujer fina* in Barcelona who was not able to engage in a conversation about any aspect of the life of the Liceo. Membership in the Círculo del Liceo, a private British-style men's club, afforded the most prestigious status in Barcelona society. With its headquarters in the very theater building, the Círculo provided direct access to the theater lobby, private salons, offices, a reading room, a dining room, and a private entrance to the noble floor of the theater.[40] The city leaders were members of the Círculo, and that clique controlled a great deal of the theater's business. At midcentury, the Círculo, which represented the political and cultural positions of Catalonian upper bourgeoisie, contributed to the shaping of a Catalonian identity by promoting the operas of some Catalan maestros—Felipe Pedrell, Jaume Pahissa, Ricard Lamote de Grignon, Enric Morera, Àngel Guimerà, and Eduardo Marquina.[41]

In time, the Círculo became more conservative politically and culturally, largely owing to changes in audience. Beginning in the late 1880s and continuing through the 1890s, the Liceo became embroiled in the cultural wars and social conflicts of Spain fin de siècle. The November 7, 1893, terrorist blast on opening night of the season violently depicted its symbolic role in Spanish culture. Two bombs thrown by an anarchist from the upper floors into the front orchestra killed twenty people and injured many others. Barcelona was horrified, and although the theater reopened months later, the seats occupied by those killed by the bombs would remain vacant for a number of years. For the Liceo this sad episode marked a before and an after, as the mood of the theater shifted toward political and cultural conservatism.

Spain's culture wars were reflected in the confrontations and debates that took place among audiences regarding the function that the theater should play. Connoisseurs, a minority group of young purists, and the anti-system bohemia of the lower-priced seats in the upper stage called *galliner,* demanded a more avant-garde repertoire. They argued for a theater exclusively oriented to the promotion of artistic creation and innovation. They won some partial victories, bringing to the program operas by Richard Wagner and Georges Bizet in addition to traditional Italian composers. Nonetheless, it was the conservative majority who prevailed, and they conceived of the theater as a space for cultivation, enjoyment, and, above all, the promotion of polite sociability. "We have to be straightforward and tell the full truth," a columnist writing in 1903 opined in the newspaper *La Vanguardia.* In regard to the function of the theater, "the Liceo is almost the only available space for proper sociability in Barcelona, and while the scenic representation attracts spectators to the theater, the principal interest is in the seats and corridors not in the scenario." For the Catalonian bourgeoisie the Liceo became the favored symbol of their historical triumph and Barcelona's economic, social, and cultural achievements.

The Teatro Real in Madrid emerged quite differently than the Liceo. While the symbolic function of both auditoriums was similar, their development reflects "a tale of two cities." Madrid was the royal capital and possessed the first opera theater in Spain, but at the beginning of the century that theater needed to be demolished. Contrasted with the three-year construction period of El Liceo, El Real took thirty-two years to complete. Its promoters were not a group of good citizens in search of improving the life of their city, but rather a complex social conglomerate composed of new and old dominant groups, including the monarchy, the old aristocracy, and the new liberal bourgeoisie. The Teatro Real was only one part of an extensive and ambitious urban project—the Plaza de Oriente, which was to create a symbolic space representing Madrid's role as the state capital of a new culturally progressive Spain.

Construction started in 1818, much earlier than that of the Liceo, but issues with funding repeatedly delayed the opening of the Teatro Real. By 1838, financial control over the initiative had been transferred from the crown to the state but progress remained slow and uneven. The inauguration finally took place on November 19, 1850. Opening day was itself delayed—the event had been planned for the queen's twentieth birthday on October 10—which underscored the theater's belated arrival. Its flamboyant interior was as plush and luxurious as that of the Liceo or any other major opera theaters of the time, but the building itself was plagued by oversights and blunders. Attendants on opening night noticed the lack of a cloakroom, overlooked by builders and administrators, and the heating system was not functional. At first the theater was quite ambitious, with the best possible programs, but its early years were plagued by financial problems.

Eventually, the government privatized Madrid's opera theater. Its new owners raised the price of seats to inaccessible levels even for well-to-do patrons, making it one of the most expensive theaters in Europe.[42] Unlike the Liceo, the life of El Real revolved around the presence of the royal family, who attracted the old aristocracy and the new plutocracy. For that reason the theater never became a genuine symbol of the city, and when the revolutionaries of 1868 overthrew the traditional monarchy—the queen and the Bourbon family—the Teatro Real changed its name to National Opera Theater. This rebranding was short-lived: in 1874, it regained the name Real along with its exclusive reputation. The theater served as a major space of Madrilenian *sociedad de buen tono,* as well as a center for cultivated entertainment. At the same time its very presence in Madrid symbolized the issues faced by Madrid's dominant society in their effort to establish solid, credible, and lasting symbols of modernity. The theater closed in 1925 due to cracks in its foundation, probably caused by the building of Madrid's first subway line.[43] It reopened in 1965 as a concert hall for classical music, and after new remodeling it reopened again in 1997 as the Opera Theater of Madrid.

It is worth mentioning that in addition to these two major opera theaters, there were many other theaters staging productions of opera and other forms of classical music in Madrid, Barcelona, as well as provincial cities around Spain. The opera season lasted through the summer in Barcelona and Madrid, often featuring the best artists of the time performing in the cities' pleasure gardens. The tradition of Barcelona's middle-class engagement with classical music is rooted in the rich and varied repertoire featured in these fashionable summer concerts. The Campos Eliseos and the Jardines de Euterpe flourished under the sponsorship of the musician Anselm Clavé. In the Barcelona Campos Eliseos there was an auditorium that in 1881 became the Teatro Lírico-Sala Beethoven, the first theater in Barcelona and Spain mainly for classical music.[44]

Madrid opened its first specialized auditorium for classical music in 1884. The musician, businessman, and inventor Antonio Romero Andía owned the largest music publishing company and shop in mid-nineteenth-century Madrid. Romero Andía sublet the Sala Capellanes, an ill-reputed but popular ballroom in old Madrid, intending to transform it into an elegant concert room.[45] A few years earlier, in 1866, the musicians Francisco Asenjo Barbieri, Federico Chueca and Joaquin Romualdo Gaztambide established the Sociedad de Conciertos de Madrid (Madrid Society of Concerts), the first private symphonic orchestra in Spain. Although the Sociedad deserves credit for promoting European classical music, as well as talented Spanish maestros such as Isaac Albeniz, Joaquin Turina, Tómas Bretón, and Ruperto Chapí, it never had its own theater. The closest Madrid had to a classical music theater was the Principe Alfonso in Paseo de Recoletos, a unique auditorium built in 1862 to be a circus following the Parisian model on the Champs-Élysées. In 1870, the Principe Alfonso was remodeled to function as a concert hall for classical music, and became popular among Madrid's elegant society. It was a place for performances by Sociedad de Conciertos, but money problems caused it to close in 1898.[46]

The Barcelonan bourgeoisie prized cultural civic initiatives. The construction of the Palau de la Música Catalana, one of the most emblematic buildings of the modernist city, provides a good example. Funding for the Palau, as for the Liceo, emerged from politics surrounding the defense and promotion of autochthonous Catalan culture, which became stronger in the Barcelona fin de siècle. The Palau was built to house the musical association Orfeó Català, established in 1891. It was to serve as an auditorium for classical music in general and Catalan music in particular.[47] Designed by architect Lluís Doménech i Montaner, the building reflects the idealization of medieval design as a model for the new bourgeois city. What stands out among its neo-gothic architectural elements is the elaborate iconography: Catalan country maidens singing and dancing, Germanic valkyries, coats-of-arms with Catalan medieval symbols, and the busts of the most consecrated German composers.[48] Interest in classical music, originally linked to the opera and later choral and instrumental music, was on the rise in midcentury in many other Spanish cities—especially Bilbao, San Sebastian, Valencia, and Cadiz.[49] Much of this heightened interest had to do with zarzuela, a popular genre among Spanish middle classes, the history of which is too rich to be covered in the limited space of this chapter.

The popularity of musical and dramatic performance underscores the critical role of celebrity in nineteenth-century bourgeois Spanish culture. Actresses, actors, and opera singers had become icons of elegance and refinement since the late eighteenth century. The most successful were admitted to the worldly *sociedad de buen tono* and other elite circles. Carlos María de Esquivel's 1846 impressive group portrait of Madrid's intellectual elite, *A Lecture by Zorrilla in the Artist's Study,* depicts the importance accorded to actors. Joaquín Romea, famous actor and theater manager, occupies the heart of the composition. Esquivel, Romea and the playwright José Zorrilla appear surrounded by Madrid's most prominent politicians, journalists, writers, poets, aristocrats, and businessmen.[50]

This cult of celebrity expanded with the development of an illustrated and specialized press in the second half of the century. All of the new theater and music magazines included articles and images about the public and private lives of the famous, with stories of their love affairs and extravagance.[51] Of major interest were opera singers such as the tenors Julián Gayarre and Enrico Tamberlik, or the famous prima donnas, among whom Adelina Patti reigned supreme. A journalist described the diva in 1908:

La Patti . . . who just turned sixty, is preparing an artistic tour around America and has imposed on her sponsors the following conditions: the astronomic stipend of two million pesetas; travel in the company of her husband, seven servants, and her dogs and birds, the number of which is not determined; lodging in the hotels of her choice with a minimum booking of seven rooms; meals prepared only by her cooks. La Patti will also set the price of the seats for each representation, and as the final condition, there must be someone poised to throw on the stage at least three bouquets of flowers at the end of each performance.[52]

Pleasure Gardens

Pleasure gardens, known in Spain as *jardines de recreo* or *jardines públicos,* were extensive privately owned, entertainment resorts within the city or in its suburbs generally seasonal, opening their gates in late spring and closing them in early autumn. Access to these parks required the payment of an entrance fee. Pleasure gardens reflected the democratic spirit of the nineteenth-century liberal bourgeoisie but at the same time its restrictive limits. Openness was controlled to ensure selectivity and order by the offering of high-priced activity programs such as opera representations, classical music concerts, and social balls that required strict etiquette for admission. Eighteenth- and nineteenth-century pleasure gardens were the antecedents of modern amusement parks.

Although the use of gardens for leisure and entertainment goes back to ancient times, its expansion occurred mainly during the Renaissance, when it became linked to courtier and aristocratic life. It was the English who first commercialized gardens, mainly in London, as open spaces for entertainment and sociability.[53] The first pleasure gardens appeared in London in the late seventeenth century, but became more popular in the second half of the eighteenth century, when Vauxhall Gardens turned into the most fashionable location for summer evening entertainment. Vauxhall on the south bank of the Thames and Ranelagh Gardens in Chelsea were the most celebrated English pleasure gardens. They became models, and several gardens named Vauxhall or Ranelagh opened in continental Europe and America. English pleasure gardens specialized in programming high-culture entertainment, mainly music. Some of the most famous musical compositions by George Frideric Handel, Joseph Haydn, Wolfgang Amadeus Mozart, and James Hook were performed for the first time at Vauxhall or at Ranelagh's rococo concert hall known as The Rotunda. In addition to music the public could enjoy a variety of spectacles such as masquerades, fireworks, hot air balloons, tightrope walkers, and battle reenactments.[54]

The first pleasure gardens on the Continent were opened in Paris in the second half of the eighteenth century. The pleasure garden was initially called *vauxhall d'été,* but soon the French changed the name to *jardin de loisir.* This new distinctly French pleasure garden was typified by the Tivoli Gardens, which opened in 1766. While English gardens offered high culture—classical music and opera—the French included mundane forms of spectacle. The Tivoli, a name inspired by ancient Roman gardens, was the largest and most popular *jardin de loisir* of Paris at the turn of the century, and it spawned gardens with the name Tivoli in many parts of Europe, including Spain. The only extant survivor of that generation of Tivoli gardens is the famous Tivoli Park of Copenhagen. Opened in 1843, it still preserves some characteristics of the old-style gardens. Although the Parisian Tivoli competed with twenty other pleasure gardens opened in the city between 1750 and 1850, it was the most profitable and famous. Marie Antoinette loved the Tivoli, and last visited on the afternoon of June 20, 1791, before the royal family's flight to Varennes. The Revolution neutralized the aristocratic tone of the gardens, but they still remained the favorite place of Paris's *beau monde*. Labeled "bourgeois gardens" during the years of the Convention, the Tivoli were the preferred leisure place of the Bonaparte family. The Parisian Tivoli Gardens had another moment of splendor under the Restoration after 1815 before closing definitively in 1842.

After the 1840s, a new style of garden, the *jardin-spectacle,* was introduced in Paris. The first *jardin-spectacle* opened along the new avenue of Champs-Élysées. There is no comprehensive study of the origins, contents, and evolution of this type of garden, which remained popular until the last third of the nineteenth century, but *jardin-spectacle* seems to have been a product of the new social order under the Second Empire. These gardens were opened to promote sociability for the new Parisian *beau monde* that arose during the rule of Napoleon III. The *jardin-spectacle* replaced frolic with the formal: instead of traditional fair and circus attractions, the new gardens concentrated on social balls, musical soirees, operas, plays, and polite sociability in cafés, restaurants, and promenades. Like its predecessors, this model of French pleasure garden was exported to other European countries.[55]

Pleasure gardens were a landscape of commodified consumption. As was the case with theater and opera, between 1800 and 1835 pleasure gardens became symbols of urban transformation and modernity. The history of the pleasure gardens belongs to the history of speculative and entrepreneurial management of urban leisure and entertainment in the nineteenth century. These gardens also featured sophisticated and imaginative machines requiring specialized labor for maintenance and improvement. Such displays of entrepreneurial, scientific, and technological development attracted national prestige. Pleasure gardens were expressions of bourgeois culture and social identity created to accommodate new bourgeois ideals of courtesy, sociability, elegance, imagination, consumption, hygiene, and comfort. As such, pleasure gardens were powerful symbols representing the modern identities of dominant national groups.

Notwithstanding Mariano José Larra's disparaging remarks at the beginning of this chapter, Madrid opened its first Spanish pleasure garden in the late seventeenth century. Called the gardens of Corregidor Juan Fernández, they were located at the site of the present Buenavista Palace near Plaza de Cibeles. The palace was built in 1769 on a private park with promenades, fountains, ponds, and a restaurant used by members of Madrid's noble families for picnics and social gatherings.[56] The most noteworthy antecedent of the nineteenth-century public pleasure gardens appeared in 1767, when King Charles III opened parts of the Retiro royal gardens to the public.[57] "The Retiro promenade is charming," wrote the Duke of Medinasidonia in 1772 to a friend who was absent from Madrid serving in a diplomatic post. "A tent has been installed near the park's menagerie with comfortable straw chairs where sweets and hot and cold beverages are served. Another tent with the same amenities has been placed by the park's lake. A third one with beverages and card games is near the Fuente de Mayo . . . I can assure you, my friend, that I never imagined I would see my country as it looks now."[58]

The first modern pleasure garden in Spain, the Jardín de Tívoli, opened in Madrid in 1821. This Spanish Tívoli was the first of many. It belonged to a French entrepreneur and was situated on the Paseo del Prado, where the Hotel Ritz presently stands, across from the Goya gate of the Prado Museum. For the writer Ramón Mesonero Romanos, the installation of that first European-style pleasure garden marked a clear change in the life of the city. He related it to the rise of the new liberal government after the revolution of 1820. "Madrid," he wrote, "is abandoning its secular lethargy, getting rid of the gag imposed by a tyrannical rule that was reluctant to allow any kind of expansion characteristic of modern societies." He added, "The new government . . . is promoting in Madrid innovative forms of business previously unknown in the city, and opening public initiatives of utility, pleasure, and recreation, the most successful of which is the magnificent Tívoli of the Prado."[59]

That same year of 1821 and in the same part of the city, construction began on a monument dedicated to the heroes of the second of May. Both projects, the monument and the garden, were part of a larger design aimed at transforming the area of Paseo del Prado into the new symbolic space of the liberal capital. The Tívoli was inaugurated in 1822 with a congratulatory atmosphere. Although more modest than the Tivoli of Paris, the new garden had enormous symbolic implications for Madrid. The park occupied a large trapezoidal block, landscaped with rows of trees creating a network of promenades and a central square. In the central area portable structures for a theater, a café, and a restaurant were installed. A wall with several gates enclosed the park, controlling access during performances. The theater was a wooden octagonal structure covered by a large tent that could be disassembled during winter.

The main promenade of the park was a public street that connected the new monument of the heroes of the second of May with the entrance of the Prado Museum. Initially that street was closed during performances, but it remained opened most of the time, as did the rest of the park.

After disappointing economic results in the first year, the Tívoli was completely enclosed and an entrance fee was charged. In 1823, the company was having trouble financially and presented a report to Madrid's city hall requesting the extension of the pleasure garden to winter months; the municipal authorities rejected the request.[60] The Tívoli had a short life as a pleasure garden. In 1829, the Madrilenian artist José Madrazo sublet the property to the municipality for the installation of a lithographic laboratory.[61] The gardens survived until the 1880s as a public park before buildings were constructed there. This instability was a characteristic of all European pleasure gardens. Several factors contributed to this precariousness: the seasonal character of the business, changing fashions, and, most important, the area they occupied was frequently absorbed by urban growth. Because the bulk of those who frequented the parks were of the middle and upper classes, they were strategically located close to old royal or aristocratic gardens, elegant quarters, or areas of the city with adequate ecological conditions, usually the urban lots of higher value for real estate development.

New kinds of pleasure gardens opened in Madrid and Barcelona during the 1830s.[62] In Madrid the most noteworthy was the already mentioned Jardín de las Delicias in Paseo de Recoletos, between the streets of Almirante and Bárbara de Braganza. This new *jardín de recreo* was better equipped than its forerunners and more in tune with the standards of European gardens. Although it was not as big as the classic gardens in France and England, it had sufficient water for a small lake and two cascades with small caves underneath. A wall enclosed the park and its main entrance had a ticket booth. Inside the park there were several permanent constructions, including a main building with a café, a restaurant, a grand salon, and a lodge for those desiring a long stay to enjoy the pleasures of the place. Located within the park were kiosks and decks for musicians as well as tables for card playing, chess, backgammon, draughts, and billiards. The rides were fairly standard: there was a carousel, games, and several kinds of swings.[63] The garden even had a spa attached to the hotel and restaurant building with private rooms for baths that featured hot water and metallic bathtubs as well as a pool "with enough room for eight people in case one wanted to bathe in company."[64] An announcement in the *Diario de Avisos de Madrid* informed its readers of nighttime entertainment: "For the convenience of our clients we have placed a line of street lamps from Plaza de Cibeles to the entrance of the garden to illuminate the boulevard."[65]

Despite the increased availability of pleasure gardens in Madrid, the difference in quality and number compared to those of the major European cities was still notable. To remedy this, Mesonero Romanos wrote an article in May 1836 proposing the transformation of Madrid's Retiro royal gardens into a modern public pleasure garden. The old gardens, wrote Mesonero, in the hands of productive and intelligent private management could be transformed into public gardens similar to those of other European capitals. He mentioned specifically the Vauxhall of London as a model to be emulated. The renovated Retiro, in his vision, would have a theater, a concert hall, belvederes, restaurants, an inn, a horse race track, games, dioramas, gondolas in the large pond at the heart of the park, and other amenities "similar to those one can find in the London parks." Mesonero worried that Madrilenian society was inclined to the boorish ambience of the tavern and the circus, and he wanted to create a space for "civilized and well mannered forms of entertainment."[66]

By the late 1830s, Madrid offered several variations of leisure garden. The Jardín de Apolo was perhaps the most popular due to its affordable entrance fee. Located in what was known as the Puerta de San Fernando (present-day Glorieta de Bilbao) it offered concerts—mainly zarzuela—theater plays, balls, and small rides. Literary references describe the place as appropriate for holiday picnics with basic landscaping. A maze provided the highlight of the gardens. Another park, the Jardín de Portici, functioned for a short time. It was located in the opposite corner of the city, by the banks of the Manzanares creek, in an estate known as the Soto de Migas Calientes. That area of Madrid, close to the royal properties of the Casa de Campo, enjoyed an abundant water supply from the river Manzanares. Midcentury maps depict rows of trees, parterres, and promenades where kiosks for beverages and food were installed.[67] The Portici's most distinctive feature was an area by the river where people could take swimming lessons. A bit distant from the city, the Portici was appropriate for daylong excursions and picnics.[68] Thus, by the beginning of 1840, Madrid had a diversified supply of pleasure gardens covering a wide social spectrum. Delicias and Portici, with higher entrance fees, were more selective, while the Apolo was more popular.[69]

In the coming years Madrilenians saw the opening of new pleasure gardens and the continuity, recycling, and disappearance of the old. Carmen Ariza Muñoz cites the existence of at least eight parks in the area of Paseo de Recoletos between the late 1840s and the late 1850s, but the city still lacked the large park Mesonero Romanos wanted to compete in size and content with the gardens of London and Paris.[70] And meanwhile, what was going on in Barcelona?

By 1853, Barcelona would inaugurate the first gardens in Spain that could fully compete in size and quality with those in the rest of Europe. This may have been its most grand, but Barcelona had long surpassed the capital in creating modern initiatives for commercial leisure. At the beginning of the nineteenth century, the number of landscaped areas for strolling and gathering within Barcelona's city limits and surroundings had been limited. Barcelona did not have old aristocratic gardens or royal gardens comparable to the Retiro of Madrid. However, the social and cultural awakening Barcelona experienced starting in the late eighteenth century did result in the rapid growth of pleasure gardens similar to the ones opened in Madrid after 1820. All the new pleasure gardens were located in Passeig de Gràcia, within Barcelona's *eixample,* after the *passeig* opened in 1827. In the beginning of the century, picnic areas were established by the convent of Franciscanos de Jesús on the old road to the village of Gràcia. This area had a famous fountain called *la fuente de Jesús,* abundant shade trees, and kiosks that served food and drinks; Barcelonians liked to gather there for *merienda* and promenade on summer afternoons.[71]

Barcelona's first conventional pleasure garden, the Jardines del Criadero, opened around 1840, twenty years later than Madrid's first gardens. Like the Portici of Madrid, the Criadero was installed in what were the municipal nurseries of the city, outside of the medieval wall. In 1849, the Jardín de Tívoli opened several meters north of Criadero on the left side of the *passeig* between today's Aragón and Valencia streets. The Tívoli, also established in a former nursery, was under private ownership. The third of these new pleasure gardens, the Prado Catalán, was inaugurated in the early 1850s also in the vicinity of Passeig de Gràcia between the current Gran Vía and Diputación streets.[72] These new gardens were very similar in structure and offerings to those in Madrid. The only difference was their close proximity, making them more accessible to the general public and giving Passeig de Gràcia a vital role in the life of the early nineteenth-century city. One can imagine what the *passeig* must have looked like on a Sunday afternoon or a holiday, filled with Barcelonians enjoying their leisure time in one of the gardens. The public who came during the day to play, drink, dance, and go on rides was socially diverse, while at night the gardens were frequented by more selective members of society attending plays, concerts, zarzuelas, and performances of acrobats and famous magicians.[73] With the passage of time the Criadero and Prado Catalán gardens became more oriented toward wider audiences, including the lower-middle and popular classes. In the Criadero the owners opened a *cafe cantante* and in 1870 built the new Teatro Español, specializing in zarzuela. El Prado Catalán incorporated a pavilion for the exhibit of dioramas and cycloramas, although its zarzuela theater was transformed in 1863 into an equestrian circus for audiences of 1,800.

The 1850s saw a new generation of pleasure gardens established in Barcelona, such as the Jardines de la Ninfa—soon to become the Jardines de Euterpe—and the Campos Eliseos or Camps Elisis. The former, open from about 1850 to 1861, was especially focused on choral music. The movement for choral music was a phenomenon of civic sociability and an expression of Catalan national identity. It became linked to those pleasure gardens that explicitly promoted cultivated leisure. The main sponsor of this movement, the musician and civic leader Anselmo Clavé, used the pleasure garden to organize and promote his choirs. In 1850, his choir La Fraternidad (The Brotherhood) began rehearsing and performing in the Jardín de Tívoli. By 1853, it had moved to the Jardines de la Ninfa.[74] The events of 1854—the cholera epidemic and political turmoil—had a negative impact on Clavé's musical and civic movement: many members of the choir were either sick or suffered from political repression, and Clavé himself was exiled to the Balearic Islands due to his support of the progressive party.

When he returned from exile in 1857, Clavé founded the Sociedad Musical Euterpe (Music Society Euterpe) with what remained of La Fraternidad and new sources of support. This new society marked the beginning of the golden age of Clavé's movement and its influence on Catalonian and Spanish social and cultural history. In 1857, the Jardines de la Ninfa changed its name to Jardines de Euterpe, after the Society. Euterpe would become one of the most emblematic pleasure gardens of Barcelona. In May 1859, the Sociedad began publishing a newsletter with the program of each concert, biographical notes, lyrics, literary comments, passages from classical mythology, and commentary on music, theater, opera, and other forms of cultivated leisure. Euterpe's repertoire included choral passages from opera and zarzuela, and compositions by Clavé and other Catalonian, Spanish, and European musicians of the moment. The

Sociedad Euterpe was a vanguard group that promoted musical and cultural innovation and contributed substantially to the making of the Catalonian Reanixença. When in 1861 the owners of the Euterpe pleasure garden decided to reconfigure the land as an investment, the Sociedad moved its performances to the more elegant Campos Eliseos.[75]

Behind these new gardens was the banker and politician Evaristo Arnús, one of the main figures in the making of modern Barcelona.[76] The Campos Eliseos, or Camps Elisis, which opened in 1853, was the biggest pleasure garden ever built in Spain. Located on the right side of Passeig de Gràcia, across from the Jardines de Tívoli, it covered 8 hectares with a wall facing the *passeig* that measured 850 meters. The Campos Eliseos was about the same size as the Cremorne Gardens of London, and its structure, purpose, and types of entertainment were also very similar.[77] Both borrowed most heavily from the traditional French *jardin de loisir*. The Campos Eliseos offered circus attractions, spectacles of visual effects, and an extensive variety of rides and sideshows. The gardens also imitated the English tradition by featuring a carefully programmed repertoire of opera and classical music. With their varied and high-quality repertoire, the Campos Eliseos competed with the most advanced pleasure gardens of Europe and outshined those in Madrid.

The Campos Eliseos featured both technological advancement and polite sociability. They were elaborately landscaped with rows of trees, flowerbeds, parterres, statues, and fountains. They promised attractive new rides, the most exciting being Spain's first roller coaster. This ride opened to the public on June 5, 1853, at 9:00 a.m. and ran until dark.[78] It functioned with a simple mechanism; it was a little train on a wavy rail that moved up and down using gravity. The Campos Eliseos, a suburban pastoral arcadia, was also the perfect place for the sociability of Barcelona's *sociedad de buen tono*. In fact, the first representations of French opera in Barcelona were given there. The north wing of the garden had two ponds connected by a canal, with gondolas built for two. Although the gardens were remodeled several times between 1853 and the late 1870s (when they closed), some features remained unchanged. One of them was the small hippodrome built for horse racing, which ended up being used for velocipede rides and races. In the north wing next to the canal there was a central square with a theater, restaurant, and café. Other attractions included several carousels, swing boats, side-shows, kiosks for bands and dancing platforms, and pistol and arrow shooting.[79] The central square was reserved for fireworks, hot air balloons, and cock fighting—a popular spectacle in Catalonia. The inclusion of the first public *sardana* dances established a long-standing tradition in the civic life of Barcelona.[80] The Grand Salon was a Vauxhall-style rotunda with space for a large audience designed by the architect Oriol Mestres and decorated by the scenographer Felix Gagé, both of whom were involved in the construction of the Theater of Liceo.[81]

In the Campos Eliseos, the best-attended and the most important activities were opera performances, orchestra concerts, and, especially, balls. The first ball was staged in the Grand Salon of the park on Saturday, June 17, 1853, at 9:30 p.m. The price of admission was 20 *reales,* about five times the price of regular admission to the park. If the exorbitant price was not enough to make the event exclusive, the tickets were not sold at the garden box, but could only be acquired at the private dwelling of one of the park managers.[82] A special moment in the life of the Campos Eliseos came in 1860, when they received the visit of Queen Isabel II. The queen went to Barcelona to inaugurate the first foundation poured in the *eixample*.[83] The occasion was celebrated with a banquet and performances in the pleasure gardens. Eventually, construction of the *eixample* brought an end to the Campos Eliseos. By 1881, all that was left of the garden was the theater: under the patronage of Evaristo Arnús it became the Teatro Lírico Sala-Beethoven, mainly dedicated to the promotion of classical music.[84] When the Teatro Lírico was demolished in 1900, the last vestige of the Campos Eliseos disappeared. In Barcelona, as in all European cities, the pleasure gardens did not survive nineteenth-century urban growth.

In 1860, Catalonian entrepreneur José Casadesús presented a new garden project to Madrid's municipal authorities. His grand pleasure garden, Campos Eliseos, was an attempt to transfer the success of Barcelona's large-scale gardens to Madrid.[85] The ambitious project included the construction of an interior square for thirty thousand people to witness grandiose spectacles of fireworks, hot air balloons, and acrobats. There would be a roller coaster, a crystal palace greenhouse, and several pavilions for dioramas, cosmoramas, and automatons. A Royal Order approved the project on January 26, 1861. This spectacular new pleasure garden would be located in the new *ensanche* (extension) proposed for Madrid in 1860.[86] After several years in the making, the gardens opened in June 1864, and despite cuts to the original plan, the Campos Eliseos became the favorite place for Madrid's *sociedad de buen tono* during the summer season.[87] By the end of June, Teatro Rossini, the theater of the gardens, presented the opera *William Tell* in homage to its author, Gioachino Antonio Rossini. The acclaimed performance, which drew an attendance of more than two thousand, started at 9:00 p.m. and lasted until 2:00 a.m. All in all, that first event was a success, with the only complaint in the morning papers being the high cost of admission. A journalist wrote: "We had to pay six *reales* for the general admission to the garden, three additional for the theater seat, plus the necessary two for the bus; it is an excessive expense!"[88]

The Rossini auditorium was located in the center of the garden. While the architectural design was not particularly innovative, it had a well decorated interior.[89] "The inside," wrote a journalist, "has a tastefully painted ceiling, nicely decorated boxes and galleries, the seats are comfortable, and there is enough space between the seats and the rows."[90] The worst feature was the poor acoustics. The famous tenor Enrico Tamberlik performed in the Rossini opera for its inaugural session.[91] The theater programs were also innovative—the first season closed with the premiere in Madrid of *Faust* by Charles Gounod, which received mixed reviews.[92]

The main gate of the Campos Eliseos was on Aragón Road, which was the continuation of Alcalá Street, across from northeast wing of the Retiro Gardens. From there the visitor accessed a semicircular square from which two wide tree-lined walks led to the center of the park. The longer path ended in a small bullring, built around the roller coaster. The other walk led the visitor to the central plaza, where the Teatro Rossini, restaurant, and café were located. From the central plaza another walk ended in a semicircular square with a small menagerie. In between the roller coaster and the menagerie were a concert hall and a ballroom, favorite spots of visitors to the garden. The concert hall was a rotunda covered by a tent that the journalist Fernández de los Ríos described as "an original and elegant camping tent."[93] Its interior was stylishly decorated with flags, coats, garlands, and other similar motifs. The poet Gustavo Adolfo Becquer described the concert hall as the highlight of the pleasure gardens due to its elegance, dimensions—it had a capacity of to three thousand visitors— and exquisite programming by maestro Francisco Asenjo Barbieri, the musical director.[94] While in charge of the musical programming of the Campos, Barbieri composed a collection of waltzes entitled *Los Campos Eliseos*.[95]

While Barcelona's pleasure gardens influenced the construction of a Catalonian identity, Madrid was somewhat different. While in Madrid there was an admiration for Clavé's work, civic choral groups were not to be found in the pleasure gardens of the capital because Barbieri preferred to offer zarzuela and more conventional music to suit the bourgeois taste of the garden's public. In Madrid it would be inconceivable to have a space dedicated to entertainment without some form of bullfighting, and Campos Eliseos did have a bullring, albeit a minor one, described in brochures and newspaper articles as a *plaza de toretes* (bullring for small bulls). Its function was complex and multipurpose: besides bullfighting, it was also used for other animal fights, such as bulls against different wild animals—tigers, elephants, and bears—a kind of spectacle that still drew an audience but was harshly criticized by most of the city's newspapers. In the Madrid garden there was no cockfighting—the tradition was stronger in Catalonia—and of course, visitors to the Madrid gardens never danced the *sardana*.

Ultimately, typical visitors went to the Campos Eliseos of Madrid to enjoy new forms of entertainment. For instance, they could ride in a carousel driven by the most modern technology available in Europe: a forty horsepower machine. After that, they could relax in the garden spa or ride a gondola through the canal that occupied the west wing of the park. Roller-skating was another popular activity. Over the seventeen years of the pleasure garden's existence, visitors could enjoy activities as diverse as attending circus performances, working out at one of the earliest public gymnasiums in the city, bowling (American style), attending a political meeting, or even riding in an aerostatic balloon. But, above all, the visitor went to the Campos Eliseos to socialize in its elegant and comfortable spaces: the concert hall, theater, ballroom, and dancing-platforms. Though the garden was multipurpose and multisocial, ultimately it was a place with an unequivocally bourgeois ethos.[96]

Like the pleasure gardens in Barcelona, the Campos Eliseos in Madrid was torn down in 1881 for the construction of apartment buildings in the new *ensanche*. Madrilenians retained fond memories of good times in the park, and in 1897 a new proposal was submitted to city hall and a new Campos Eliseos park opened in 1900 in the northeast side of Madrid, not far from the new Ventas bullring. While retaining some elements from the past, the new park included many new features. For instance, there was a three hundred-square-meter greenhouse made of iron and glass for winter gardens that housed an aquarium. Surrounding this crystal palace was a three-kilometer-long promenade for coaches, horses, and the first automobiles. There was also a velodrome, considered the best in Spain at the time, for bicycle practice and racing. The new Campos Eliseos was intended to be the largest and most modern amusement park in Europe, and its owners planned to build roller coasters, a casino, an ice arena, and other innovations. Before that could happen, the company declared bankruptcy and the park closed abruptly in 1902. A final attempt to revive the Campos Elíseos occurred in the late 1920s, but this project, which would have ushered in the era of mass leisure in Spain, never became a reality due to the civil unrest leading up to the Spanish Civil War in the 1930s.[97]

In the last two decades of the nineteenth century, a new style of pleasure garden delighted Madrid and Barcelona's *sociedades de buen tono*. This new style of garden was modeled after the *jardin-spectacle* of Paris, and the most famous was the Jardines del Buen Retiro in Madrid. The fact that Pio Baroja dedicated a novel to it—entitled *Las Noches del Buen Retiro*—speaks to the importance of that garden in *fin de siècle* Madrid. The Buen Retiro, wrote Baroja, was "a strategic and important point for the bourgeoisie of Madrid."[98] Baroja, who had frequented the gardens in his youth, describes summer nights in the Buen Retiro as "the meeting place for politicians, aristocrats, bankers and other members of Madrid's elegant society."[99] The park was constructed within the former royal Retiro Gardens in a section originally known as the Huerta de San Juan, which became municipal property after the Revolution of 1868.[100]

Inaugurated in the summer of 1876, the Buen Retiro closed in 1905 to make way for the construction of the Palacio de Comunicaciones (Post Office Palace) by the emblematic Plaza de Cibeles. Several factors accounted for the success of the Jardines del Buen Retiro. First of all, the location of the garden was unique— in the very heart of Madrid. The area was exceptionally well landscaped, with tall old shade trees and other exquisite elements retained from the former royal gardens, and the restaurant of El Buen Retiro was considered one of the best in Madrid.[101] The program focused on musical performances, plays, and social balls. Nighttime plays, operas, social balls, and concerts were the highlight of the Jardines. The Jardines del Buen Retiro was Madrid's first large public space to install electric light,[102]

The Jardines' main business competitors were the grand international exhibitions of the end of the century. The World Fairs marked a turning point in the history of modern commercial leisure: they brought about the definitive end of the nineteenth-century pleasure garden and introduced many of the elements of the twentieth-century amusement park. In Spain, the 1888 World Fair of Barcelona and the 1887 World Fair of the Philippine Islands in Madrid left a number of emblematic buildings in both cities, as well as a legacy of change and innovation. Traditional pleasure gardens appeared obsolete when compared to modern-looking grand expositions. By 1920, the classic pleasure gardens, with their mix of business, entertainment, and polite sociability, seemed a thing of the past. They were another component of nineteenth-century bourgeois society that was swallowed by mass society.

Casinos, Athenaeums, Museums, and Expositions

Like pleasure gardens, Spain's casinos, athenaeums, museums, and art expositions facilitated the rise of bourgeois sociability in the nineteenth century. Spanish casinos were not exclusively for gambling; they provided cultural activities and spaces for male sociability. In the provinces casinos served to articulate polite male society.[103] Athenaeums, exclusively cultural, scientific, and academic in character, provided the backbone of Spanish intellectual life prior to the government's educational reforms in the late nineteenth century. Museums also helped to articulate polite bourgeois society, largely through exhibitions that portrayed the historical underpinnings of national identity.[104] Art expositions, as Mesonero Romanos pointed out, also helped to foster refined sociability. These spaces served major roles in the creation and articulation of bourgeois culture.[105]

In nineteenth-century Spain casinos were social and cultural organizations. While their institutional and political dimensions are well known, historians have paid less attention to the role played by casinos in relation to the making of bourgeois identities and lifestyles. At the beginning of the century, casinos did not even exist in Spain. The first opened in the 1830s, and within 30 years there were 575—operating in all Spanish provinces except for Soria.[106] By 1895, there were more than two thousand active casinos in Spain, with the largest concentration in Andalusia. As casinos grew in number, their purpose, function, and ideological orientation became more diverse. Early casinos were run by local elites, and provided spaces for sociability, leisure, and cultural activities. Agustín Guimerá describes nineteenth-century casinos as a combination of an English club and an Italian public café: it was a private organization based on selective membership and funded by maintenance fees that served an essentially recreational function centered on board games, drinking, and male sociability.[107]

The first casinos were segregated along gender and class lines—they admitted men from local middle and upper groups. As more casinos opened, they became more diverse: popular casinos were created with leftist political orientation and some even allowed female membership. This evolution points to their role in a broader transition from restrictive liberal bourgeois society to democratic mass society. Some casinos—such as Madrid's first, established in 1837—were luxurious and elitist, the exclusive realm of the *beau monde*. Other casinos in provincial towns and villages were quite modest.

The wealthy casinos of provincial capitals such as San Sebastian, Santander, and Murcia occupied sumptuous buildings that remain among the most emblematic of their respective cities. The first casinos emerged as initiatives sponsored by private citizens who had already established some sort of *tertulia* (discussion group). Casinos began as places for privileged classes who had leisure time and money to spend in an atmosphere of comfort and exclusivity. In the major cities casino membership came from the upper to the middle classes, including the old aristocracy and the new bourgeoisie. In the provinces the casino was the realm of local bosses (*caciques*) and the different segments of local bourgeois groups—professionals, merchants, and bureaucrats. The casino of Madrid, for instance, was created by a group of notables who had been gathering for many years in a café located near the old Teatro del Príncipe— today's Teatro Español.[108] Its first site occupied the second floor of that café in several rooms sublet by General Fernández de Córdoba, one of the founding members. The founders stated that they wanted to establish a casino, not a club or a society, "to eliminate any suspicion of political intentions."[109]

Casinos were used for gambling, but above all they were thought of as community organizations for social interaction. Every casino had a reading room, mainly for daily newspapers, and some had well-stocked libraries that provided opportunities for educating their respective communities. Parties and balls for members and invitees were also frequent activities. On these occasions casinos opened their doors to women and children, and thus became spaces for polite sociability. Most casinos institutionalized certain celebrations as part of their yearly calendar of activities.

Casinos also promoted cultural activities such as concerts, zarzuelas, theater performances, public talks, and even political speeches. In the beginning owners of casinos avoided political or religious affiliations to remain apolitical. Additionally, many included articles in their bylaws that prohibited political or religious discussion among members. However, since the members of these institutions were educated people, some of them highly politicized, political discussion was inevitable. For example, it was not possible for Madrid's casino to escape politics since its members included people like the Marquis of Salamanca, General Juan Prim, Antonio Cánovas, and Práxeles Mateo Sagasta—all central figures in nineteenth-century Spanish political life. After the 1870s, many new casinos based on political or religious affiliations were founded, and by 1895 at least 165 of the 2,000 casinos registered in Spain professed an ideological identification.[110]

In contrast, athenaeums promoted cultural, scientific, and political debate as well as scholarship, with the ultimate goal of contributing to the moral and intellectual formation of citizens. Urban institutions established by public initiative, athenaeums were the most influential and durable institutions of the nineteenth-century bourgeois public sphere in Spain.[111] The first were established at the beginning of the century, to some extent as a continuation of eighteenth-century Enlightenment economic societies and academies.[112] The first athenaeum opened in Madrid in 1835 and became a model to export to other parts of Spain.[113] After 1830, the number of athenaeums expanded, reaching a peak at the end of the century. After Madrid, they appeared in León, Cádiz, Coruña, Badajoz, and Barcelona. By midcentury, there were fifty-four active athenaeums in Spain's provincial capitals and major cities. Polite society required the *hombre fino* to participate knowledgeably in conversation about literature, science, and politics. The athenaeum was the place where the up-and-coming bourgeois acquired the cultural capital needed to succeed in the circles of *sociedad de buen tono*.

Of course, the goals of athenaeums were more far-reaching than simply providing symbols and tools to foster performance in polite society. In a country where academic institutions remained attached to and controlled by tradition, the athenaeums represented alternative platforms for freedom. Their organization and practices were democratic, endorsing individual rights in contrast to corporate practices of established universities. Athenaeums also promoted academic innovation and initiatives to galvanize change.[114] The athenaeum of Madrid, for instance, endowed a number of professorships in a variety of disciplines, some which had yet to be offered in the traditional curriculums of established universities.

Following a trajectory similar to that of casinos, in the second half of the century and up to the 1930s some new athenaeums adopted ideological or religious orientations. By the beginning of the Spanish Civil War, there were about five hundred athenaeums in different parts of Spain.[115] Early athenaeums, created by the liberal bourgeoisie, had been inspired by the rational scientific tradition of the Enlightenment. However, after the revolutions of 1868, the social composition and ideological orientation of athenaeums became more diverse, and working-class, republican, and socialist athenaeums appeared. The revolution caused athenaeums to become less academic and more oriented toward the left politically, which alienated substantial segments of the conservative bourgeoisie. Athenaeums attracted professionals and intellectuals with advanced ideas and positions, but did not have a following among financiers, entrepreneurs, managers, or even large segments of the petit bourgeoisie.

Commitment to intellectual community accentuated the academic character of athenaeums. Manuel Azaña, president of the Second Republic, declared that the main mission of the athenaeum was to "activate scientific inquisitiveness among youth attending the university."[116] Situated at the vanguard of intellectual life, they became one of the main platforms for political activism against the old liberal state, which was controlled by a conservative bourgeoisie. In these circumstances, the enlightened rational-liberal spirit that inspired the first athenaeums was swept away by the impulse of the new experimental ideologies arising in the context of mass society. Athenaeums were key forums for the spread of democratic republicanism, the liberalization of social practices, and the introduction of social justice. Politicization may have enriched the intellectual life of some athenaeums, but in general it brought polarization and sectarianism to the life of an institution whose original purpose was the promotion of freedom and unity.

Madrid's athenaeum was not only the first but also the most active and innovative. It introduced poetic soirées in 1876, and hosted public talk series in 1878. In 1880, the athenaeum began celebrating anniversaries of symbolic importance for Spanish national identity, such as the fourth centennial of Columbus's first voyage to the New World and the first publication of *Don Quixote*.[117] Barcelona did the same thing, except that the effort focused on the building of a Catalonian identity.[118] The daily life of these institutions flourished, with members making use of libraries and reading rooms, and taking advantage of a large variety of culture events such as discussion groups, conferences, presentations, art exhibits, and musical concerts and plays. A small number of athenaeums have survived to the present day thanks to their libraries, which were at the center of athenaeum life; the case of Madrid is the best example. Besides promoting intellectual debate, athenaeums also sponsored scientific laboratories, art exhibits, and university extensions.

Museums and art expositions had, since the late eighteenth century, provided venues for civic entertainment, sociability, and the acquisition of cultural capital for the middle classes. Expositions of art and antiques were linked to the development of art collecting, a practice that changed during the nineteenth century when middle classes joined the collectors' market. Oscar Vazquez has demonstrated that in Spain as in the rest of Europe, between 1830 and 1870 an unprecedented expansion of printed texts and manuscripts dealing with different aspects of art collecting reached a wide circulation.[119] While this phenomenon began in Spain later than in France and England, by the second half of the nineteenth century the main Spanish cities had established art markets that served a public that increasingly integrated members of the bourgeoisie. Auctions and private galleries, well-established in London before 1850, did not appear in Barcelona and Madrid until the last years of the century. Nonetheless, new practices of art and antique acquisition reached segments of society never before involved in that kind of consumption.

Much decorative arts purchasing still took place in unregulated and informal markets served by local fairs and itinerant vendors. Yet, since the 1830s, Madrid and Barcelona had shops specializing in paintings, antique furniture, and other objects of art—such as the *tiendas* on Montera Street in Madrid.[120] These shops proliferated with demand. This heightened interest in art and antiques was spurred by two significant developments: first, the work of the official academies and museums to enhance artistic education and sponsor artistic production; and second, the influence of the press, which included art critiques and promoted art events, young artists, and art museums as part of their modernizing agenda.[121] The new liberal state also sponsored art through its support of institutions such as the Royal Academy of Arts of San Fernando and the Prado Museum—called Museo Real de Pintura y Escultura—which opened November 19, 1819. Although entry was initially restricted—it was open only one day a week and visitors needed special permission from the royal administration—in a few decades it became a national museum, open to all citizens.

While the Prado was not the first public museum created in Spain it was certainly the most important. New liberal states used institutions like museums to articulate a unified national identity and effect its citizens' incorporation into modernity. Museums are part of the "realm of memory" defined by Pierre Nora: they are symbols of collective remembrance representing a specific community. The Prado, for example, featured national artists whose work highlighted national themes.[122] Before they became spaces for education and entertainment of the masses in the first third of the twentieth century, museums were spaces used mainly by the middle classes to display civility and modernity. Museums, as spaces for civility and refined sociability, played a role in the acquisition of respectability.[123]

In nineteenth-century Spain, the major museums were located in Madrid. The earliest was the National Museum of Natural Sciences, which opened to the public in 1815. Originating in the Cabinet of Natural History established by King Charles III in 1772, it had been a restricted museum since 1776. It contained objects from the royal and private collections as well as diverse items collected by scientists and archaeologists. The Natural Sciences Museum was first located on Alcala Street, in the Royal Academy of Arts of San Fernando. In 1901, the museum moved to its current location on the Paseo de la Castellana as part of a new urban project to create Madrid's first scientific park. Its arrangement followed the Victorian model, with showcases displaying minerals, insects, and plants, elaborate dioramas, and exotic dissected animals. In 1867, its archaeological objects were moved to a different site to establish the National Museum of Archaeology, inaugurated four years later by King Amadeo de Saboya. In 1895, the Museum of Archaeology was definitively installed in a new complex of buildings near the new National Library, where it remains today.[124]

The Prado Museum, established in 1819 with paintings and sculptures from the royal collections, soon became an institution of international reputation. It was Spain's main museum and the only one in the country comparable to the major museums in Europe.[125] The National Library and the Museum of Archaeology were conceived in the 1860s, but they took close to thirty years to complete, so until the 1890s the Prado was the symbolic centerpiece of a complex of buildings and gardens dedicated to the arts and sciences in the capital of the new liberal state. Further, the Glorious Revolution of 1868 had transformed the institution into a public national museum open to all citizens. By the beginning of the twentieth century, Madrid had three emblematic cultural sites—the Prado and the Archaeological and the Natural Science museums—symbols of progress made toward the re-creation of a city to represent Spanish national civilization and modernity.[126]

THE APPEAL OF HEDONISM AND HYGIENE

In addition to its practice of cultivated leisure, nineteenth-century bourgeois culture also had a hedonistic and hygienic side. Some forms of bourgeois leisure activity, such as traveling to new places, combined intellectual enrichment with sensuality. Others, for example, summer vacationing, pursued the relaxation of the spirit and the pleasure of the senses. The bourgeois obsession with health and hygiene was manifest in this social group's preoccupation with the care of the body. In the following sections we will consider these aspects of the bourgeois experience by looking at the birth of modern tourism as an outcome of the bourgeois practice of vacationing, and the spread of modern sports as a result of bourgeois concern with the body.

Vacations and Tourism

In the summer of 1871, the journalist Julio Nombela pointed out in his weekly magazine column that recreational traveling was becoming contagious. He wrote, "Judging by the aspect of Madrid this summer and the activity we see in seaside resorts anyone would think that we are prosperous and joyful."[127] Two weeks later, the same journalist wrote his weekly contribution from a beach in the Basque Country where he was vacationing. "The English," wrote Nombela, "have passed to us the practice of summer traveling . . . [In the summer] Madrid is a jail for the imagination; emotions are as necessary as food; it is convenient to travel. Traveling is life. Here you find an old friend; there you make some new acquaintances; in an unexpected place and moment you have an exciting adventure; in that location you engage in a quarrel; in that other you help a lady to escape from an embarrassing situation; in a hotel you forget your wallet; all this revitalizes, enhances conversations; one has occasions for clapping, laughing, crying; in travels there is life, there are emotions."[128] Nombela's eloquent words express the meaning and purpose people like him attached to summer vacations and the practice of tourism in general.

Modern tourism arose in the tradition established by the English aristocratic classes of undertaking a European Grand Tour. At a certain age, affluent youngsters traveled southward to through the main regions of the Continent, the intent being that they would learn from the art, history, language, and taste of continental Europeans, but also to enjoy the rewards that travel promised. During the nineteenth century, the Grand Tour tradition was embraced by many other elites across Europe, and became an extended practice among the bourgeoisie. Historians estimate that during the nineteenth century less than 10 percent of Europeans could afford to travel for pleasure.[129] In southern Europe that proportion might have been even lower. Nonetheless, Nombela's slightly inflated comments demonstrate a tendency beginning in the nineteenth century and expanding up to present day—in a recent poll in Spain 59 percent of people interviewed reported traveling to a foreign country at least once in their life, and 61 percent confirmed habitual travel for vacation.[130]

Historians find the first hints of modern tourism during the Renaissance. Travel was of course not new, but what defines modern tourism is the motif for engaging in travel.[131] In ancient and medieval times people traveled for religious reasons, to obtain economic necessities, or to escape war and disease. Almost nobody traveled for pleasure, and it was not widely considered an act of social distinction. During the Renaissance, voyages of discovery captivated the imaginations of the well-to-do, and gave new meaning to the idea of travel. Travel came to be associated with discovery, research, science, and education. At the same time, kings and courtiers popularized the idea of countryside palaces for seasonal escapes.

In England, travel to the Continent became a requisite for gentlemanly identity. Travel became what Marc Boyer calls an "invention of distinction."[132] Young men all over Europe wanted to emulate the practice of English tourism. Travelers of the Grand Tour, in search of the historical and cultural roots of Western civilization, became the epitome of the modern tourist.[133] In England people also began traveling to health spas. Bath was one of the most famous of these. Starting in 1709, Beau Nash, the master of ceremonies at Bath, made the spa one of the most fashionable places in Europe. In the ancient Roman baths it was possible to combine medical treatment while participating in an atmosphere of refinement and elegance.[134] In Bath the aristocracy socialized with the petit bourgeoisie as long as everyone accepted the established codes of genteel behavior.

Bath transformed itself into the second most important center for conspicuous consumption (after London).[135] Visits to fashionable spas became a central part of the Grand Tour itinerary. According to Boyer, the invention of the spa and the tradition of the Grand Tour were synchronic processes that brought about a "touristic revolution" simultaneous to all the other revolutions that characterized the progress of Great Britain in the eighteenth century.[136]

Whether the influence of Bath was as important as historians maintain, the truth is that on the other side of the Channel there were spas functioning as therapeutic centers and vacationing resorts since the last third of the eighteenth century. A guide to the Belgium spa baths published in 1782 stated that of the more than two thousand foreign visitors that year only two hundred were there for medical reasons. The rest were attracted by "curiosity, leisure, the desire of breathing fresh air; some wanted to enjoy the atmosphere of freedom of the place, others were looking for games."[137] In the first half of the nineteenth century, spas became popular from the Iberian Peninsula to eastern Europe. First was the inland spa, often situated by mountains, and next came the seaside spa, known in Spain as *baños de ola* or *oleaje* (baths of sea wave).[138] A variety of small old baths mainly in central Europe were helped by visits from members of the royalty, the aristocracy, and the bourgeoisie. Baden Baden, Homburg, Wiesbaden, and Aix-en-Savoy are some of the names resounding in the history of the spa by the luxury of their installations and the quality of their services.

The expansion of the spa came from three main impulses. The first one was economic growth from industrialization, making it possible for the middle classes to engage in new forms of consumption. Without the existence of new social groups with enough acquisitive power the growth of spas would not have happened.[139] The second impulse came from science. Concerning the use of the spa as a health practice there were two scientific schools in vogue during the nineteenth century: hygienics and balneology (or balneotherapy). Hygienists saw the new city's poor sanitation systems, insufficient air circulation, and stressful lifestyles as major factors contributing to contagious and nervous diseases, for which spa treatment was recommended. Balneologists concluded that mineral waters had medical properties capable of curing diseases.[140] People went to spas to drink medicinal waters (crenotherapy), to take baths (hydrotherapy), and to relax in a quiet place that was close to nature, with fresh air, comfortable lodging, and an exciting social life.[141] This combination of therapy, leisure, and refined sociability points to the third impulse leading to the proliferation of spas in the nineteenth century. As Dominique Jarrassé writes, the spa evolved into a prototypical space for the implementation of bourgeois cultural modernity—similar to the theater, the opera, and the pleasure garden. The main function of the spa was to improve personal physical and mental health, a purpose that was in tune with bourgeois ideals.[142] The romantic movement, with its emphasis on the genuine and its fascination with nature, also helped popularize the spa. Spas tended to be located in picturesque settings, with water flowing from mysterious dark cavities or exuberant falls, and visitors relaxed amid leafy forests or creatively landscaped gardens. Such settings were widely acknowledged to evoke emotions, sensitivities, and even patriotic identities.[143] Balneology was linked to the beginnings of mountain sports in the Alps and the Pyrenees, another essential component of the development of modern tourism.[144]

By the second half of the nineteenth century, a large number of European spas were transformed into bourgeois summer vacation centers.[145] The old sanatorium spa had almost totally disappeared. In the new baths of the end of the century, ballrooms and playrooms were as important as the hydrotherapy rooms. A visitor at Wiesbaden, the most popular European spa around 1900, could enjoy long walks through the Roman and medieval remains, gamble in the Kursaal, go hunting, attend the theater, or appear at one of the several balls available every night. Of course, they could also stop by the baths to take the worldwide famous mineral waters.

The seaside spa was also an important aspect of bourgeois tourism. Doctors and chemists had emphasized the curative qualities of seawater since the eighteenth century. Seawater therapy was founded in three convictions: first, that salty cold water was better for some treatments; second. that sea wave massages had healing properties; and third. that the relaxation of a sea bath and the quietness of the seacoast helped in the treatment of nervous conditions.[146] English doctors pioneered this therapy, and established the early paradigms of knowledge. English patients were the first to take advantage of systematic treatments of drinking seawater. Doctors thought that drinking saltwater could also protect the glandular system, and eliminate "body impurities and viscosities." Sea baths were believed to help skin conditions, strengthen muscles, and cure impotence and infertility.[147]

It would be an exaggeration to say that in nineteenth-century Spain there was a "touristic revolution," yet Spain made interesting contributions that anticipated the developments of the twentieth century.[148] While Spain's adoption of this modern trend occurred in the 1960s, its nineteenth-century roots can be traced to the subtle ascent of the middle classes. Bourgeois tourism and vacationing started in the 1820s and found its moment of maturity during the Restoration (1874–1923) in the last third of the nineteenth century. The historical steps taken by the social groups who popularized this practice in Spain were similar to those in the rest of Europe. There were three main elements. It began with summer vacations in villas or rural houses in the countryside near the cities. Next came seasonal stays in inland spas or seaside spas. The third step involved Grand Tours, lengthy long-distance international vacations. In this development the expansion of the railway in the 1860s was a crucial factor—specially the building of the Madrid-Irun line in 1864.

Since the 1830s, writers and journalists reported the exodus that occurred every summer in the major cities in Spain, especially Madrid. Most well-to-do groups escaped from Madrid and Barcelona during the hottest weeks of the summer to vacation in nearby countryside areas. This practice would influence future suburbanization. In Madrid, there were a series of preferred locations. The most exclusive were El Escorial and La Granja, both with long traditions of distinguished vacationing that featured royal palaces. Less exclusive were the villages of Pozuelo and Carabanchel, where some old and new aristocratic families possessed estates styled after Italian villas or British country houses. Some members of the upper bourgeoisie emulated this tradition. For instance, in 1859, José de Salamanca acquired Maria Cristina's former royal palace in Vista Alegre, near Madrid, to transform it into a sumptuous summer villa.

The least exclusive summer country spots were the small agrarian villages in the proximity of the city. Journalists viewed these middle-class locations with ambivalence. For instance, the columnist for the *El Museo Universal,* Raimundo Fernández-Cuesta, saw Getafe as well-connected by train and stagecoach to Madrid, with a decent supply of lodging, enjoyable cereal fields, and pure air.[149] The same reporter mentioned other places in southern Madrid such as Valdemoro, Leganés, and Navalcarnero with similar conditions. The Sierra, located on the north side of Madrid, was still an economically depressed region in comparison to the more prosperous agrarian plains south of Madrid. Other writers showed less enthusiasm for the dusty villages south of the capital. Mesonero Romanos in his travel book *Recuerdos de viaje por Francia y Bélgica* considered the surroundings of Madrid of an unbearable rusticity compared with what he sought in Paris and Brussels.[150]

In their study of the bourgeoisie of Valencia, Anaclet Pons and Justo Serna describe the summer villas of prominent families in the proximities of the city. In contrast to the nobility, who built houses as symbols of power, the bourgeoisie built places to escape from the city's insalubrious environment. At the same time they were spaces for the practice of refined sociability, and symbolized distinction. For instance, Gaspar Dotres's villa near the village of Godella was mentioned in the first travel guides for the city published in the 1840s.[151] These villas were not necessarily profitable investments; their surplus was attained mainly in the form of symbolic capital. In the summer, Dotres's villa became a center for exquisite sociability and was renowned for its social parties with theater performances and music concerts.

Spanish villas were also spaces for family reunion, symbolically important at a time when modern apartments for nuclear families began to replace the traditional large houses of the bourgeois extended family. Above all, the villas allowed the affluent to spend the summer months in leisure, far from the routines of urban life. By the 1830s, the habit of taking summer vacations away from the city began to include the middle classes, whether they owned their villas or rented them.[152] At present Spain is the country in Europe with the most houses per inhabitant, a high portion of which are owned by middle-class Spaniards as second homes for vacations—a practice that emerged in the nineteenth century.

Owning a villa was nonetheless the privilege of a few; most Spanish nineteenth-century vacationers rented rural houses or single rooms, or, most likely, found their lodging in spa resorts. Balneology flourished in Spain after the mid-eighteenth century. New spas combined spaces for both drinking water and taking baths. The main resorts, such as Solán de Cabras, Trillo, and Caldas, were built by well-known architects and many of these places were promoted by institutions and initiatives of the Enlightenment to stimulate regional modernization—such was the case for the Basque Society of the Friends of the Country and the Vergara Seminar.[153] Gómez de Bedoya registered up to forty establishments in Spain after 1750.[154] None of them were as famous as Bath, but they were intensely popular among Spanish elites. In 1817, the government dictated the first legislation for the functioning of Spanish spas, completed with an additional bill in 1834. Since that moment and up to the 1930s, the number of spas continued growing. Pedro María Rubio in his *Tratado Completo de Aguas Minero Medicianles,* published in 1853, registered the existence of 103 spas. In

1884, the number was 146, and 8 years later, in 1892, that number rose up to 152 with a total of 152,000 visitors, according to the data in the guide written by Federico de Botella y Hornos.[155] Using different historical sources, it is possible to ascertain who went to the spas, what these establishments were like, and how Spanish baths contributed to the history of modern tourism.

Dominique Jarrassé writes that mid-nineteenth-century spas functioned as the "parlors of Europe": chosen centers of sociability frequented by polite society during the summer season.[156] This assertion also applies to Spanish spas. Up to the 1830s, spas in Spain were places mainly to receive medical treatment. However, the relaxing nature of the treatment combined with their seasonal locations made spas attractive to everyone; the spa would prove beneficial for visitors, sick or healthy. By the mid-nineteenth century, baths became popular vacation spots. This transformation is reflected in public and personal accounts. The travel diaries of José Inocencio del Llano, member of a prominent bourgeois family of nineteenth-century Valencia, describe his visit to the spa of Panticosa during the summer of 1854. Del Llano chose Panticosa for its location in the Pyrenees, its specialization in respiratory illnesses, and its popularity among the affluent classes of the time. The Pyrenees, according to Pons and Serna, became a favorite destination for bourgeois vacationers who were discovering the joys of high mountain activities.[157] Panticosa was far from Valencia, more than six days' travel on difficult roads, yet del Llano arrived there with other distinguished members of his Valencian social circle who decided to vacation in the same distant spot.

In 1854, Panticosa offered an attractive social life along with modern lodging, first-quality medical services, an exuberant environment, and entertainment. The spa had a new lodge called Casa de la Pradera (House of the Prairie), where del Llano rented two rooms for his stay.[158] The lodge had been completed two years earlier and del Llano notes the cleanliness and space of the rooms. The dining room had large round tables to foster social interaction among guests.[159] He recognized that Panticosa was not yet a "city spa," but its installations were comparable to the average or above average European offering. Del Llano describes the typical daily routine of the spa user. Guests got up early to drink the waters before breakfast. The morning was spent taking baths, walking, and drinking until lunch. After lunch, at minimum a one-hour nap was recommended. In the afternoon there was more walking and drinking until the hour for mail collection. Around five thirty, it was time for *merienda* (snack) and leisure activities. Some used that time for reading, writing letters, engaging in early evening gatherings at the piano room, or going outside to row in a boat, shoot pistols, or walk in the promenades of the spa garden. Dinner was served at eight, and after dinner guests indulged in games and occasional balls.[160] Out of this routine the best fitted and more adventurous took hiking excursions, even to the permanent snows of the Gabarnie's glacier.

Del Llano's account at midcentury recounts the beginnings of the spa fever in Spain, the peak of which would happen later, during the Restoration years after 1874. In fact, Panticosa achieved its greatest period between 1880 and 1930, when the site reached the level of *ciudad balneario* (city spa). By that time, it had expanded to accommodate more than fifteen thousand visitors. In the 1870s, the spa's medical team included several internationally renowned specialists in balneology. In 1868, the Casa de la Pradera was transformed into a grand hotel with all the amenities and services offered in the best European spas. Lodging was expanded with boarding houses, and bed and breakfasts affordable to middle-class patrons. Cafés, restaurants, gardens, and other forms of entertainment also opened to serve the demands of an international clientele, mainly from Spain and France. The building in 1875 of a church under the advocacy of Our Lady of Panticosa and Saint Nicholas gave the site the official character of *villa* (village). The development of railroad lines near the spa, as well as regular stagecoach (and later bus) service, contributed to the site's prominence.[161]

The example of Panticosa reflects other cases in the spa history of Spain. A grand hotel was the starting point for creating a tourist center. As Urkia Etxabe has argued, the difference between second-rank places serving local clients, and centers for interregional or international tourism, was the hotel. Once the hotel was built, the management of the spa shifted from doctors to owners, and the focus from medical installations to vacation services.[162] The grand hotel usually included a casino, ballrooms, a theater auditorium, a restaurant, and side gardens. By looking at the construction of grand hotels in Spain after 1880, there were three main areas of spa expansion: Catalonia, Cantabria, and the Basque Country. These were the areas with the most renowned fin de siècle spas—Cestona, Vichy, L'Espluga, Liérganes, and Puente Viesgo. Grand hotels were not totally limited to certain areas; in fact, they arose all over Spain.[163] Molina Villar, writing about Catalonia, has demonstrated that spas fostered the development of regional economies and societies. The large spas contributed to the modernization of provincial life in many ways. The *ciudad balneario* (city spa) transformed agrarian economies into service economies, contributed to the custom of vacationing during the summer, and created new urban architectonical forms and new forms of entrepreneurship. It is true that very few Spanish spas reached the international prestige of the grand European spas. But, the spa was an essential institution in the process of Spanish modernization and the hegemony of middle-class culture.[164]

We can better observe the contribution of Spain to the history of vacationing and tourism in Europe by looking at the seaside. Seaside resorts developed in Spain at the same time as those on the Dutch Baltic coasts and the German coasts of the North Sea.[165] Spanish seaside resorts began appearing in the 1820s and were well established by the 1840s.[166] Because the seaside offered the curative properties of salty cold water, Spanish spas were first established in the cold waters of the north and not on the Mediterranean. English tourism to the French Riviera and the French Midi was not sea bath–motivated; it was a practice of escape from cold northern winters.[167] The myth of exceptional medical qualities of Cantabrian seawaters attracted the aristocracy first and the bourgeoisie later to the beaches of San Sebastian and Santander, and other smaller places such as Zarauz, Deva, Abra, Lequeitio, and Laredo.[168] The first visitors to these Sebastian beach were clients of the inland spas by the mountains, mainly from Cestona, who wanted to test the benefits of seawater. Most visitors came from Madrid, and one of the main stagecoach companies in the country established the first direct regular service Madrid-Irún to shorten to five days a journey that previously took a whole week.[169]

In 1830, San Sebastian became the summer destination of some members of the royal family, culminating with the presence of Queen Isabel II after 1854. Thus, since the 1850s, San Sebastian was the favorite summer destination of Spanish *sociedad de buen tono*, with a strong presence of Madrilenians. Social and leisured life of the Spanish capital was transported during the summer months to San Sebastian, which featured military parades, music concerts, operas, and fireworks. In 1864, the Madrid-Irún-Paris railroad made it possible to travel from the capital to San Sebastian in one day. Further, the urban remodeling plan referred to as the Plan Cortázar transformed what was a mercantile and fishing town into a modern, elegant, and fancy city with modern accommodations.[170] This urban reform included hotels, casinos, boulevards, cafés, restaurants, seaport marinas, and one of the best hippodromes in Spain.

When in August 1871 the journalist Julio Nombela arrived by train in San Sebastian to cover his traditional summer reporting, he could not find a place to stay. All of the elegant hotels and comfortable lodging houses in the new part of the city were booked, so he had to accept a room in a less fancy boarding house in the old town. The whole city, he wrote, was a party: "there are announcements in every corner for opera, theater, equestrian and acrobatic circus, excursions by boat to Santa Catalina Island, balls and concerts in the Kursaal, roulette in the Indo palace, and on Thursdays and Sundays military bands and fashion parades in the Glorieta square."[171] And still the city had not yet reached its peak as a tourist destination. That moment arrived between 1880 and 1930, with the building of the Royal Palace of Miramar, the Grand Casino, and a number of grand hotels and other amenities that transformed San Sebastian into one of the most attractive European tourist resorts of the Belle Époque.[172]

"Sea wave" tourism attracted people to other cities and villages of northern Spain as well. In 1900, tourist guides registered up to twenty-one seaside resorts in the northern Atlantic coast of the Iberian Peninsula, three in the French coast and eighteen in the Spanish side. Santander was the second most important seaside resort after San Sebastian. It was a safer place during the Carlist wars, and would feature the presence of the royal family at the end of the century. Its seaside offerings were the initiative of a number of families from the city's bourgeoisie who sponsored the transformation of El Sardinero beach into a sea spa. Santander as a seaside resort reached its peak around 1908 with the construction of the royal palace of La Magdalena and the presence there of King Alphonse XIII every summer.

On the other side of the peninsula, in the Mediterranean, some areas initiated a development similar to the French Riviera, though on much smaller scale. Since the eighteenth century, the Andalusian city of Malaga and its coastal counties attracted a number of English tourists. Some were Grand Tourists, others connected to international trade networks of Mediterranean products established in that part of Spain. These groups chose the future Costa del Sol not for the therapeutic quality of seawater, but rather for its mild Mediterranean climate. These travelers pioneered the touristic explosion in the region after 1960.[173] Cadiz and Sanlucar were also early touristic places, promoted by local bourgeoisies who built villas in beach areas and attracted the interest of some aristocrats from northern Europe. By the end of the century, some segments of the Madrid middle class started to vacation on the eastern coast of Spain by the Mediterranean. Since 1860, journalists of *El Museo Universal*, later *La Ilustración Española y Americana,* when writing on summer vacation habits, had mentioned the attraction to Madrilenians of Cabañal beach in Valencia and the beach of Alicante. Historians generally assume that this process started in the 1960s, but what happened then reflected a much longer trend.

The Grand Tour also linked tourism in Spain with the rise of bourgeois culture. Some of these practitioners of international tourism left firsthand testimonies in their diaries, memoirs, and books. Historians of tourism emphasize the perspective of English and other northern Europeans traveling to the south. The most influential were young romantics from industrial cities looking for the authentic and the exotic. They found their "arcadias" in the French Riviera, in the countryside of the French Midi, in the exuberant alpine valleys, and, above all, in the exotic rural areas of Italy, Greece, and southern Spain. There was, however, another version of the European Grand Tour that helped define modern tourism. That version was the reverse of the northern European Grand Tour, as southern and eastern Europeans traveled from the exotic and less developed south and east to the modern urbanized and industrialized north and west.

José Inocencio del Llano undertook a reverse Grand Tour (1842–95). He traveled north from the Mediterranean city of Valencia. Pons and Serna note the frequency of accidental or planned encounters with members of his Valencian social circle as he visited tourist attractions in northern Europe. He ran into fellow countrymen on the boulevards of Paris, when visiting the exhibitions of London's Crystal Palace, or while at the Panticosa spa. On other occasions he went to specific places to meet up with friends and relatives who were also traveling for pleasure or for business.[174] It was not uncommon for families of the industrial bourgeoisie of Catalonia and the Basque Country to send their sons to English factories or French commercial houses to acquire experience in manufacturing or international finances.[175] Del Llano's account demonstrates a culture of traveling among the new Spanish middle classes similar to what historians of modern tourism have described for Britain and France. The difference is that these Spaniards, like their Italian, Portuguese, or Russian counterparts, traveled to the heart of advanced Europe seeking experiences of modernity.

The most meaningful episodes in del Llano's journeys were his repeated visits to northern Europe's capitals and most prosperous regions. He details his astonishment with the scientific discoveries and technological innovations on display at London's Great Exhibition of 1851. He enjoys the elegance of Parisian boulevards, but his account reflects the most excitement when he describes the stock market, the business district, and the variety of shopping.[176] Del Llano, like most young Spanish travelers, went to the prosperous urbanized and industrialized north in search of experiences of modernization. These "tourists of modernity" left abundant testimonies, and their perspective on the value of traveling offers fascinating insights into the history of modern tourism.

The expansion of the railroad after 1850 made travel more accessible to the new middle classes because of new forms of transportation.[177] International travelers shared their experiences with the distinguished summer vacationers in the Cantabrian beaches, the diverse clientele of the spas, and the most modest tenants of rooms in rural houses near the big cities: all were the pioneers of the modern practice of touristic traveling and vacationing. Once again we see how bourgeois habits spread during the nineteenth century have become essential components of the hegemonic culture of today's Spain.

Sports

As both practice and entertainment, sports form a substantial part of hegemonic Spanish culture. Sociologists characterize today's Spain as a sports-oriented society, and consider its culture of sport as one of the main features of Spanish modernity.[178] Historians of sport agree that present-day developments originated in the nineteenth century with rising prominence of the middle class.[179] The ubiquity of sport as a practice and as a business is yet another component of nineteenth-century bourgeois culture. The origin of modern sports-oriented society is linked to scientific discoveries of the body, the influence of hygiene theory, the expansion of education, and the commercialization of leisure.

In 1913, there were about 360 societies dedicated to the promotion of sports in Spain. The majority of these associations were football (soccer) clubs, though all sports of the time were represented and groups were spread all over the Spanish map. There were clubs in all provincial capitals and in many secondary cities, but major cities had the greatest numbers: Barcelona had the highest concentration with seventy-one associations, Madrid had twenty-seven, and Valencia had twenty-six. Membership in these sports associations was drawn mainly from the middle and upper classes.[180] Media coverage included twenty illustrated sports magazines and one newspaper in Barcelona, *El Mundo Deportivo*.[181]

Not counting the tradition in Spain, as in the rest of the Old Continent, of games that involved physical exercise and competition, the first writing about the benefits of sport appeared in the conduct manuals of the early nineteenth century. For instance, in *El hombre fino al gusto del día* there was a full chapter dedicated to horseback riding, the practice of which was recommended because it was healthy and distinguished.[182] The recommendation of physical exercise to remain healthy and presentable was a feature of all books devoted to elegance, taste, and manners. Ultimately, these references became more explicit and diverse—for example, bicycle riding was appropriate for men, but not women; tennis was recommended for young ladies, horseback riding for everyone. Some manuals even outlined specific etiquette for refined men and women to follow when undertaking certain sports.[183] The ideal bourgeois was to appreciate the value of sports as a practice of distinction as well as a way to maintain a healthy body.

The practice of modern sports in Spain originated with the army. Like in most places in Europe, the military in Spain understood and promoted the value of physical education for the formation of good professionals. They fostered pedagogical initiatives such as the Pestalozzian Royal Military Institute of Madrid, opened in 1806, which placed sports at the center of the educational curriculum. The first major sports educator and scholar was Colonel Francisco Amorós, Marquis of Sotelo (1770–1848), who helped create the aforementioned institute and devoted his professional career to writing, researching, and promoting physical education.[184] Because of his support of the French during the Napoleonic wars, Amorós was exiled in 1814, and spent most of his remaining years in Paris. There, around 1830, he opened one of the first public gymnasiums in the city.[185] In 1839, Amorós returned to his home in Valencia, commissioned by the Royal Society of Friends of the Valencian Country to create a program where members of the Spanish military could go to Paris and visit his installations and attend his lectures.[186]

This exchange led to the creation of the Central Gymnasium of the Guadalajara Military School in 1847. José Aparici, a pupil of Amorós's who participated in the exchange, published a number of manuals for physical education, promoted the opening of new gymnasiums in a variety of military venues, and organized the first competitions of shooting, swimming, and horseback riding within the army. King Alphonse XIII acknowledged Aparici's contribution at the Barcelona World Fair of 1888, offering a ceremony and a medal in his honor. Aparici's program of physical education spread beyond the military. Francisco de Aguilera, Count of Villalobos, was a key figure in this process. He left the army early in his career to promote the practice of physical exercise among civilians. In 1842, he published *Ojeada sobre la jimnasia* (Overview on gymnastics) in which he argued that exercise was a way to "make ourselves respected and even feared by other people around the world."[187] Aguilera opened the first public gymnasium in Spain in the 1840s, installed in a facility for the School for the Humanities in Madrid. The influence of the military in these nineteenth-century gymnasiums prevailed even when the owners and most of the clients were not members of the army or navy. Marcelo Sanz y Mariano Ordáx's installations on Prado Street of Madrid, opened in 1880, were considered the first grand gymnasiums in the history of the city—the Gimnasio Higiénico y Sala de Armas (Hygienic Gymnasium and Arms Room).[188]

Horseback riding, a practice essential for the military but also enjoyed by the aristocracy and the bourgeoisie, was other major factor in the spread of modern sports in the West. The transformation of horseback riding into a commercial form of entertainment occurred in Spain much later than in Britain and France.[189] The earliest known initiatives for horse racing in Spain took place in 1835, under the patronage of the Duke of Osuna, who used his estates near Madrid known as the Alameda de Osuna. In 1841, a group of aristocrats and members of the Madrid bourgeoisie established the Sociedad de Fomento de la Cría Caballar (Society for the Promotion of Horse Breeding) that organized its first race in 1843. Events sponsored by Sociedad de Fomento were staged in private estates and in the royal gardens of Madrid's Casa de Campo until the construction of the first hippodrome in 1846.

Horse racing moved to different locations within the city of Madrid and in other parts of Spain. The first hippodrome in Madrid and Spain was located in the continuation of Paseo de la Castellana, beyond the old wall that surrounded the city and close to the urbanized areas where the pleasure gardens were installed. It had all elements of modern horse race parks, including a restaurant and an outdoor stand for music. The life of this first hippodrome was short: in two years the site was closed and the land sold to build apartments. The second grand hippodrome in Spain opened in the Andalusian city of Jerez in 1868.[190] Horse racing finally matured as a form of commercialized leisure and modern sport with the construction of long-standing hippodromes in Madrid and Barcelona. The new hippodrome in Madrid was inaugurated in 1878, again in Paseo de la Castellana. Barcelona opened its horse race park in 1886 in the Gran Via of the *eixample*. During the last third of the nineteenth century, the government established norms for the regulation of horse racing and the number of initiatives and events expanded to many cities in Spain.

After 1880, the Spanish government started to take seriously the promotion of sports in Spain. In 1881, the state created the first sports school in Madrid for the formation of physical education instructors—the Escuela Central Gimnástica. Behind this pedagogical initiative were some of the early contributors to the promotion of civil sports in Spain. Its directors, Mariano Ordáx and Marcelo Sanz, one of the first school graduates, were also the owners of the Gimnasio Higiénico y Sala de Armas on Prado Street in Madrid.[191] Ordáx and Sanz sponsored a number of publications and groups related to the practice of sports. The government passed new legislative initiatives to back this activity. A series of bills between 1892 and 1894 introduced the requirement of physical education in school curriculums, endowed the first college professorships, raised the salaries of sports instructors, and established an academic degree in physical education.[192] Of special importance in introducing sports in schools was the role of the private Institución Libre de Enseñanza (Free Educational Institution). The Institución was the first school in Spain to require competitive sports and outdoor activities for graduation. It followed the experiences of some British, French, and German schools by introducing field trips to archaeological settings, natural parks, and other sites of scientific interest. The practice of dedicating Thursday afternoons for intra-school sport competitions and activities has been followed by many schools in Spain up to present day. An example of the contribution of the Institución to modern sports was the creation by alumni of the Madrid Foot-Ball Sky Club in 1895, later transformed into Madrid Foot-ball Club, and finally into Real Madrid FC.[193]

For all the activity happening in Madrid, the first large sports competitions in Spain took place in Barcelona at the 1888 World Fair. Among the attractions for the inaugural ceremonies of the fair there were horse, velocipede, and rowing races, *juegos de pelota* (ball games), and race walking competitions.[194] This event marks the beginning of Barcelona's leadership in the creation of civil initiatives for sport activities, in contrast to Madrid, where the spread of sports involved both the state as well as civil society. Barcelona's bourgeoisie was captivated by outdoor velocipede rides. They formed competitive velocipede clubs to bike in the countryside. Excursions were part of the agenda of civic and political groups interested in the construction of a Catalan national identity. Landscapes fascinated nationalists, and these early bicycles offered easy and healthy access to the countryside.

Cycling evolved as a powerful engine for the expansion of other sports among Barcelona's civil society. When the Sociedad Gimnástica Española (Gymnastic Spanish Society) was established in 1887, it was not a coincidence that three out of the four founding members were from Catalonia, one from a well-known industrial family of Barcelona.[195] This Society became the most active promoter of encounters, publications, and public speeches of the time. Its members sponsored the opening of gymnasiums and sports clubs in Barcelona and many other cities within Spain. Because of their dedication there were enough organizations and members in 1898 to transform the Sociedad Gimnástica into the most ambitious Federación Gimnástica Española (Gymnastic Spanish Federation). The Federación had chapters in sixteen provinces. At that point Barcelona produced six sports magazines and the first sports diary in Spain, while Madrid had five magazines. Football remained "foot-ball" instead of the Spanish *fútbol,* and Spaniards used the English term "sports," instead of the Spanish *deportes.* This lack of an autochthonous vocabulary indicates that sport continued to be the practice of a social minority, mainly upper and middle classes. Yet, before too long, Spain embraced football as a mass spectacle and national activity, joining other European nations in competition. Sports provide a critical and widespread manifestation of the historical transcendence of nineteenth-century bourgeois culture into the mainstream culture of modern Spain.

Conclusion

URRENT narratives of the history of nineteenth-century Spain, especially of the second half of the century, coincide in highlighting the central role played by the bourgeoisie. The culmination of the liberal state and its society in the system of the Restoration, after the Glorious Revolution of 1868, is described in history books as a bourgeois creation. At the same time, Spanish historians debate about the insufficient democratic, economic, and social achievements of this regime, and some attribute these insufficiencies to the many shortcomings of that social group. These historians find fault with the bourgeoisie due to their cultural and social subordination to the old aristocracy and the Catholic Church, the two main remaining forces of the Spanish Old Regime. According to this approach, bourgeois fascination with the lifestyles and value system of the aristocracy during the Restoration is an atavism characteristic of Spanish society, and the Catholic Church's turn toward reactionary anti-liberal positions is a factor behind the resistance to democratic reform among Restoration's political class. Consequently, these scholars portray the Spanish bourgeoisie as a timid and hesitant group that decided to side with the anti-modernizing and anti-democratic forces in order to secure its domination. This book demonstrates that this picture of the nineteenth-century bourgeoisie is only partially accurate.

It is true that Spain did not become a middle-class society until the 1960s, and that in comparison with most developed European societies of the modern era, its bourgeoisie was smaller and less influential within its own territory and, above all, in the international context. But the image of a social group that remained subordinated to the manners and styles of the old aristocracy, and that manifested less commitment to modernity than their European counterparts, does not fully respond to the reality depicted in this study.

Bourgeois admiration of aristocratic social rituals, conduct norms, and lifestyles was not exclusive to the Spanish. As a matter of fact, the fascination of the British and French middle classes for the aristocracy and the *beau monde* surpassed that of the Spaniards. The adoption of aristocratic forms of social behavior was not in contradiction with the establishment of a new and genuine bourgeois polite society. The bourgeoisie displaced the aristocracy from many of their positions of power but still admired their lavishness and chic. What marked the new bourgeois polite society as different is that it was open to wider social segments. In theory, any individual willing to adopt the norms established in conduct manuals automatically acquired gentility and was able to be part of exclusive society. The first step in the building of a bourgeois culture was the establishment and dissemination of gentility norms during the eighteenth century. As this book shows, bourgeois civility did not fully develop in Spain until the first third of the nineteenth century, but over the course of the century Spanish dominant groups made significant progress to catch up with European standards of conduct. In the early stages of this process Spaniards translated European manuals of behavior, transferring foreign molds only slightly adapted to the conditions of Spanish society. After 1850, a more genuinely Spanish set of conduct manuals reached the publishing market. These manuals reflected the characteristics of Spanish polite society—known by Spaniards as *sociedad de buen tono*. As in other parts of Europe, Spanish *sociedad de buen tono* was part of the bourgeois public sphere and was shaped by ideals drawn from a mix of aristocratic traditions and new bourgeois norms. Spanish *sociedad de buen tono* emerged as solid evidence of the imposition of bourgeois lifestyles in Spain.

Bourgeois culture was also a consumer culture as consumption was a central element of *buen tono*. In quantitative terms, consumer patterns of nineteenth-century Spain lagged far behind from those of the industrial societies of northern Europe. England was a mass consumer society by end of the nineteenth century, a stage that Spain did reach until the 1960s. But while Spanish consumption was limited, our evidence demonstrates that Spanish urban middle classes embraced a vigorous consumer culture beginning in the last third of the eighteenth century, following a path similar to that of other European societies. The main manifestations of the rise of consumer culture in

Spain were the adoption of the ideals of domesticity by wider segments of the urban middle classes, as well as a slow but steady expansion of varied consumer practices by the middle classes in the cities and the countryside.

The culture of domesticity is linked to the birth of the bourgeois home. By looking at a variety of historical sources—from probate family inventories to representations of the home in the novel, in conduct literature, and in journalism—we can see that by the second half of the nineteenth century the bourgeois home was both an ideal and a material reality. As a matter of fact, the actual transformation of house interiors into functional and comfortable bourgeois dwellings preceded the conceptualization of the bourgeois home as an ideal.

Inventory analysis also shows a modest but sustained rise of consumer practices. The middle classes of Madrid and Barcelona and other smaller urban centers display an increasingly varied material culture with the presence of diverse objects of gentility in their homes. Evidence about nineteenth-century consumer trends is still meager and sketchy, but what we know presents a picture of slow progress. The spread of consumer culture is more evident in other manifestations of the modernization of Spanish society, such as the development of a fashion press, a fashion industry, and the transformation of the retailing sector. Literary analysts have approached Spanish fashion literature from the perspective of women's and feminist studies. This book highlights this form of journalism as a manifestation of the spread of consumer culture in Spain. Successful magazines, besides being profitable businesses, played a decisive role in igniting consumer habits among the groups that could afford what they featured and advertised. Fashion magazines were a notable part of the new illustrated press that projected the aesthetic values, social habits, and psychological anxieties of the bourgeois groups. For the most part they propagated conservative visions of the social function of women and their position in the private and public spheres. But over time some of these magazines advocated a more dynamic role for women in modern society and even adopted feminist points of view. The evolution of fashion culture in Spain also reflects the ascent of Barcelona to become the main Spanish node of nineteenth-century bourgeois modernity. In the last third of the century, Barcelona arose as a contentious competitor with Madrid for the fashion market with the production of new successful fashion periodicals. Barcelona displaced

Cadiz from the role it had played up to the mid-nineteenth century as a fashion hub, reflecting the vitality of Catalonia as the most industrialized and socially developed region within Spain. Catalonia's lead in the development of middle-class consumer initiatives is palpable in the dynamism of Barcelona's shopping sector after 1850. The city surpassed Madrid as the major retailing nucleus in nineteenth-century Spain. The opening of the first Spanish department store in 1881 put Barcelona on a par with the most commercially advanced fin-de-siècle Western cities. All in all, the evidence compiled in this book demonstrates that Spain deserves to have a more explicit space within the historiography of the origins and evolution of Western consumer culture and the making of modern middle-class consumer society.

Final proof of the transcendence of bourgeois culture presented in this study is the role played by the bourgeoisie in the transformation of the nineteenth-century Spanish city and the development of the society of leisure. The city extensions (*ensanches*) developed in major Spanish urban centers during the second half of the century are seen as a way of adapting the cities to the social needs, aesthetic values, and political conceptions of the bourgeoisie. The new nineteenth-century Spanish city, with its straight avenues, artificial parks, and spaces for polite sociability, was a creation of the bourgeoisie, who considered urban improvement to be a sign of progress and a symbol of modernity. Since the early nineteenth century, the elites of Madrid and Barcelona engaged in open competition for the implementation of initiatives of urban modernity. In the second half of the century, Barcelona showed clear signs of being ahead in the game, as evidenced in the implementation of the *eixample,* the hosting of the World Fair in 1888, and the building of a diversity of public and private spaces for bourgeois social interaction. By the first third of the twentieth century, Barcelona became one of the most vibrant examples of urban modernism, the roots of which can be traced to the nineteenth century. This is not to say that Madrid failed as a bourgeois urban project. As this book has argued, the Madrilenian ruling groups pursued modernizing projects with the same energy, initiative, and goals as their counterparts in Barcelona. If they did not attain similar results it is because Madrid did not have a strong autochthonous bourgeoisie like that of Barcelona. The bourgeoisie of Madrid consisted of the Spanish political and business classes, integrated by people of diverse regional origins, not an industrial and commercial group of individuals born in the city or its surroundings, as was the case of Barcelona. Without a homogenous civic group to provide stable support, Madrid's urbanizing project was hostage to complicated political negotiations and slow and uneven funding.

In 1900, the dominant cultural system in Spain was that of the modernizing bourgeoisie. To modernize meant the homologation of Spanish society with the most developed societies of Europe. For that reason Spanish bourgeois culture was emulative in a significant portion of its conceptions and developments. Europeanism was a leitmotif omnipresent in the discourses and actions of Spanish bourgeois modernizers. To be like the developed societies of Europe meant to attain the level of prosperity and social welfare of the most economically and socially advanced countries of the time. The bourgeois was, for that reason, a culture that exercised an unquestionable attraction over wide segments of Spanish society, still underdeveloped and characterized by a deep divide between poor and rich.

Most of the elements of the bourgeois lifestyle studied in this book not only appealed to Spaniards of diverse social extraction, they specially served to create a common ground for the making of a bourgeois identity. Politics and religion divided the bourgeoisie. The exercise of *buen tono,* cultivated leisure, and consumerism gave this group a sense of belonging. Of course, in nineteenth-century Spain the material and spiritual joys of the bourgeois way of life were restricted to a minority who failed to create the economic and social conditions to ensure their spread to wider sectors of society. The country paid a high price for that failure in political instability, social turmoil, and repression during a large portion of the twentieth century. But the essence of the values, norms, habits, meanings, styles, and symbols that made up nineteenth-century bourgeois culture are today's hegemonic system of Spanish middle-class consumer society.

NOTES

CHAPTER ONE

1. Bestard de la Torre (1898) p. 224.

2. Curiously, some French cook books include a recipe called *galette des rois espagnole* or *gateau des rois espagnole*. This is a variation of what at present is still called *gateau des rois* and is baked in Provence. The *galette des rois* comes from the north and is the most popular in today's France.

3. I follow Manuel Castells's definition of identity as an "organizing principle . . . the process by which a social actor recognizes itself and constructs meaning." Castells (1996) p. 22.

4. For a good overview of recent historiography on modern Spain, see Cabrera (2005).

5. Ringrose (1996); Fusi and Palafox (1997); Vincent (2007).

6. See, for instance, Valis (2002); Parsons (2003); Labanyi (2005); Larson and Woods (2005); Resina (2008); Frost (2008).

7. Valis (2002) p. 11.

8. On the role of middle-class culture as a safeguard of social and political order, see Blumin (1989) p. 10; Bushman (1993) p. 402; Wahrman (1995) p. 12; Searle (1993); Grier (1997); Young (2003) p. 6.

9. Ringrose (1996) p. 392.

10. See Sebastiá and Piqueras (1987). On the bourgeois revolution debate in Spain, see Petit (1990); Cruz (1996) chap. VIII.

11. See Cabrera (2005) pp. 1000–1002.

12. Maza points out a striking resemblance of the bourgeois "other" with the American and the Jew in French society, groups all marked by "unearned privilege and cultural deficiency." See Maza (2003) pp. 13 and 195

13. On this revisionist point of view, see also Roche (1988); Darnton (1979) and (1990); Garrioch (1996).

14. Álvarez de Miranda (2001) pp. 15–21.

15. Pons and Serna (1997) p. 35.

16. Battaner (1977).

17. See Botrel and Le Bouil (1973).

18. In the language of some documents written during the seventeenth and eighteenth centuries, it is common to find expressions and concepts such as "el estado de los medianos," "estado de la medianía," or "el mediano estado." See Thompson (1991) p. 56.

19. See Jovellanos (2003); Toreno (2003); Goldman (1992) pp. 9–15.

20. Mesonero Romanos (1926) p. 14.

21. Bretón de los Herreros (1883) vol. 5, p. 501.

22. Pons and Serna (1997) pp. 36–37.

23. Gay (2002) pp. 4–5.

24. Romanelli (1997) p. 5; Romanelli (1991) pp. 717–39.

25. Jarvis (1997) p. 16; Decker (1997) p. 23.

26. Juan Manuel de Manzanedo y González made a fortune in Cuba trading in sugar and slaves as well as in the banking sector. In 1845, he moved to Madrid, where he achieved a political career and attained an aristocratic title. Eusebio Güell Bacigalupi, first Count of Güell, transformed his family into one of the wealthiest and most influential of early twentieth-century Spain. See Cayuela and Bahamonde (1991) pp. 60–72; Bahamonde and Cayuela (1992); McDonogh (1986) p. 213.

27. Shubert (1990) pp. 46–48.

28. Shubert (1990) pp. 110–16.

29. Villacorta Baños (1989).

30. Ringrose (1996) pp. 369–88; Bahamonde and Martínez (1994) p. 462.

31. Cruz (1996) chap. VIII.

32. Hughes (1993) p. 374.

33. Functional sociology based on quantitative analysis considers that Spanish society became middle class dominated only at the end of the 1960s. That was the moment when conventional middle-class occupations such as professionals, managers, government employees, agents, salesmen, foremen, and the self-employed became the largest single portion of Spanish social spectrum—40 percent in 1960, 70 percent in 2000.

34. On the role of consumer culture in the creation of discourses of modernity in Spain, see Labanyi's study on late nineteenth-century realist novel: Labanyi (2000) chap. 5.

35. See Hunt (1989) pp. 7–11; Appleby and Hunt (1994).

36. Martínez Martín (2003) pp. 1–17.

37. Fusi and Palafox (1997) p. 8; Ringrose (1996) p. 389.

38. See Burke (2004) pp. 2 and 33–37; Bonnell and Hunt (1999) pp. 3–7; Kuper (1999).

39. For a definition of culture, see Williams (1981) pp. 10–13; Hatch (1973).

40. Cohen (1994) pp. 206–7; Geertz (1973) pp. 6–12.

41. Valis (2002) p. 21.

42. Elias (1978) and (1983).

43. Bourdieu (1984) p. 111.

44. Jenkins (2002) pp. 84–85.

45. Bourdieu (1991) pp. 229–31; Bourdieu (1984) p. 254.

46. Bourdieu (1988) pp. 127 and 128.

47. The history of material culture has been quite prolific, above all in English-speaking countries and France. Among some of the most inspiring works for this study are Frykman and Löfgren (1987); Garrison (1991); Bushman (1993); Perrot (1995); Grier (1997); Hardyment (1997); Roche (2000); Brosterman (2000); Ulrich (2001); Briggs (2003).

48. See Mckendrick, Brewer, and Plumb (1982); Brewer and Porter (1993); Stearns (2001).

49. See Kotkin (2005); Gunn and Morris (2001); Czaplicka and Ruble (2003).

50. Parsons (2003); Frost (2008); Resina (2008).

51. See Daumard (1987) and (1996); Montclos (2005); Harrison (1999); Tiersten (2001); Bushman (1993).

52. Young (2003) p. 6.

53. Some of the most significant studies are Erice Sebares (1980) and (1995); Bahamonde (1981); Jutglar (1984); Ramos Santana (1987); Otazu (1987); Herán (1990); Maruri Villanueva (1990).

54. Gary McDonogh's (1986) study on the industrial elites of Barcelona was a pioneer of this genre. See also Pons and Serna (1992); Romeo Mateo (1993); Martínez López (1996); Baladía (2003); Pons and Serna (2006).

55. Valis (2002) chaps. 1 and 5; Frost (2008) pp. 21–23.

CHAPTER TWO

1. Barbazza, Simon Palmer, and Guereña (1995) pp. 103–93.

2. The first edition of *The Civilizing Process* (*Über den Prozess der Zivilisation*) in 1939 was virtually ignored. Elias's thesis started to be taken into account after 1969, when his works were translated into English. That is the reason for the scarce number of compilations on the history of conduct published between 1940 and 1980. Schlesinger (1946), Wildeblood (1965), and Aresty (1970) did not mention Elias's works and either focused on collective identities, or were mere descriptions of the evolution of manners in history. For an understanding of the impact of Elias in recent historiography, see Burke (2004) p. 2.

3. See Woodman (1989); Piper (1997); St. George (1993); Kelly (2001).

4. See Davidson (2004); Wouters (1995); Carter (2001).

5. See Kasson (1990); Newton (1994); Bryson (1998); Arditi (1998); Muchembled (1998); Goodwin (1999); Hemphill (1999).

6. See Lichter (1998); Himmelfarb (1995).

7. See Montandon (1994) and (1995); Duroux (1995); Blanco (1994); Guereña (1995).

8. See Laspalas (2003); Miguel (1995).

9. Blanco (1994) p. 113.

10. The Spanish translator of François de Callières was Ignacio Benito Avalle, and Francisco Mariano Nipho translated the manual of Marquis of Caraccioli.

11. Amann (2008) p. 96.

12. Bushman (1993) p. 37. Bushman states that as time went by, the courtly ideal extended beyond the court. By the end of the seventeenth century, the upper echelons of the English middle class were absorbing and adapting courtliness under the name of gentility. For Linda Young the culture of gentility broadened at the turn of the nineteenth century as it became linked to the growth of the middle classes as a product of self-control. People adopted self-controlled gentility for strategic reasons, for instance, in order to find personal identity in group affiliation and to improve both the physical and emotional aspects of their lives. Young (2003) pp. 4–6. Concerning the model of *l'honnête home,* see Montandon (1994) p. 402.

13. Feijóo (1863) p. 388.

14. Feijóo (1863) p. 388.

15. Feijóo (1863) p. 390.

16. Feijóo (1863) p. 391.

17. Feijóo (1863) p. 392.

18. Feijóo (1863) p. 394.

19. Feijóo (1863) p. 395.

20. Clavijo y Fajardo (1999) vol. 2, pp. 40–42.

21. Pons and Serna (1992) p. 215.

22. Mariano Rementería y Fica (1786–1841) was a writer born in Bilbao who lived in Madrid most of his life and wrote during the romantic period. He was a professor in the Escuela Normal, a mediocre writer, an uneven journalist, and a compulsive translator. Like most writers of the time, Rementería was a convinced liberal who suffered the consequences of realist repression in 1823. In one point of his life his main source of income was the translation of texts mainly from French. His death, wrote Antonio de Iza Zamacola, came early and in a non-romantic form: on December 15, 1841, on the corner of a street in Madrid by a sudden heart attack when he was taking an afternoon stroll. See Escobar Arronis (1970) p. 559.

23. The first edition of this manual appeared in Madrid (Imprenta de Moreno, 1829) with the long title *(El) hombre fino al gusto del día, ó manual completo de urbanidad, cortesia y buen tono, con las reglas aplicaciones y egemplos del arte de presentarse y conducirse en toda clase de reuniones, visitas, etc., en el que se enseña la etiqueta y ceremonial que la sensatez y la costumbre han establecido, con la guía del tocador y un tratado del arte cisoria.* For this chapter I have used the 1837 facsimile edition published by Maxtor in 2001.

24. Sebold (1992) p. 375. The term *dandi* did not appear in the dictionary of the *RAE (Real Academia Española)* until 1927 and was understood as an Anglicism of *petimetre.* In the edition of 1950 it is still considered an Anglicism but this time of *lechuguino* and *pisaverde,* concepts of derogatory meaning. It was not until the edition of 1983 that the word was no longer considered an Anglicism with negative connotations and was defined as a man who is distinguished by his extreme elegance and politeness.

25. In the 1732 *Diccionario de Autoridades* etiquette is defined as "the protocol for styles, uses, and customs that should be observed and respected in the royal houses, where the king and queen dwelled." The word was of French origin, specifically from the royal court of Burgundy from where it was introduced into Spain and other European countries.

26. Wouters (1995) pp. 108–9; Arditi (1998) p. 182.

27. Rementería (1837) p. iv.

28. Rementería (1837) p. 2.

29. Rementería (1837) p. 7.

30. Rementería (1837) p. 15.

31. Rementería (1837) pp. 27–30.

32. Rementería (1837) p. 72.

33. Rementería (1837) p. 75.

34. Rementería (1837) p. 76.

35. Rementería (1837) p. 176.

36. Rementería (1837) p. 177.

37. Manjarés (1854) p. 10.

38. Rementería (1837) p. 2.

39. Bestard de la Torre (1898) p. 100. Viscountess of Barrantes Bestard de la Torre was one of

the pseudonyms of Alfredo Pallardó (1851–1928), journalist and playwright of Catalonian origin. Pallardó was a clear example of a self-made man. He came from a working-class family. He started earning a living as an apprentice in a printing press, became a typesetter, rose to the position of proofreader, was a successful writer, and ended up as a journalist. He obtained a degree in philosophy and arts in only two years when he was forty. At this point Pallardó was already an acclaimed journalist and contributor to various national newspapers. In Madrid he founded the *Centro Catalán* (the Catalonian Center) and in Barcelona the magazine *Juventud Ilustrada* (Illustrated Youth). He wrote in Castilian and Catalan. He traveled extensively, translated from French, and of course had a fascination with the *beau monde* and polite society.

40. Bertrán de Lis (1859) p. 16.

41. Bertrán de Lis (1859) p. 18.

42. Colbert (2005) p. 34; Alharaca (1991) p. 13.

43. Alharaca (1991) p. 24.

44. Cabeza (1859) p. 36.

45. Bertrán de Lis (1859) p. 26.

46. Orberá (1875) pp. 18–22.

47. St. George (1993) p. 86.

48. Manjarrés (1854) p. 15; Aresty (1970) p. 169.

49. Jagoe (1994) p. 41.

50. Tasca (2004) p. 205.

51. Aresty (1970) p. 182.

52. Uría (2008) p. 254.

53. *La cortesanía* (1850) p. 8.

54. Day (1845) p. 23.

55. Dufaux (1890) p. 61; *La cortesanía* (1850) p. 88.

56. Pons and Serna (1992) p. 219.

57. Aresty (1970) p. 169; St George (1993) p. 114; Lichter (1998) p. 211.

58. Bestard de la Torre (1898) p. 43.

59. Fabra (1883) p. 31.

60. *La cortesanía* (1850) p. 42.

61. *La cortesanía* (1850) pp. 50–57.

62. Bestard de la Torre (1898) pp. 46–48.

63. Bestard de la Torre (1898) p. 68.

64. Mesonero Romanos (1991) p. 46.

65. Dufaux (1883) pp. 88–90; Rementería (1837) p. 98.

66. Bestard de la Torre (1898) p. 49.

67. There was a series of basic rules of etiquette for introductions that established the difference; for example, when making an introduction between a gentleman and a lady, the gentleman was always introduced, when making introductions between two gentlemen, the younger man was always introduced, and so on. Bestard de la Torre (1898) p. 70; Mata García (1885) p. 42.

68. For a recent reflection on the cultural dimensions of this process, see Labanyi (2005) pp. 168–70; Alvárez Junco (2001).

69. For Bestard de la Torre this was "one of the most delicate points of life in society." Bestard de la Torre (1898) pp. 192–95.

70. Rementería (1837) pp. 127–34.

71. Pons and Serna (1992) p. 161.

72. Muñoz López (2001) pp. 112–14.

73. See Bestard de la Torre (1898); Ossorio y Bernard (1997); Burgos (1897); Fabra (1883); Pomés Soler (1902).

74. Profeti (1995) pp. 203 and 208.

75. In the eighteenth century, it became fashionable among wealthy families to organize, after a stroll, a gathering, or *tertulia,* in their homes, which when accompanied with dance was called *sarao.* Saraos were quite expensive, since besides the customary refreshments consisting of the traditional chocolate, sponge cake, marzipan, and sweetened waters, they required a comfortable space for the dancers and the hiring of musicians. See Martín Gaite (1987) pp. 36 and 38.

76. *La cortesanía* (1850) p. 168.

77. Sánchez Moreno (1925) pp. 148–90.

78. See Otero (1912); Pons and Serna (1992) pp. 215–19; Frost (2008) pp. 316–17.

79. We find a good example in some manuals of *urbanidad* from the end of the nineteenth century in which sections are dedicated to rules of behavior for trains, carriages, streetcars, and other modern means of transportation. Osorio y Bernard (1897) pp. 18–21.

80. On the importance of the stroll, see Pons and Serna (1992) pp. 215–19.

81. Rementería (1837) p. 111.

82. *La cortesanía* (1850) pp. 64–66.

83. All the treatises on urbanity gave rules about how to care for the body in order to keep it elegant and clean, what in the language of the moment was called *toilette.* The first manuals specifically dedicated to elegance, hygiene, and cosmetics appeared after 1850. Toward the end of the century, there had already been assembled a wide range of literature dedicated to the care of the body that was summed up in texts of urbanity and etiquette, in texts on domestic economy, in fashion magazines, and in the daily press through advertising and sports sections.

84. See Fresquet Febrer (1990). The introduction of hygiene as an educational discipline is attributed to the Catalonian Pedro Felipe Monlau, author of the first Spanish manual of hygiene, published in Barcelona in 1846.

85. See Rementería and more explicitly the translation of the manual of Horace Raisson on elegance and hygiene published in 1849. See also Cabeza (1859); *El libro de las familias* (The book of families) (1856).

86. Raisson (1849) p. 7.

87. Raisson (1849) p. 35.

88. Dufaux (1890) p. 68.

89. Bestard de la Torre (1898) p. 95.

90. Burgos (1897) p. 103.

91. Almagro (1944) p. 221. Melchor de Almagro San Martín attributes this reflection to Pío Baroja.

92. The introduction to a popular manual of *urbanidad* and etiquette published only a few years before the arrival of the Second Republic clearly reflects this spirit: "The (World) War with all its devastation brought one more: the abrupt change of social positions, in which persons of little social stature introduced vulgar behavior adopted by youth originally as a way to have fun and developed into bad habits . . . Poorly understood love of foreign customs . . . has disseminated in some branches of society changes in the ways of conducting oneself that are hardly pleasant for sensible and educated persons . . . Our intention is that this book serves as a barrier against that overwhelming barrage of evil words and deeds." Sánchez Moreno (1925) pp. 6–7.

93. See *Nuevo manual de urbanidad* (The new manual of urbanity) (1850) pp. 11–12.

94. Ossorio y Bernard (1897) p. 20.

95. See Tasca (2004) p. 205.

96. Bestard de la Torre (1897) pp. 26–28.

97. Burgos (1877–1920); on the evolution of the education of women in the nineteenth century, see Escolano Benito (2001) pp. 9–39.

98. On children's urbanity in the nineteenth century, see Guereña (1995) pp. 287–304; Morales Muñoz (1995) pp. 277–85.

CHAPTER THREE

1. *El Hogar* (1867) p. 19. On this publication, see Sarasúa (1994) p. 20.

2. *El Hogar* (1866) p. 1.

3. The best example of this journalism oriented toward the family was *El Museo de las Familias*.

4. Flanders (2004) p. 4.

5. Rybczynski (1987) pp. 51f.

6. On this debate for the case of Spain, see Labanyi (2000) chaps. 1 and 2.

7. Bannet (2000) p. 23.

8. Archibald (2002). On the public and private spheres debate and the development of domestic novel, see Cohen (2005); Johnston (2001); Harrow (2004).

9. See Eiland (1996); Franits (1993) and (2004).

10. See Blanco (2001) p. 23; Jagoe (1998) pp. 26–28; Aldaraca (1991) chap. 1. In English-speaking societies this development was carried out by the evangelical movement and the Methodist and similar dissenting sects. See Davidoff and Hall (1987) chap. 2; Epstein (1981).

11. See Mckendrick, Brewer, and Plumb (1982) pp. 9–33; on the contents of this debate, see Clunas (1999) pp. 1497–1500; Stearns (2006); Gottdiener (2000) pp. 3–29.

12. Other home and family periodicals were *El Gabinete de Lectura gaceta de las Familias* (Madrid, 1841); *El Álbum de las Familias* (Barcelona, 1858); *El Hogar* (Madrid, 1866); *La familia: Revista del Hogar* (Madrid, 1876); *El Seguro de la Vida o Almanaque del Hogar* (Madrid, 1877); *El Amigo de Casa* (Madrid, 1877); *El Amigo del Hogar* (Madrid, 1880); *Semanario de las familias* (Madrid, 1882); *Tesoro de las Familias* compilation from *El Eco de la Moda* (Barcelona, 1890); *La Escuela y el Hogar* (Pamplona, 1893); *La Mujer en su Casa* (Madrid, 1902) *El Hogar y la Moda* (Barcelona, 1909).

13. Cabarrús (1990) p. 133. Some years ago Lawrence Stone postulated the expansion of a new

value system in the West founded on the principle of "affective individualism," which had a revolutionary effect on the conception of marriage and sentimental relations. Stone (1979).

14. Coontz (2005) pp. 146f. The origins of affective love for marriage is the object of an ongoing debate. Some historians argue that it existed before the eighteenth century. See Hartman (2004) chap. 8.

15. See Ariès (1973). Recent approaches to the history of childhood can be found in Stearns (2006) pp. 54–63; Heywood (2001) pp. 23–31.

16. On the evolution of the nineteenth-century Spanish population, see Tortella (1998) pp. 32–45.

17. Kirkpatrick (1989); Aldaraca (1991); Charnon-Deutsch (1994); Charnon-Deutsch and Labanyi (1995); Jagoe (1994); Bolufer Peruga (1998), Bolufer Peruga and Morán Deusa (1994); Labanyi (2000); Blanco (2001); Ballarín Domingo (2001); Ramos and Vera (2002); Baquero Escudero (2003); Rabaté (2007).

18. Blanco (2001) p. 11.

19. Blanco (2001) p. 23.

20. Kirkpatrick (1989) p. 23.

21. Pérez Galdós (1998) pp. 138 and 152

22. Oller (1986) pp. 34f.

23. Pérez Galdós (1998) pp. 123 and 165.

24. Pérez Galdós (1998) p. 165.

25. Rementería y Fica (1837) pp. 95–97.

26. *Nuevo manual de urbanidad* (1850) chap. XXV.

27. *Nuevo manual de urbanidad* (1850) p. 150.

28. *Nuevo manual de urbanidad* (1850) p. 152.

29. *Nuevo manual de urbanidad* (1850) p. 153.

30. See, for instance, Dufaux (1890) p. 11.

31. Dufaux (1890) p. 12.

32. Dufaux (1890) p. 15.

33. Dufaux (1890) p. 18.

34. This compilation was published in 1902 under the title of *Tesoro de las Familias* and was advertised in the fashion magazine *El Eco de la Moda* and distributed by its editors.

35. See, for instance, Ossorio y Bernard (1897) pp. 128–33.

36. The catalogues of Madrid's National Library register a total of sixty-three domestic economy entries of books published between 1829 and 1924. Only two were published in the first half of the century—1829 and 1830. Of the sixty-one left, 27 percent were published between 1850 and 1880, and 73 percent between 1880 and 1920.

37. Pons and Serna (1992) p. 228.

38. See Ossorio y Bernard (1897) p. 130.

39. Bestard de la Torre (1898) p. 262.

40. *Tesoro de las Familias* (1902) p. 32.

41. *Tesoro de las Familias* (1902) p. 34.

42. Yeves (1879) chap. V; Burgos (1897) p. 150.

43. *Tesoro de las Familias* (1902) pp. 36–37.

44. Alvarez Carretero (1889) p. 98.

45. *La Parisien* was owned by V. Sociats and Son in Rambla dels Studis of Barcelona; *Tesoro de las Familias* (1890) pp. 30–31.

46. Burgos (1897) p. 152.

47. Roche (2000) p. 170.

48. Edwards (2005) pp. 4–5.

49. An additional recommended activity to grasp the material reality of nineteenth-century upper-middle-class domestic life is the visit of the recently remodeled Museo del Romanticismo in Madrid. The museum displays decorative possessions from the home of well-known upper-class Madrilenian family. It constitutes one of the most complete examples of a mid-nineteenth-century Spanish bourgeois home.

50. On the role of Madrid as an imperial capital, see Ringrose (1985) chap. 1.

51. On the concept of the nineteenth-century Madrid dual economy, see Bahamonde Magro and Otero Carvajal (1999) pp. 22–26.

52. Inventories have been used by scholars in recent times to study the historical evolution of consumption, material culture, and standards of living, especially for the early modern period. Some examples are Pardailhé-Galabrun (1988); Torras and Yun Casalilla (1999); Sarti (2002); Edwards (2005).

53. As Bartolomé Yun has pointed out, inventories are rich historical sources but are not without problems. See Torras and Yun Casalilla (1999) p. 30.

54. Burns (2005) p. 355.

55. See Sambricio (1985) pp. 490–495; Sambricio and Terán (1999); Sambricio and Lopezosa Aparicio (2001); Ruiz Palomeque (1985); Pinto Crespo and Madrazo Madrazo (1995–2001).

56. Mesonero Romanos (1991), p. 88.

57. This feature characterized the material culture of the house in the Middle Ages. See Carson (1994) p. 523.

58. Schama (1987) pp. 316f.

59. Late eighteenth-century plays feature *petimetres* in their nightgowns entertaining visitors in their private alcoves while grooming at a dressing table. The most classic examples can be found in Ramón de la Cruz's *sainetes*. See Martín Gaite (1987).

60. Like in Parisian houses of the same period. See Pardailhé-Galabrun (1988) p. 58.

61. Archivo Histórico de Protocolos de Madrid (AHPM), Protocolo (P) 11038, folio (f.) 48

62. AHPM, P. 11517, f. 999.

63. Descriptions of *estrados* were more frequent in literary sources of the seventeenth century. One of the best known is Zabaleta (1977), pp. 32f.; see Deleito y Piñuela (1966) pp. 32 and 85f; Burr (1964) p. 42. The dictionary of *Autoridades,* in the 1732 edition, defines *estrado* as "the set of jewels that serves to cover and to adorn the place or piece where the ladies sit to receive visits, which are made up of carpets, pillows, stools or low chairs." For the most complete analysis of the meaning and content of *estrado,* see Abad (2003).

64. AHPM, P. 11527, f. 1180

65. See, for instance, AHPM, P. 24775, f. 851(Inventory of Francisco Sánchez de las Pastoras, Oficial de la Contaduría del Reino, 1682); AHPM, P. 11527, f. 814 (Inventory of Francisco Aguado,

Portero de los Reales Consejos, 1677); AHPM, p. 24775, f. 153 (Inventory of Francisco González, barber master, 1674).

66. Sarmiento (1966) p. 185.

67. Abad (2003) pp. 376–80.

68. See Sarti (2002) p. 132; Thornton (1991) pp. 206–14; Thornton (1998) p. 63.

69. Sarti (2002)p. 124; Simoncini (1995) vol. 1, pp. 165–79.

70. On the function and style of *estrado* chairs, see Abad (2003) p. 388.

71. Martín Gaite (1987) p. 42.

72. This lack of functionality in the distribution of household interiors is characteristic of most of Europe up to the seventeenth century, although it appears to be more persistent in peripheral areas such as Spain or Scotland. See Nenadic (1994) p. 148.

73. One of the main aspects that the enlightened minister Gaspar Melchor Jovellanos emphasized when he remodeled his old provincial family estate in 1800 was, precisely, the conversion of former large spaces he considered too cold and austere into smaller comfortable rooms for private use. See Jovellanos (1952) p. 204.

74. See AHPM, P. 22961 f. 450f.

75. See Eleb and Debarre (1995) pp. 106f.; Flanders (2004) p. 168.

76. Aguiló Alonso (1987) p. 132.

77. See Shammas (1990) pp. 310–17; De Vries (1993) p. 95; Fairchilds (1993) pp. 851–55; Berg and Clifford (1999); Brewer and Porter (1993).

78. See Clunas (1999) p. 1510; Matthee (2005).

79. Recent scholarship points toward the existence in Spain of a slow but sustained transition to new consumer habits since the seventeenth century. This long-term transformation intensified during the second half of the eighteenth century, but did not evolve into a "consumer revolution" until the first third of the twentieth century. See the contributions by Xavier Lencina Pérez, Monserrat Durán, Lidia Torra Fernández, Máximo García Fernández, Fernando Carlos Ramos Palencia, Ramón Maruri, and Juan Carlos Sola in the collective volume edited by Jaume Torras and Bartolomé Yun (1999). The historical evolution of consumption in Spain fits better into Carole Shammas's evolutionary pattern than into the paradigm of the consumer revolution. See Shammas (1990) and (1993); Mckendrick, Brewer, and Plumb (1982) p. 9.

80. Mckendrick, Brewer, and Plumb (1982) p. 9.

81. On the study of the meaning of objects to define identities, see Marcus (1995); Csikszentmihalyi (1981); Roche (2000).

82. For more details on the history of this family, see Cruz (1986).

83. Archivo Histórico del Banco de España, Section of Secretaría Book 18648.

84. AHPM, P. 22280, f. 503.

85. Mesonero Romanos (1991) p. 90.

86. Hall (1997) p. 47; Benevolo (1993), pp. 171f.

87. Díez Baldeón (1987) p. 132f.; Hall (1977) pp. 144–45.

88. For similar processes in other Spanish cities, see Pons and Serna (1992) pp. 120f.; McDonogh (1986) pp. 181f.

89. Marcus (1995), pp. 17–18; Bryden and Floyd (2000) pp. 13f.

90. In Madrid's apartments, semi-public spaces served as a transition between the public and the private spheres. These spaces indicate that the traditional conception of the existence of sealed private interiors separated from their public realms needs to be reconsidered. Evidence in this chapter joins scholarship that argues for the connection between the public civic and the private household interiors. For the classic argument in favor of sphere separation, see Perrot (1987) vol. 4, p. 341. On the approaches arguing in favor of connection. see Marcus (1995) p. 6.

91. The concepts "front stage" and "back stage" are borrowed from Weatherill (1988).

92. The Casa de Cisneros is the only *plateresco*-style building in Madrid and has a long and varied history, having served as an Episcopal palace, a jail, an aristocratic residence, and part of the city hall—its present function.

93. AHPM, P. 27896, f. 2116f.

94. AHPM, P. 28758, f. 125f.

95. AHPM. P. 27896, f. 2121f.

96. As described by Teófilo Gautier, quoted by Díaz-Plaja (1993) p. 50.

97. See Davidoff and Hall (1987). For the case of Spain, see Pons and Serna (1992) pp. 171–73.

98. Some of Pérez Galdós's examples can be found in *Fortunata y Jacinta, Tormento, La de Bringas and Lo Prohibido*. For Palacio Valdés, see *La Espuma*.

99. José Garcia de la Torre minister of *Gracia y Justicia* in 1820. AHPM, P. 25446, f. 118.

100. AHPM P. 27271.

101. Perrot (1987) p. 342.

102. AHPM, P. 27272, f. 1381.

103. AHPM, P. 3573, f. 5522.

104. El inventario de Otondo se realizó en 1818: AHMP, P. 22280, f. 503. El de Aguirre Labroche es de 1883: AHPM, 23558, j. 333.

105. AHPM, P. 28758, f. 1016f.

106. AHPM, P. 22848, f. 588f.

CHAPTER FOUR

1. *La Moda Ilustrada,* Madrid, January 10, 1882.

2. Goodman and Cohen (2004) p. 18.

3. Stearns (2001) p. 16.

4. Mckendrick, Brewer, and Plumb (1982) p. 9.

5. Campbell (1987) p. 2.

6. Burke (1993) p. 158; Clunas (1999) p. 1498; Clunas (2004) pp. 170–73.

7. De Vries (2008) p. xi.

8. Martín Gaite (1987) pp. 27f.

9. Because of their tendency to mimic the French, they were termed *petimetres* by some Spanish writers. This terminology was elaborated over the course of the century with a much broader pejorative vocabulary that included terms such as *currutaco* (dandy) for men and *bachillera* (know-it-all) and *madamita* (flashy dame) for women. See Martín Gaite (1987) pp. 35–37.

10. Martín Gaite (1987) pp. 35f. and 44f.

11. Norton (2008) p. 175; Norton (2006) p. 670.

12. This scholarship is the product of several team projects under the direction of Bartolomé Yun Casalilla and Jaume Torras. The results are the subject of two edited volumes and several journal articles and dissertations. See Torras and Yun (1999) and a special number of the *Revista de Historia Económica* dedicated to this topic (2003).

13. Torras and Torra (1999) p. 68.

14. Torra (1999) pp. 93–98.

15. Moreno Claverías (1999) p. 88.

16. Torra (2003) pp. 90–93; Torra (2002) pp. 15–18.

17. Vicente (2007) pp. 9–15.

18. Vicente (2007) pp. 69–74.

19. Vicente (2007) p. 55.

20. Dávila Corona and García Fernández (2001) pp. 158–60; García Fernández (1999) pp. 152–53; García Fernández (2004) pp. 726–30.

21. Ramos Palencia (1999) pp. 127–28; Ramos Palencia (2003) pp. 143 and 173–74.

22. Maruri (1999) pp. 165–68; Hoyo and Maruri (2003) pp. 132–35.

23. Maruri (1999) p. 179; Maruri (1990) pp. 252f.

24. A comprehensive summary of this literature can be found in De Vries (2008) p. 124.

25. Moreno Lázaro (2006) p. 18; Hernández and Moreno Lázaro (2009) pp. 153–56.

26. Torras and Yun Casililla (2003) p. 23.

27. De Vries (2008) chap. 3.

28. Thomson (1992) pp. 72–75; Vicente (2007) pp. 11–15.

29. See some examples in the following notarial records: AHPM. P. 18489, p. 591; P. 20446, 11/11/1765; P. 20479, p. 84; P. 20258, 1/4/1784; P. 20371, p. 377; P. 20479, 21/8/1766.

30. See, for instance, AHPM P. 20258.

31. Data extracted from *Almanak mercantil o Guía de comerciantes* (1795).

32. Sánchez (2000) p. 519.

33. Shammas (1994); De Vries (2008) p. 135; Torras and Yun Casalilla (2003) p. 33.

34. AHPM P. 27272.

35. AHPM, P. 35022.

36. AHPM, P. 26622.

37. AHPM, P. 27127.

38. Gronow (1997) p. xi.

39. McCracken (1988) p. 11.

40. Laver (1995) p. 113.

41. DeJean (2005) pp. 63–69.

42. Jones (2004) p. 181.

43. Roche (1989) pp. 464–65; Sama (2004) p. 400.

44. Bozal (1982) p. 9.

45. Seoane (1983) p. 21.

46. Simón Palmer (2005) p. 53.

47. The first fashion magazine in Spanish was published in Cuba: *La Moda o Recreo Semanal*

del Bello Sexo (1829–30). It was the initiative of the Cuban writer and publisher Domingo del Monte and was inspired mainly by models from England that the author might have observed during his stay in the United States. *La Moda* contributed to the introduction of romantic aesthetics and taste in the island. It was also the first publication that treated women as consumer subjects. The influence of *La Moda* over the early fashion magazines published in the peninsula is nonetheless uncertain.

48. Pena (2001) p. 367.

49. Calefato (2004) p. 11.

50. The main contributions to this approach are Perinat and Marradés (1980); Roig Castellanos (1986); Kirkpatrick (1989); Jiménez Morell (1992); Simón Palmer (1993); Sánchez Llama (2000); Blanco (2001); Cantizano Márquez (2004); Espigado (2006).

51. Espigado (2006) p. 102.

52. They were *El Diario del Bello Sexo* and *Lyceo General del Bello Sexo,* denied authorization by King Charles IV. See Roig Castellanos (1986) p. 10.

53. Cited by Sánchez Llama (2000) p. 127.

54. González Díez and Pérez Cuadrado (2009) p. 59.

55. Copeland (1995) p. 6.

56. *Correo de las Damas: Periódico de Música, Amena Literatura, Teatros y Modas,* June 3, 1833.

57. *Correo de las Damas,* December 31, 1835.

58. These were *La Psiquis, Periódico del Bello Sexo* (Valencia, 1840); *La Esmeralda* (Madrid, 1842); *La Moda* later called *La Moda Elegante Ilustrada* (Cadiz-Madrid, 1842–1927); *El Espósito, Periódio de Literatura* (Córdoba, 1843); *El Defensor del Bello Sexo: Periódico de Literatura, Moral y Modas, Dedicado Exclusivamente a las Mugeres* (Madrid, 1844–46); *El Vergel de Andalucía* (Córdoba, 1845); *El Tocador: Gacetín del Bello Sexo* (Madrid, 1844–45); *El Pensil del Bello Sexo* (Madrid, 1845–46); *La Aurora* (Sevilla, 1846); *La Sílfide: Periódico Mensual de Literatura, Ciencias, Artes y Modas Dedicado al Bello Sexo* (Madrid, 1845–46); *Gaceta de las Mujeres Redactada por Ellas Mismas* (Madrid, 1845); *La Elegancia: Boletín de Gran Tono* (Madrid, 1846–47); *Álbum de Teatros y de la Moda* (Madrid, 1846); *El Cupido* (Madrid, 1848); *El Pensamiento* (Madrid, 1848); *Ellas. Órgano Oficial del Sexo Femenino* (Madrid, 1851–53); *La Gaceta del Bello Sexo* (Cadiz, 1851–53); *El Correo de la Moda* (Madrid, 1851–93); *El Mensajero de las Modas* (Madrid, 1852); *La Caprichosa: Periódico de Buen Tono* (Paris, 1857–58). A brief review of the evolution of the fashion press in nineteenth-century Spain can be found in *La Ilustración Española y Americana,* December 22, 1907.

59. Sánchez Llama (2000) p. 107.

60. Pena (2001) p. 377.

61. Sánchez Llama (2000) p. 142.

62. These were *La Nueva Caprichosa,* edited by Emilia Serrano de Wilson (1861); *La Educanda,* sponsored by Angela Grassi (1862–63); *La Violeta,* founded by Faustina Sáez de Melgar and Pilar Sinués de Marco (1862–66); *El ángel del hogar,* founded and edited by Pilar Sinués de Marco; *La Guirnalda* (1867–82); *La Mariposa,* edited by Fernánda Gómez (1866 and 1876); *El Último Figurín,* edited by Emilia Serrano de Wilson (1871); *Día de Moda* (1880–81); *La Moda Ilustrada* (1882); *El Figurín Artístico* (1882–84); *La Moda de Madrid* (1884–87); *El Salón de la Moda* (1884–1911); *La Última Moda* (1888–1927); *El Eco de la Moda* (1897–?)

63. *La Ilustración Española y Americana,* December 22, 1907.

64. See *La Moda Elegante Ilustrada,* December 20, 1863, p. 416.

65. Francisco Flores Arenas was a multifaceted individual, engineer by formation, medical doctor by profession, and journalist by vocation. He was involved in a variety of publishing enterprises in mid-nineteenth-century Cádiz and Madrid. See Márquez (2005) p. 189.

66. *La Ilustración Española y Americana,* April 4, 1884. This issue includes an obituary of Abelardo de Carlos written by José Castro Serrano with information about his life and career.

67. *La Moda Elegante Ilustrada,* January 1, 1861.

68. *La Ilustración Española y Americana,* April 4, 1884.

69. See the following issues of *La Moda Elegante Ilustrada,* January 6, 1881; January 6, 1886; July 6, 1889.

70. *La Guirnalda,* December 5, 1880.

71. The main short-lived publishing initiatives from Barcelona were *La Abeja* (1867), with a focus on embroidery; *La Elegancia: Revista Semanal de Modas, Labores, Literatura y Novelas* (1867); *Modas y Labors: Suplement al Diari Català* (1880); *Revista de Modas y Salones* (1883–85); *La Moda de los Niños* (186); *El Mundo de las Damas* (1887); *El Bordado Económico* (1889); *El Hogar* (1895). See Segura and Selva (1984).

72. See, for instance, the following issues: *El Eco de la Moda,* April 11, 1897, and December 23, 1900.

73. *El Eco de la Moda,* July 4, 1897, and July 11, 1897.

74. See *Tesoro de las Familias,* supplement to *El Eco de la Moda,* February 1902.

75. Checa Godoy (2007) p. 29.

76. Checa Godoy (2007) p. 40.

77. Loeb (1994) p. 5.

78. Benson and Ugolini (2006) p. 27.

79. Stearns (2001) p. 16.

80. Benson and Shaw (1992) p. 200; Walsh (1999) p. 46; Bowlby (2001) pp. 114f.

81. Crossick and Jaumain (1999) p. 7.

82. Cruz (1996).

83. *Semanario Pintoresco,* Madrid, May 8, 1836, p. 36.

84. *Semanario Pintoresco,* Madrid, October 16, 1836, p. 233.

85. The two major studies on this topic focus on the twentieth century. See Cuartas (2005); Toboso Sánchez (2001).

86. Cruz (1996) p. 27.

87. Archivo del Banco de España, Secretaría, libro 18648.

88. The firm of Francisco Antonio Bringas had estimated assets of 36 million *reales,* the firms of the Caballero brothers combined assets of 30 million *reales,* and the firm of García de la Prada had assets valued at 20 million *reales.* Of a total of 11 establishments cited in the Bonapartist survey, 8 had assets worth more than 14 million *reales* and all of them had more than 5 million *reales* in assets. See Cruz (1996) p. 19. For the García de la Prada and Caballero families, see AHPM, P. 21098 and 21782.

89. Marrey (1979) p. 14; Perrot (1994) p. 42.

90. Mesonero Romanos (1991) p. 83.

91. See, for instance, *Diario de Avisos de Madrid,* March 14, 1836, p. 3.

92. *Diario de Avisos de Madrid,* March 15, 1836, p. 3.

93. Perrot (1994) p. 53; Nielfa (1985) p. 30.

94. See, for instance, the commercial by Almacenes de Generos Superiores in *Diario de Avisos de Madrid,* March 15, 1836, p. 2.

95. See *Diario de Avisos de Madrid,* March 28, 1836, p. 2.

96. The Pasaje the Matheu in Madrid—also known as Pasaje de la Villa de Madrid—was the first of these arcades built between 1843 and 1847. It connected the streets of Espoz y Mina and La Victoria and was the most successful and long-lived among the Madrid arcades. Also in Madrid the Pasaje de Murga (1845) connected the streets of Montera and Tres Cruces. In Barcelona the Passatge Bacardi (1856) still functions as a commercial arcade connecting the Rambla de Caputxins with Plaça Reial.

97. Benson and Ugolini (2006) p. 16.

98. Benson and Shaw (1992) p. 138.

99. Cited by Pasalodos (2004) p. 933.

100. Pasalodos (2004) p. 933. Other large shops in Madrid were Le Tout Paris on Príncipe Street, which sold clothes, cosmetics, corsets, and jewelry; Walewyk-Lacloche, with shops in Madrid and Biarritz; Bazar X; and La Villa de Madrid. See Pasalodos (2004) pp. 923–30.

101. *La Vanguardia,* January 28, 1882.

102. *La Vanguardia,* January 1, 1882.

103. *La Vanguardia,* January 30, 1882.

104. Pasalodos (2004) p. 923.

105. An example was the *Almacenes El Siglo Valenciano,* established in 1879 as a drapery large shop in an emblematic building of several floors open to an interior patio covered by an iron and crystal transparent structure. At present the building has been remodeled to house the Centre de Cultura Contemporània of Valencia.

106. Some details about the recent history of El Aguila department store can be found in an article written by Roger Jiménez in *El Mundo* (ed. Barcelona), Sunday, February 13, 2005.

107. Other late nineteenth-century multiple shops that deserve further research are Almacenes La Torre Eiffel (Madrid, Carmen, 42 and Barcelona Doctor Dou, 1); Almacenes New England, founded in Madrid by Agustín Mansó in 1887 with stores in Madrid and Barcelona; Almacenes Pons y Bonet with shops in Palma de Mallorca and Madrid, specialized in linen and wedding apparel. See Pasalodos (2004) p. 943. Local stores in Madrid with two or more shops after 1880 include Ruiz Velasco y Martínez, which operated since 1879 and sold shirts, trousseaus, wedding dresses, and men's, women's, and children's clothes (had three shops in Madrid, main two on 11–13 Mayor Street and a monster shop on 10–18 Postas Street); José María Baranda, sold linen and clothing (two shops in Madrid); El Buen Consejo, linen, shirts, children (two shops); Adela García, shawls and women's clothes (two shops); García Mustieles, haberdasher (two shops); Palacios Brothers, imported and national textile fabrics, women's and men's clothing (three shops); Azas, drapery (two shops); Manuel de Diego, still in business *nowadays,* selling umbrellas, parasols, fans, canes (two shops). See Pasalodos (2004) pp. 904–15.

108. *La Vanguardia,* October 13, 1882.

109. Whitaker (2006) pp. 7–10.

110. *La Vanguardia,* October 2, 1881, and October 18, 1881.

111. *Fin de temporada de invierno 1898–99: Grandes Almacenes de El Siglo. Gran rebaja de precios del 1 al 15 de Febrero,* Barcelona, Gracia, 1899. Biblioteca Nacional Madrid, VC/4899/109.

112. Faciabén (2003).

113. Miller (1981) p. 3.

114. Clark (2006) p. 16.

CHAPTER FIVE

1. Tortella (1998) p. 45.

2. Reher (1986) pp. 57f.

3. Resina (2008) p. 40.

4. Parsons (2003) p. 35.

5. See Lowe (1982) p. 129; Sennett (1994) p. 340.

6. On the idea of the "spatial turn," see Gunn and Morris (2001) pp. 1–14.

7. Umbach (2005) pp. 659–60.

8. Berman (1981) pp. 143–50. For Paris, see Harvey (2003) pp. 10–14; Moncan (2002). For Berlin, see Fritzsche (1996).

9. The concept of *gouvernementalité* was introduced by Foucault in his conferences at the Collège de France during the last years of his life. Since then, a number of social scientists from the United States and the United Kingdom have been providing content. See Dean (1999); Lemke (2001) pp. 190–95.

10. Otter (2002) p. 3.

11. For a critical view of the concept of *gouvernementalité,* see Kerr (1999) pp. 173–203.

12. On this process in the colonial cities of North America, see Bushman (1993) p. 140.

13. Pons and Serna detected this reality in various parts of their work on the bourgeoisie of Valencia and illustrate it with some examples. See Pons and Serna (1992) pp. 215f.

14. Hughes (1993) p. 5.

15. Cadalso (1793) p. 72.

16. Tatjer (1985) p. 35.

17. See Caballé and Nicolau (1993).

18. McDonogh (1986) p. 21.

19. Alberch i Fugueras (1999) p. 100.

20. The building known as Porxos d'En Xifré, in the vicinity of the Lltoja, was built at the request of D. Joseph Xifré i Casas (1777–1856), one of the wealthiest men of the city. Xifré was a Catalan *indiano* who settled in Cuba, where he made a fortune exporting coffee, sugar, and hides and trafficking in slaves. In 1831, he returned to Barcelona, where he became the most important urban landowner and financier of his time. The Porxos building is decorated with allegorical bas-reliefs of the somewhat exotic and gaunt business world of the protagonists of the later Spanish colonialism: cherubs hauling sugarcane, sacks of coffee, or tobacco leaves, cornucopias full of bananas, mulatto women wearing turbans, and Indian women wearing feathered headdresses. These motifs

can be found in some façades in Barcelona and other places in Spain as testimony of a colonial bourgeoisie that played a relevant role in nineteenth-century Spain. See Alberch i Fugueras (1999) p. 103; Hughes (1993) 226. On the history of *indianos,* see Bahamonde and Cayuela (1992).

21. Duran i Sanpere (1972) vol. I, p. 493.

22. See Alcaide González (2005); Fernández-Armesto (1992) p. 170.

23. Robert Hughes refers to this project as "Barcelona's Gardens of Luxembourg." See Hughes (1993) p. 273.

24. Corominas i Ayala (2002) p. 69.

25. Corominas i Ayala (2002) p. 75

26. The subject generated a discussion known in its time as "the battle of the extensions." See Grau (1988).

27. See Sagarra i Trias (1996) p. 46.

28. Scholars have called attention to the influence of the French architect César Daly on the plans of Rovira i Trias y Garriga i Roca. See Resina (2008) p. 65. On Daly, see Papayanis (2006) pp. 325–29.

29. Fuensanta Muro and Pilar Rivas found them in the Administrative Archives of Alcalá de Henares. Their content was published quite quickly in two volumes: *Teoría de la Construcción de las Ciudades, Cerdà i Barcelona* and *Teoría de la Viabilidad Urbana,* both published in 1991 by the municipalities of Barcelona and Madrid. See Rivas and Muro (1999) pp. 222–27.

30. Pla (1945) p. 133.

31. Hughes (1993) pp. 283–84; Permanyer (1990) pp. 81–82.

32. Stewart (2003) pp. 6–18.

33. On the origins of the Escuela de Caminos, see Lucena Giraldo (2005).

34. On the introduction of hygiene studies and movement in Spain, see Alcaide González (1999).

35. Corominas i Ayala (2002) p. 27.

36. Grau and López (1988) pp. 191–229.

37. Aibar and Bijker (1997) p. 10.

38. On the intellectual and political principles of this debate, see Bonet (1985); Sagarra i Trias (1996); Permanyer (1990) pp. 61–65.

39. Sagarra i Trias (1996) p. 63.

40. Permanyer (1990) p. 114.

41. The Teatro Lírico was the last remains of the garden of the Campos Elíseos. Between 1880 and 1900, under the sponsorship of the banker Evaristo Arnús, it became the main center of promotion of symphonism and the most innovative tendencies in the field of music and dramatic arts. See Guardiet (2006). On the Maison Dorée, see Permanyer (1994) pp. 23–36.

42. See Fabré i Carreras (1988) p. 32; Grau and López (1988); Vergés and Sarrias (1988).

43. See Sambricio (1997).

44. The works of Lopezosa Aparicio (1991–1992) and (2002) provide abundant information regarding the history of the urban transformations of Madrid's Prado.

45. Resina (2008) p. 40.

46. Mainer (2003) pp. 107–9.

47. Mercader Riba (1983) p. 380.

48. Ringrose (1985) pp. 164–69.

49. See Comín, Martín Azeña, and Castro (2004).

50. Ringrose (1996) pp. 262–90; Castro (1987) pp. 116f.

51. Regarding the composition and functioning of the dominant Madrid society during the first half of the nineteenth century, see Cruz (1996).

52. Mesonero Romanos (1989); Mesonero Romanos (1926) chap. VIII.

53. Navascués Palacio (1993) pp. 416–17.

54. See Cruz (1996) p. 268.

55. Ruiz Palomeque (1983) pp. 19–27. Regarding the relevance of Mesonero's proposals, see Ruiz Palomeque (1985) pp. 505f.

56. See Mesonero Romanos (1989) p. x.

57. I use, with some modifications, the thematic interpretation developed by Edward Baker in the introduction to the 1989 edition of Mesonero's *Rápida ojeada*. See Mesonero Romanos (1989) pp. i–xxiii.

58. Regarding the demographic growth of Madrid, see Carbajo Isla (1987) pp. 214f.

59. Sambricio (1979) p. 493.

60. Mesonero Romanos (1989) p. 25.

61. Regarding the displays of commemorative gardens, see Prieto González and Rodríguez Romero (1998) pp. 402f.

62. Until the 1840s, Madrid did not have a large scale manufacturing industry. What is classified as industrial population and activity in census and statistics did not exceed for the most part the artisan level. This situation began to change in 1839, with the inauguration of the Bonaplata iron foundry and the subsequent opening of the Sanfort and Sanfort foundries and machine companies. Because of an ancient ban against locating large workshops in the interior of the city, these new factories were placed in the poorer sections of the city. See Sambricio and Terán (1999) p. 46.

63. See Díez Baldeón (1987) p. 416.

64. Navascués Palacio (1993) p. 416.

65. The *maragatos* make up a distinctive group connected to the history of Madrid since its transformation into a capital. It was a community of immigrants originally from the region of Maragatería, also known as Somoza, in the province of León whose most important urban center is Astorga. For a number of cultural, social and economic reasons, a substantial segment of individuals from this part of Castile were devoted to the transportation of merchandise by mule train over long distances, eventually controlling the most substantial portion of the supply of products to Madrid from the north: cereal, wine, manufactured textiles, fish, and sausage. Our personage, "el Maragato" Alonso Cordero, was without a doubt the most famous dignitary from that curious society of muleskinners who liked to wear their ancestral and exotic regional costumes. Alonso Cordero created an authentic emporium of transport companies of his time, not just of merchandise but also of travelers. He went from mule to industry when he obtained a concession for transport service between Madrid and the ports of Cantabria. Even Queen Isabel II used his modern carriages for her travels to the northern provinces.

66. The details of the renovation of Puerta del Sol have been studied by Quirós Linares (1985); Navascués Palacio (1993) pp. 418–20.

67. See Bahamonde and Otero (1989).

68. Sambricio (1997) p. 47.

69. Albó (1846) and (1857).

70. Mas Hernández (1982) pp. 22–24.

71. See Caballero (1840); Mellado (1845).

72. Sambricio (1997) p. 49.

73. Regarding his contribution, see Saavedra Moragas (1895).

74. See Castro (1978).

75. Pallol Trigueros (2004) pp. 77–82.

76. Parsons (2003) p. 35.

77. Navascués Palacio (1993) p. 430; González Yanci (2004) pp. 23f.

78. *Biblioteca Nacional,* Madrid, Maps and Cartography Section. Madrid. Population Charts: 1807, 1808, 1812 and 1880. A copy of that of Facundo Cañada López can be studied at the Cartoteca de la Biblioteca de Humanidades (Facultad de Geografía, Historia y Arte, Universidad Complutense Madrid).

79. Regarding the nature of and the problems generated by Madrid's capital-city duality, see Bahamonde and Otero (1999); Juliá Díaz (2000).

80. Carlos Sambricio utilizes the concept "liberal city" to define the new city arising from the urban transformations of the nineteenth century. See Sambricio (2004) p. 15.

81. Sambricio and Terán (1999) pp. 56 and 60.

82. Castells (2000) pp. 283–95.

83. Martín Ramos (2004) p. 32.

84. Walton (2002) pp. 3–12.

85. Pons and Serna (1992) pp. 25–28.

86. See Piñón (1988).

87. Taberner (1987) p. 68.

88. *El Ensanche* (1984) chap. 1.

89. Regarding the stages and problems in the development of the extension until the mid-twentieth century, see *Historia de la Ciudad* (2000–2004) vol. 3; Azagra y Ros (1998) pp. 134–37.

90. See Basurto Ferro, Rodríguez-Escudero, and Velilla Iriondo (1999); Glas (1997).

91. Yeste Navarro (1999–2000) pp. 188f.

92. See Ponga Mayo (1997).

93. Otero Carvajal records a chronology of expansion plans of Spanish cities at the end of the nineteenth century. Not including those already mentioned, the list adds Vitoria (1865), Sabadell (1865), Gijón (1867), Alicante (1874), Alcoy (1874), Villanova y la Geltrú (1876), Santander (1877), Málaga (1878), Vigo (1878), Tarrasa (1878), Mataró (1878), Avilés (1895), Tarragona (1899), Cádiz (1900). Some of these plans, among them those of Vitoria and Alicante, began to be implemented in the nineteenth century, but their full development did not occur until the following century. See Otero Carvajal (2005) p. 19.

CHAPTER SIX

1. Larra (1833).

2. Baker (1991) p. 26.

3. Larra (1984) pp. 168–82.

4. Bullfighting was the most popular form of entertainment in nineteenth-century Spain, but it cannot be considered a characteristically bourgeois form of leisure. It is true that the bourgeoisie patronized the *corrida* by getting involved in the spectacle's business and politics, but it is also true that this social group produced the main manifestations of opposition. Much of the critique of bullfighting came from bourgeois writers, including women. For a review of the role of the bourgeoisie in the history of the *corrida* during the nineteenth century, see Shubert (1999) pp. 162–74.

5. Larra (1834).

6. The metaphor "pleasures of the imagination" has been borrowed from John Brewer's insightful book on eighteenth-century English culture. See Brewer (1997).

7. Koshar (2002) p. 4.

8. Brewer (1997) p. xix.

9. Corbin and Csergo (1995); Cross (1990) pp. 87–99.

10. Thompson (1967) pp. 60–66. E. P. Thompson linked the history of leisure in England to labor and productivity. The middle classes felt the benefits of industrialization in the distribution of productive time and the availability of surplus capital for consumption. In the early stages of this process the will to enjoy the delights of high culture and costly entertainment was motivated by the desire to emulate the aristocracy.

11. On the use of cultural capital accumulation for the making of bourgeois identities, see Young (2003) pp. 17f.

12. Tranter (1998); Withey (1997); Jones and Wills (2005).

13. On the origins of commercial leisure in modern Spain, see Otero Carvajal (2003) pp. 169–98; Bermejo Berros (2005); Estomba and de Pablo Contreras (2002) pp. 155–59; Bahamonde (2002); Salaün (1990).

14. Gies (1994) p. 38.

15. Gies (1994) p. 176.

16. Gies (1994) p. 351.

17. Gies (2002) p. 177.

18. Gies (2002) p. 182.

19. Gies (2002) pp. 182–83.

20. Pons and Serna (1992) p. 240.

21. Mesonero Romanos (1991) pp. 564–73.

22. Biographical information on Salamanca has been extracted from the following works: Hernández Girbál (1992); Torrente Fortuño (1969); Romanones (1962); Rico (1994).

23. Pérez Galdós (1949) vol. IV, p. 1662.

24. *La Luneta,* December 27, 1846.

25. Some examples of this kind of journalism can be found in the following provincial papers: *La Lealtad* (Granada, 1874–75); *El Defensor de Granada* (1880); *El Noticiero Granadino* (1892).

26. In Madrid, Teatro del Principe and Teatro de la Cruz. Barcelona had only one, Teatro de la Cruz.

27. The author of this article complains about the excessive number of available seats in the 101 Spanish bullrings, a total of 526,000, 4 times the number of theater seats. *El museo Universal*, August 10, 1867, p. 2.

28. Gies (1994) p. 15.

29. Pérez Galdós (1949) vol. V, p. 573; on this same theme, see the article by Mesonero "La comedia casera" publicado en 1832, in Mesonero Romanos (1991) pp. 34–42.

30. Valera (1947–49) vol. 3, pp. 607–9.

31. On this development, see Alier (2002); Headington, Westbrook, and Barfoot (1987) pp. 12–37; Lacombe (2001) pp. 226–51.

32. Gerhard (1998) p. 5.

33. Fiedler (2001) p. 5.

34. Díaz de Escovar and Lasso de la Vega (1924) vol. I, pp. 377–78.

35. Paradoxically, the Coliseo de los Caños del Peral had to close in 1817 due to damage from the war as well as the instable soil of its construction site.

36. Compiled information on the history of Teatro Liceo comes from the following works: Bertrán (1931); Radigales (1998); Alier and Guerra (2004); Pla i Arxé (1999); Nadal (1999); Aviñola (1999).

37. In some areas of Catalonia constitutional monarchy under Queen Isabel was threatened by strong supporters of absolutist Carlism.

38. Cited by Pla i Arxé (1999).

39. McDonogh (1986) p. 190.

40. McDonogh (1986) p. 188.

41. Fontbona (1991).

42. In the beginning, programs focused mainly on traditional Italian *bel canto*. There was an intermediate period dedicated to national opera—mainly Giuseppe Verdi, who visited El Real in 1863 to conduct the Spanish premiere of *La forza del destino*. Later programs moved toward Wagnerian and French opera.

43. The information about the history of Teatro Real has been compiled from the following works: Díaz de Escovar and Lasso de la Vega (1924); Muñoz (1946); Velasco Zazo (1956); Gómez de la Serna (1976); Martínez Ibáñez (1993); Iglesias (1996); Turina Gómez (1997); Subirá (1997).

44. Guardiet i Bergé (2006) p. 81f.

45. *La Dinastía. Diario político, literario y mercantil*, Barcelona, May 1, 1884, p. 18.

46. Sobrino (1992).

47. Carbonell i Guberna (2003); Narváez Ferri (2005) pp. 63–65.

48. See Umbach (2005) p. 671.

49. Sobrino (1995); Sancho García (2005) pp. 66–68.

50. Details on the history of the social circle in Esquivel's painting can be found in Mesonero Romanos (1926) chap. XIII.

51. Some examples of this type of journalism in Spain after 1850 are *El Museo Universal* (Madrid); *Album Salón* (Barcelona); *Arca* (Barcelona); *Almanaque Literario Ilustrado* (Madrid); *La*

Ilustración (Barcelona); *Alrededor del Mundo* (Madrid); *El Arte del Teatro* (Madrid); Comedias y comediantes (Madrid); *La Ilustración Artística* (Barcelona); *La Ilustración Española y Americana* (Madrid y Barcelona); *Pluma y Lápiz* (Barcelona); *La Moda Elegante* (Madrid); *Respetable Público* (Madrid); *El Viajero Ilustrado* (Barcelona).

52. *Alrededor del Mundo,* Madrid, April 10, 1908, p. 235.

53. Brewer (1997) pp. 57–70.

54. For the history of English pleasure gardens, see Wroth (1979); Boulton (1901); Edelstein (1983); Southworth (1941); Conlin (2006).

55. All data on French gardens have been obtained from Langlois (1991).

56. Ariza Muñoz (1988a) p. 343.

57. Ariza Muñoz (1988b) p. 181; Ariza Muñoz (1990).

58. Cited by Martín Gaite (1987) p. 51.

59. Mesonero Romanos (1926) pp. 273–78.

60. Archivo de la Villa de Madrid (AVM) Secretaría, 1-203-41.

61. Lopezosa Aparicio (2005).

62. Nineteenth-century pleasure gardens were often built on the site of an older garden. Mesonero Romanos describes the rejuvenation of gardens dating from the beginning of the eighteenth century, for example: "The house and famous gardens known as Las Delicias owned by Count of Baños, later property of Count of Alatamira, and finally of Duke of Medina de Torres." Mesonero Romanos (1881) vol. II, p. 98.

63. AVM, Secretaría 3-464-2.

64. Larra (1834).

65. *Diario de Avisos,* June 5, 1834. See Baker (1991) p. 44.

66. Ramón Mesonero Romanos, 'El Buen-Retiro,' *Semanario Pintoresco* (May 8, 1836), 51–53. On Mesonero's attitudes and purposes concerning public gardens and the transformation of Madrid's Retiro, see Baker (1991) p. 41; Frost (2005) pp. 329–31.

67. Biblioteca Nacional, Madrid, Planos de población, 1830–1870 (Dower, John).

68. Information on the Portici gardens i from AVM, Secretaría, 4-198-9; 4-22-87 and 6-147-28.

69. Ariza Muñoz (1988b) pp. 230–31.

70. El Eliseo Madrileño, a small garden located in Paseo de Recoletos near the new palace of the banker José de Salamanca, was inaugurated in 1860. According to Ariza, it became the favorite gathering place for lower middle classes. In 1862, the old Jardín de las Delicias was remodeled and transformed into Jardín del Paraíso, a garden following the model of the French jardin-spectacle, specialized in music and social balls. See Ariza Muñoz (1988b) p. 233.

71. Guardiet i Bergé (2006) p. 29.

72. Guardiet i Bergé (2006) p. 32.

73. *El Áncora,* June 20, 1852.

74. Located on the left side of Paseo de Gracia, about five hundred meters north of the Jardines de Tívoli, in the area that is presently the city blocks located between Diagonal Avenue and Provenza Street.

75. *El Eco de Euterpe,* May 15, 1889. On Anselmo Clave's choral movement, see Carbonell i Guberna (2000) and (2003).

76. On Evaristo Arnús, see Guardiet i Bergé (2006) pp. 53–69.

77. Nead (2000) p. 110.

78. *El Áncora,* June 5, 1853.

79. Corominas i Ayala (2002) p. 71.

80. According to Guardiet i Bergé, this first public *sardana* dance took place in 1859. Guardiet i Bergé (2006) p. 39.

81. Guardiet i Bergé (2006) p. 41.

82. *El Áncora,* June 17, 1853.

83. It was for the building of the Casa Gibert, which was later demolished to create the Plaza de Cataluña.

84. Guardiet i Bergé (2006) p. 82; Bonastre (2004–5) p. 58.

85. AVM, Secretaría, 4-260-16 and 4-203-90.

86. It was built at the heart of the future Barrio de Salamanca, in the area spanning what at present day are the streets of Alcalá, Velazquez, Goya, and Castelló.

87. AVM, Corregimiento, 3-121-223; Ariza Muñoz (1988b) pp. 234–36.

88. *El museo universal,* July 3, 1864.

89. Díaz de Escovar y Lasso de la Vega (1924) vol. 2, pp. 76–77.

90. *El museo universal,* June 26, 1864.

91. *El museo universal,* August 21, 1864.

92. *El museo universal,* September 11, 1864.

93. Cited by Ariza Muñoz (1988a) p. 348.

94. Gustavo Adolfo Bécquer "Los Campos Eliseos," in *El Contemporáneo,* August 7, 1864.

95. Biblioteca Nacional, Archivo Barbieri, Los Campos Elíseos (música manuscrita): valses, 1867.

96. Contents of programmed activities in the gardens can be found in AVM, Corregimiento, 3-34-57; 3-34-80 and 3-34-81.

97. Ariza Muñoz (1988a) pp. 350–51.

98. Baroja (1997) p. 7.

99. Baroja (1955) p. 261.

100. AVM, Secretaría, 10-204-19.

101. AVM, Secretaría 6-353-54 and 7-246-2.

102. Ariza Muñoz (1988b) p. 248.

103. Villena Espinosa and López Villaverde (2003) p. 444.

104. Prior (2002) p. 28.

105. Mesonero Romanos (1991) pp. 573–81.

106. Rueda Herranz (2000) pp. 54–55.

107. Guimerá Ravina (1992) p. 27.

108. Mesonero Romanos (1926) p. 63.

109. Zozaya Montes (2002); Montero Alonso (1971) pp. 8–10.

110. Villena Espinosa and López Villaverde (2003) p. 459.

111. In the same line as the institutions studied by Roger Chartier in pre-revolutionary France. Chartier (2000).

112. Villacorta Baños (2003) p. 417.

113. Villacorta Baños (1985).

114. On the history of university life in nineteenth-century Spain, see Peset Reig (2003); Rodríguez-San Pedro Bezares (2000).

115. Sánchez García (1998) pp. 3–12; Villacorta Baños (2003) pp. 423–24.

116. Cited by Villacorta Baños (2003) p. 425.

117. Villacorta Baños (2003)p. 430.

118. Villacorta Baños (2003) p. 436.

119. Vázquez (2001) p. 7.

120. For instance the article "Las tiendas" in *Escenas Matritenses* by Mesonero Romanos (1991).

121. Campaigns in newspapers and magazines for the promotion of art exhibits were frequent and with some impact. A good example can be found in *El Museo Universal,* October 9, 1864.

122. According to Nora, a site of memory is any significant entity, whether material or nonmaterial in nature, which by dint of human will or the work of time has become a symbolic element of the memorial heritage of any community (in his case, the French community). See Nora (1984) vol. I, p. xvii.

123. See Prior (2002); Preziosi (2003); Lorente (1998); Duncan (1995); McClellan (1994); Bennett (1995).

124. See Bolaños (1997).

125. In his handbook for Spain Richard Ford dedicates forty-two pages to the description of museum collections. See Ford (1845) vol. 3, pp. 1109–51.

126. See Bolaños (1997); Géal (2005); Villafranca Jiménez (1998); García (1997).

127. *La Ilustración Española y Americana,* Madrid, July 28, 1871.

128. *La Ilustración Española y Americana,* August 15, 1871.

129. Boyer (2005) chap. 8.

130. Data from *Barómetro del Centro de Investigaciones Sociológicas,* February 2007.

131. Boyer (2005) pp. 14–26.

132. Boyer (2002) p. 14; Towner (1996) p. 97.

133. Pons and Serna (2006) p. 25.

134. Aresty (1970) p. 133.

135. Towner (1996) pp. 64–95.

136. Boyer (2000) pp. 30f.

137. Cited by Jarrasé (2002) p. 35.

138. Walton (1983) chap. 2; Corbin (1994) pp. 254–63.

139. Porter (1995) p. 36.

140. Urkia Etxabe (2004) pp. 105–11; Urkia Etxabe (1985).

141. Mackaman (1998).

142. Jarrassé (2002) p. 36.

143. Jarrassé (2002) pp. 37–40.

144. Hoibian (2000); Ring (2000).

145. Penez (2005) pp. 185–88.

146. Corbin (1994) p. 57.

147. Corbin (1994) pp. 64–67.

148. At present, Spain's tourist industry is among the three largest in the world; vacationing is a recognized right by Spanish labor law, and Spaniards practice tourism like their wealthier European neighbors.

149. *El Museo Universal,* Madrid, July 10, 1864.

150. Mesonero Romanos (1983) p. 63.

151. Pons and Serna (1992) pp. 235–36.

152. Barke and Towner (1996) pp. 24–25.

153. Sánchez Ferré (1992) p. 17; Urkia Etxabe (2004) p. 110.

154. The *Historia universal de las fuentes minerals en España* (General history of mineral springs in Spain) by Pedro Gómez Bedoya (1765), opened a historical cycle completed with the opening in 1790 of the first modern spas.

155. Information compiled from the work of Sánchez Ferré (2000) pp. 219 and 222.

156. Jarrasé (1999) p. 93.

157. Pons and Serna (2006) pp. 110–11.

158. Pons and Serna (2006) p. 112.

159. Pons and Serna (2006) p. 113.

160. Pons and Serna (2006) p. 115.

161. Montserrat Zapater (1998).

162. Urkia Etxabe (2004) p. 115.

163. Such as La Toja, Archena, Caldas de Oviedo, Mondariz, Carratraca.

164. Molina Villar (2004) pp. 805–25.

165. Walton and Smith (1996) p. 36.

166. Towner (1996) pp. 184–92.

167. Walton and Smith (1996) p. 36.

168. Larrinaga (2005) p. 88.

169. Aguirre Franco (1995) p. 90.

170. Larrinaga Rodríguez (2006) pp. 785–90.

171. *La Ilustración Española y Americana,* Madrid, August 15, 1871.

172. Aguirre Franco (1995) p. 112.

173. Larrinaga Rodríguez (2002) pp. 176–77.

174. Pons and Serna (2006) p. 56.

175. Baladía (2003) chap. I.

176. In his July 1842 visit to Paris, for instance, he went to the office of Dr. Malagou Désirabode, an internationally known dentist who probably did dental procedures not yet available in Valencia. Pons and Serna (2006) p. 60.

177. A symptom of the spread of a traveling culture in Spain was the publication after 1878 in Barcelona of the weekly magazine *El Viajero Ilustrado,* first Spanish periodical on traveling, inspired by the French *Le Tour de Monde* (1860). Among other things, *El Viajero Ilustrado* narrated for Spanish readers the journeys of David Livingstone and Henry Stanley to the heart of Africa.

178. Lagardera Otero (1995–96) pp. 152–53.

179. McFarland (2004) p. 28.

180. McFarland (2004) p. 40.

181. McFarland (2004) p. 48. What is interesting about this development was its speed. It started a in the mid-1870s, later than England and France, at the same time but with less intensity than in Austria or Belgium, and at the same time and same intensity than in Italy, Sweden, and Norway

182. Rementería y Fica (1837) chap. III (third part).

183. Burgos (1897); Sánchez Moreno (1925) pp. 159–63.

184. Fernández Sirvent (2007) p. 38.

185. Fernández Sirvent (2002) pp. 171–78.

186. Fernández Sirvent (2007) p. 39.

187. Fernandez Sirvent (2007) p. 41.

188. McFarland (2004) pp. 45–46 and 67.

189. Huggins (2000) p. 68f.

190. Andalusia's long tradition of horseback riding flourished in the mid-nineteenth century owing to sponsorship by members of the aristocracy and the urban bourgeoisie.

191. García Bonafe (1986) p. 40; Calatayud Miquel (2002).

192. McFarland (2004) pp. 46–47.

193. McFarland (2004) pp. 50–63.

194. Museu Nacional d'Art de Catalunya (2002).

195. Their names: Narciso Masferrer, Emilio Coll, Eduardo Charles, and Emilio Fernández.

Bibliography

Abad, Carmen. "El estrado: continuidad de la herencia islámica en los interiores domésticos zaragozanos de las primeras cortes borbónicas (1700-1759)." *Artigrama: Revista del Departamento de Historia del Arte de la Universidad de Zaragoza*, no.18 (2003): 375–92.

Aguiló Alonso, María Paz. *El mueble clásico español*. Madrid: CSIC, 1987.

Aguirre Franco, Rafael. *El turismo en el País Vasco: vida e historia*. Donostia–San Sebastian: Txertoa, 1995.

Aibar, Eduardo, and Wiebe E. Bijker. "Constructing a City: The Cerdà Plan for the Extension of Barcelona." *Science, Technology, & Human Values* (1997): 3–30.

Alberch i Fugueras, Ramón, ed. *Els barris de Barcelona*. 3 vols. Barcelona: Ajuntament de Barcelona, 1997–99.

Albó, Mariano de. *Observaciones sobre mejoras de Madrid y proyecto de ensanche de la Puerta del Sol*. Madrid: Imprenta de M. González, 1857.

Albó, Mariano de. *Sobre las principales causas que dependiendo esencialmente de la Policía Urbana, y del arte de edificar: han influido en el mal estado de riqueza, población y aspecto público en que se encuentra la capital de España, con respecto a las demás de Europa*. Por Mariano Albó coronel de infantería, ingeniero militar y arquitecto de la Real Academia de San Fernando, Madrid, 2 de febrero de 1846, Servicio Histórico Militar, Manuscritos.

Alcaide González, Rafael. "La introducción y el desarrollo del higienismo en España durante el siglo XIX. Precursores, continuadores, y marco legal de un proyecto científico y social." *Scripta Nova, Revista Electrónica de Geografía y Ciencias Sociales*. Universidad de Barcelona, 1999, 50 (www.ub.es/geocrit/nova1.htm).

Alcaide González, Rafael. "El ferrocarril como elemento estructurador de la morfología urbana: el caso de Barcelona 1848–1900." *Scripta Nova, Revista Electrónica de Geografía y Ciencias Sociales*. Universidad de Barcelona, 2005, 65 (www.ub.es/geocrit/nova1.htm).

Aldaraca, Bridget. *El ángel del hogar: Galdós and the Ideology of Domesticity in Spain*. Chapel Hill: University of North Carolina Press, 1991.

Alier, Roger. *Historia de la ópera*. Teià: Ma Non Troppo, 2002.

Alier, Roger, et al. *El libro de la zarzuela*. Madrid: Daimon, 1982.

Alier, Roger, and Carles Guerra. *El gran llibre del Liceu*. Barcelona: Edicions 62, 2004.

Almagro San Martín, Melchor de. *Biografía del 1900*. Madrid: Revista de Occidente, 1944.

Almanak mercantil o Guía de comerciantes. Madrid: Viuda de Joaquín Ibarra, 1795.

Álvarez Carretero, Antonio. *Catecismo de higiene y economía doméstica precedido de unas nociones de fisiología.* Burgos: Librería de S. Rodríguez Alonso, 1889.

Álvarez de Miranda, Pedro. "Léxico y sociedad en la España del siglo XVIII (Con un excurso sobre la historia de *burgués*)." In *Historia social y literature*, ed. Roberto Fernández and Jacques Soubeyroux, vol. 2, pp. 7–28. Lleida: Milenio; Saint-Étienne: Université Jean Monnet, 2001.

Álvarez Junco, José. *Mater Dolorosa: la idea de España en el siglo XIX.* Madrid: Taurus, 2001.

Amann, Elizabeth. "Scarlet Letters: Translation, Fashion, and Revolution in 1790s Spain." *Dieciocho* 31, no. 1 (Spring 2008): 93–114.

Appleby, Joyce, and Lynn Hunt. *Telling the Truth about History.* New York: Norton, 1994.

Archibald, Diana C. *Domesticity, Imperialism, and Emigration in the Victorian Novel.* Columbia: University of Missouri Press, 2002.

Arditi, Jorge. *A Genealogy of Manners: Transformations of Social Relations in France and England from the Fourteenth to the Eighteenth Century.* Chicago: University of Chicago Press, 1998.

Aresty, Esther B. *The Best Behavior: The Course of Good Manners—from Antiquity to the Present—as Seen through Courtesy and Etiquette Books.* New York: Simon and Schuster, 1970.

Ariès, Philippe. *L'enfant et la vie familiale sous l'ancien régime.* Paris: Éditions du Seuil, 1973.

Ariza Muñoz, Carmen. "Jardines de recreo de Madrid: los llamados Campos Elíseos." *Goya: Revista de arte* 1988/204a, pp. 342–51.

Ariza Muñoz, Carmen. *Los jardines de Madrid en el siglo XIX.* Madrid: El Avapiés, 1988.

Ariza Muñoz, Carmen. *Los jardines del Buen Retiro de Madrid.* 2 vols. Barcelona: Lunwerg, 1990.

Aviñola, Xosé. "L'afició operística a Barcelona." *Barcelona. Metròpolis Mediterrània* 48 (1999).

Azagra y Ros, Joaquín Pedro. "Urban Growth and 'Ensanches': Neighbours and Householders in 1930s Valencia." *Bulletin of Spanish Studies: Hispanic Studies and Research on Spain, Portugal, and Latin America* 75, no. 5 (1998): 133–56.

Bahamonde Magro, Angel. *El horizonte económico de la burguesía isabelina: Madrid 1856–1866.* Madrid: Universidad Complutense, 1981.

Bahamonde Magro, Ángel. *El Real Madrid en la historia de España.* Madrid: Taurus, 2002.

Bahamonde Magro, Ángel, and José Cayuela. *Hacer las Américas: las élites coloniales españolas en el siglo XIX.* Madrid: Alianza, 1992.

Bahamonde Magro, Ángel, and Jesús A. Martínez. *Historia de España, siglo XIX.* Madrid: Cátedra, 1994.

Bahamonde Magro, Ángel, and Luis Enrique Otero Carvajal. "Madrid, de capital imperial a región metropolitana. Cinco siglos de terciarización." In *Papeles de Economía Española. Economía de las Comunidades Autónomas: Madrid*, pp. 18–30. Madrid: Papeles de Economía Española, 1999.

Bahamonde Magro, Ángel, and Luis Enrique Otero Carvajal. "Madrid. De territorio fronterizo a región metropolitan." In *España. Autonomias*, ed. Juan Pablo Fusi, pp. 519–615. Madrid: Espasa-Calpe, 1989.

Baker, Edward, *Materiales para escribir Madrid. Literatura y espacios urbanos de Moratín a Galdós*. Madrid: Siglo XXI, 1991.

Baladía, F. Javier. *Antes de que el tiempo lo borre: recuerdos de los años de esplendor y bohemia de la burguesía catalana*. Barcelona: Editorial Juventud, 2003.

Ballarín Domingo, Pilar. *La educación de las mujeres en la España contemporánea (siglos XIX–XX)*. Madrid: Síntesis, 2001.

Bannet, Eve Tavor. *The Domestic Revolution: Enlightenment Feminisms and the Novel*. Baltimore: Johns Hopkins University Press, 2000.

Baquero Escudero, Ana. *La voz femenina en la narrativa epistolar*. Cádiz: Universidad de Cádiz, 2003.

Barbazza, Marie-Catherine, Simon Palmer, Maria del Carmen, and Jean-Louis Guereña. "Bibliographie des traités de savoir vivre espagnols." In *Bibliographie des traités de savoir-vivre en Europe*, ed. Alain Montandon, pp. 103–93. Clermont-Ferrand: Faculté des Lettres et Sciences Humaines, 1995.

Barke, M., and J. Towner. "Exploring the History of Leisure and Tourism in Spain." In *Tourism in Spain: Critical Issues*, ed. M. Barke, J. Towner, and M. T. Newton, pp. 3–33. Wallingford, England: CAB International, 1996.

Baroja, Pío. *Memorias*. Madrid: Ediciones Minotauro, 1955.

Baroja, Pío. *Las noches del Buen Retiro*. Madrid: Caro Raggio, 1997.

Basurto, Ferro, Nieves, Paloma Rodríguez-Escudero Sánchez, and Jaione Velilla Iriondo. *El Bilbao que pudo ser: proyectos para una ciudad, 1800–1940*. Bilbao: Diputación Foral de Bizkaia, Departamento de Urbanismo, 1999.

Battaner, María Paz. *Vocabulario político-social en España (1868–1873)*. Madrid: Real Academia Española, 1977.

Benevolo, Leonardo. *The European City*. Oxford: Blackwell, 1993.

Bennett, Tony. *The Birth of the Museum: History, Theory, Politics*. London: Routledge, 1995.

Benson, John, and Gareth Shaw, eds. *The Evolution of Retail Systems, c. 1800–1914*. Leicester: Leicester University Press, 1992.

Benson, John, and Laura Ugolini. *Cultures of Selling: Perspectives on Consumption and Society since 1700*. Aldershot, England, and Burlington, Vt.: Ashgate, 2006.

Berg, Maxine, and Helen Clifford, eds. *Consumers and Luxury: Consumer Culture in Europe, 1650–1850*. Manchester: Manchester University Press, 1999.

Berman, Marshall. *All That Is Solid Melts into Air: The Experience of Modernity.* New York: Simon and Schuster, 1981.

Bermejo Berros, Jesús, ed. *Publicidad y cambio social: contribuciones históricas y perspectivas de futuro.* Sevilla: Comunicación Social, 2005.

Bertrán de Lis, Fernando. *Reglas de urbanidad para uso de las señoritas.* Valencia: Librerías "París-Valencia," 1995. Reprod. de la ed. de Valencia: Imprenta de Julián Mariana, 1859.

Bertrán, Marc Jesús. *El Gran Teatre del Liceu de Barcelona.* Barcelona: Oliva de Vilanova, 1931.

Bestard de la Torre, Vizcondesa de Barrantes (pseud. of Alfredo Pallardó). *La elegancia en el trato social: reglas de etiqueta y cortesanía en todos los actos de la vida.* Madrid: A. P. Guillot y Compañía, 1898.

Blanco, Alda. *Escritoras virtuosas: narradoras de la domesticidad en la España isabelina.* Granada: Editorial Universidad de Granada, 2001.

Blanco, Mercedes. "Les discours sur le savoir-vivre dans l'Espagne du siècle d'or." In *Pour une histoire des traités de savoir-vivre en Europe,* ed. Alain Montandon, pp. 111–49. Clermont-Ferrand: Association des Publications de la Faculté des Lettres et Sciences Humaines de Clermont-Ferrand, 1994.

Blumin, Stuart M. *The Emergence of the Middle Class: Social Experience in the American City, 1760–1900.* Cambridge: Cambridge University Press, 1989.

Bolaños, María. *Historia de los museos en España: memoria, cultura, sociedad.* Gijón: Trea, 1997.

Bolufer Peruga, Mónica, and Morán Deusa Isabel. *Amor, matrimonio, y familia. La construcción histórica de la familia moderna.* Madrid: Síntesis, 1994.

Bolufer Peruga, Mónica. *Mujeres e ilustración: la construcción de la feminidad en la España del siglo XVIII.* Valencia, Diputació de València: Institució Alfons el Magnànim, 1998.

Bonastre, Francesc. "Els models simfònics." *Recerca musicològica* 14–15 (2004–5): 57–76.

Bonet Correa, Antonio, Soledad Lorenzo Fornés, and Fátima Miranda Regojo. *La polémica ingenieros-arquitectos en España, siglo XIX.* Madrid: Colegio de Ingenieros de Caminos, Canales y Puertos, Turner, 1985.

Bonnell, Victoria E., and Lynn Hunt, eds. *Beyond the Cultural Turn: New Directions in the Study of Society and Culture.* Berkeley: University of California Press, 1999.

Botrel, Jean F., and J. La Bouil. "Sur le concept de 'clase media' dans la pensée bourgeois en Espagne au XIXe siècle." In *La question de la "bourgeoisie" dans le monde hispanique au XIXe siècle,* pp. 137–60. Bordeaux: Éditions Bière, 1973.

Boulton, William Biggs. *The Amusements of Old London; Being a Survey of the Sports and Pastimes, Tea Gardens and Parks, Playhouses and Other Diversions of the People of London from the 17th to the Beginning of the 19th Century.* London: J. C. Nimmo, 1901.

Bourdieu, Pierre. *Distinction: A Social Critique of the Judgement of Taste.* Cambridge: Harvard University Press, 1984.

Bourdieu, Pierre. *Cosas dichas.* Madrid: Gedisa, 1988.

Bourdieu, Pierre. *Language and Symbolic Power.* Cambridge: Harvard University Press, 1991.

Bowlby, Rachel. *Carried Away: The Invention of Modern Shopping.* New York: Columbia University Press, 2001.

Boyer, Marc. *Histoire de l'invention du tourisme, XVIe–XIXe siècles: origine et développement du tourisme dans le sud-est de la France.* La Tour d'Aigue: Éditions de l'Aube, 2000.

Boyer, Marc. "El turismo en Europa, de la Edad Moderna al siglo XX." *Historia contemporánea* 25 (2002): 13–31.

Boyer, Marc. *Histoire générale du tourisme du XVIe au XXIe siècle.* Paris: L'Harmattan, 2005.

Bozal, Valeriano, and A. Rodríguez. *Colección General de trages que en la actualidad se usan en España principiada en el año 1801.* Madrid: Visor, 1982.

Bretón de los Herreros, Manuel. *Obras de Don Manuel Bretón de los Herreros.* Vol. 1. Madrid: Imprenta de Miguel Ginesta, 1883.

Brewer, John. *The Pleasures of the Imagination: English Culture in the Eighteenth Century.* London: HarperCollins, 1997.

Brewer, John, and Roy Porter, eds. *Consumption and the World of Goods.* New York: Routledge, 1993.

Briggs, Asa. *Victorian Things.* Stroud, Gloucestershire: Sutton, 2003.

Brosterman, Norman. *Out of Time: Designs for the Twentieth-Century Future.* New York: Harry N. Abrams, 2000.

Bryden, Ingra, and Janet Floyd. *Domestic Space: Reading the Nineteenth-Century Interior.* Manchester: Manchester University Press, 2000.

Bryson, Anna. *From Courtesy to Civility: Changing Codes of Conduct in Early Modern England.* Oxford: Clarendon, 1998.

Burgos, Carmen de. *Arte de la elegancia.* Valencia: F. Sempere y Cia, [n.d.].

Burgos, Carmen de. *Arte de saber vivir. Prácticas sociales recopiladas por Carmen de Burgos Seguí (Colombine).* Valencia: F. Sempere y Cia., 1897.

Burgos, Carmen de. *El arte de ser mujer: Belleza y perfección.* Madrid: Juan Pueyo, 1920.

Burke, Peter. "*Rest et verba*: Conspicuous Consumption in the Early Modern World." In *Consumption and the World of Goods,* ed. John Brewer and Roy Porter, pp. 148–61. New York: Routledge, 1993.

Burke, Peter. *The Fortunes of the Courtier: The European Reception of Castiglione's Cortegiano.* Cambridge: Polity, 1995.

Burke, Peter. *What is Cultural History?* Cambridge: Polity, 2004.

Burns, Kathryn. "Notaries, Truth, and Consequences." *American Historical Review* 110, no. 2 (2005): 350–79.

Burr, Grace H. *Hispanic Furniture: From the Fifteenth through the Eighteenth Century.* New York: Archive, 1964.

Bushman, Richard L. *The Refinement of America: Persons, Houses, Cities.* New York: Vintage Books, 1993.

Caballé, F., and A. Nicolau. "Industria i ciutat a la primera meitat del segle XIX. . . ." Vol. 2. III Congrés d'Història de Barcelona, Barcelona, Ajuntament, 1993.

Caballero, Fermín. *Noticias topográfico-estadísticas sobre la administración de Madrid.* Madrid: Yenes, 1840.

Cabarrús, Conde de. *Cartas sobre los obstáculos que la naturaleza, la opinión y las leyes oponen a la felicidad pública.* Madrid: Fundación Banco Exterior, 1990.

Cabeza, Felipa Máxima de. *La Señorita instruida, ó sea Manual del bello sexo.* Madrid: Imprenta de las Escuelas Pías, 1859.

Cabrera, Miguel A. "Developments in Contemporary Spanish Historiography: From Social History to the New Cultural History." *Journal of Modern History* 77 (2005): 988–1023.

Cadalso, José. *Cartas Marruecas.* Madrid: Imprenta de Sancha, 1793.

Calatayud Miquel, Francisco. *De la gimnasia de Amorós al deporte de masas (1770–1993): una aproximación histórica a la educación física y el deporte en España.* València: Ajuntament de València, 2002.

Calefato, Patrizia. *The Clothed Body.* Oxford: Berg, 2004.

Calhoun, Craig, ed. *Habermas and the Public Sphere.* Cambridge: MIT Press, 1992.

Callières, François de. *La urbanidad y la cortesía universal que se practica entre las personas de distinction.* Trans. and ed. from the French by D. Ignacio Benito Avalle. Madrid: Imprenta de Miguèl Escribano, 1762. (First ed., 1744, reed., 1778).

Campbell, Colin. *The Romantic Ethic and the Spirit of Modern Consumerism.* Oxford and New York: Blackwell, 1987.

Cantizano Márquez, Blasina. "La mujer en la prensa femenina del XIX." *Ambitos: Revista internacional de comunicación* 11–12 (2004): 281–98.

Caraccioli, Marqués de. *El verdadero mentor o educación de la nobleza.* Trans. Francisco Mariano Nipho. Madrid: Imprenta de Andrés Ramírez, 1787.

Carandell, Luis. *La familia Cortés: manual de la vieja urbanidad.* Madrid: Aguilar, 2000.

Carbajo Isla, María. *La población de la villa de Madrid: desde finales del siglo XVI hasta mediados del siglo XIX.* Madrid: Siglo XXI, 1987.

Carbonell i Guberna, Jaume. *Josep Anselm Clavé i el naixement del cant coral a Catalunya, 1850–1874.* Cabrera de Mar: Galerada, 2000.

Carbonell i Guberna, Jaume. "Aportaciones al estudio de la sociabilidad coral en la España contemporánea." *Hispania, Revista española de historia* 214 (2003): 485–504.

Carson, Cary, Ronald Hoffman, and Peter J. Albert, eds. *Of Consuming Interests: The Style of Life in the Eighteenth Century.* Charlottesville: University Press of Virginia, 1994.

Carter, Philip. *Men and the Emergence of Polite Society: Britain, 1660–1800.* New York: Longman, 2001.

Castells, L. "La Bella Easo: 1864–1936." In *Historia de Donostia–San Sebastián,* ed. Miguel Artola, pp. 283–386. San Sebastian: Nerea, 2000.

Castells, Manuel. *The Rise of the Network Society.* Cambridge: Blackwell, 1996.

Castro, Carlos María de. *Plan Castro,* estudio preliminar de Antonio Bonet Correa. Madrid: Colegio Oficial de Arquitectos, 1978.

Castro, Concepción de. *El pan de Madrid: el abasto de las ciudades españolas del antiguo régimen.* Madrid: Alianza Editorial, 1987.

Cayuela Fernández, José Gregorio, and Ángel Bahamonde Magro. "La creación de nobleza en Cuba durante el siglo XIX." *Historia social* 11 (1991): 57–82.

Charnon-Deutsch, Lou. *Narratives of Desire: Nineteenth-Century Spanish Fiction by Women.* University Park: Pennsylvania State University Press, 1994.

Charnon-Deutsch, Lou, and Jo Labanyi, eds. *Culture and Gender in Nineteenth-Century Spain.* Oxford: Oxford University Press, 1995.

Chartier, Roger. *Les origines culturelles de la Révolution française.* Paris: Éditions du Seuil, 2000.

Checa Godoy, Fernando. *Historia de la publicidad.* Madrid: Netbiblo, 2007.

Clark, Walter Aaron. *Enrique Granados: Poet of the Piano.* Oxford: Oxford University Press, 2006.

Clavijo y Fajardo, José. *El pensador (1762–1767).* Ed. Yolanda Arencibia. 7 vols. Las Palmas: Universidad de Las Palmas de Gran Canaria, 1999.

Clunas, Craig. "Modernity Global and Local: Consumption and the Rise of the West." *American Historical Review* 104 (1999): 1497–1511.

Clunas, Craig. *Superfluous Things: Material Culture and Social Status in Early Modern China.* Honolulu: University of Hawai'i Press, 2004.

Cohen, Anthony P. *Self Consciousness: An Alternative Anthropology of Identity.* London: Routledge, 1994.

Cohen, Monica F. *Professional Domesticity in the Victorian Novel: Women, Work, and Home.* Cambridge: Cambridge University Press, 2005.

Colbert, María. *Reading the Ideology of Domesticity: Women, Identity, and the Market in Restoration Madrid.* Ph.D. dissertation, Harvard University, 2005.

Comín, Francisco, Pablo Martín Aceña, and Concepción de Castro. *Campomanes y su obra económica.* Madrid: Instituto de Estudios Fiscales, 2004.

Conlin, Jonathan, "Vauxhall Revisited: The Afterlife of a London Pleasure Garden, 1770–1859." *Journal of British Studies,* no. 45 (October 2006): 718–43.

Coontz, Stephanie. *Marriage, a History: From Obedience to Intimacy, or How Love Conquered Marriage.* New York: Viking, 2005.

Copeland, Edward. *Women Writing about Money: Women's Fiction in England, 1790–1820.* Cambridge: Cambridge University Press, 1995.

Corbin, Alain. *The Lure of the Sea: The Discovery of the Seaside in the Western World, 1750–1840.* Berkeley: University of California Press, 1994.

Corbin, Alain, Julia Csergo, et al. *L'avènement des loisirs, 1850–1960.* Paris: Aubier, 1995.

Corominas i Ayala, Miquel. *Los orígenes del Ensanche de Barcelona: suelo, técnica, e iniciativa.* Barcelona: Edicions UPC, 2002.

Cotarelo y Mori, E. *Colección de entremeses, Loas, Bailes, Jácaras y Mojigangas desde fines del siglo XVI a mediados del XVIII.* Madrid: NBAE, 17, 1911, pp. clxiv–cclxxiii.

Cross, Gary S. *A Social History of Leisure since 1600.* State College, Pa.: Venture, 1990.

Crossick, Geoffrey, and Serge Jaumain. "The World of the Department Store: Distribution, Culture and Social Change." In *Cathedrals of Consumption: The European Department Store, 1850–1939,* ed. Geoffrey Crossick and Serge Jaumain, pp. 1–45. Aldershot, England, and Brookfield, Vt.: Ashgate, 1999.

Cruz, Jesús. "Cambistas madrileños en la segunda mitad del siglo XVIII." In *Madrid en la sociedad del siglo XIX,* ed. A. Bahamonde Magro, and L. E. Otero Carvajal, vol. 1, pp. 454–74. Madrid: CIDUR, 1986.

Cruz, Jesús. *Gentlemen, Bourgeois, and Revolutionaries: Political Change and Cultural Persistence among the Spanish Dominant Groups, 1750–1850.* Cambridge: Cambridge University Press, 1996.

Cruz, Jesús. "Building Liberal Identities in Nineteenth-Century Madrid: The Role of Middle Class Material Culture." *Americas* 60, no. 3 (January 2004): 391–410.

Cruz, Ramón de la. *Sainetes.* Ed. and notes by J. M. Sala Valldaura, Nathalie Bittoun-Debruyne, and Mireille Coulon. Barcelona: Crítica, 1996.

Csikszentmihalyi, Mihaly. *The Meaning of Things: Domestic Symbols and the Self.* Cambridge: Cambridge University Press, 1981.

Cuartas, Javier. *Biografía de el corte inglés.* Barcelona: Dictext, 2005.

Czaplicka, John J., and Blair A. Ruble, eds. *Composing Urban History and the Constitution of Civic Identities.* Baltimore: Johns Hopkins University Press, 2003.

Darnton, Robert. *The Business of Enlightenment: A Publishing History of the Encyclopédie, 1775–1800.* Cambridge: Belknap Press, 1979.

Darnton, Robert. *What Was Revolutionary about the French Revolution?* Waco: Baylor University Press, 1990.

Daumard, Adeline. *Les bourgeois et la bourgeoisie en France depuis 1815.* Paris: Aubier, 1987.

Daumard, Adeline. *La bourgeoisie parisienne de 1815 à 1848.* Paris: Albin Michel, 1996.

Davidoff, Leonor, and Catherine Hall. *Family Fortunes: Men and Women of the English*

Middle Class, 1780–1850. Chicago: University of Chicago Press, 1987.

Davidson, Jenny. *Hypocrisy and the Politics of Politeness: Manners and Morals from Locke to Austen*. Cambridge: Cambridge University Press, 2004.

Dávila Corona, Rosa María, and Máximo García Fernández. "El consumo de productos textiles en Valladolid: 1750–1850." In *Investigaciones Históricas: Época moderna y contemporánea* 2001, pp. 133–80.

Day, Charles William. *Etiquette*. New York: Wilson & Company, 1845.

De Vries, Jan. "Between Purchasing Power and the World of Goods: Understanding the Household Economy in Early Modern Europe." In *Consumption and the World of Goods*, ed. John Brewer and Roy Porter, pp. 85–132. New York: Routledge, 1993.

De Vries, Jan. *The Industrious Revolution: Consumer Behavior and the Household Economy, 1650 to the Present*. Cambridge and New York: Cambridge University Press, 2008.

Dean, M. *Governmentality: Power and Rule in Modern Society*. London: Sage, 1999.

Decker, Jeffrey Louis. *Made in America: Self-Styled Success from Horatio Alger to Oprah Winfrey*. Minneapolis: University of Minnesota Press, 1997.

DeJean, Joan E. *The Essence of Style: How the French Invented High Fashion, Fine Food, Chic Cafés, Style, Sophistication, and Glamour*. New York: Free Press, 2005.

Deleito y Piñuaela, José. *La mujer, la casa, y la moda en la España del rey poeta*. Madrid: Espasa, 1966.

Díaz de Escovar, Narciso, and Francisco de P. Lasso de la Vega. *Historia del teatro español. Comediantes. Escritores. Curiosidades escénicas*. 2 vols. Barcelona: Montaner y Simón, 1924.

Díaz-Plaja, Fernando. *La vida cotidiana en la España Romántica*. Madrid: Edaf, 1993.

Díez Baldeón, Clementina. *Arquitectura y clases sociales en el Madrid del siglo XIX*. Madrid: Siglo XXI, 1987.

Dufaux, Ermance. *El buen gusto en el trato social y en las ceremonias civiles y religiosas, versión castellana de Miguel de Toro y Gómez*. Paris: Garnier, 1890.

Duncan, Carol. *Civilizing Rituals: Inside Public Art Museums*. London: Routledge, 1995.

Duran i Sanpere, Agustí. *Barcelona i la seva historia*. 3 vols. Barcelona: Curial, 1972.

Duroux, Rose, ed. *Les traités de savoir-vivre en Espagne et au Portugal du Moyen Âge à nos jours*. Clermont Ferrand: Centre de Recherche sur les Littératures Modernes et Contemporaines, 1995.

Dyer, Christopher. *Standards of Living in the Later Middle Ages: Social Change in England, 1200–1520*. Cambridge: Cambridge University Press, 1989.

Edelstein, T. J. *Vauxhall Gardens*. New Haven, Conn.: Yale Center for British Art, 1983.

Edwards, Clive. *Turning Houses into Homes: A History of the Retailing and Consumption of Domestic Furnishings*. Aldershot, England, and Burlington, Vt.: Ashgate, 2005.

Eijoecente, Luis de. *Libro del agrado, impreso por la virtud en la imprenta del gusto, a la moda y al ayre del presente siglo*. Madrid: Joachin Ibarra, 1785.

Eiland, William U., ed. *Images of Women in Seventeenth-Century Dutch Art: Domesticity and the Representation of the Peasant.* Athens: University of Georgia Press, 1996.

El ensanche de la ciudad de Valencia de 1884. Valencia: Colegio Oficial de Arquitectos, Centro de Servicios e Informes, 1984.

El Instructor del bellosexo, ó sea breves tratados de religion, moral, gramática, aritmética, higiene, economía doméstica y urbanidad: Para uso de las escuelas de niñas. Zaragoza: Imprenta de V. Andrés, 1857.

El libro de las familias y novísimo manual de cocina, higiene y economía doméstica: Contiene mas de dos mil fórmulas de ejecución sencilla y fácil, el arte de trinchar. Madrid: Imprenta de M. Rivadeneyra, 1856.

Eleb, Monique, and Anne Debarre. *L'invention de l'habitation moderne: Paris, 1880–1914.* Paris: Hazan; Brussels: Archives d'architecture moderne, 1995.

Elias, Norbert. *The Civilizing Process.* 2 vols. Vol. 1: *The History of Manners.* Vol. 2: *Power and Civility.* New York: Urizen Books, 1978.

Elias, Norbert. *The Court Society.* Oxford: Blackwell, 1983.

Epstein, Barbara Leslie. *The Politics of Domesticity: Women, Evangelism, and Temperance in Nineteenth-Century America.* Middletown, Conn.: Wesleyan University Press, 1981.

Erice Sebares, Francisco. *La burguesía industrial asturiana (1885–1920), aproximación a su estudio.* Gijón: Silverio Cañada, 1980.

Erice Sebares, Francisco. *Propietarios, comerciantes, e industriales: burguesía y desarrollo capitalista en la Asturias del siglo XIX (1830–1885).* 2 vols. Oviedo: Universidad de Oviedo, Servicio de Publicaciones, 1995.

Escobar Arronis, José. "Sobre la formación del artículo de costumbres: Mariano de Rementería y Fica, redactor del 'Correo literario y mercantil.'" *Boletín de la Real Academia Española* 50 (1970): 559–73.

Escolano Benito, Agustín. *El pensil de las niñas: la educación de la mujer. Invención de una tradición.* Madrid: Aguilar, 2004.

Espigado, Gloria. "Women and Publishing in Nineteenth-Century Spain." In *Women, Business, and Finance in Nineteenth-Century Europe: Rethinking Separate Spheres,* ed. Robert Beachy, Béatrice Craig, and Alastair Owens, pp. 96–109. Oxford: Berg, 2006.

Estomba, Fernando, and Santiago de Pablo Contreras. "Deporte y sociedad en el País Vasco durante la II República: de diversión amateur a espectáculo profesional." *Cuadernos de Alzate: revista vasca de la cultura y las ideas* 27 (2002): 155–77.

Faciabén Lacorte, Patricia. "Los grandes almacenes en Barcelona." In *Scripta Nova. Revista Electrónica de Geografía y Ciencias Sociales.* Universidad de Barcelona, 2003, vol. VII, núm. 194 (www.ub.es/geocrit/nova1.htm).

Fabra, Camilo. *Código o deberes de buena sociedad.* Barcelona: Librería de Juan y Antonio Bastinos, 1883.

Fabré i Carreras, Xavier, et al. *Arquitectura i ciutat a l'Exposició Universal de Barcelona, 1888.* Barcelona: Universitat Politècnica de Catalunya, 1988.

Fairchilds, Cissie. "Consumption in Early Modern Europe: A Review Article." *Comparative Studies in Society and History* 35 (1993): 850–58.

Faret, Nicolas. *L'Honneste homme, ou l'art de plaire à la court.* Édition critique de M. Magendie. Paris: Presses universitaires de France, 1925.

Feijoo, Fr. Benito Jerónimo. *Obras escogidas del padre fray Benito Jerónimo Feijoo y Montenegro.* Biblioteca de Autores Españoles. Vol. 56. Madrid: M. Rivadeneyra, 1863–1961.

Fernández de los Ríos, Ángel. *El futuro Madrid: paseos mentales por la capital de España, tal cual es y tal cual debe dejarla transformada la revolución.* Madrid: Imprenta de la Biblioteca Universal Económica, 1868. Facsimile ed., intro. by Antonio Bonet Correa, Barcelona: José Batlló, 1975.

Fernández de los Ríos, Ángel. *Guía de Madrid. Manual del Madrileño y del forastero.* Madrid: La Ilustración Española y Americana, 1876. Facsimile ed., Madrid: La Librería, 2002.

Fernández Sirvent, Rafael. "Aproximación a la obra educativa de un afrancesado: el coronel Francisco Amorós y Ondeano." *Revista de historia contemporánea* 1 (2002): 167–82.

Fernández Sirvent, Rafael. "Memoria y olvido de Francisco Amorós y de su modelo educativo gimnástico y moral." *Revista Internacional de Ciencias del Deporte* 6 (2007): 24–51.

Fernández-Armesto, Felipe. *Barcelona: A Thousand Years of the City's Past.* Oxford: Oxford University Press, 1992.

Ferrer, Antonio Carlos. *Paseo por Madrid, 1835.* Madrid: Colección Almenara, 1952.

Fiedler, Johanna. *Molto agitato: The Mayhem behind the Music at the Metropolitan Opera.* New York: Nan A. Talese/Doubleday, 2001.

Flanders, Judith. *Inside the Victorian Home: A Portrait of Domestic Life in Victorian England.* New York: Norton, 2004.

Fluvià i Escorsa, Armand de. *Repertori de grandeses, títols i corporacions nobiliàries de Catalunya.* 2 vols. Sant Cugat del Vallès: Institut d'Estudis Nobiliaris Catalans, 1998–2004.

Fontbona, Francesc, ed. *El Cercle del Liceu: història, art, cultura.* Barcelona: Catalanes, 1991.

Ford, Richard. *A Hand-book for Travellers in Spain.* 3 vols. London: J. Murray, 1845.

Franits, Wayne E. *Paragons of Virtue: Women and Domesticity in Seventeenth-Century Dutch Art.* Cambridge: Cambridge University Press, 1993.

Franits, Wayne E. *Dutch Seventeenth-Century Genre Painting: Its Stylistic and Thematic Evolution.* New Haven: Yale University Press, 2004.

Fresquet Febrer, José Luis. *Francisco Méndez Alvaro (1806–1883) y las ideas sanitarias del liberalismo moderado.* Madrid: Ministerio de Sanidad y Consumo, 1990.

Fritzsche, Peter. *Reading Berlin 1900.* Cambridge: Harvard University Press, 1996.

Frost, Daniel. "Mesonero's Modern Landscapes." *Journal of Spanish Cultural Studies* 3 (2005): 319–34.

Frost, Daniel. *Cultivating Madrid: Public Space and Middle-Class Culture in the Spanish Capital, 1833–1890.* Lewisburg, Pa.: Bucknell University Press, 2008.

Frykman, Jonas, and Orvar Löfgren. *Culture Builders: A Historical Anthropology of Middle-Class Life.* New Brunswick, N.J.: Rutgers University Press, 1987.

Fusi Aizpurúa, Juan Pablo, and Jordi Palafox Gámir. *España, 1808–1996: el desafío de la modernidad.* Madrid: Espasa, 1997.

García Bonafe, Milagros. "Notas para una historia del deporte en España." *Revista de Occidente* 62–63 (1986): 35–50.

García Fernández, Máximo. "Los bienes dotales en la ciudad de Valladolid, 1700–1850: el ajuar doméstico y la evolución del consumo y la demanda." In *Consumo, condiciones de vida, y comercialización: Cataluña y Castilla, siglos XVII–XIX,* ed. Jaume Torras and Bartolomé Yun Casalilla, pp. 133–58. Valladolid: Consejería de Educación y Cultura, 1999.

García Fernández, Máximo. "El consumo, la demanda, y el mercado en Castilla, 1750–1850." In *Política y cultura en la época moderna: (cambios dinásticos, milenarismos, mesianismos, y utopías),* ed. Jaime Contreras Contreras, Alfredo Alvar Ezquerra, and José Ignacio Ruiz Rodríguez, pp. 725–34. Universidad de Alcalá de Henares, Servicio de Publicaciones, 2004.

García, Andrea A. *Museus d'art de Barcelona: antecedents, genesi, i desenvolupament fins l'any 1915.* Barcelona: Lunwerg, 1997.

Garrioch, David. *The Formation of the Parisian Bourgeoisie, 1690–1830.* Cambridge: Harvard University Press, 1996.

Garrison, J. Ritchie. *Landscape and Material Life in Franklin County, Massachusetts, 1770–1860.* Knoxville: University of Tennessee Press, 1991.

Gay, Peter. *The Bourgeois Experience: Victoria to Freud.* New York: Oxford University Press, 1984.

Gay, Peter. *Schnitzler's Century: The Making of Middle-Class Culture, 1815–1914.* New York: Norton, 2002.

Géal, Pierre. *La naissance des musées d'art en Espagne: (XVIIIe–XIXe siècles).* Madrid: Casa de Velázquez, 2005.

Geertz, Clifford. *The Interpretation of Cultures: Selected Essays.* New York: Basic Books, 1973.

Gerhard, Anselm. *The Urbanization of Opera: Music Theater in Paris in the Nineteenth Century.* Chicago: University of Chicago Press, 1998.

Gies, David T. *The Theatre in Nineteenth-Century Spain.* Cambridge: Cambridge University Press, 1994.

Gies, David T. "«Pentimento»: El anti-canon de la literatura decimonónica española." In *La elaboración del canon en la literatura española del siglo XIX, Sociedad de Literatura Española del Siglo XIX,* ed. Luis F. Díaz Larios et al., pp. 175–84. Coloquio 2°, 1999, Barcelona. Barcelona Universitat, 2002.

Glas, Eduardo Jorge. *Bilbao's Modern Business Elite.* Reno: University of Nevada Press, 1997.

Goldman, Peter. "What's in a Word? 'Class' and Its Evolution in the Eighteenth Century." *Romance Quarterly* 29, no. 1 (1992): 7–16.

Gómez de la Serna, Gaspar. *Gracias y desgracias del Teatro Real: (Abreviatura de su historia).* Madrid: Servicio de Publicaciones del Ministerio de Educación y Ciencia, 1976.

González Díez, Laura, and Pedro Pérez Cuadrado. "La Moda elegante ilustrada y el Correo de las Damas, dos publicaciones especializadas en moda en el siglo XIX." *Doxa Comunicación: revista interdisciplinar de estudios de comunicación y ciencias sociales,* no. 8 (2009): 53–72.

González Yanci, María del Pilar. *Fernández de los Ríos, el republicano que soñó la transformación de Madrid.* Madrid: Artes Gráficas Municipales, Área de Régimen Interior y Patrimonio, 2002.

González Yanci, María Pilar. Visión de "Madrid en la obra de Fernández de los Ríos desde su exilio en Francia." In *Palabras y recuerdos: homenaje a Rosa María Calvet Lora,* ed. María Rosario Ozaeta Gálvez and Doina Popa-Lisseanu, pp. 89–93. Madrid: Universidad Nacional de Educación a Distancia, 2004.

Goodman, Douglas J., and Mirelle Cohen. *Consumer Culture: A Reference Handbook.* Santa Barbara, Calif.: ABC-CLIO, 2004.

Goodwin, Lorinda. *An Archaeology of Manners: The Polite World of the Merchant Elite in Colonial Massachusetts.* New York: Kluwer Academic/Plenum, 1999.

Gottdiener, M. "Approaches to Consumption: Classical and Contemporary Perspectives." In *New Forms of Consumption: Consumers, Culture, and Commodification,* ed. Mark Gottdiener. Lanham, Md.: Rowman & Littlefield, 2000.

Gracián, Baltasar. *Obras completas de Baltasar Gracián.* 2 vols. Madrid: Turner, 1993.

Gracián, Baltasar. *El discreto.* Ed. Aurora Egido. Madrid: Alianza Editorial, 1997.

Gracián, Baltasar. *El héroe.* Ed. Aurora Egido. Zaragoza: Gobierno de Aragón, 2001.

Grau, Ramón, et al. "Las batallas por el Ensanche." In *Exposición universal de Barcelona: llibre del centenario, 1888–1988,* ed. Ramón Grau and Marina López. Barcelona: L'Avenç, 1988.

Grau, Ramón, and Marina López, eds. *Exposició universal de Barcelona: llibre del centenario, 1888–1988.* Barcelona: L'Avenç, 1988.

Grau, Ramón, and Marina López. "Les batalles per l'Eixample." In *Exposició universal de Barcelona: llibre del centenario, 1888–1988,* ed. Ramón Grau and Marina López, pp. 191–229. Barcelona: L'Avenç, 1988.

Grier, Katherine C. *Culture and Comfort: Parlor Making and Middle-Class Identity, 1850–1930.* Washington, D.C.: Smithsonian Institution Press, 1997.

Gronow, Jukka. *The Sociology of Taste.* London: Routledge, 1997.

Guardiet i Bergé, Monserrat. *El teatre Líric de l'Eixample (1881–1900).* Barcelona: Portic, 2006.

Guereña, Jean Louis. "École et socialisation. Les manuals de civilité à l'usage des écoles primaires en Espagne au XIXe siècle." In *Les traités de savoir-vivre en Espagne et au Portugal du Moyen Âge à nos jours,* ed. Rose Duroux, pp. 287–304. Clermont-Ferrand: Centre de Recherche sur les Littératures Modernes et Contemporaines, 1995.

Guimerá Ravina, Agustín, and Alberto Darias Príncipe. *El casino de Tenerife (1840–1990).* Santa Cruz de Tenerife: Casino de Tenerife, 1992.

Gunn, Simon, and Robert J. Morris, eds. *Identities in Space: Contested Terrains in the Western City since 1850.* Aldershot, England, and Burlington, Vt.: Ashgate, 2001.

Habermas, Jürgen. *The Structural Transformation of the Public Sphere: An Inquiry into a Category of Bourgeois Society.* Cambridge: Cambridge University Press, 1989.

Haidt, Rebecca. *Embodying Enlightenment: Knowing the Body in Eighteenth-Century Spanish Literature and Culture.* New York: St. Martin's, 1998.

Haidt, Rebecca. "Luxury, Consumption, and Desire: Theorizing the Petimetra." *Arizona Journal of Hispanic Cultural Studies* 3 (1999): 33–50.

Haidt, Rebecca. "A Well-Dressed Woman Will Not Work: Petimetras, Economics, and Eighteenth-Century Fashion Plates." *Revista Canadiense de Estudios Hispánicos* 28, no. 1 (2003): 137–57.

Hall, Thomas. *Planning Europe's Capital Cities: Aspects of Nineteenth-Century Urban Development.* Oxford: Chapman & Hall, 1997.

Hardyment, Christina. *Behind the Scenes: Domestic Arrangements in Historic Houses.* London: National Trust, 1997.

Harrison, Carol E. *The Bourgeois Citizen in Nineteenth-Century France: Gender, Sociability, and the Uses of Emulation.* Oxford: Oxford University Press, 1999.

Harrow, Sharon. *Adventures in Domesticity: Gender and Colonial Adulteration in Eighteenth-Century British Literature.* New York: AMS, 2004.

Hartman, Mary S. *The Household and the Making of History: A Subversive View of the Western Past.* Cambridge and New York: Cambridge University Press, 2004.

Harvey, David. *Paris: Capital of Modernity.* New York: Routledge, 2003.

Hatch, E. *Theories of Man and Culture.* New York: Columbia University Press, 1973.

Headington, Christopher, Roy Westbrook, and Terry Barfoot. *Opera: A History.* London: Bodley Head, 1987.

Hemphill, C. Dallett. *Bowing to Necessities: A History of Manners in America, 1620–1860.* New York: Oxford University Press, 1999.

Herán, F. *Le bourgeois de Séville. Terre et parenté en Andalousie.* Paris: Presses universitaires de France, 1990.

Hernández García, Ricardo, and Javier Moreno Lázaro. "El nivel de vida en el medio rural de Castilla y León: una constatación antropométrica, 1840–1970." *Historia agraria: Revista de agricultura e historia rural* 47 (2009): 143–66.

Hernández Girbal, F. *José de Salamanca, Marqués de Salamanca (el Montecristo español).* 2nd ed. Madrid: Lira, 1992.

Heywood, Colin. *A History of Childhood: Children and Childhood in the West from Medieval to Modern Times.* Malden: Blackwell, 2001.

Himmelfarb, Gertrude. *The De-Moralization of Society: From Victorian Virtues to Modern Values.* New York: Knopf, 1995.

Hoibian, Olivier. *Les alpinistes en France, 1870–1950. Une histoire culturelle.* Paris: Harmattan, 2000.

Hoyo Aparicio, Andrés, and Ramón Maruri Villanueva. "Pautas de consumo textil en una sociedad rural: Liébana (Cantabria), 1700–1860." *Revista de Historia Económica—Journal of Iberian and Latin American Economic History* 21, no. 4 (2003): 107–40.

Huggins, Mike. *Flat Racing and British Society, 1790–1914: A Social and Economic History.* London: Frank Cass, 2000.

Hughes, Robert. *Barcelona.* New York: Vintage Books, 1993.

Hunt, Lynn, ed. *The New Cultural History.* Berkeley: University of California Press, 1989.

Iglesias, Antonio, ed. *El Teatro Real de Madrid. Teatro de la Ópera.* Madrid: Universidad Complutense, Cursos de Verano del Escorial, 1996.

Jagoe, Catherine. *Ambiguous Angels: Gender in the Novels of Galdós.* Berkeley: University of California Press, 1994.

Jagoe, Catherine, Alda Blanco, and Cristina Enríquez de Salamanca. *La mujer en los discursos de género: textos y contextos en el siglo XIX.* Barcelona: Icaria, 1998.

Jarrassé, Dominique. *Les thermes romantiques: bains et villégiatures en France de 1800 à 1850.* Clermont-Ferrand: Institut d'études du Massif Central, Centre d'histoire des entreprises et des communautés, 1992.

Jarrassé, Dominique. "Los salones de Europa, balnearios y literature." In *Ciudades termales en Europa,* ed. Mihail Moldoveanu. Barcelona: Lunwerg, 1999.

Jarrassé, Dominique. "La importancia del termalismo en el nacimiento y desarrollo del turismo en Europa en el siglo XIX." *Historia contemporánea* 25 (2002): 33–49.

Jarvis, Adrian. *Samuel Smiles and the Construction of Victorian Values.* Gloucestershire: Sutton, 1997.

Jenkins, Richard. *Pierre Bourdieu.* London: Routledge, 2002.

Jiménez Morell, Inmaculada. *La prensa femenina en España (desde sus orígenes a 1868)*. Madrid: Ediciones de la Torre, 1992.

Johnston, Susan. *Women and Domestic Experience in Victorian Political Fiction*. Westport, Conn.: Greenwood, 2001.

Jones, Jennifer Michelle. *Sexing la mode: Gender, Fashion, and Commercial Culture in Old Regime France*. Oxford: Berg, 2004.

Jones, Karen R., and John Wills. *The Invention of the Park: From the Garden of Eden to Disney's Magic Kingdom*. Cambridge: Polity, 2005.

Jovellanos, Gaspar Melchor de. *Obras publicadas e inéditas de Melchor Gaspar de Jovellanos*. Vol. 50. Madrid: Biblioteca de Autores Españoles, 1952.

Jovellanos, Gaspar Melchor de. *Cartas a lord Holland sobre la forma de reunión de las Cortes de Cádiz*. Alicante: Biblioteca Virtual Miguel de Cervantes, 2003.

Juliá Díaz, Santos, David Ringrose, and Cristina Segura. *Madrid, historia de una capital*. Madrid: Alianza Editorial, 2000.

Jürgens, Oskar. *Ciudades españolas: su desarrollo y configuración urbanística*. Madrid: Instituto Nacional de Administración Pública, 1992.

Jutglar, Antoni. *Historia crítica de la burguesía*. Barcelona: Anthropos, 1984.

Kasson, John F. *Rudeness and Civility: Manners in Nineteenth-Century Urban America*. New York: Hill and Wang, 1990.

Kelly, Catriona. *Refining Russia: Advice Literature, Polite Culture, and Gender From Catherine to Yeltsin*. Oxford: Oxford University Press, 2001.

Kerr, D. "Beheading the King and Enthroning the Market: A Critique of Foucauldian Governmentality." *Science & Society* 63, no. 2 (1999): 173–203.

Kirkpatrick, Susan. *Las románticas: Women Writers and Subjectivity in Spain, 1835–1850*. Berkeley: University of California Press, 1989.

Koshar, Rudy, ed. *Histories of Leisure*. Oxford: Berg, 2002.

Kotkin, Joel. *The City: A Global History*. New York: Modern Library, 2005.

Kuper, Adam. *Culture: The Anthropologists' Account*. Cambridge: Harvard University Press, 1999.

La cortesanía. *Nuevo manual práctico de Urbanidad,* by D. V. J. B. Barcelona: Imprenta de J. Piferrer, 1850.

Labanyi, Jo. *Gender and Modernization in the Spanish Realist Novel*. Oxford: Oxford University Press, 2000.

Labanyi, Jo. "Relocating Difference: Cultural History and Modernity in Late Nineteenth-Century Spain." In *Spain beyond Spain: Modernity, Literary History, and National Identity,* ed. Brad Epps and Luis Fernández Cifuentes. Lewisburg, Pa.: Bucknell University Press, 2005.

Lacombe, Hervé. *The Keys to French Opera in the Nineteenth Century*. Berkeley: University of California Press, 2001.

Lagardera Otero, Francisco. "Notas para una historia social del deporte en España." *Historia de la educación: Revista interuniversitaria* 14–15 (1995–96): 151–72.

Langlois, Gilles-Antoine. *Folies, Tivolis, et attractions: Les premiers parcs de loisirs parisiens.* Paris: Editions Aavp-Action Artistique, 1991.

Larra, Mariano José de. "El castellano Viejo." In *El Pobrecito Hablador. Revista Satírica de Costumbres,* by el Bachiller don Juan Pérez de Munguía (pseud. of Mariano José de Larra). Madrid: Imprenta de Repullés, 1832.

Larra, Mariano, José de. "La fonda nueva." *La Revista Española, Periódico Dedicado a la Reina Ntra. Sra.* Madrid, no. 88, 23 August 1833.

Larra, Mariano, José de. "Los jardines públicos." *La Revista Española, Periódico Dedicado a la Reina Ntra. Sra.* Madrid, no. 246, 20 June 1834.

Larra, Mariano, José de. *Artículos varios.* Ed. E. Correa Calderón. Madrid: Castalia, 1984.

Larrinaga Rodríguez, Carlos. "El turismo en la España del siglo XIX." *Historia contemporánea* 25 (2002): 157–79.

Larrinaga Rodríguez, Carlos. "Turismo y ordenación urbana en San Sebastián desde mediados del siglo XIX a 1936." In *La ciudad contemporánea, espacio, y sociedad,* ed. José María Beascoechea Gangoiti, Manuel González Portilla, and Pedro A. Novo López, pp. 785–800. Bilbao: Universidad del País Vasco, 2006.

Larrinaga, Carlos. "A Century of Tourism in Northern Spain: The Development of High-Quality Provision between 1815 and 1914." In *Histories of Tourism: Representation, Identity, and Conflict,* ed. John K. Walton, pp. 88–103. Clevedon, England, and Buffalo, N.Y.: Channel View Publications, 2005.

Larson, Susan, and Eva Woods. *Visualizing Spanish Modernity.* New York: Berg, 2005.

Laspalas, Javier. "La 'cortesía' como forma de participación social." *Anuario filosófico* 36, no. 1 (2003): 311–43.

Laver, James. *Costume and Fashion: A Concise History.* New York: Thames and Hudson, 1995.

Lemke, T. "The Birth of Bio-Politics: Michael Foucault's Lectures at the College de France on Neo-Liberal Governmentality." *Economy and Society* 30, no. 2 (2001): 190–207.

Lichter, Linda S. *Simple Social Graces: The Lost Art of Gracious Victorian Living.* New York: Regan Books, 1998.

Loeb, Lori Anne. *Consuming Angels: Advertising and Victorian Women.* New York: Oxford University Press, 1994.

Lopezosa Aparicio, Concepción. "Consideraciones y síntesis de un proyecto: El Paseo del Prado." *Anales de historia del arte* 3 (1991–92): 215–30.

Lopezosa Aparicio, Concepción. "Fiesta oficial y configuración de la ciudad. El caso del Prado madrileño." *Anales de historia del arte* 12 (2002): 79–92.

Lopezosa Aparicio, Concepción. "Ocio y negocio: El jardín del Tívoli en el Paseo del Prado de Madrid." *Anales de historia del arte* 15 (2005): 269–79.

Lorente, Jesús Pedro. *Cathedrals of Urban Modernity: The First Museums of Contemporary Art, 1800–1930.* Aldershot, England, and Brookfield, Vt.: Ashgate, 1998.

Lowe, Donald M. *History of Bourgeois Perception.* Chicago: University of Chicago Press, 1982.

Lucena Giraldo, Manuel. *Historia de un cosmopolita: José María de Lanz y la fundación de la Ingeniería de Caminos en España y América.* Madrid: Colegio de Ingenieros de Caminos, Canales y Puertos, 2005.

Mackaman, Douglas Peter. *Leisure Settings: Bourgeois Culture, Medicine, and the Spa in Modern France.* Chicago: University of Chicago Press, 1998.

Mainer, José Carlos. "La creación de un centro: Madrid, capital del siglo XIX." In *Capitales y corte en la historia de España,* ed. Humberto Baquero Moreno et al. Valladolid: Secretariado de Publicaciones e Intercambio Editorial, Universidad de Valladolid, 2003.

Manjarrés, José de. *Guía de señoritas en el gran mundo.* Barcelona: Tomás Gordes, 1854.

Marcus, Clare Cooper. *House as a Mirror of Self: Exploring the Deeper Meaning of Home.* Berkeley: Conari, 1995.

Marcus, Sharon. *Apartment Stories: City and Home in Nineteenth-Century Paris and London.* Berkeley: University of California Press, 1999.

Márquez, Miguel B. "D. Abelardo de Carlos y la ilustración española y americana." *Ambitos: Revista internacional de comunicación* 13–14 (2005): 185–209.

Marrey, Bernard. *Les grands magasins: des origines à 1939.* Paris: Picard, 1979.

Martín Gaite, Carmen. *Los usos amorosos del dieciocho en España.* Barcelona: Anagrama, 1987.

Martín Ramos, Ángel. *Los orígenes del ensanche Cortázar de San Sebastián.* Barcelona: Fundación Caja de Arquitectos, 2004.

Martínez Ibáñez, María Antonia. *El Teatro Real en la época de Isabel II.* Madrid: Instituto de Estudios Madrileños, 1993.

Martínez López, David. *Tierra, herencia, y matrimonio: un modelo sobre la formación de la burguesía agraria andaluza (siglos XVIII–XIX).* Jaén: Universidad de Jaén, 1996.

Martínez Martín, Jesús A., ed. *Orígenes culturales de la sociedad liberal (España siglo XIX).* Madrid: Biblioteca Nueva, 2003.

Maruri Villanueva, R. *La burguesía mercantil santanderina, 1700–1850. Cambio social y mentalidad.* Santander: Universidad de Cantabria, 1990.

Maruri Villanueva, R. "Vestir el cuerpo, vestir la casa: el consumo de textiles en la burguesía mercantil de Santander, 1750–1850." In *Consumo, condiciones de vida, y comercialización: Cataluña y Castilla, siglos XVII–XIX,* ed. Jaume Torras and Bartolomé Yun Casalilla, pp. 159–82. Valladolid: Consejería de Educación y Cultura, 1999.

Mas Hernández, Rafael. *El barrio de Salamanca: planteamiento y propiedad inmobiliaria en el ensanche de Madrid.* Madrid: Instituto de Estudios de Administración Local, 1982.

Mata García, Juan de. *La urbanidad deducida de sus principios mas ciertos y civilizadores: aplicados a todas las circunstancias de la vida.* Almeria: Imprenta de D. Joaquin Robles Martinez, 1885.

Matthee, Rudolph P. *The Pursuit of Pleasure: Drugs and Stimulants in Iranian History, 1500–1900.* Princeton: Princeton University Press, 2005.

Maza, Sarah. *The Myth of the French Bourgeoisie: An Essay on the Social Imaginary, 1750–1850.* Cambridge: Harvard University Press, 2003.

McClellan, Andrew. *Inventing the Louvre: Art, Politics, and the Origins of the Modern Museum in Eighteenth-Century Paris.* Cambridge: Cambridge University Press, 1994.

McCracken, Grant David. *Culture and Consumption: New Approaches to the Symbolic Character of Consumer Goods and Activities.* Bloomington: Indiana University Press, 1988.

McDonogh, Gary W. *Good Families of Barcelona: A Social History of Power in the Industrial Era.* Princeton: Princeton University Press, 1986.

McFarland, Andrew Michael. *Creating a National Passion: Football, Nationalism, and Mass Consumerism in Modern Spain.* Ph.D. dissertation, University of Texas at Austin, 2004.

McKendrick, Neil, John Brewer, and J. H. Plumb. *The Birth of a Consumer Society: The Commercialization of Eighteenth-Century England.* Bloomington: Indiana University Press, 1982.

Mellado, Francisco de Paula. *España geográfica, histórica, estadística, y pintoresca: Descripción de los pueblos mas notables.* Madrid: Mellado, Editor, 1845.

Mercader Riba, Juan. *José Bonaparte, rey de España (1808–1813): estructura del estado español bonapartista.* Madrid: Consejo Superior de Investigaciones Científicas, Instituto de Historia "Jerónimo Zurita," 1983.

Mesonero Romanos, Ramón. *El antiguo Madrid: paseos históricos-anedócticos por las calles y casas de esta villa.* 2 vols. Madrid: Oficinas de la Ilustración Española y Americana, 1881.

Mesonero Romanos, Ramón. *Memorias de un setentón, natural y vecino de Madrid.* Vol. 8 of *Obras completas.* Madrid: Renacimiento, 1926.

Mesonero Romanos, Ramón. *Recuerdos de viaje por Francia y Bélgica.* Madrid: Miraguano, 1983.

Mesonero Romanos, Ramón. *Rápida ojeada sobre el estado de la capital y los medios de mejorarla.* Intro. by Edward Baker. Madrid: CIDUR, 1989.

Mesonero Romanos, Ramón. *Escenas Matritenses.* Madrid: Fernando Plaza del Amo, 1991.

Miguel, Armando de. *Cien años de urbanidad: crítica de costumbres de la vida Española.* Barcelona: Planeta, 1995.

Miller, Michael Barry. *The Bon Marché: Bourgeois Culture and the Department Store, 1869–1920.* Princeton: Princeton University Press, 1981.

Molina Villar, Juan José. *Termalismo y turismo en Catalunya: un estudio geohistórico contemporáneo*. Ph.D. dissertation, Universidad de Barcelona, 2004.

Moncan, Patrice de. *Le Paris d'Haussmann*. Paris: Les Editions du Mécène, 2002.

Monlau, Pedro Felipe. *Higiene del matrimonio o el libro de los casado*. Madrid: Imp. y Estereot. de M. Rivadeneyra, 1858.

Monserrat Zapater, Octavio. *El Balneario de Panticosa (1826–1936): historia de un espacio de salud y ocio en el Pirineo Aragonés*. Zaragoza: Departamento de Educación y Cultura, 1998.

Montandon, Alain, ed. *Pour une histoire des traités de savoir-vivreen Europe*. Clermont-Ferrand: Association des Publications de la Faculté des Lettres et Sciences Humaines de Clermont-Ferrand, 1994.

Montandon, Alain, ed. *Bibliographie des traités de savoir-vivre en Europe*. 2 vols. Clermont-Ferrand: Faculté des Lettres et Sciences Humaines, 1995.

Montclos, Xavier de. *L'ancienne bourgeoisie en France du XVIe au XXe siècle*. Paris: Éditions Christian, 2005.

Montero Alonso, José. *Historia del Casino de Madrid y su época*. Madrid: Rayca, 1971.

Morales Muñoz, Manuel. "Las enseñanzas de la virtud: reglas cívico-morales en los catecismos del siglo XIX." In *Les traités de savoir-vivre en Espagne et au Portugal du Moyen Âge à nos jours,* ed. Rose Duroux, pp. 277–85. Clermont-Ferrand: Centre de Recherche sur les Littératures Modernes et Contemporaines, 1995.

Moreno Claverías, Belén. "La burguesía local de las letrs y los negocios a través de los inventarios post-mortem. El Penedés del siglo XVIII." In *Consumo, condiciones de vida, y comercialización: Cataluña y Castilla, siglos XVII–XIX,* ed. Jaume Torras and Bartolomé Yun Casalilla, pp. 71–88. Valladolid: Consejería de Educación y Cultura, 1999.

Moreno Lázaro, Javier. "El nivel de vida en la España atrasada entre 1800 y 1936: el caso de Palencia." *Investigaciones de historia económica: revista de la Asociación Española de Historia Económica* 4 (2006): 9–50.

Muchembled, Robert. *La société policée: politique et politesse en France du XVIe au XXe siècle*. Paris: Éditions du Seuil, 1998.

Muñoz López, Pilar. *Sangre, amor einterés. La familia en la España de la Restauración*. Madrid: Marcial Pons, 2001.

Muñoz, Matilde. *Historia del Teatro Real*. Madrid: Tesoro, 1946.

Museu Nacional d'Art de Catalunya. *Les arts industrials als cartells modernistes: exposició, del 25 de juliol al 24 de setembre de 2002*. Barcelona: MNAC, 2002.

Nadal, Joaquín María de. *Memóries d'un estudiant barceloni: Cromos de la vida vuitcentista*. Barcelona: Dalmay i Jover, 1952.

"Nadal, Pau, Caruso, Tebaldi, Callas, Kraus, Caballé . . . ." *Barcelona. Metròpolis Mediterrània* 48 (1999).

Narváez Ferri, Manuela. *L'Orfeó Català, cant coral i catalanisme (1891–1951)*. Ph.D. dissertation, Universidad de Barcelona, 2005.

Navascués Palacio, Pedro. "Madrid, ciudad y arquitectura (1808–1898)." In *Historia de Madrid*, ed. Antonio Fernández García. Madrid: Editorial Complutense, 1993.

Nead, Lynda. *Victorian Babylon: People, Streets, and Images in Nineteenth-Century London*. New Haven: Yale University Press, 2000.

Nenadic, Stana. "Household Possessions and the Modernising City: Scotland, c. 1720 to 1840." In *Material Culture: Consumption, Life-Style, Standard of Living, 1500–1900*, ed. Anton J. Schuurman and Lorena Walsh. Proceedings of the 11th International Economic History Congress. Milan: Università Bocconi, 1994.

Newton, Sarah E. *Learning to Behave: A Guide to American Conduct Books before 1900*. Westport, Conn.: Greenwood, 1994.

Nielfa Cristobal, Gloria. *Los sectores mercantiles en Madrid en el primer tercio del siglo XX: tiendas, comerciantes, y dependientes de comercio*. Madrid: Ministerio de Trabajo y Seguridad Social, 1985.

Nora, Pierre. *Les Lieux de mémoire*. 3 vols. Paris: Gallimard, 1984.

Norton, Marcy. "Tasting Empire: Chocolate and the European Internalization of Mesoamerican Aesthetics." *American Historical Review* 111, no. 3 (2006): 660–91.

Norton, Marcy. *Sacred Gifts, Profane Pleasures: A History of Tobacco and Chocolate in the Atlantic World*. Ithaca, N.Y.: Cornell University Press, 2008.

Nuevo manual de urbanidad, cortesía, decoro, y etiqueta; ó el hombre fino. Madrid: Llorenci, 1850.

Orberá, María. *La joven bien educada. Lecciones de urbanidad para niñas y adultas*. Valencia: Imprenta Católica de Piles, 1875.

Ossorio y Bernard, Manuel. *La vida en sociedad: cartas familiares dadas a la publicidad*. Madrid: Hijos de Miguel Guijarro, 1897.

Otazu, Alfonso de. *Los Rothchild y sus socios en España, 1820–1850*. Madrid: O. Hs. Ediciones, 1987.

Otero Carvajal, Luis Enrique. "Ocio y deporte en el nacimiento de la sociedad de masas: la socialización del deporte como práctica y espectáculo en la España del primer tercio del siglo XX." *Cuadernos de historia contemporánea* 25 (2003): 169–98.

Otero Carvajal, Luis Enrique. "Las ciudades en la España de la Restauración, 1868–1939." Comunicación presentada a las VII Jornadas de investigación de Castilla-La Mancha, sobre investigación en archivos. España entre Repúblicas 1868–1939, Guadalajara, 2005.

Otero, José. *Tratado de bailes de sociedad, regionales españoles, especialmente andaluces, con historia y modo de ejecutarlos*. Sevilla: Tip. de la Guía Oficial, 1912.

Otter, Chris. "Making Liberalism Durable: Vision and Civility in the Late Victorian City." *Social History* 27, no. 1 (January 2002): 1–15.

Palacio Valdés, Armando. *La espuma*. Vol. 2: *Obras completas*. Madrid: Aguilar, 1959.

Pallol Trigueros, Rubén. "Chamberí, ¿un nuevo Madrid? El primer desarrollo del ensanche norte madrileño, 1860–1880." *Cuadernos de historia contemporánea* 26 (2004): 77–98.

Papayanis, Nicholas. "César Daly, Paris, and the Emergence of Modern Urban Planning." *Planning Perspectives* 21, no. 4 (2006): 325–46.

Pardailhé-Galabrun, Annik. *La naissance de l'intime: 3000 foyers parisiens XVIIe–XVIIIe siècles*. Paris: Presses Universitaires de France, 1988.

Parsons, Deborah L. *A Cultural History of Madrid: Modernism and the Urban Spectacle*. Oxford: Berg, 2003.

Pasalodos, Mercedes. *El traje como reflejo de lo femenino: evolución y significado, Madrid 1898–1915*. Ph.D. dissertation, Madrid, Universidad Complutense, Servicio de Publicaciones, 2004.

Pena, Pablo. "Análisis semiológico de la revista de modas romántica." *Estudios sobre el mensaje periodístico* 7 (2001): 365–81.

Penez, Jérôme. *Histoire du thermalisme en France au XIXe siècle: eau, médecine, et loisirs*. Paris: Economica, 2005.

Pereda, José María de. *Al primer vuelo (idilio vulgar)*. Barcelona: Imprenta de Henrich y Cia., 1891.

Pérez Galdós, Benito. *Obras completas*. 6 vols. Madrid: Aguilar, 1949.

Pérez Galdos, Benito. *Inferno*. London: Phoenix House, 1998.

Perinat, Adolfo, and María Isabel Marrades. *Mujer, prensa, y sociedad en España, 1800–1939*. Madrid: Centro de Investigaciones Sociológicas, 1980.

Permanyer, Lluís. *Historia del Eixample*. Esplugu es de Llobregat, Barcelona: Plaza & Janés, 1990.

Permanyer, Lluís. *Biografia del Passeig de Gràcia*. Barcelona: La Campana, 1994.

Perrot, Michelle. "At Home." In *A History of Private Life*, ed. Philippe Ariès and Georges Duby. Cambridge: Harvard University Press, 1987.

Perrot, Philippe. *Fashioning the Bourgeoisie: A History of Clothing in the Nineteenth Century*. Princeton: Princeton University Press, 1994.

Perrot, Philippe. *Le luxe: une richesse entre faste et confort, XVIIIe–XIXe siècle*. Paris: Éditions du Seuil, 1995.

Peset Reig, Mariano. "Universidad y liberalismo en España y América Latina." In *Orígenes del liberalismo: universidad, política, economía*, ed. Ricardo Robledo Hernández, María Cruz Romeo Mateo, and Irene Castells Oliván, pp. 17–47. Salamanca: Ediciones Universidad de Salamanca, 2003.

Petit, Carlos, ed. *Derecho privado y revolución burguesa*. Madrid: Marcial Pons, 1990.

Piferrer, Juan Francisco. *Reglas de la buena crianza civil y cristiana, utilísimas para todos singularmente para los que cuidan la educación de los niños: añadido un nuevo método de trinchar en la mesa.* Barcelona: por Juan Francisco Píferrer, 1840. (First ed., 1781).

Piñón, Juan Luis. *Los orígenes de la Valencia moderna: notas sobre la reedificación urbana de la primera mitad del siglo XIX.* Valencia: Edicions Alfons el Magnànim, 1988.

Pinto Crespo, Virgilio, and Santos Madrazo Madrazo. *Madrid, atlas histórico de la ciudad.* 2 vols. Madrid: Fundación Caja de Madrid, Lunwerg, 1995–2001.

Piper, William Bowman. *Common Courtesy in Eighteenth-Century English Literature.* Newark: University of Delaware Press, 1997.

Pla i Arxé, Ramon. "La formación de un gran teatro de ópera." *Barcelona. Metròpolis Mediterrània* 48 (1999).

Pla, José. *Un señor de Barcelona.* Barcelona: Destino, 1945.

Pomés Soler, Ramon. *Cortesanía, higiene, sport: la educación social y familiar.* Barcelona: Hijos de Jaime Jepús, 1902.

Ponga Mayo, Juan Carlos. *El ensanche de la ciudad de León, 1900–1950: cincuenta años de arquitectura.* Colegio Oficial de Arquitectos de León, 1997.

Pons, Anaclet, and Justo Serna. *Diario de un Burgués. La Europa del siglo XIX vista por un valenciano distinguido.* Valencia: Los libros de la memoria, 2006.

Pons, Anaclet, and Justo Serna. *La ciudad extensa. La burguesía comercial financiera en la Valencia de mediados del XIX.* Valencia: Diputació de València, 1992.

Pons, Anaclet, and Justo Serna. "La palabra y los mundos posibles. Lo burgués, la burguesía, y la historia conceptual." In *A qué llamamos burguesía. Historia social e historia conceptual,* ed. Raffaele Romanelli, Anaclet Pons, and Justo Serna. Colección Eutopías, Ed. Episteme, 1997, vol. 177–78.

Porter, Roy. "Les Anglais et les loisirs." In *L'avènement des loisirs, 1850–1960,* ed. Alain Corbin. Paris: Aubier, 1995.

Preziosi, Donald. *Brain of the Earth's Body: Art, Museums, and the Phantasms of Modernity.* Minneapolis: University of Minnesota Press, 2003.

Prieto González, José Manuel, and Eva J. Rodríguez Romero. "'Caprichos' en el jardín: Ficción y realidad en la escenografía de los ámbitos de recreo público decimonónico." *Archivo español de arte* 71, no. 284 (1998): 391–406.

Prior, Nick. "Museums: Leisure between State and Distinction." In *Histories of Leisure,* ed. Rudy Koshar, pp. 27–44. Oxford: Berg, 2002.

Prior, Nick. *Museums and Modernity: Art Galleries and the Making of Modern Culture.* Oxford: Berg, 2002.

Profeti, Maria Gracia. "La danza como 'Savoir Vivre' en la España del siglo XVII." In *Les traités de savoir-vivre en Espagne et au Portugal du Moyen Âge à nos jours,* ed. Rose Duroux, pp. 205–13. Clermont-Ferrand: Centre de Recherche sur les Littératures Modernes et Contemporaines, 1995.

Quirós Linares, Francisco. "Política y especulación en la reforma de la Puerta del Sol (1853–1862)." In *Urbanismo e historia urbana en el mundo hispano: segundo simposio, 1982*, ed. Antonio Bonet Correa, pp. 957–68. Madrid: Universidad Complutense, 1985.

Rabaté, Colette. *¿Eva o Maria? Ser mujer en la época Isabelina (1833–1868)*. Salamanca: Ediciones universidad de Salamanca, 2007.

Radigales, Jaume. *Els orígens del Gran Teatre del Liceu (1837–1847): de la plaça de Santa Anna a la Rambla. Història del Liceu Filharmònic d'Isabel II o Liceu Filodramàtic de Barcelona*. Barcelona: Publicacions de l'Abadia de Montserrat, 1998.

Raisson, Horace. *Manual de la elegancia y de la higiene, ó segunda parte del Manual de Cortesania. Traducido del francés y arreglado á nuestras costumbres por Carlos Nicolás Rebolledo*. Madrid: Imprenta de Repullés, 1849.

Ramage, Edwin S. *Urbanitas: Ancient Sophistication and Refinement*. Norman: University of Oklahoma Press, 1973.

Ramos Palencia, Fernando. "Una aproximación al consumo en el mundo rural castellano: Palencia, 1750–1840." In *Consumo, condiciones de vida, y comercialización: Cataluña y Castilla, siglos XVII–XIX*, ed. Jaume Torras and Bartolomé Yun Casalilla, pp. 61–69. Valladolid: Consejería de Educación y Cultura, 1999.

Ramos Palencia, Fernando. "La demanda de textiles de las familias castellanas a finales del Antiguo Régimen, 1750–1850: ¿aumento del consumo sin industrialización?" *Revista de Historia Económica—Journal of Iberian and Latin American Economic History* 21, no. 4 (2003): 141–80.

Ramos Santana, A. *La Burguesía Gaditana en la época Isabelina*. Cádiz: Cátedra Adolfo de Castro, Fundación Municipal de Cultura, 1987.

Ramos, María Dolores, and M. Teresa Vera, eds. *Discursos, realidades, utopías. La construcción del sujeto femenino en los siglos XIX y XX*. Barcelona: Anthropos, 2002.

Reher, David Sven. "Desarrollo urbano y evolución de la población: España 1787–1930." *Revista de historia económica* 4, no. 1 (1986): 39–66.

Rementería y Fica, Mariano. *El hombre fino al gusto del día: manual completo de urbanidad, cortesía y buen tono*. Valladolid: Maxtor, 2001. (Facsimile reproduction of the 3rd ed., Madrid: Imprenta del Colegio de Sordo-mudos, 1837.)

Resina, Joan Ramon. *Barcelona's Vocation of Modernity: Rise and Decline of an Urban Image*. Stanford: Stanford University Press, 2008.

Rico, Eduardo G. *Yo, José de Salamanca, el "Gran bribón."* Barcelona: Planeta, 1994.

Ring, Jim. *How the English Made the Alps*. London: John Murray, 2000.

Ringrose, David. "Inmigración, estructuras demográficas, y tendencias económicas en Madrid a comienzos de la Epoca Moderna." *Moneda y Crédito* 138 (1976): 9–55.

Ringrose, David. *Madrid y la economía española, 1560–1850: ciudad, corte, y país en el antiguo régimen*. Madrid: Alianza Editorial, 1985.

Ringrose, David. *Imperio y península: Ensayos sobre la historia económica de España (Siglos XVI–XIX)*. Madrid: Siglo XXI, 1987.

Ringrose, David. *Spain, Europe, and the "Spanish Miracle," 1700–1900*. Cambridge: Cambridge University Press, 1996.

Rivas Quinzaños, Pilar, and Fuensanta Muro García-Villalba. "El intento de patentar un invento teórico: la tramitación de la Teoría de la Viabilidad Urbana." *Ciudad y territorio: Estudios territoriales* 119–20 (1999): 221–33.

Roche, Daniel. *Les républicains des lettres: gens de culture et lumières au XVIIIe siècle.* Paris: Fayard, 1988.

Roche, Daniel, *La Culture des apparences: une histoire du vêtement (XVIIe–XVIIIe siècle).* Paris: Fayard, 1989.

Roche, Daniel. *A History of Everyday Things: The Birth of Consumption in France, 1600–1800*. Cambridge: Cambridge University Press, 2000.

Rodríguez San Pedro Bezares, Luis Enrique, ed. *Las universidades hispánicas: de la monarquía de los Austrias al centralismo liberal.* V Congreso Internacional sobre Historia de las Universidades Hispánicas, Salamanca, Univeridad de Salamanca, 2000.

Roig Castellanos, Mercedes. *La mujer en la historia a través de la prensa: (Francia, Italia, España) (S. XVIII–XX).* Madrid: Instituto de la Mujer, 1986.

Romanelli, Raffaele. "Political Debate, Social History, and the Italian Borghesia: Changing Perspectives in Historical Research." *Journal of Modern History* 63, no. 4 (1991): 717–39.

Romanelli, Raffaele. "Borghesia, bürgertum, bourgeoisie, itinerarios europeos de un concepto." In *A qué llamamos burguesía. Historia social e historia conceptual,* ed. Raffaele Romanelli, Anaclet Pons, and Justo Serna. Colección Eutopías, Ed. Episteme, 1997, vol. 177–78.

Romanones, Álvaro de Figueroa y Torres, Conde de. *Salamanca, conquistador de riqueza, gran señor.* Madrid: Espasa-Calpe, 1962.

Romeo Mateo, María Cruz. *Entre el orden y la revolución: la formación de la burguesía liberal en la crisis de la monarquía absoluta (1814–1833).* Alicante: Instituto de Cultura Juan Gil-Albert, 1993.

Rueda Herranz, Germán. "Formas de sociabilidad y condiciones de vida en la segunda mitad del siglo XIX." In *En torno al "98." España en el tránsito del siglo XIX al XX,* ed. Rafael Sánchez Mantero, vol. 1, pp. 47–90. Huelva, Universidad de Huelva, 2000.

Ruiz Palomeque, Eulalia. "Ordenación y realidad urbana del casco antiguo madrileño en el siglo XIX." *Revista de la Universidad Complutense* 115 (1979): 501–16.

Ruiz Palomeque, Eulalia. *Geografía urbana del Madrid del siglo XIX (el casco antiguo).* Madrid: Instituto de Estudios Madrileños, 1983.

Ruiz Palomeque, Eulalia. "Ordenación y realidad urbana del casco antiguo madrileño en el siglo XIX." In *Urbanismo e historia urbana de España,* pp. 501–16. Madrid, 1985.

Rybczynsky, Witold. *Home: A Short History of an Idea.* New York: Viking, 1987.

Rybczynsky, Witold. *La casa: historia de una idea.* San Sebastian: Nerea, 2003.

Saavedra Moragas, Eduardo. "Carlos María de Castro." *Revista de obras públicas* 43, no. 1 (1895): 73–77.

Sagarra i Trias, Ferran. *Barcelona, ciutat de transició (1848–1868): el projecte urbà a través dels treballs de l'arquitecte Miquel Garriga i Roca.* Barcelona: Institut d'Estudis Catalans, 1996.

Salaün, Serge. *El cuplé (1900–1936).* Madrid: Espasa Calpe, 1990.

Sama, Catherine M. "Liberty, Equality, Frivolity! An Italian Critique of Fashion Periodicals." *Eighteenth-Century Studies* 37, no. 3 (2004): 389–414.

Sambricio, Carlos. "Sobre el proyecto y desarrollo urbano de Madrid en la segunda mitad del siglo XVIII." In *Urbanismo e historia urbana de España,* pp. 489–500. Madrid, 1979.

Sambricio, Carlos. *Territorio y ciudad en la España de la Ilustración.* Madrid: Ministerio de Obras Públicas y Transportes, 1991.

Sambricio, Carlos. "Imagen de una calle: la configuración de Bailén." *Reales Sitios: Revista del Patrimonio Nacional* 132 (1997): 46–52.

Sambricio, Carlos. "Ideología, política, y especulación urbanas en Madrid en la primera mitad del siglo XIX. El caso de la Castellana." *Quintana: revista de estudios do Departamento de Historia da Arte, Santiago de Compostela* 3 (2004): 13–24.

Sambricio, Carlos, and Concepción Lopezosa Aparicio. *Cartografía histórica: Madrid región capital.* Madrid: Dirección General de Urbanismo y Planificación Regional, 2001.

Sambricio, Carlos, and Fernando Terán. *Madrid, ciudad-región.* 2 vols. Madrid: Dirección General de Urbanismo y Planificación Regional, 1999.

Sánchez Ferre, José. *Guía de establecimientos balnearios de España.* Madrid: Centro de Publicaciones, MOPT, 1992.

Sánchez Ferré, José. "Historia de los balnearios en España. Arquitectura, patrimonio, sociedad." In *Panorama actual de las aguas minerales y minero-medicinales en España,* ed. Juan Antonio López Geta and J. L. Pinuaga Espejel, pp. 213–30. Madrid: Ministerio de Medio Ambiente, 2000.

Sánchez García, José Luis. "Ateneísmo y ateneos en España." In *La voluntad regeneracionista. Esfuerzo e inercia del Ateneo de Valladolid, 1872–1936,* pp. 3–23. Palencia: J. L. Sánchez, 1998.

Sánchez Llama, Iñigo. *Galería de escritoras isabelinas: la prensa periódica entre 1833 y 1895.* Madrid: Cátedra, 2000.

Sánchez Moreno, José. *Tratado práctico de etiqueta y distinción social.* Barcelona: A. Pons, 1925.

Sánchez, Alex. "Crisis económica y respuesta empresarial: los inicios del sistema fabril en la industria algodonera catalana, 1797–1839." *Revista de Historia Económica—Journal of Iberian and Latin American Economic History* 3 (2000): 485–524.

Sancho García, Manuel. *El sinfonismo en Valencia durante la restauración (1878–1916).* Ph.D. dissertation, Universidad de Valencia, 2005.

Sarasúa, Carmen. *Criados, nodrizas y amos: el servicio doméstico en la formación del mercado de trabajo madrileño, 1758–1868.* Madrid: Siglo XXI, 1994.

Sarmiento, Domingo F. *Recuerdos de Provincia.* Buenos Aires: Editorial Kapelusz, 1966.

Sarti, Raffaella. *Europe at Home: Family and Material Culture, 1500–1800.* New Haven: Yale University Press, 2002.

Schama, Simon. *The Embarrassment of Riches: An Interpretation of Dutch Culture in the Golden Age.* New York: Knopf, 1987.

Schlesinger, Arthur. *Learning How to Behave: A Historical Study of American Etiquette Books.* New York: Macmillan, 1946.

Searle, G. R. *Entrepreneurial Politics in Mid-Victorian Britain.* New York: Oxford University Press, 1993.

Sebastiá, E., and J. A. Piqueras. *Pervivencias feudales y revolución democrática.* Valencia: Edicions Alfons el Magnanim, 1987.

Sebold, Russel. "Figaro y el hombre fino." In *De ilustrados y románticos,* pp. 209–13. Madrid: Ediciones El Museo Universal, 1992.

Segura, Isabel, and Marta Selva. *Revistes de dones (1846–1935).* Barcelona: Edhasa, 1984.

Sennett, Richard. *Flesh and Stone: The Body and the City in Western Civilization.* New York : Norton, 1994.

Seoane, Maria Cruz. *Historia del periodismo en España. El siglo XIX.* Madrid: Alianza Editorial, 1983.

Shammas, Carole. *The Pre-Industrial Consumer in England and America.* Oxford: Clarendon, 1990.

Shammas, Carole. "Changes in English and Anglo-American Consumption from 1550 to 1800." In *Consumption and the World of Goods,* ed. John Brewer and Roy Porter, pp. 177–305. New York: Routledge, 1993.

Shammas, Carole. "The Decline of Textile Prices in England and British America prior to the Industrial Revolution." *Economic History Review* 47 (1994): 483–507.

Shubert, Adrian. *A Social History of Modern Spain.* London: Unwin Hyman, 1990.

Shubert, Adrian. *Death and Money in the Afternoon: A History of the Spanish Bullfight.* New York: Oxford University Press, 1999.

Simón Palmer, María del Carmen. *Revistas femeninas madrileñas.* Madrid: Artes Gráficas Municipales, 1993.

Simón Palmer, María del Carmen. "El impresor-editor Don León de Amarita." In *Prensa, impresos, lectura en el mundo hispánico contemporáneo: homenaje a Jean-François*

Botrel, ed. Jean Michel Desvois, pp. 43–60. Institut d'études ibériques & ibéro-améri-caines, Université Michel de Montaigne-Bordeaux, 2005.

Simoncini, Giorgio. *L'uso dello spazio privato nell'età dell'Illuminismo.* 2 vols. Firenze: Leo S. Olschki, 1995.

Sinué, María del Pilar. *Biblioteca moral y recreativa.* 10 vols. (*El ángel del hogar* vols. 3, 4, and 5). Madrid: Imprenta Española, 1862–63.

Sobrino, Ramón. *El sinfonismo español en el siglo XIX: la sociedad de conciertos de Madrid.* Ph.D. dissertation, Universidad de Oviedo, Departamento de Historia y Artes, 1992.

Sobrino, Ramón. "La música sinfónica en el siglo XIX." In VV. AA., *La música española en el siglo XIX.* Gijón: Universidad de Oviedo, 1995.

Southworth, James Granville. *Vauxhall Gardens: A Chapter in the Social History of England.* New York: Columbia University Press, 1941.

St. George, Andrew. *The Descent of Manners: Etiquette, Rules, and the Victorians.* London: Chatto & Windus, 1993.

Stearns, Peter N. *Consumerism in World History: The Global Transformation of Desire.* London: Routledge, 2001.

Stearns, Peter N. *Childhood in World History.* New York: Routledge, 2006.

Stearns, Peter N. *Consumerism in World History: The Global Transformation of Desire.* New York: Routledge, 2006.

Stewart, Matthew. *Monturiol's Dream: The Extraordinary Story of the Submarine Inventor Who Wanted to Save the World.* New York: Pantheon Books, 2003.

Stone, Lawrence. *Family and Fortune: Studies in Aristocratic Finance in the Sixteenth and Seventeenth Centuries.* Oxford: Clarendon, 1973.

Stone, Lawrence. *The Family, Sex and Marriage in England, 1500–1800.* New York: Harper & Row, 1979.

Subirá, José. *Historia y anecdotario del Teatro Real.* Madrid: Fundación Caja Madrid, 1997.

Taberner, Francisco. *Valencia entre el ensanche y la reforma interior.* Valencia: Edicions Alfons el Magnànim, Valenciana, 1987.

Tasca, Luisa. *Galatei: buone maniere e cultura borghese nell'Italia dell'Ottocento.* Firenze: Le lettere, 2004.

Tatjer Mir, Mercedes. *La Barceloneta: del siglo XVIII al Plan de la Ribera.* Barcelona: Los libros de la Frontera, 1985.

Tesoro de las Familias: recopilación de los almanaques de la casa en El Eco de la Moda. Barcelona: E. Richardin, P. Lamb y Cia., 1902.

Thompson, E. P. "Time, Work Discipline, and Industrial Capitalism." *Past and Present* 38 (1967): 59–91.

Thompson, I. A. A. "Hidalgo and Pechero: The Language of 'Estates' and 'Classes' in Early-Modern Castile." In *Language, History, and Class*, ed. Penelope J. Corfield, pp. 53–78. Oxford: Blackwell, 1991.

Thomson, James K. J. *A Distinctive Industrialization: Cotton in Barcelona, 1728–1832.* Cambridge: Cambridge University Press, 1992.

Thornton, Peter. *The Italian Renaissance Interior, 1400–1600.* New York: Harry N. Abrams, 1991.

Thornton, Peter. *Form and Decoration: Innovation in the Decorative Arts, 1470–1870.* New York: Harry N. Abrams, 1998.

Tiersten, Lisa. *Marianne in the Market: Envisioning Consumer Society in Fin-de-Siècle France.* Berkeley: University of California Press, 2001.

Toboso Sánchez, Pilar. *Pepín Fernández, 1891–1982: el pionero de los grandes almacenes, Galerías Preciados.* Madrid: LID, 2001.

Toreno, José María Queipo de Llano Ruiz de Saravia, conde de. *Historia del levantamiento, guerra y revolución de España (extracto sobre la Constitución del 12).* Alicante: Biblioteca Virtual Miguel de Cervantes, 2003.

Torra Fernández, Lídia. "Pautas del consumo textil en la Cataluña del siglo XVIII: una visión a partir de los inventaios 'post-mortem.'" In *Consumo, condiciones de vida, y comercialización: Cataluña y Castilla, siglos XVII–XIX*, ed. Jaume Torras and Bartolomé Yun Casalilla, pp. 89–106. Valladolid: Consejería de Educación y Cultura, 1999.

Torra Fernández, Lídia. "Cambios en la oferta y la demanda textil en Barcelona (1650–1800)." *Revista de historia industrial* 22 (2002): 13–44.

Torra Fernández, Lídia. "Las botigues de teles de Barcelona: aportación al estudio de la oferta de tejidos y del crédito al consumo (1650–1800)." *Revista de Historia Económica—Journal of Iberian and Latin American Economic History* 21 (2003): 89–106.

Torras, Jaume, and Lidia Torra. "El ajuar de la novia." In *Consumo, condiciones de vida, y comercialización: Cataluña y Castilla, siglos XVII–XIX*, ed. Jaume Torras and Bartolomé Yun Casalilla, pp. 61–69. Valladolid: Consejería de Educación y Cultura, 1999.

Torras, Jaume, and Bartolomé Yun Casalilla, eds. *Consumo, condiciones de vida, y comercialización: Cataluña y Castilla, siglos XVII–XIX.* Valladolid: Consejería de Educación y Cultura, 1999.

Torras, Jaume, and Bartolomé Yun Casalilla. "Historia del consumo e historia del crecimiento. El consumo de tejidos en España, 1700-1850." *Revista de Historia Económica—Journal of Iberian and Latin American Economic History* 21, no. 4 (2003): 17–41.

Torrente Fortuño, José Antonio. *Salamanca, bolsista romántico.* Madrid: Taurus, 1969.

Tortella Casares, Gabriel. *El desarrollo de la España contemporánea: historia económica de los siglos XIX y XX.* Madrid: Alianza Editorial, 1998.

Towner, John. *An Historical Geography of Recreation and Tourism in the Western World, 1540–1940.* New York: Wiley, 1996.

Tranter, Neil L. *Sport, Economy, and Society in Britain, 1750–1914.* Cambridge: Cambridge University Press, 1998.

Turina Gómez, Joaquín. *Historia del Teatro Real.* Madrid: Alianza Editorial, 1997.

Ulrich, Laurel. *The Age of Homespun: Objects and Stories in the Creation of an American Myth.* New York: Knopf, 2001.

Umbach, Maiken. "A Tale of Second Cities: Autonomy, Culture, and the Law in Hamburg and Barcelona in the Late Nineteenth Century." *American Historical Review* 110, no. 3 (2005): 659–92.

Uría, Jorge. *La España liberal (1868–1917): cultura y vida cotidiana.* Madrid: Síntesis, 2008.

Urkia Etxabe, José María. *Historia de los balnearios guipuzcoanos.* Bilbao: Euskal Medikuntzaren Historia-mintegia, 1985.

Urkia Etxabe, José María. "El esplendor de los balnearios." In *Historia de las ciencias y de las técnicas,* ed. Luis Español González, José Javier Escribano Benito, and María de los Angeles Martínez García, eds., vol. 1, pp. 105–20. Logroño: Universidad de la Rioja, 2004.

Valera, Juan. *Obras completas.* 3 vols. Madrid: M. Aguilar, 1947–49.

Valis, Noël M. *The Culture of Cursilería: Bad Taste, Kitsch, and Class in Modern Spain.* Durham: Duke University Press, 2002.

Vázquez, Óscar Enrique. *Inventing the Art Collection: Patrons, Markets, and the State in Nineteenth-Century Spain.* University Park: Pennsylvania State University Press, 2001.

Velasco Zazo, Antonio. *Historia del Real.* Madrid: Victoriano Suárez, 1956.

Vergés, Oriol y Sarrias. Ignasi, *Barbes i bigotis a l'Exposició Universal de 1888.* Barcelona: Abadia de Montserrat, 1988.

Vicente, Marta V. *Clothing the Spanish Empire: Families and the Calico Trade in the Early Modern Atlantic World.* New York: Palgrave Macmillan, 2007.

Villacorta Baños, Francisco. *El ateneo científico, literario, y artístico de Madrid.* Madrid: Centro de Estudios Históricos, 1985.

Villacorta Baños, Francisco. *Profesionales y burócratas: estado y poder corporativo en la España del siglo XX, 1890–1923.* Madrid: Siglo XXI, 1989.

Villacorta Baños, Francisco. "Los ateneos liberales: política, cultura, y sociabilidad intelectual." *Hispania, Revista española de historia* 214 (2003): 415–42.

Villafranca Jiménez, María del Mar. *Los museos de Granada: génesis y evolución histórica (1835–1975).* Granada: Diputación de Granada, 1998.

Villena Espinosa, Rafael, and Angel Luis López Villaverde. "Espacio privado, dimensión pública: hacia una caracterización del casino en la España contemporánea." *Hispania, Revista española de historia* 214 (2003): 443–66.

Vincent, Mary. *Spain, 1833–2002: People and State.* Oxford: Oxford University Press, 2007.

VV. AA. *Historia de la ciudad.* 3 vols. Valencia: Instituto para la Comunicación, Asesoría, Reciclaje, y Orientación Profesional del Colegio Territorial de Arquitectos de Valencia, 2000–2004.

Wahrman, Dror. *Imagining the Middle Class: The Political Representation of Class in Britain, c. 1780–1840.* Cambridge: Cambridge University Press, 1995.

Walsh, Claire, "The Newness of the Department Store: A View from the Eighteenth Century." In *Cathedrals of Consumption: The European Department Store, 1850–1939,* ed. Geoffrey Crossick and Serge Jaumain, pp. 46–71. Aldershot, England, and Brookfield, Vt.: Ashgate, 1999.

Walton, J. K., and J. Smith. "The First Century of Beach Tourism in Spain: *San Sebastián* and the *Playas del Norte* from the 1830s to the 1930s." In *Tourism in Spain: Critical Issues,* ed. M. Barke, J. Towner, and M. T. Newton, pp. 35–61. Wallingford, England: CAB International, 1996.

Walton, John K. *The English Seaside Resort: A Social History, 1750–1914.* Leicester: Leicester University Press, 1983.

Walton, John K. "Planning and Seaside Tourism: San Sebastián, 1863–1936." *Planning Perspectives* 17, no. 1 (January 2002): 1–20.

Weatherill, Lorna. *Consumer Behavior and Material Culture in Britain, 1660–1760.* London: Routledge, 1988.

Whitaker, Jan. *Service and Style: How the American Department Store Fashioned the Middle Class.* New York: St. Martin's, 2006.

Wildeblood, Joan. *The Polite World: A Guide to English Manners and Deportment from the Thirteenth to the Nineteenth Century.* New York: Oxford University Press, 1965.

Williams, R. *Culture.* London: Fontana, 1981.

Withey, Lynne. *Grand Tours and Cooks' Tours: A History of Leisure Travel, 1750–1915.* New York: W. Morrow, 1997.

Woodman, Thomas. *Politeness and Poetry in the Age of Pope.* Rutherford, N.J.: Fairleigh Dickinson University Press, 1989.

Wouters, Cas. "The Integration of Social Classes. (Etiquette Books and Emotion Management in the 20th Century, Part 1)." *Journal of Social History* 29, no. 1 (Fall 1995): 107–25.

Wroth, Warwick William. *The London Pleasure Gardens of the Eighteenth Century.* Hamden, Conn.: Archon Books, 1979.

Yeste Navarro, Isabel A. "Una aproximación al urbanismo de Félix Navarro: El ensanche de Zaragoza de 1880." *Turiaso* 15 (1999–2000): 175–90.

Yeves, Carlos. *Guía del ama de casa, ó principios de economía é higiene domésticas con aplicación á la moral.* Madrid: Librería de Hernando, 1879.

Young, Linda. *Middle-Class Culture in the Nineteenth Century: America, Australia, and Britain.* Houndmills: Palgrave, 2003.

Zabaleta, Juan. *El día de fiesta.* Ed. De José M. Díaz Borque. Madrid: Cupsa, D.L., 1977.

Zozaya Montes, María. *El Casino de Madrid, orígenes y primera andadura.* Madrid: Casino de Madrid, 2002.

INDEX

self-made man, 11–12; in Anglo-Saxon societies, 11; in European societies, 11–12
Serna, Justo, 8, 19, 165, 209, 210, 230n80,
235n88, 240n13
Serrano de Wilson, Emilia, 115
sewing machines, 112
Shammas, Carole, 234n79
shops and shopping, 121–30; the department
store, 127–30; and fixed prices, 125; the
fixed shop, 122, 124; in France, 122, 125, 126,
129; in Great Britain, 122, 125, 126; the large
shop (*almacén, bazar,* or *galeria*), 125–26,
239n100; the *magasin de noveautés,* 124;
the multiple shop (chain store), 125, 126–27,
239–40n107; and ready-made clothing,
124–25; and sales, 125; the shop arcade
(French *galerie*), 124, 125, 239n96; and
window displays, 124. *See also specific shops*
Shubert, Adrian, 12, 244n4
Sinesio Delgado, Isidro, 128
Sinués de Marco, Pilar, 35, 115
smoking, 33
sociedad de buen tono (polite society), 27, 30,
38, 50, 172, 221; stratified social circles of,
34, 47
Sociedad de Conciertos de Madrid (Madrid
Society of Concerts), 184
Sociedad Gimnástica Española (Gymnastic
Spanish Society), 219
Sociedad Musical Euterpe (Music Society
Euterpe), 192–93
Southworth, James Granville, 246n54
Spain: conduct manuals published in, 20;
demographic growth in, 12, 56; as a middle
class-dominated society, 226n33; tourist industry in, 249n148; urbanization of, 56–57
spas, 205–7, 209–12; in Bath, 205–6; the *ciudad
balneario* (city spa), 211; and the grand
hotel, 211, 249n163; the inland spa, 206;
main impulses leading to the expansion
of (economic growth, science [hygienic
and balneology], bourgeois cultural mo-

dernity), 206–7; the seaside spa, 206; and
seawater therapy, 207
spatial turn, 132, 240n6
sports, 4, 215–19; bicycle riding, 216; in conduct
manuals, 216; cycling, 219; football, 219;
and health and beauty, 4, 46–47; horseback
riding, 216, 217; media coverage of, 215–16;
and the military, 216–17; societies dedicated to the promotion of, 215; the Spanish
government's promotion of, 218; sports
competitions, 218–19; tennis, 216
Stearns, Peter N., 232n15; on the "retail revolution," 121
Stone, Lawrence, on "affective individualism,"
232n13
Stübben, Josef, 167
Sureda, Juan, 173

Tamberlik, Enrico, 185, 185
Tarazona, Pedro Angel, 120
Tesoro de la lengua castellana o española
(Cobarruvias), 8
Tesoro de las Familias, 65, 66, 232n34
textile products, 97–102; in Catalonia, 97–99;
in Madrid (*ropa blanca/ropa de casa* and
vestidos), 99–102, 101 (table), 102 (table),
103 (table), 105–7; in Old Castile (the
Valladolid-Palencia-Santander axis),
97–99; and *tiendas de generous catalanes*
(stores of Catalan textiles), 104–5
textiles: calicoes (*indianas*), 97, 135, 102; cotton,
102; linen, 101; muslin, 102; silk, 101–2;
wool, 101
theater, 172–77; coverage of in weekly magazines and newspapers, 175–76, 245n25;
informal theater, 176–77; main themes of
plays (nation, sexuality, and finances), 173;
as portrayed in novels, 175; and the Royal
Decree of 1847; *teatros por horas* (theaters
by hours), 177; theater etiquette, 44
Thompson, E. P., 14, 244n10
Tivoli Gardens, 186–87